Universal Teaching Strategies

H. Jerome Freiberg

Professor of Education
University of Houston

Amy Driscoll

Associate Professor of Education
Portland State University

ALLYN AND BACON

Boston   London   Toronto   Sydney   Tokyo   Singapore

Series Editor: *Sean W. Wakely*
Series Editorial Assistant: *Carol L. Chernaik*
Production Administrator: *Annette Joseph*
Production Coordinator: *Holly Crawford*
Editorial-Production Service: *Lynda Griffiths/TKM Productions*
Cover Administrator: *Linda K. Dickinson*
Manufacturing Buyer: *Louise Richardson*

Copyright © 1992 by Allyn and Bacon
A Division of Simon & Schuster, Inc.
160 Gould Street
Needham Heights, MA 02194

Library of Congress Cataloging-in-Publication Data

Freiberg, H. Jerome.
    Universal teaching strategies / H. Jerome Freiberg and Amy
Driscoll.
      p.   cm.
    Includes bibliographical references and index.
    ISBN 0-205-13197-2
    1. Teaching. 2. Classroom management. I. Driscoll, Amy.
  II. Title.
LB1025.3.F74 1991   91-30636
371.1′02—dc20   CIP

Printed in the United States of America
10 9 8 7 6 5 4 3 2 1   96 95 94 93 92 91

Photo credits: Chapters 1, 2, 3, 5, 6, 7, 9, 11, 13, and 14: © Frank Siteman 1990.
Chapters 4, 8, 10, and 15 were taken at the Preston High School and the Academic Center in Kingswood, West Virginia; © H. Jerome Freiberg. Chapter 12 by Brad Eliot.

Cartoon credits: Pages 11, 80, 164, 214, 253, 269, 339, 362, and 404: © 1991 Ford Button. Pages 23, 26, 100, 141, 195, 300, 312, and 418: © 1991 Ford Button and H. Jerome Freiberg.

Figure on page 66 from *HBJ Geometry* by James Ulrich, copyright © 1984 by Harcourt Brace Jovanovich, Inc., reprinted by permission of the publisher.

Brief Contents

Contents

Preface

Universal Teaching Strategies will provide you with an understanding of instruction from a variety of expert perspectives. Your authors will share with you their 40 years of collective teaching and research experience. In addition to the authors' expertise, other expert perspectives are provided throughout the text, through innovative focal points including **Snapshots, Teacher Talks, Research Vignettes, and Samples and Examples.**

The authors see teachers as a valuable source of information and ideas that should be shared with all current and prospective teaching professionals. The Snapshots, Teacher Talks, and Samples and Examples are derived from classroom experience. Research Vignettes are drawn from the study of teaching that has evolved over the last 20 years to allow the teaching profession to move beyond anecdotes to produce a knowledge base of instruction.

Snapshots give a teacher's detailed perspective on a topic discussed in the text. For example, in Chapter 2 (Planning for Instruction: Visualizing What Could Be) a veteran fifth-grade teacher shares her experience of including the students in the planning process. Snapshots appear throughout the text, drawing on a wealth of expertise that is found in our nation's classrooms.

Teacher Talk inserts are brief words of wisdom, strategies, and philosophy from teachers in our elementary, middle, and high schools. For example, in Chapter 15 (Self-Improvement through Self-Assessment) a high-school teacher talks about the first time he tape-recorded a class and listened to classroom interactions.

Research Vignettes are summaries of research studies that relate to the chapter topics. For example, Chapter 8 (Questioning and Discussion: Creating a Dialogue) discusses a study by Kenneth Tobin that examined the effects on achievement of giving students 3 to 5 seconds (wait time) to answer teacher questions. The study design, procedures, research results, and implications for the classroom are included for each Research Vignette.

Samples and Examples are included at the end of each chapter to provide materials that may be used or adapted to meet your present or future classroom needs. For example, in Chapter 3 (Designing Effective Instruction: Creating a Blueprint) three examples of different lesson plans are provided. In Chapter 2 (Planning for Instruction: Visualizing What Could Be) "A Year at a Glance" calendar is included.

At the beginning of each chapter, *Universal Teaching Strategies* lists **Chapter Outcomes** as well as **Key Terms and Concepts**. The Chapter Outcomes identify what you should expect to learn from each chapter. The Key Terms and Concepts present the most important ideas for your review and study. The summary at the end of each chapter provides a complete review of the chapter.

Universal Teaching Strategies presents teaching from three specific actions:

organizing, instructing, and assessing. The book is divided into three sections that reflect each of these teaching actions. The strategies mirror the universal nature of teaching in that they cut across grade levels, subject areas, and teaching situations.

Decisions about which actions to take in a busy classroom require an understanding of the **context**, the place in which the teaching will occur; the **content**, what will be taught; and, most important, the **learners**, those who will be taught. The thread of the context, content, and learner runs through all the chapters and the three sections of the book.

The first section, Organizing Strategies, includes Chapters 1 through 6, beginning with a look at teaching for tomorrow, planning, design, effective use of time, and two approaches to classroom management. Organizing strategies create the conditions necessary for teaching and learning.

The second section, Instructing Strategies, includes Chapters 7 through 13. Each chapter provides a repertoire of teaching strategies that will expand your knowledge about what and how to teach.

The third section, Assessing Strategies, includes Chapters 14 and 15. Chapter 14 will help you diversify student assessment to accommodate varied content, context, and learners to assess student learning. The last chapter of the text describes strategies for looking at your teaching and determining your effectiveness.

Every chapter has been taught to veteran, mentor, and beginning teachers as well as student teachers and beginning teacher education students. We trust you will find *Universal Teaching Strategies* applicable to both your current and future teaching and learning positions.

ACKNOWLEDGMENTS

We are indebted to many people for their assistance in creating this book, including Susanne Canavan, who convinced us to write the text and to publish it with Allyn and Bacon.

A very special acknowledgment is due to our spouses—to Linda Freiberg for her substantial intellectual and psychological contributions, to Brad Eliot for his clarity, wisdom, and expert critique; and to both for their endless loving support. Thanks also go to our wonderful children, Ariel and Oren Freiberg and Kerry, Kelly, Katy, and Keenan Driscoll. They have given our work in education greater meaning.

Recognition must be given to the many teachers and colleagues who provided insights, examples, and resources from their classroom and experiences. Thank you Ken Peterson, Jane Stallings, Robin Lindsley, Carolyn Turkanis, Jeff Cresswell, Maryellen Synder, Kathleen Gandin-Russell, Myrna Cohen, Gwen Ruttledge, and Melinda Irwin for enriching this work. We also extend our gratitude to the reviewers of this book: Douglas Brooks, Miami University; Ronald Doll, Professor Emeritus, The City University of New York; Diane Lawler, Arkansas State University; David Payton, New York State Education Department; and Dennie L. Smith, Memphis State University.

Finally, this text would not be possible without the creative and diligent efforts of the editorial team at Allyn and Bacon, including Sean Wakely, Senior Education Editor, Carol Chernaik, Allison Sylvia, and Annette Joseph, and of freelancers, Lynda Griffiths, TKM Productions, and Holly Crawford. Thanks are also given to Ford Button, who added images to the humor of teaching.

CHAPTER 1

Teaching for Tomorrow: Context, Content, and Learners

CHAPTER OUTCOMES

At the conclusion of this chapter you will be able to:

1. Define a universal teaching strategy.
2. Describe how you may expand your teaching repertoire.
3. Identify and describe organizing, instructing, and assessing teaching strategies.
4. Describe learners of tomorrow, based on demographic trends.
5. Describe the role of context, content, and learner in determining the selection of teaching strategies.

KEY TERMS AND CONCEPTS

Teaching Repertoire
Universal Teaching Strategies
Framework of Strategies
Organizing Strategies
Instructing Strategies
Assessing Strategies
Context of Teaching Tomorrow
Content of Teaching Tomorrow
Learners of Tomorrow

> *The average teacher tells. The good teacher explains.*
> *The superior teacher models. The great teacher inspires.*
> Unknown.

INTRODUCTION

Listen to the Teachers

Each year one event links all teachers, regardless of location, grade level, or content being taught—it is the first day of school. The first day, like other firsts in a child's education, sets the stage for the future. When we listen to teachers, we hear a common voice: Teaching is exciting, hopeful, and full of challenge.

TEACHER TALK

It's the first day of school. I didn't sleep much last night and it's unusually early for me to be awake. You would think that after 10 years of teaching, the excitement and anticipation would wear off, but this feels like every other first day of school. I'm anxious to see those young people and to try out some of the new activities I've planned for them.

Felicia Gomez
Secondary English Literature Teacher

It's a warm sunny day. I'm trying to relax. After all, I've been in schools before. I've spent 16 years going to school, but always as a student, never as the person on the other side of the desk. Memories of my own student experiences flood my mind. I want to be like the best of those teachers I've known. Some made me learn, some made me want to learn, some made me laugh, some made me angry, some made me hope, and some made me despair. I remember feeling smart and I remember feeling quite dumb. I want to be like those who nurtured me.

Eric Adams
Middle-School Environmental Science Teacher

I'm really energized for this. In fact, I've been waiting for weeks to get started. Last year I really made progress toward my goals. It's funny—I almost didn't want the school year to end. I've never felt like that before. This summer the workshops I attended and the reading I've done have given me ideas and confidence about my work. This year will be great. I'm going to really inspire my students.

Pam Rossio
Fourth-Grade Teacher

Meet the Teachers

Felicia Gomez, in her early 50s, is a former training director for a large bank corporation. She made a career change 10 year ago. Her minor in English literature influenced her choice of teaching secondary-school literature courses. She updated her background of novels, short stories, and poetry while pursuing her teaching certificate. Her training background made it possible for her to learn how to teach through a nontraditional teacher education program. The program and career change were right for Felicia and soon she was enthusiastically accepted by students and peers. Her goals for the students in a large urban public school focus on the love for reading that she values so highly.

Eric Adams is a 24-year-old with a degree in environmental science. He just completed a graduate program in teacher education in order to teach middle-school students. He is passionate about his concerns for the environment, is involved in advocacy groups, and spends most of his free time outdoors, hiking and bicycling. He also volunteers with a group of teens in an outdoor recreation program. His goals for the students in his suburban middle school include cooperation and responsible citizenship.

Pam Rossio is a single parent who returned to school once her children were all in elementary classrooms. She completed the college coursework begun 10 years earlier through a four-year education program, and has been teaching for four years. She is completing a master's degree, one course at a time, in the evening. She puts in long hours preparing for her teaching and is respected and admired by parents, other teachers, and administrators. An extraordinary number of students return to visit her each year. Her goals for her fourth-grade students in a rural elementary school are focused on thinking skills. She wants them to think critically and creatively, and to be able to solve problems and make decisions.

Felicia Gomez, Eric Adams, and Pam Rossio are pseudonyms but they represent the real teachers we observe and listen to in schools. They are the teachers of tomorrow. They chose a teaching career through careful decision making, acutely aware of the problems, criticisms, and challenges so well publicized by the media. After considering other options, and even trying them out, they prepared for the teaching role through varied means: traditional four-year, graduate or fifth-year, and alternative programs. They each joined the teaching profession, having spent at least 16 years in schools, influenced by those student experiences, and thoughtful about their own school memories. They entered their first classrooms with commitments to the kind of teachers they wanted to be, and almost immediately formulated some personal goals for their work. Felicia, Eric, and Pam are teachers who seek knowledge to expand their teaching repertoires.

Teaching Repertoires

A teaching repertoire is an accumulation of skills, concepts, and attitudes based on a person's universe of knowledge and experiences. Each of the three teachers' repertoires is unique, depending on the range of his or her contact with children or adolescents. Although Eric's repertoire is limited by his newness to teaching in public school classrooms, it has already developed through his recent graduate studies in teacher education and his volunteer work with teens.

Pam's repertoire has been expanded by each of her four years of teaching, but is constantly influenced by her own children and the visits of former students. She also subscribes to *The Reading Teacher* and *Elementary School Journal*. She just completed a research project for her graduate class on cooperative learning.

Felicia's work with adult learners brought her into teaching with an already developed repertoire from her training work—one that she has adjusted and flexed to the content and learners of her high-school classroom. Felicia has also expanded her repertoire by attending a nationally recognized summer institute on creative writing.

Building a Teaching Repertoire

The process of building a teaching repertoire is never ending. It may be built from a variety of formal and informal sources. Pam is constantly expanding her repertoire through her graduate work, her frequent attendance at workshops, and her journal reading. Felicia's love of reading literature continues to expand her content knowledge, and this often inspires teaching strategies and activities. After a summer of reading, she is bursting with enthusiasm and new ideas. Eric's formal knowledge of both teaching and science content is fresh. His experiences during this first year will build an informal knowledge base, but it will take time for Eric to build a developed teaching repertoire, which will be influenced by the context, content, and students during the next few years. A veteran teacher like Felicia has a well-developed repertoire, and yet it could become less effective as students or curriculum change.

Like Pam, Eric, and Felicia, you have a range of opportunities for building and expanding your teaching repertoire. It expands each time you try out a new idea in your classroom or share an idea with other teachers. Building a repertoire does not require the reinvention of the wheel. Many sources are available beyond your own immediate experiences. You expand your repertoire when you:

1. Observe other teachers.
2. Receive feedback from other professionals about your teaching.
3. Receive feedback from students (Freiberg & Waxman, 1988).
4. Analyze your own teaching.
5. Conduct research in your classroom.
6. Read books, journals, and research studies.
7. Join with other teachers to work on projects.

The frequency of these opportunities, the amount of practice you engage in (Joyce & Showers, 1988), and the support you receive for developing and trying out your new ideas will all help to determine the range of your teaching repertoire. Eric will be teaching next door to a veteran teacher who has already shared activity ideas and a few management routines for lab work. She agreed to review his plans for the first weeks of school. Her feedback was appreciated and he made some changes based on her suggestions. He approaches the first week feeling better prepared. Furthermore, his new mentor discovered that her teaching repertoire was also enriched by the interaction and sharing of ideas.

The three teachers represent their profession well in their efforts to build a teaching repertoire. Felicia, Eric, and Pam know that they will need an expanded repertoire to meet the challenges of teaching for tomorrow. This book's universal teaching strategies respond to that need.

UNIVERSAL TEACHING STRATEGIES

Effective teaching for tomorrow demands teaching strategies that can accommodate the variety of contexts in which teachers will teach, the variety of content that must be taught, and the variety of learners with different backgrounds, needs, and problems. The strategies of this text have been identified as being universal to the act of teaching.

Definition of Terms

The word *universal*, from Latin, means comprehensively broad and versatile. The word *teaching* comes from Greek, meaning to show, point out, direct, or guide. The word *strategy*, from the Greek *strategia*, is defined as the art of devising or employing plans toward a goal. This book, *Universal Teaching Strategies*, can be used to reach a variety of content goals at a variety of grade levels, and is thereby effective with different learners and in different contexts.

Framework of Strategies

This book is designed to add to your teaching repertoire with three kinds of strategies. Figure 1.1 displays a framework of teaching strategies based on our

FIGURE 1.1   *Framework of Universal Teaching Strategies*

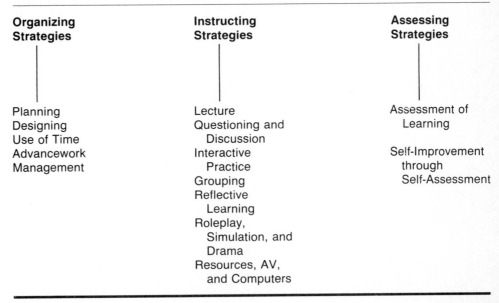

Organizing Strategies	Instructing Strategies	Assessing Strategies
Planning	Lecture	Assessment of
Designing	Questioning and	Learning
Use of Time	Discussion	
Advancework	Interactive	Self-Improvement
Management	Practice	through
	Grouping	Self-Assessment
	Reflective	
	Learning	
	Roleplay,	
	Simulation, and	
	Drama	
	Resources, AV,	
	and Computers	

analysis of research and practice (Wittrock, 1986; Houston, 1990). The framework provides strategies for organizing your teaching, for instructing, and for assessing teaching and learning. *Organizing strategies* describe much of the work that precedes teaching. They provide a foundation for your instruction—they pave the way for you to teach. *Instructing strategies* are more directly observable. You can see and hear a lecture, a roleplay, or a videotape. They focus on the "how" question to be raised throughout this chapter—how to teach content and learners of tomorrow. *Assessing strategies* are aimed at the measurement of teaching and learning. They provide information about the organization and the instruction.

The chapters of *Universal Teaching Strategies* are arranged as shown in this framework. A preview will show you how they will contribute to your teaching repertoire.

Chapter Previews

CHAPTER 2   Planning for Instruction:
Visualizing What Could Be

Eric Adams's mentor teacher and Felicia Gomez have many years of teaching experience and engage in the planning we describe in Chapter 2. They visualize and make decisions as they prepare to teach. Their planning gives them an overview of their day, provides order for instruction and management, ensures purposeful learning, indicates an appropriate pace and sequence, connects classroom events with community resources, documents their instruction, helps them order supplies, reduces duplication of effort, and assists them in using a wide repertoire of strategies. Chapter 2 describes those phases of planning in which teachers think through their alternatives and classroom possibilities. Eric does and will continue to do a great deal of preplanning, whereas Felicia and Pam make numerous "in-flight" decisions as they teach. In Chapter 2, you will hear many examples of Teacher Talk about planning experiences to guide your own planning process.

CHAPTER 3   Designing Effective Instruction:
Creating a Blueprint

We provide a range of design formats that help you prepare for teaching: lesson designs, unit designs, and daily and weekly designs. Eric will benefit from expert design models as he experiments with different ways to prepare for his classes. Regardless of the format you use, you will need to attend to goals, objectives, teaching and learning strategies, materials, feedback, and assessment. We describe each and provide examples in Chapter 3. Effective beginnings and endings are emphasized and demonstrations are provided by various teachers. You will see examples of the kind of designs that teachers like Pam and Felicia use for their planning— designs personalized to meet their needs, reflect their priorities and beliefs, and illustrate efficiency. We will encourage you to do the same.

CHAPTER 4   Effective Use of Time:
Doing More with Less

Felicia, Eric, and Pam are faced with time constraints as they try to incorporate an expanding curriculum in their already full days. Chapter 4 will help them and you decide how to use time well for teaching and learning. We provide theory and research related to time management, as well as a description of the demands and limits you will be facing. You will read about a teacher whose commitment to her goals for students directs the way she uses her time. And you will find ways to identify and reduce the time losses and wasters that exist in most classrooms.

CHAPTER 5   Classroom Management:
Advancework

Our secondary teacher, Felicia Gomez, has few discipline problems in her teaching. She has created many of her teaching and learning activities to reflect the lives of her students, and she involves them in the selection of literature so that content is meaningful to them. The strategy of advancework has enabled her to do so. Chapter 5 discusses advancework—an information-gathering strategy that promotes awareness. Advancework is necessary for making decisions and planning your classroom management. We suggest ways to conduct advancework in the context of your students' neighborhood, classroom, school, and district. Advancework with your curriculum will help you provide the kind of relevant and useful content that Felicia provides for her students. Advancework with students works toward physically and mentally active learning, social learning, confidence, motivation for your learners, and a safe environment for learning.

CHAPTER 6   Classroom Management:
Beyond Discipline

Snapshots of classroom management models will assist you in developing a cooperative community for your students, much like the one you would find in Pam Rossio's room. We encourage your study of the models in order to develop a system of your own. Much of the climate and routines of your class will be established during the beginning of the year, and we make recommendations for getting started. Your classroom will be affected by transitions, interruptions, crises, and behavior problems, all of which can be addressed effectively. In the final section of Chapter 6, we encourage cooperative work with parents as a way of extending your classroom community.

CHAPTER 7   Lecture: From Passive to
Active Learning

Felicia decided to make a change from a formal lecture approach, which she had experienced through most of her years in school, to an interactive use of the strategy. She had student groups discuss points in the lecture, provided guided note-taking techniques, and had students prepare outlines on transparencies for the overhead projector. Chapter 7 presents additional ways to make the strategy of lecturing highly interactive and to reduce the level of passivity usually associated with it. We present suggestions that will help you use lecture for informational, motivational, or critical thinking outcomes. You will see how teachers can manage new variations of the old lecture theme.

CHAPTER 8   Questioning and Discussion: Creating a Dialogue

Pam, Eric, and Felicia realize how limited they are in using questions or discussion strategies to promote student thinking. They have listened to tapes of their classrooms and are concerned about the low levels of questions and the limited amount of time students are given to answer. Chapter 8 responds to their concerns with strategies for effective questioning and discussion. The chapter describes types of questions as well as questioning for a variety of purposes. Cautions are given about using questions to intimidate or control students, and about the length of time you give students to answer question. The chapter also provides guidelines and strategies for the effective use of discussion. To use discussion, you and your students will need to learn how to listen, reflect, and respond in meaningful ways.

CHAPTER 9   Interactive Practice for Learning: Beyond Drill

Chapter 9 describes outcomes for student learning that match the goal Pam Rossio has set for her fourth-graders—critical thinking. We describe how to incorporate learning strategies with your practice activities in order to help students "learn how to learn." By using the examples in the chapter, you will be able to plan practice activities with different levels of complexity. You will also gain ideas for working with the problems learners often have with practice. We provide descriptions of five practice strategies: recitation, review, seatwork, homework, and learning centers. You will learn how to use each strategy in a variety of interesting ways.

CHAPTER 10   Grouping for Instruction: Involvement and Interaction

Chapter 10 examines the context, content, and learner for information that can help you make grouping decisions. We suggest a repertoire of grouping arrangements for accommodating the differences you have in your classroom: different curriculum outcomes, different physical environments, and different student personalities and needs. To support your use of grouping for involvement and interaction, we describe routines and procedures for management and guidelines for using the assistance of volunteers and aides.

CHAPTER 11   Reflective Teaching: Students as Shareholders

This chapter will also be helpful to Pam in her efforts to teach critical thinking. In it, we guide you in promoting students as sources of curriculum—as "shareholders" in teaching and learning. A climate of trust, necessary for such teaching, is one in which students' thinking and point of view are valued. The strategies of mapping and brainstorming are described to expand students' participation and experiences prior to using the actual processes of critical thinking and guided discovery.

CHAPTER 12   Roleplay, Simulation, and Drama: Making Learning Real

During his teacher education coursework and practicum, Eric Adams saw the potential for improvisation strategies to provide vicarious experiences for students. With many areas of curriculum, those experiences are necessary for students to be able to learn by doing, thinking, feeling, and responding within the safety of the classroom. Improvisation describes the three strategies of Chapter 12. We help you become aware of and sensitive to your community while using its resources for improvisation, and help you set up your classroom physically and emotionally to support this type of teaching. The use of roleplay, simulation, and drama is encouraged for all content areas, but especially for the problem solving and decision making you will find in tomorrow's curriculum. You will find step-by-step models for roleplay and simulation, guidelines for using drama as a teaching strategy, and a description of the important roles you play in supporting learning through the three strategies.

CHAPTER 13   Using Community Resources, Audiovisuals, and Computers: Varying the Stimuli

Drawing on her banking experience, Felicia enjoys the challenges of incorporating technology in her curriculum but feels limited by the resources and policies of her school. In Chapter 13, we describe the technology available in most schools, from the simplest chalkboards to the most complex computer programs, and recognize the limits Felicia faces. We remind you and her of the purposes that technology can serve, and of the contextual and content considerations that influence the use of resources, audiovisuals, and computers. To employ these as stimuli for teaching, we suggest effective and unusual ways to make them part of teaching and learning.

CHAPTER 14   Assessment of Learning: Let Me Count the Ways

Our three teachers will need another repertoire for their teaching—a repertoire of strategies to assess learning. Chapter 14 works to develop that repertoire for the varying content and learners they face. Assessment questions and issues fall into three groupings: diagnostic, formative, and summative. We describe the many purposes of assessment: planning, decision making, motivating, and communicating to students, parents, other teachers, and the general public. You will find over a dozen strategies for assessing student learning, described with guidelines for selection or for development.

CHAPTER 15   Self-Improvement through Self-Assessment

Chapter 15 identifies sources of data to improve your teaching. Measures of self-assessment to analyze your teaching are provided, as well as strategies for using student feedback and peer observations for additional information. We describe formal and informal ways of looking at yourself, learning about yourself, and improving yourself in the classroom. The theme of Chapter 15 is that learning to be an effective teacher is a lifelong pursuit and requires a variety of information sources.

The chapters of this book are arranged in the framework of organizing strategies, instructing strategies, and assessing strategies. Within each chapter you will find opportunities for building and expanding your teaching repertoire. The chapters have common themes that will make the content more usable for your teaching. Considerations of the *context, content,* and *learners* are developed within the descriptions of each teaching strategy and guidelines for use are given. We look at those themes as we proceed to *teaching for tomorrow.* The challenge of tomorrow's context, tomorrow's content, and tomorrow's learners awaits you.

THE CONTEXT OF TEACHING TOMORROW

Context is another word for setting or environment. The context for teaching may include physical environments such as a country, state, school district, neighborhood, school, or classroom. It may include less concrete settings such as the political or economic climate. The context for teaching is influenced by the status of the education profession as well as the public's awareness and satisfaction with education.

Each of our three teachers is aware that tomorrow holds change for their professional context. Even as he prepared to teach, Eric witnessed revision in teacher certification requirements and in teacher education programs. Pam has been involved on a committee that is attempting to reform what is taught and the way student progress is assessed. Felicia and her colleagues have discussed the changes they see in their students, and have developed a student/faculty committee to address concerns they have about the climate of their school and the lack of school readiness skills they see in their students. All three teachers will work in a context of reform or change due to concern from within teaching and from outside of the profession.

Projected Context for Tomorrow

Although it is impossible to predict exactly what they will look and feel like, there are definite indications of contextual characteristics to come. Education is being thought of in a much broader sense to include home, neighborhoods, and society. Thus, a better term for the teaching context may be *community.* We suggest that teaching for tomorrow may take place in a "wired" community and one that is characterized by cooperation.

"Then in 1978 it was back to basics . . ."

A "Wired" Community

In a time when video term papers are being used (Landfried, 1990) and teleconferencing brings together a wider audience of parents and teachers (West, 1990), a wired community may already be close. Tomorrow's prediction and prescription are for "education that relies on electronic learning" (Mecklenburger, 1990, p. 105), but tomorrow's reality calls for huge restructuring of schools if the prediction is to come true.

Today's technological conditions include trends and statistics, including the following:

1. In 1985, the number of microcomputers in public schools was approximately 500,000 (*Condition of Education*, 1987), and by 1988, between 2.5 to 4 million were available (Weinstein & Roschwalb, 1990).
2. Approximately 50,000 teachers will be teaching computer technology as their main course between 1990 and 1995 (Smith & Dunn, 1987).
3. Two-thirds of U.S. teachers now use computers, and a majority of them feel "less computer literate than their students" (Crum, 1989).

In addition to preparing themselves to be more computer literate, teachers like Felicia, Eric, and Pam are faced with multiple challenges. They must make decisions about the role of computers in their teaching, appropriate curriculum, quality software, and equal access for students.

Tomorrow's challenge in a wired community is for educators to be involved in major decisions about technology that will impact both home and school. We do not want to be faced with conclusions such as, "Clearly, we are approaching the time when a publicly financed and managed satellite-based telecommunications network dedicated to educational purposes will be in the nation's best interest" (Weinstein & Roschwalb, 1990) without having a say in the decision. The challenge calls for an energetic and active role in policy development and decision making on issues of technology.

Our next challenge is one of scale, as school-based technology can only be described as small scale. To change from small scale to large scale, Mecklenburger (1990) recommends and challenges us to:

1. *Invent new systems or adapt old systems in ways that will serve every learner, every teacher, and every community (p. 106).*
2. *Expand our vision of classroom to accommodate a larger number of learners, to encompass settings on and off our school grounds (p. 107).*
3. *Revise the economic base of educational technology with increased budgets and, simultaneously, efficient spending (p. 108).*

These challenges alone represent major restructuring of the context of teaching. Felicia, with her banking experience, sees many possibilities for meeting the second challenge—expanding the vision of classroom—but feels limited by the resources and policies of her school. Pam, an advocate for educational equality, has already used creative scheduling with her limited computer resources to increase learning opportunities for her students. The challenges of a wired community are many.

A Community of Cooperation

We are facing the challenge of helping students become responsible citizens. This goal, which has been with us since the beginning of our nation, often gets pushed aside when achievement scores are unsatisfactory, or when reform focuses on basic skills, or when economics drive educational change (Boyer, 1990). There is a resurgent push from within and outside of education to produce higher social responsibility scores. It will be difficult to reach that goal without attending to the emotional context of schools.

When you consider how much time students spend in school, it seems ideal to conceptualize classrooms as small-scale versions of neighborhoods, state, national, and world communities. School can be a place to practice the thoughts and actions of responsible citizenship. There are model programs in place that demonstrate that classrooms can be caring communities where students can practice being responsible citizens: the Child Development Project in California (Schaps & Solomon, 1990), the Stanford University Program for Complex Instruction (Cohen & DeAvila, 1983), and the Education for Living in a Nuclear Age Project (Sagor, 1990). The success of these programs is attributed to collaboration of many people and multilevels of interaction.

The impact of cooperative learning strategies on the climate of schools is widespread. The technique has been successful in diverse settings—from inner-city, to bilingual and multilingual, to academically heterogeneous settings. The recommendations coming from the use of cooperative learning and from participants of model programs in place provide a challenging list of what may be ahead for communities of cooperation:

1. A greater understanding of the concepts of community, interdependence, and collaboration for both teachers and students (Berman, 1990)
2. The development of more curriculum material and strategies that require cooperation and promote interaction (Cohen, 1990)
3. Support for teachers working toward cooperative communities through inservice programs, expert mentors, and collaborative arrangements between teachers, parents, and community members (Cohen, 1990)

We will need classrooms with high levels of communication, interaction, and collaboration. Classroom problems need to be solved by class members, feelings need to be expressed, and the consequences of behavior need to be experienced. A challenge of teaching for tomorrow will be creating classrooms characterized by cooperation.

THE CONTENT OF TEACHING TOMORROW

We have been talking about the context demanded for the schools of tomorrow. Now let us discuss the content—the pool of information, skills, and values that our students are expected to learn. Content is often called curriculum or subject matter. It can be structured with specifically stated goals and objectives, teaching and learning activities, and materials found in curriculum guides developed by states and school districts. It can also be unstructured and in the control and thinking of individual teachers. Sometimes content refers strictly to what is contained in a textbook. Whatever the source, content changes with the changes in society. Content reflects problems, concerns, values, and priorities of people, as you will see in our projections for the content of tomorrow.

Projected Content for Tomorrow

Our three teachers, Felicia, Eric, and Pam, teach different content (English literature, environmental science, and elementary everything), but all three will be affected by the curricular trends of tomorrow. The content associated with social responsibility, which we just described, will influence Eric's science curriculum and Felicia's literature selections. All of the subject matter that Pam teaches will be influenced by the resurgent focus on civics.

Another example of a content trend for tomorrow is higher-level thinking or critical thinking. It is the kind of content that will cross other curriculum areas; that is, you will be able to teach critical thinking while teaching something else. Another content prediction for tomorrow's teaching is information associated with the health of our students: curriculum about AIDS, drugs and alcohol, nutrition, and stress. Health content will be taught separately but will also be integrated with other subject matter at all levels of school.

Thinking Skills Content

Much of the push for thinking skills content has resulted from an awareness that we live in a society that requires us to make complex decisions. It is not likely that tomorrow will be simpler and require less of such thinking and reasoning; in fact, is likely to require more.

Currently, there are thinking skills programs operating successfully in some school systems: Philosophy for Children (Lipman, 1982), The CoRT Thinking Program (DeBono, 1984), and Instrumental Enrichment (Feuerstein, 1980). Unfortunately, much of the work on thinking skills content has been directed only toward such particular schools or programs, specific populations of learners such as gifted students (Torrance, 1986), and limited curricular areas such as mathematics and computer programming (Upchurch & Lochhead, 1987). There is also controversy over how to teach, or help, or guide students to think critically. Some advocate special curriculum or courses, some advocate teaching basic skills first as a knowledge base for thinking skills, and some advocate teaching thinking skills as a way to learn other knowledge and skills (Romanish, 1986).

In the midst of limited efforts and controversy, there is a direction for tomorrow's thinking skills content—to teach students "to think in a way that prepares them for life outside of school, not just life in classrooms" (Sternberg, 1990, p. 43). Such a goal sounds simple, but it holds much challenge. To achieve it with our students, we must develop teaching strategies, resources, and assessment focused on critical thinking that also accommodates cultural differences and learning styles (Cohen, 1990).

We must provide specialized preparation for teachers as well as support for their efforts in critical thinking content. Pam Rossio has been working on curriculum reform and actively implements critical thinking curriculum with her fourth-graders. But she often feels isolated in her efforts and frustrated by lack of resources. We must provide support for her and other professionals in their efforts by means of workshops, seminars, resources, materials, and recognition.

Student Health Content

The general public has an intense interest in the issue of health, and more people are actively involved in promoting health than ever before. Governmental agencies and the education profession are advocating an effective and comprehensive program of health education for U.S. schools (Koop, 1986; U.S. Department of Health and Human Services, 1980; Cortese, 1985; Iverson & Kolbe, 1983). The question for the 1990s is how to teach and promote health effectively for all students. The question is further complicated by the threats of AIDS and drug and alcohol abuse, and the social, political, and emotional issues associated with the two killers.

A recent study entitled "Code Blue" (National Commission, 1990) presents a picture of adolescents who are not healthy and who are ill-prepared to be productive members of society. The study's findings related to schools (see Figure 1.2)

FIGURE 1.2 *Code Blue: A Medical Emergency*

- 1 million teen-age girls—nearly one in 10—get pregnant each year.
- 39 percent of high-school seniors reported they had been drunk (had five or more drinks in a row) within the two previous years.
- Alcohol-related accidents are the leading cause of death among teenagers.
- The suicide rate for teens has doubled since 1968, making it the second-leading cause of death among adolescents. Some 10 percent of teen-age boys and 18 percent of girls have attempted suicide.
- Teen-age (14 to 17 years old) arrests are up thirty-fold since 1950.
- Homicide is the leading cause of death among minority youths between ages 15 and 19.

Source: National Commission on the Role of the Schools and the Community in Improving Adolescent Health. (1990). *Code blue: Uniting for healthier youth.* Atlanta: Center for Disease Control.

raise serious concerns about the well-being of adolescent learners today and in the future.

The findings from "Code Blue" were reported at the end of 1990. The seeds for the problems, however, were planted when today's adolescents were very young. We know that education begins at birth. If we are to influence thinking and habits, then we must address all levels of education.

As we struggle with the complications of how best to accomplish that influence, two issues are especially prominent. One issue is sensitivity—a sensitivity toward individual student differences, family backgrounds, and cultural values when making content decisions about what information and how much information. When student health content is added to an already full elementary school day or an already full load of secondary coursework, time becomes a second issue.

We have limited research data to help us determine how to teach and promote health effectively for all students. There are indications from successful programs that the involvement of parents or families holds promise (Beck & Summons, 1990) and that complete and accurate information must be provided as a basis of decision making (Healy & Coleman, 1989).

We are faced with the need to continue with increased comprehensive health education for all students. Since educators have the potential to reach 95 percent of the nation's young (Haffner, 1987), we have a huge responsibility for the country's overall well-being. To meet our obligations, we must have the most current and accurate information available, develop sensitive strategies for sharing the information, and promote attitudes and practices of personal and social responsibility.

On a practical level, individual teachers must find and allocate time for sharing information and promoting those attitudes and practices, must keep themselves up to date in terms of information, and must be sensitive to community, family, and student differences that influence how information is best shared. It may seem to be an overwhelming task, but there are plentiful resources to help, and most states have developed programs and support.

Eric Johnson is especially concerned about his role in health education for his young adolescent students. His concerns are more comprehensive because he is knowledgeable about environmental influences on health. All three teachers, Felicia, Eric, and Pam, will be faced with the issue of not enough time as they try to incorporate health issues and other new curricula in their already full days.

We have discussed two of the major influences on teaching—context and content. Predictions were made about contextual trends related to technology and cooperation, and content trends related to critical thinking and health. Now we look at the third major influence—the learners—and predict what they will look like tomorrow.

THE LEARNERS OF TOMORROW

Today's students are tomorrow's adults. The attitudes, knowledge, skills, and hope provided during growth and development will be the foundations of adulthood. The prophecy is well stated by Freiberg (1990): "Today's children are our leaders for the future and the generation we will depend upon to care for us in our twilight years. We will reap the legacy of both our successes and our mistakes."

Today's children and adolescents are a challenge to teach. They are distracted by a world of videos, CDs, and electronic games. They come from varied family structures and bring to classrooms a myriad of problems to address. A look at the demographics of families of the 1990s and the leading school discipline problems will give you a preview of the challenges of teaching the learners of tomorrow.

Families of Tomorrow

A picture of families of the 1990s gives us some clues about the students we will be teaching. Figure 1.3 illustrates the picture. In addition to the items mentioned in Figure 1.3, we have indications that 25 percent of our students will come to school with limited economic resources and the problems often associated with poverty. We are currently describing those students as "educationally disadvantaged" by the mismatch between home and community and school. Poverty is only one influence.

FIGURE 1.3 *Families in the 1990s*

- Today, fewer than 10 percent of U.S. families have a mother who stays home and raises the children while the father works outside the home.
- By 1995, more than three-quarters of all school-age children and two-thirds of preschoolers will have mothers in the labor force.
- Between one-fourth and one-third of children under age 13 must care for themselves one part of their day.
- Some 59 percent of children born in 1983 will live with only one parent at some time before reaching the age of 18.

Source: Adapted from *Newsweek 1990: The twenty-first century family*. Special edition (Winter/Spring). New York, New York.

Others include cultural and language differences and lack of parent education. The lack of match between the values, experiences, and resources of the home and community and that of the school puts students at a disadvantage for success in school. It is currently predicted that by the year 2020, nearly half of the nation's students will be educationally disadvantaged (Pallas, Natriello, & McDill, 1989).

The demographics of families and future students tell us that there is a need for a complex teaching repertoire—one with the variation necessary to meet the diversity of needs. Research indicates that if we are to be effective in teaching amidst such diversity, our repertoire must not include teaching strategies that make students passive learners (Mullis, Owen, & Phillips, 1990). Students of today and tomorrow require interactive teaching that promotes high levels of personal involvement.

Problems of the Learners

Comparing teacher concerns about discipline in 1980 with those of 1940 produced startling differences, as seen in Figure 1.4.

School discipline problems deter some people from entering the field of teaching and cause others to leave the profession. Those who choose to join and stay have learned to address discipline problems with both instructional and management strategies. Instructional strategies that promote relevant content and high levels of student involvement are effective in reducing discipline problems. Management strategies that consider the needs and interests of learners, their families, and communities are effective in preventing discipline problems.

Felicia has few discipline problems in her teaching. She uses teaching strategies that keep her students involved: interpreting dialogue, creating their own endings to stories, dramatizing scenes, and so on. She also involves her secondary students in the selection of literature so that the content is more meaningful to them.

As Eric contemplates the students in his middle-school classroom, he sees the

FIGURE 1.4   *Discipline Problems Then and Now*

1940s	1980s
Talking	Drug abuse
Chewing gum	Alcohol abuse
Making noise	Pregnancy
Running in the hallways	Rape
Getting out of place in line	Robbery
Wearing improper clothing	Assault
Not putting paper in wastebaskets	Burglary
	Arson
	Bombing

Source: Dr. Howard L. Hodgkinson, Director, Center Demographic Policy, Institute for Educational Leadership, Inc. Washington, DC. Used with permission.

problems of tomorrow's learners as the core of his work toward the goal of social responsibility. He brings insights from his volunteer work with teens and a repertoire of activities to work toward his goal.

FACING TOMORROW

In addition to the challenges predicted for the context, content, and learners of tomorrow, the teaching profession is faced with demands for improving assessment of teaching and learning as well as improving teaching strategies (Cheney, 1990; Cuban, 1984).

Changes in content and the realization that current assessment practices do not accurately measure much of what students learn have prompted a call for states to revamp assessment procedures (Pipho, 1990). As for the assessment of teaching practices, the National Board for Professional Teaching Standards has begun to award contracts for the development of such assessment. Development efforts are aimed toward "concrete examples of the types of assessment which must be created if superior teaching is to be recognized" (Bradley, 1990). Individual school districts have been working on such developments and many systems that discriminate between effective and ineffective teachers are in operation (Peterson, Stevens, & Driscoll, 1990).

Pam, Eric, and Felicia face these demands for changes in assessment, as well as many other challenges in their teaching. Their future is full of challenges. It is evident from the demographics of the future that teaching will require greater expertise and a broader repertoire from which to select teaching strategies.

SUMMARY

Teaching is a never-ending quest for new knowledge and ideas to expand our teaching repertoires to meet the needs of a changing world (context, content, and learners). We leave Felicia Gomez, Eric Adams, and Pam Rossio as we conclude this first chapter. However, throughout the remaining chapters you will meet expert teachers who will share their thoughts, strategies, and experiences.

We must begin today if we are to teach for the future and to provide tomorrow's adults with the necessary knowledge, skills, attitudes, and dreams for the twenty-first century. This challenge will require us to break from the mold of a limited approach to teaching and expand our options to meet the needs of every learner. This is the challenge of teaching for tomorrow.

REFERENCES

Baron, J. B., & Sternberg, R. J. (1987). *Teaching thinking skills: Theory and practice.* New York: W. H. Freeman.

Beck, K. H., & Summons, T. G. (1990). Sources of information about drugs and alcohol for black and white suburban high school students. *Health Education*, *21*(2), 21–24.

Berman, S. (1990). Educating for social responsibility. *Educational Leadership*, *48*(3), 75–80.

Boyer, E. L. (1990). Civic education for responsible citizens. *Educational Leadership*, *48*(3), 4–9.

Bradley, A. (1990). National board lets its first contract for teacher assessment. *Education*

Week, *10*(11), 1, 19.

Cheney, L. V. (1990). *Tyrannical machines: A report on educational practices gone wrong and our best hopes for setting them right.* Washington, DC: Office of Publications and Public Affairs, National Endowment for the Humanities.

Cohen, D. L. (1990). Higher-order instruction is essential for every child, state chiefs assert. *Education Week,* *10*(11), 9.

Cohen, E. G. (1990). Continuing to cooperate: Prerequisites for persistence. *Kappan,* *72*(2), 134–138.

Cohen, E. G., & DeAvila, E. (1983). *Learning to think in math and science: Improving local education for minority children, Final Report.* Stanford, CA: Stanford University Program for Complex Instruction.

Condition of Education. (1987). Washington, DC: U.S. Government Printing Office.

Cortese, P. A. (1985). Why school health education: A synthesis. *Health Education,* *16*, 3–5.

Crum, M. (1989). *The computer report card—How teachers grade computers in the classroom.* New York: The Wirthlin Group.

Cuban, L. (1984). *How teachers taught: Constancy and change in American classrooms 1890–1980.* New York: Longman.

DeBono, E. (1984). *The CoRT thinking program.* Elmsford, NY: Pergamon.

Duffy, G. G., & Roehler, L. (1987). Improving reading instruction through the use of responsive elaboration. *The Reading Teacher,* *6*, 514–521.

Feuerstein, R. (1990). *Instrumental enrichment.* Washington, DC: Curriculum Development Associates.

Footlick, J. (1990). The 21st century family. *Newsweek,* pp. 14–92.

Freiberg, H. J. (1990). School and teacher effectiveness for the 21st century child. Speech given to the West Virginia State Department of Education, Morgantown, WV.

Freiberg, H. J., & Waxman, H. W. (1988). Alternative feedback approaches for improving student teachers' classroom instruction. *Journal of Teacher Education,* *39*(4), 8–14.

Haffner, D. W. (1987). *AIDS and adolescents: The time for prevention is now.* Washington, DC: Center for Population Options.

Healey, R. M., & Coleman, T. (1989, December). A primer on AIDS for health professionals. *Health Education,* 4–11.

Houston, R. W. (1990). *Handbook of research on teacher education.* New York: Macmillan.

Iverson, D. C., & Kolbe, L. J. (1983). Evaluation of the national disease prevention and health promotion strategy: Establishing a role for the schools. *Journal of School Health,* *53*(5), 294–302.

Joyce, B., & Showers, B. (1988). *Student achievement through staff development.* New York: Longman.

Koop, C. E. (1986). The quest for a smoke-free young America by the year 2000. *Journal of School Health,* *56*, 8–9.

Landfried, S. E. (1990). Video term papers teach research and social responsibility. *Educational Leadership,* *48*(3), 46–48.

Lipman, M. (1982). *Philosophy for children.* Montclair, NJ: First Mountain Foundations.

Martin, D. S. (1989). Restructuring teacher education programs for higher-order thinking skills. *Journal of Teacher Education,* *40*(3), 2–8.

Mecklenburger, J. A. (1990). Educational technology is not enough. *Kappan,* *72*(2), 104–108.

Mullis, I., Owen, E. H., & Phillips, G. (1990). *America's challenge: Accelerating academic achievement—Summary of findings from 20 years of the National Assessment of Education Program.* Princeton, NJ: Educational Testing Service.

National Commission on the Role of the Schools and the Community in Improving Adolescent Health. (1990). *Code blue: Uniting for healthier youth.* Atlanta: Center for Disease Control.

Pallas, A., Natriello, G., & McDill, E. (1989). The changing nature of the disadvantaged population: Current dimensions and future trends. *Educational Researcher,* *8*(5), 16–22.

Peterson, K., Stevens, D., & Driscoll, A. (1990). Student reports: Sources of assessment data. *Journal of Personnel Evaluation,* *4*(2), 165–173.

Pipho, C. (1990). Budgets, politics, and testing. *Kappan,* *72*(2), 102–103.

Romanish, B. (1986). Critical thinking. *The*

Educational Forum, 45(1), 45–56.

Sagor, R. (1990). Educating for living in a nuclear age. *Educational Leadership, 48*(3), 81–83.

Schaps, E., & Solomon, D. (1990). Schools and classrooms as caring communities. *Educational Leadership, 48*(3), 38–40.

Smith, P. P., & Dunn, S. (1987). Human and quality considerations in high tech education. *Educational Technology, 27*(2), 35–39.

Sternberg, R. J. (1990). Critical thinking in the everyday world. In A. C. Ornstein (Ed.), *Strategies for effective teaching.* New York: Harper Collins Publishers.

Torrance, E. P. (1986). Teaching creative and gifted learners. In M. C. Wittrock (Ed.), *Handbook of research on teaching,* (3rd ed.). New York: Macmillan.

Upchurch, R. L., & Lochhead, J. (1987). Computers and higher-order thinking skills. In V. Richardson-Koehler (Ed.), *Educators' handbook.* New York: Longman.

U.S. Department of Health and Human Services. (1980). *Promoting health, preventing disease: Objectives for the nation.* Washington, DC: U.S. Government Printing Office.

Weinstein, S., & Roschwalb, S. A. (1990). Is there a role for educators in telecommunications policy? *Kappan, 72*(2), 115–117.

West, P. (1990). Schools turning to teleconferences to reach broader audiences. *Education Week, 10*(11), 8.

Wittrock M. C. (1986). Students' thought processes. In M. C. Wittrock (Ed.), *Handbook of research on teaching* (3rd ed.). New York: Macmillan.

CHAPTER 2

Planning for Instruction: Visualizing What Could Be

CHAPTER OUTCOMES

At the conclusion of this chapter you will be able to:

1. Describe the functions of planning.
2. Describe four planning stages.
3. Identify considerations of the learner, content, and context in planning.
4. Describe how you could initiate or improve your planning.

KEY TERMS AND CONCEPTS

Definition of Planning
Importance of Planning
Functions of Planning
Limitations of Planning
Preplanning
Active Planning
Ongoing Planning
Postplanning
Mental Process
Learner
Content
Context

INTRODUCTION

Planning

Teacher planning is the thread that weaves the curriculum, or the *what* of teaching, with the instruction, or the *how* of teaching. The classroom is a highly interactive and demanding place. Planning provides for some measure of order in an uncertain and changing environment.

SNAPSHOT

As I become more experienced, I find myself sharing my plans more with my students. In my fifth-grade class, for instance, each Friday I write on a chalkboard, which is set up as a calendar, the major assignments to come for the following week. It is understood that adjustments may be made, yet the students get a preview of what is to come and it allows them to practice budgeting their homework time. In addition, at the outset of each lesson, I share with the students the planned agenda for the day.

I did not always teach in this fashion. Often, especially when I taught high school, I liked incorporating an element of surprise in my lessons. I felt that the pupils would be more alert if they kept guessing about what was to come next. That worked for me then. But now I feel that sharing my organization with the pupils is more valuable. It gives them a feeling of security. The goals of the lesson become more distinct. Attention spans increase. I find that for slightly learning-disabled pupils, this method is extremely beneficial. Once the students are aware of and can follow the schedule, the material becomes familiar because it can be related to as small manageable units. (Myrna Cohen, 5th-grade teacher)

Reseach during the past 30 years on teaching effectiveness supports what most experienced teachers have concluded: Effective teaching is not a haphazard process. Expert teachers plan ahead to create an environment that is conducive for both their teaching style and student learning. Although all effective teachers incorporate some form of planning in their lessons, how a teacher plans seems to be unique to the individual.

Planning Defined

Visualizing

Planning is the ability to visualize into the future; creating, arranging, organizing, and designing events in the mind that may occur in the classroom. Planning allows for purposeful instruction. Consistent planning provides an instructional guide for both teacher and students. It helps with self- and classroom management and allows for easier decision making about the what and how to teach. The goal of planning should always be student learning.

Guiding
Planning for instruction provides a type of road map or guide that assists you in creating a flow of events that have a starting and ending point. Planning is a process that begins with preplanning thoughts and ideas and moves to active planning preparations. Ongoing planning and "in-flight" corrections occur during actual implementation of instruction as events in the classrooms necessitate change. Finally, postanalysis of strengths and weaknesses of instruction and discrepancies between what was planned and what occurred during instruction are noted and become part of the planning process for future lessons.

Managing
Planning is a way of managing time and events. Your plans may be short or long term. A middle-school or junior or senior high-school teacher may plan for five or six 55-minute time periods throughout the day. An elementary teacher may plan for 15- to 30-minute segments of instruction. Teachers also develop plans for larger units of time, including daily, weekly, monthly, and yearly plans. The amount of time a teacher plans may be a function of the time allocated by the state or district for the school day, the curriculum or content to be taught, and the knowledge and motivational levels of the students.

Decision Making
Planning for teaching is the ability to make decisions about the how and what of teaching. These decisions are based on three primary considerations: (1) the students' prior (affective and cognitive) learning experiences in the classroom; (2) the con-

tent derived from curriculum guides, textbooks, study guides, and teacher-developed materials; and (3) the context or conditions in which the instruction will take place.

Decision making is the ability to select from among several alternatives and implement one or more alternatives within a fixed period of time. During instruction, decision making is almost instantaneous. Planning allows for some decisions to become routine, enabling you to limit the time and energy expended on events that occur frequently. For example, deciding each day how to distribute or collect papers would be an ineffective use of instructional time. Once a routine is established for passing out papers by row and returning the finished papers to a "grading box," the need to make further decisions about assignments is limited to possible future revisions.

FUNCTIONS OF PLANNING

Many travel advisors suggest the local library as a good starting point in planning a trip. Knowledge is an important tool in planning a journey; it is also an important starting point in planning to teach. Planning gives you the advantage of controlling classroom instruction in a positive way. Planning has several benefits, ranging from providing an overview of instruction to establishing a repertoire of instructional strategies that build from daily successes and accumulate from year to year. The following list highlights the functions of planning.

1. *Planning gives an overview of instruction.* A plan presents you with a total picture of the lesson for the day or for the entire year. Knowing where you are going enables you to coordinate the development of materials, resources, and activities that will enrich instruction.

Many experienced teachers take a calendar at the beginning of the school year and divide the content to be taught for the remainder of the year. (See Samples and Examples, at the end of this chapter, for "A Year at a Glance" planning calendar.) Knowing what should be achieved by specific blocks of time provides guideposts for instruction. Experienced teachers include vacation times, standardized testing periods, site visits from state or regional accrediting agencies, and other important dates that diminish or change actual teaching time. Knowing what will interfere or alter the presentation of a lesson or unit enables you to plan around or incorporate these events.

2. *Planning facilitates good management and instruction.* Planning provides for a sense of order for the teacher and the students. Order is an important part of good management and discipline (Doyle, 1986). It is evident to a student as well as a classroom when the teacher has a clear direction for what is next. Learning flourishes in an environment of order. Students will flounder if you wander from activity to activity without any clear sense of direction or purpose. Valuable instructional time is lost and students become restless when they need to wait for the lesson to begin.

Experienced classroom teachers recognize the difference in the effectiveness of their lessons when they have not planned. Effective planning reduces the opportunities for student disruptions by providing a smooth flow of instructional events and activities during and between lessons. Order and purpose, however, should not be confused with rigidity and inflexibility. It is easier to change plans to meet student learning needs if you begin with a plan.

3. *Planning makes learning purposeful.* Research on teaching effectiveness strongly supports the belief that purpose must be provided in the instructional process (Wittrock, 1986). The teacher who thinks about the reasons for specific behaviors in the classroom and communicates academic and behavioral expectations to the students will increase student opportunities for learning and reduce anxiety and uncertainty.

The previous Snapshot on page 22 describes how sharing plans can make learning purposeful. The Samples and Examples section (at the end of this chapter) contains copies of a weekly calendar and syllabus, which may also assist you and the students in planning and learning.

4. *Planning provides for sequencing and pacing.* Most textbooks, workbooks, or district curriculum guides present a sequencing of the content. The teacher needs to review these materials at the beginning of the lesson or year to determine if the sequence is reasonable for the students and to decide what enriching activities should be provided along with the text materials. Planning enables you to place one content area in juxtaposition to previous and future instruction. Once information about the content has been reviewed, decisions about the daily, weekly, and monthly sequencing can be determined.

5. *Planning ties classroom instructional events with community resources.* Without planning, those teachable moments where school, home, and community are linked will occur less often. Knowing what will occur, at least in a general sense, two or three months ahead will allow you to coordinate community events with classroom instruction. Exhibits, guest speakers, special television programs, special performances by local arts groups all could be missed opportunities if reservations are required several weeks or months in advance and the scope of the content for the year is not evident. Teaching is clearly more than transmitting information from the textbook to the student. The teacher's ability to provide richness to the lessons requires going beyond basic classroom resources.

6. *Planning reduces the impact of intrusions.* There are over 300 teacher/student interactions in a typical 50-minute period at both the elementary and secondary

TEACHER TALK_____

If I am interrupted during a lesson, I am usually able to pick up where we stopped when I have a well thought-out lesson plan. However, those days when I haven't spent the time planning can be a problem. It seems the number of things that can go wrong on those days always escalates.

11th-Grade Science Teacher

levels. Add to these interactions the intrusions from the PA system or office, visitors at the door, lost lunch money, or students arriving late to class, and one can easily see that the classroom is a busy place. Planning reduces the need to wait until the last moment to organize materials or identify resources. Intrusions into the teaching day are unfortunate but without planning the intrusions would take a much greater toll on instructional time. Teachers who have a plan for the day report that they are less affected by the daily intrusions into the classroom.

7. *Planning for economy of time.* Time is the greatest natural resource for the classroom teacher. Like any resource, it can be easily wasted. Time is lost when material are not ready, equipment has not been tested, students are unaware of what comes next, and the teacher lacks a plan for the day. Planning enables you to portion out time for specific activities and lessons throughout the day. Many lesson plans include a space for the time a particular activity will take during a lesson. Beginning teachers may benefit from a timed lesson plan (see Figure 2.1), whereas most experienced teachers usually internalize the timing sequence or make brief notes about the time needed for specific activities.

8. *Planning makes learner success more measurable, which assists in reteaching.* It is easy to lose track of student learning in the dynamics of day-to-day interactions. You need to determine the specific outcomes as well as level of mastery for instruction before moving on to the next lesson or unit. By identifying the outcomes of learning before instruction begins, the teacher has a better gauge of student success and teaching effectiveness. For example, a 95 percent accuracy level for addition is a

FIGURE 2.1 *Lesson Plan*

Focus:	To identify the bones, functions, and some diseases of the human skeleton.
Population:	9th grade
Subject:	Biology
Objective:	Student will identify 22 bones of the human skeleton with a minimum of 80 percent accuracy. (To be continued the next day.)
Rationale:	To aid the students in understanding their own body.
Room Set-Up:	Availability of a human skeleton, blackboard, and two computers with database for the one-week lesson.

Time (in Minutes)		Activities	Materials
5.0	*Anticipatory Set:*	What are the functions of the bones of your body?	Overhead
3.0	*Objective:*	Student will identify major leg bones of the human skeleton.	Blackboard Skeleton Handout
	Instructional Input:	Common names and scientific names of the bones.	Skeleton
	Modeling:	Students write the names of the bones on corresponding handout.	Blackboard Handout Skeleton
35.0	*Guided Practice:*		
	Independent Practice:	To be achieved on the computer database in pairs.	Computer software of human skeleton
5.0	*Evaluation:*	What did you learn about leg bones of the human skeleton?	Overhead
2.0	*Closure:*	Tomorrow we will continue with the human skeleton, focusing on the arms (show x-ray).	Overhead

Source: Michelle Brightwell. Reprinted by permission.

reasonable expectation for first-graders. Moving on to subtraction before mastering addition will present serious problems for the students and their future teachers.

9. *Planning provides for a variety of instructional activities.* Incorporating new instructional strategies into your current teaching practices requires conscious

effort and practice. Many veteran classroom teachers have expressed concerns about attempting new instructional strategies. Planning plays an important role in making unfamiliar strategies more familiar. New instructional strategies, such as cooperative learning groups or peer tutoring, initially require more planning and preparation time for successful implementation. An absence of planning also reduces the options for incorporating or enriching more complex lessons that require audiovisual equipment, guest speakers, or manipulative materials into the learning experience.

The following Snapshot supports the importance of planning for incorporating new instructional activities into the classroom. The teacher is planning a unit on environmental science, and the lesson described in the Snapshot focuses on the effects of civilization on animal habitat. The teacher, Maryellen Snyder (1988), has decided to develop a simulation for the students, entitled "Habitat: A Game of Chance," which simulates the problems wild animals face in coping with civilization. Each student selects a card, which describes the type of animal he or she is to be for the game (e.g., deer, rabbit, or racoon). The object of the game is for the animal and its habitat to survive the challenges faced by interacting with civilization. The Snapshot describes the development of the game and the teacher's thinking about the planning process.

SNAPSHOT

I learned more about the benefits of planning with this lesson. Because I was using a complicated strategy and was designing a complex game from scratch, a lot of preparation went into this lesson. During the process of making the cards for the game, I was able to think through the game. Up to teaching time I was still making minor revisions and additions. The fact that the game went smoothly and was successful made all the planning worthwhile.

I knew that for any chance of success with this game I was going to have to be on top of things. I often take lectures for granted and do not do the planning and preparation that I should. An aspect that I overplanned for in my lesson plan I feared would not be reached—that of an emotional connection—developed as a result of the game. I wanted something more than just a detached acquiring of information.

I did not have the time in the lesson to have an activity focused specifically in the affective domain, but it came out on its own. After being an animal struggling through this game, students had a much better feeling about the fragile life situations of animals. It made the students stop and think. The simulation game took a great deal of planning and preparation, but the students benefited and I realized the importance that planning plays in adding new strategies to my teaching repertoire. (Snyder, 1988)

---

10. *Planning creates the opportunity for higher-level questioning.* Most teachers ask lower-order factual questions of their students (e.g., Who was the first president of the United States?) (Dillon, 1984). Incorporating higher-level thinking skills begins

with higher-level questions (e.g., How would you feel if you were a deer in the "Habitat: A Game of Chance"?). Additional effort is needed if you are to make higher-level questioning a normal part of the lesson. Writing higher-level questions (on 3 × 5 cards or a sheet of paper) prior to the lesson in the lesson plan book will reduce the chance that key questions will be omitted during instruction.

11. *Planning assists in ordering supplies.* Planning for next year begins now. The lesson that lacked enough manipulatives for the students will need to be noted if the same problem is to be avoided the next time the lesson is taught. Most districts collect supply requisitions during the spring and order them during the summer. Knowing the requisition system of your district will greatly reduce the disappointment faced by many teachers who forgot to make a list of needed instructional materials and supplies for the following year.

12. *Planning guides substitute teachers.* The hard work of creating order and routine in the classroom may be sidetracked by a substitute teacher who has no plan to follow. If the school district does not have a specific format for substitutes, then a detailed lesson plan should be provided. (See the sample substitute lesson letter in the Samples and Examples section at the end of this chapter.)

13. *Planning provides documentation of instruction.* We live in a highly legalized bureaucratic society. Teachers need to provide documentation for evaluation purposes as well as to reduce the possibility of liability. Most school districts require some form of lesson planning. Principals may require daily plans be turned in at the end of the week. Also, most evaluators require a lesson plan prior to observing in the classroom. According to Richard Henak (1980), who writes for the National Educational Association, teachers may be held liable for not teaching proper safety procedures in laboratory settings: "If the teacher can offer proof that safety procedures are taught in certain classes, it is more difficult to show negligence on the teacher's part. A lesson plan which includes safety content is one way to help establish such proof" (p. 22).

14. *Planning establishes a repertoire of instructional strategies.* Planning enables you to build on the past, examining and changing those elements of teaching that were ineffective and including those elements that were successful. Expertness in teaching is more than years of doing the same lessons. It requires building a repertoire of instructional strategies that are both global and specific in responding to changing teaching situations.

Planning Limitations

There are some limitations in the planning process. In a study on the effects of planning on teaching, Zahorik (1970) indicated that "planning makes the teacher's thinking rigid and puts him on a track that is nearly derail-proof" (p. 149). Zahorik suggested that greater flexibility on the part of the teacher, as well as sensitivity to the needs of students, would alleviate teacher inflexibility that may occur in planning. Beginning teachers may see planning as a script to follow rather than as a guide through the lesson.

Planning provides a framework for instruction that is constantly being buffeted by the events of the school day. Fire drills, shortened class schedules, assemblies, guest speakers, bomb threats, and severe weather are but a few of the events that impact on the instructional plans for the day.

Planning takes time, and many beginning as well as experienced classroom teachers find time to be in short supply. Most teachers indicate that out-of-school time must be used for planning. Some school districts provide a planning period, however, parent conferences, grade-level or team meetings, school functions coordination, student tutorials, and other tasks compete for time that may be designated for planning during the school day.

Although there are no absolutes for teaching and change is an inevitable part of the teaching profession, the limitations of planning are outweighed by the benefits.

PLANNING PHASES

The action of planning is a highly developed process of thinking through various alternatives and possibilities. There are several distinct phases of planning: (1) *Preplanning*, (2) *Active planning*, (3) *Ongoing planning*, and (4) *Postplanning*. Each phase has a function in the planning process, and key decisions are made at each level, which determines movement to the next phase (see Figures 2.2 and 2.3).

The first two phases, Preplanning and Active planning, occur prior to actual instruction. During the *preplanning* phase, tentative mental plans are developed and decisions are made regarding the design and implementation of a lesson or larger instructional unit. *Active planning* entails the physical gathering of resources and materials in preparation for teaching. Written lesson plans are usually developed during this phase of the planning process. *Ongoing planning* occurs during instruction and requires the teacher to think quickly to modify a plan that is not working. These corrections are an everyday part of teaching. Rigid adherence to a plan that does not help students learn is clearly counterproductive. *Postplanning* is the self-assessment and the last stage in the planning process. Making notes of postplanning is feedback to you for future lessons. It also becomes part of the planning repertoire each teacher acquires through reflective assessments of the lessons and the teaching day.

Preplanning

During the Preplanning stage, information is being gathered about the students' past and present achievements and motivational levels, the content that is to be

FIGURE 2.2 *Planning Phases*

Type:	Preplanning	Active Planning	Ongoing Planning	Postplanning
Activity:	Mental Plan	Written Plan	Fine-Tune Plan	Evaluate Plan
When:		Before Instruction	During	After

FIGURE 2.3 *Planning Phases*

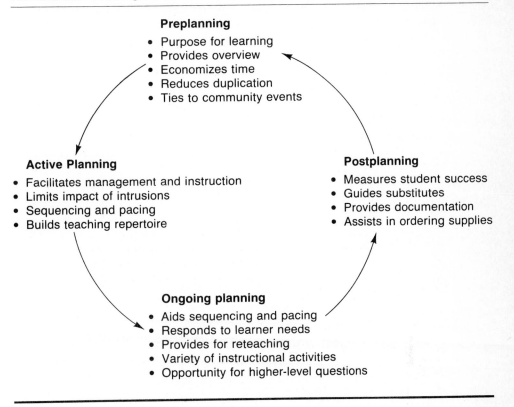

Preplanning
- Purpose for learning
- Provides overview
- Economizes time
- Reduces duplication
- Ties to community events

Active Planning
- Facilitates management and instruction
- Limits impact of intrusions
- Sequencing and pacing
- Builds teaching repertoire

Postplanning
- Measures student success
- Guides substitutes
- Provides documentation
- Assists in ordering supplies

Ongoing planning
- Aids sequencing and pacing
- Responds to learner needs
- Provides for reteaching
- Variety of instructional activities
- Opportunity for higher-level questions

presented, and the conditions in which the instruction is to be presented. The Preplanning stage represents the mental process of considering various instructional alternatives and deciding on one or several approaches for teaching. It is also during this stage that a mental picture of the sequence of instructional events and the resources needed to implement instruction are considered. Expert teachers report their ability to visualize a lesson from beginning to end by mentally testing their plans against the teaching/learning environment. The ability to visualize what has yet to occur requires either a repertoire of past experiences or a systematic plan to gather enough information to create the image.

Mental Processes
Preplanning may occur during the summer months, driving to school, during lunch, after school, and on weekends. Preplanning activities for the first day of school are very different from preplanning activities for the 51st day of school. Planning is a cumulative process that builds on previous experiences. The more familiar a teacher becomes with the course content, students, and school and classroom environment, the easier it is to plan.

Cognitive Monitoring

Manning (1984) describes four times when teachers could monitor their own thinking. This process, called *cognitive monitoring*, may occur during (1) planning, (2) instructing and interacting with students, (3) listening to students, and (4) evaluating instruction.

The monitoring points suggested by Manning parallel the four phases of planning described in this chapter. Cognitive monitoring could occur during preplanning and active planning (planning); ongoing planning (instructing and interacting with students, and listening to students); and postplanning (evaluating instruction). Awareness of what is occurring during planning and instruction will enable you continually to build on past experiences in a systematic manner.

In her research using cognitive monitoring, Neely (1986) identified 16 questions teachers should ask themselves to improve the quality of the planning process:

1. *How should I plan for the seating arrangement to use during this lesson?*
2. *Which students have special needs that should be attended to during the lesson?*
3. *What discipline and management techniques will I incorporate?*
4. *What role will I take on during this lesson?*
5. *Where will I place the materials I have listed?*
6. *How well do I understand the content of the lesson?*
7. *What changes will I feel most comfortable with during the lesson?*
8. *Why should I teach this lesson?*
9. *Is this going to be too easy/difficult for this group?*
10. *What attention do I need to give the other students while I'm working with this small group?*
11. *How will I handle interruptions to limit interference in this lesson?*
12. *How will I check on student understanding?*
13. *What are my alternative plans if problems arise in this first plan?*
14. *How will I conclude the lesson?*
15. *What will students do as this lesson ends?*
16. *How will I make transitions to the next lesson? (Neely, 1986, p. 31)*

The self-probing that occurs during the preplanning stage of instruction will enable thoughts to effectively influence subsequent actions in the implementation of a lesson. The Research Vignette discusses more of Neely's research on cognitive monitoring.

Thoughts to Actions

The mental actions of deciding what to do is a continuous process once a plan is selected. The decision to move from the preplanning to the active planning stage is identifiable in talking to experienced teachers. We asked three teachers, a first-grade teacher, a seventh-grade social studies teacher, and an eleventh-grade science teacher, to think aloud about their planning. The first-grade teacher was planning a phonics lesson for the letter *a*.

TEACHER TALK

I am going to teach the *a* sounds on Monday and Tuesday during language arts time. I have 15 to 20 minutes each day in the mornings. I will use the phonics program, which includes hand puppets and a cassette tape with songs that sound out the different combinations for the *a* sound. I need to have the children practice the different *a* sounds in small groups so I can hear them. What I don't finish on Monday I will continue on Tuesday.

AUTHOR'S NOTE: *The first part of this teacher's preplanning includes a global overview of the lesson. She is an experienced classroom teacher, so this segment took her only a few seconds to determine. She then moved on to some specific sequences:*

I will hold up the puppet with a big letter on his front and ask the children to tell me what the letter is. Most of my students will be able to identify the letter. From there, we will move on to identifying other words that begin with the letter *a*. I will then play the cassette to reinforce with songs what we have discussed and to introduce the different *a* sounds. To keep the noise levels manageable, I will pair the students and ask them to whisper the sounds to each other. I will also want each child to talk into a tape recorder (giving the *a* sounds) and to listen to themselves.

1st-Grade Teacher

The more specific steps of the lesson begin to take form as the teacher concludes the preplanning stage and moves to the active planning stage.

It is during the active planning stage that materials and other resources are physically gathered. The lesson that requires maps, stories, handouts, manipulatives, or materials the teacher will need are prepared. The active planning stage is the preparation stage for teaching. The first-grade teacher will need to check the cassette tape recorder, and the availability of the song tape and puppets, which are shared by four first-grade teachers.

A seventh-grade social studies teacher described his third-period class: "They come to history very unmotivated and I need to give them a sense of being there before learning will occur." He is going to start a unit on the American Civil War.

TEACHER TALK

I decided, given their lack of motivation, I would try to create a feeling of the times. I plan on going to the local library and photocopy some newspaper stories and editorials from 1855 to 1860. I will select my stories and editorials from the northern and southern newspapers. I want them to see how the political climate changed during the five years prior to the Civil War and read what were the key issues. The newspaper stories will be more on their reading level than the textbook we are currently using.

Teacher Education Research Vignette

INTRODUCTION

Ann Neely (1986) studied the effects of cognitive monitoring—the ability to monitor one's thinking—on preservice lesson planning. Both lesson planning and implementation were more effective for preservice teachers who used cognitive monitoring in their classrooms.

STUDY DESIGN

Neely selected 76 undergraduate early childhood teacher education students in their first methods class. The 76 students were randomly assigned to control and experimental groups for their placement in elementary schools for their field experiences: 42 were in the experimental group and 34 were in the control group. The experimental group received training in cognitive monitoring and learned to probe their plans through self-questioning, self-reinforcement, and goal setting. Each student answered the 16 questions on page 32. Students were asked to use these questions when planning, instructing, listening to students, and making student evaluations.

Students in the experimental group were asked to keep a log of their self-probes and to identify, on their lesson plans, the questions and self-probes. Each of the 76 students taught a 30-minute lesson on creative writing. The Georgia Teacher Performance Assessment Instrument was used in part to evaluate the lesson plans and the lessons. The observers did not know which students had training in cognitive monitoring.

RESULTS

As the table below shows, the total number of points earned for the lesson written was 25 and the maximum score for the lesson was 140. The group trained in cognitive monitoring scored 21 points and 127 points, whereas the control group, which received no self-monitoring training, scored 16 and 120, respectively. The differences in the scores were judged to be statistically significant.

Neely reported that cognitive monitoring improved the students' ability to "identify goals and objectives, organize lessons, predict outcomes, establish alternate plans and be sensitive to student needs" (p. 32).

CONCLUSIONS AND IMPLICATIONS FOR PRACTICE

Cognitive monitoring allowed for the teacher's own behavior to become part of the lesson plan. Whereas most lesson plans identify what the students will learn, the use of self-probes can make you aware of what your own behavior will be in the lesson. This study was conducted with preservice teachers. We shared the list of questions (see page 32) with veteran teachers and they found it very useful with their own planning. Without some thought and reflection of instructional plans before, during, and after the lesson, potential growth for improvement could be lost.

Treatment and Control Group Differences for Adequacy of Written Plans and Classroom Implementation

| Variable | Maximum Possible Scores | Group | | | | | |
| | | Experimental (N = 42) | | Control (N = 34) | | | |
		X	SD	X	SD	t	P
Written Plans	25	20.48	3.29	16.21	2.79	6.01	0.0001*
Classroom implementation	140	126.81	7.79	120.09	10.93	3.02	0.0038*

*$p<.05$

Source: Neely, A. (1986). Planning and problem solving in teacher education. Journal of Teacher Education, 37(3), 29–33. Reprinted with permission from the Journal of Teacher Education.

I plan to divide the class into a northern and a southern group and give each group the news articles and editorials from their region. Then I will ask the students to debate the issues from their articles' perspective. If time allows, I will have the groups switch sides and read the other group's articles and take a new position. I may have the students take the articles home for homework to read if I find the lesson is taking too much time.

This is the first time I have started the unit this way, but I recently read in my professional journal about more motivating approaches to the Civil War. I plan to spend two classes on the lesson. This is a lot for a warm-up, but I am hoping the added interest will pay dividends during the remainder of the Civil War unit.

7th-Grade Social Studies Teacher

This teacher is developing a lesson that incorporates a new teaching approach. Additional thought at the preplanning stage is required due to the newness of the format. The details of the lesson are still to be developed. His decision to use a "you-are-there" approach to the Civil War topic was based on his understanding of the students, the difficulty of the textbook for their reading levels, and the need to motivate them. He had prior experience with teaching the Civil War unit and was familiar with the use of original source materials from reading his professional journals.

The eleventh-grade chemistry teacher is about to teach a unit on periodic laws, and the starting point for her unit is the periodic table.

TEACHER TALK

I presented a lecture on the development of the periodic table developed by Dmitry Mendeleyev in 1869 to my eleventh-grade chemistry class. I described how Mendeleyev put small slips of paper on the wall with the known elements of his time and their atomic weights and how he arranged the elements according to the magnitude of their atomic weights (for example, H-1 hydrogen would be first on the list and H-2 helium would be second). Based on this chart, Mendeleyev was able to predict the atomic weights of elements still undiscovered. I presented the periodic table as it exists today and discussed the importance of this discovery to modern chemistry.

I felt the presentation was effective, but when I gave my students a quiz the next day the results were dismal. The students had memorized the specifics about the periodic table, but they failed to understand the relationships of the elements to each other.

I decided to teach it a different way to my seventh-period class, which was a day behind my fifth-period class. This time, I had them go through the same process that Mendeleyev experienced in developing the periodic table. I gave them the elements and atomic weights known in 1869 (without being in any order) and asked the students working in their table teams to develop some logical order for the elements. Once they achieved this, I asked them if they could predict the atomic weights of any future elements. I then showed them the current periodic table and they compared their predictions with the existing table. The results were exciting and the students began to see the relationships between the elements.

This seventh-period lesson took much more planning, preparation, and thinking before I felt comfortable with the approach. I only had one day and was up until 11:30 that night preparing for the lesson. I needed to prepare 3 × 5 cards for each of the six groups in my class. After the lesson started and one group began to place the elements on the blackboard, I discovered that the cards were too small for the class to see. So, in the middle of the lesson, I handed out blank sheets of 8½ × 11 ditto paper for them to write the elements. They needed the 3 × 5 cards to do the sorting and the larger ditto sheets took only one or two minutes to create, with each student in the team having a few elements to complete.

Sometimes you need to make in-flight corrections while teaching. I was too tired to think about the size of the cards the previous evening, but I was able to readjust during the lesson. The results were well worth the extra effort. The students all passed the quiz and I felt a real sense of excitement on their part when they discovered Mendeleyev's periodic table.

11th-Grade Science Teacher

This chemistry teacher provides us with an example of how assessing the impact of learning (postplanning) in one class (fifth period) changed the plans for the same lesson with another class (seventh period). The following day, in this case, the teacher's postplanning led back to the preplanning and active planning stages to rethink the lesson. The changes made during the lesson with the larger sheets is a good example of the types of ongoing or in-flight changes made during the lesson.

The mental process of planning is rarely discussed or taught in any formal way, yet it represents an important part of teaching. Veteran teachers have the advantage of using past experiences with similar contexts, contents, and learners. New teachers are at a disadvantage with these three important frames of reference. Becoming more aware of the planning process of other teachers and developing a repertoire of planning strategies will provide new teachers and experienced teachers who are not satisfied with their planning, or face changing conditions, a better foundation for planning.

Active Planning

The active planning stage indicates a decision and commitment have been made toward one specific plan. Active planning and preplanning include all the actions that occur prior to teaching in the classroom. The self-probes and questions have been answered and the teacher's mental plan is beginning to take form. It is during this stage that the content (what to teach) takes on greater meaning. A plan to teach specific facts, ideas, or concepts revolves around your understanding of the students, district curriculum, teacher guides, textbook materials, and the instructional methods needed to communicate, translate, transfer, and create an environment in which students will learn. The methods of teaching (how to teach) are only as effective as your knowledge level of the subject matter to be taught. The how and what of teaching both take on greater importance as the teacher moves from the preplanning to the active planning stage.

Content Focus

Although curriculum guides and textbooks exist for most subject areas, it is evident that what is taught is a condition of the mastery of the content by the teacher. Mastery, or at least a level of comfort, with the content is the starting point for many teachers. Some teachers may be content poor and this may be the greatest limitation in the planning process and in teaching. Many elementary teachers, for example, avoid science instruction because of their limited exposure to advanced science courses in high school and college. This avoidance is evident when students from the United states are compared with students from other nations in science achievement. A deficiency in content knowledge requires the teacher to take the initiative and seek out additional resources. Excellent sources of information include textbooks, other than the one being used for instruction, district curriculum guides, college texts, and college courses with a focus on content as well as methods.

Teaching Strategies

The active planning stage brings together the content to be taught with the strategies for teaching. The strategies or methods of instruction include the ways in which the content is transformed into new learning for the students. The content can be transformed directly from the teacher to the student through lecture, demonstration, drill, and questioning. The content may also be transformed more indirectly, where the teacher's role is to facilitate learning situations through grouping, discovery, inquiry, roleplay, and simulations.

Including unfamiliar strategies in your teaching repertoire requires more planning than using strategies that you have experienced or utilized previously. In the Snapshot on page 28, Maryellen Snyder, the environmental science teacher, used a simulation strategy to teach her students the impact of civilization on animal habitats. Moving away from the lecture format for this lesson, which was her usual strategy, to a simulation required additional planning. She had to consider that students would be working in groups of four, materials had to be distributed, and rules and time frames needed to be established and communicated to the students. The Habitat simulation is now part of her curriculum on environmental science and she will be able to fine-tune the simulation as she uses it with different groups of students.

Ongoing Planning

The ongoing planning stage arises during instruction. The realities of the rapidly changing classroom, lack of student mastery of previous lessons, and school scheduling changes frequently require modifications of teaching plans during the lesson. Many teachers describe changes in their plans while teaching as *in-flight corrections*. The term is common for airplane pilots who are required to submit a flight plan with air traffic controllers before departing. The best flight plans may need to be changed once a plane is airborn. In-flight corrections allow the pilot to adapt to changing conditions in the weather, at the landing site, or with the mechanical state of the airplane.

In teaching, conditions can change more rapidly than in flying. Being able to adjust to these changes is the mark of an adaptive teacher. McNair (1978–1979) conducted 60 interviews with 10 teachers to examine the in-flight decisions they make during reading lessons. The types of decisions teachers made while teaching included "whom to call upon, how to provide corrective feedback, when to discipline a given student, [and] how fast to proceed through the lesson . . ." (p. 26).

These corrections center around the transitions that are necessary to move from one part of the lesson to another, student understanding of lesson content, and the pace or timing of the lesson. Teachers who check for student understanding frequently during the lesson may realize some instances when the lesson may need to be retaught during the day (at the elementary level) or the next day (at the secondary level). Intrusions and student disruptions may also require changes in the initial plans. It is during this stage that changes are made in response to changing conditions that were not evident during the preplanning or active planning stages.

Fine Tuning

Ongoing planning is also known as *fine tuning* the lesson. As the plan for the day meets the reality of early dismissals, shortened classes, an assembly, a high-school pep rally, or a Halloween carnival, you are faced with fine tuning, changing, or completely scraping your well-designed plan. Fortunately, these events are more the exception than the rule, but they happen often enough to be an important consideration in the planning process. Strategies for fine tuning a lesson include lengthening or shortening a lesson, integrating the events for the day into the lesson, or reviewing the material taught over the last several weeks rather than beginning new instruction that will be interrupted.

Planning provides a framework for instruction, but the execution of the plan may require several adjustments along the way. There are few absolutes in teaching. The changing dynamics of the classroom reduce the certainties of the lesson plan. However, there are strategies that will assist you in reducing the need for major changes during instructional time. Consider the following:

1. Have all the resources prepared ahead of time, including handouts, materials for and other manipulatives for labs, extra paper, and pencils.
2. Create a checklist of the materials needed for the lesson. Check the clarity of handouts to eliminate going over illegible instructions or questions.

3. Prior to the students entering the class, post or display the objectives and activities of the day on the chalkboard or overhead. This will give the students and yourself a clear picture of the sequence of learning activities.
4. As they walk into the room, involve the students in an activity that reinforces prior learning. This will provide an academic focus for the lesson of the day and will determine the level of understanding of prior instruction.
5. Using 3 × 5 cards, write notes to yourself about specific points to be made during the lesson or higher-level questions you want to ask the students. Many elementary-level teachers will write notes on the chalkboard as a reminder of important tasks for both the teacher and students.

It is always helpful for the success of future lessons to review the day's activities that were effective or that needed revision. This becomes an important part of postplanning, which is the final stage of the planning process.

Postplanning

The final level in the planning process may occur as an afterthought of the lesson. The lesson is over and the plan book page is turned to the next day. Many teachers will make notes in the margins of their plan book about changes they need to make in the lesson when they teach it again next year. Our interviews with teachers indicate they keep journals, looseleaf books, or large monthly calendars to write down ideas and make notes for themselves. Postplanning affects planning for the next day as well as planning for future use of the lesson, usually for the following year.

Expert teachers realize that the freshness of ideas and feelings about the lesson will diminish with time. Trying to recall a year later, or even a day later, what went well or what needed to be changed is a frustrating task. In addition to assisting in the design of a lesson the following year, notes made about the lesson could assist in reviewing the content two or three months later. The following is a sample checklist of questions to be considered in the postplanning stage:

_____ What were the strengths and weaknesses of the lesson?
_____ Were the original objectives met in the lesson?
_____ What percentage of the class mastered the objective/content of the lesson?
_____ Was there too much or too little content for the time?
_____ Were the transitions between activities smooth?
_____ What additional resources or materials would be needed next time to make the lesson more successful?
_____ Did the activities fit the content being taught?
_____ Were the students active or passive learners?
_____ Were the support materials (text or workbooks, printed or visual materials) appropriate and available for the lesson?
_____ What changes in the lesson plan would be required to make the lesson more successful?

This list is designed to provide a framework for revising the lesson for future use, rather than be an exhaustive list. You may need to add other questions.

The four phases represent a framework for teacher planning that is cyclical in nature. The decisions made during the preplanning phase are influenced by the results of previous lessons and experiences in the postplanning stage. The active planning and ongoing planning phases denote the most intensive part of the planning process. The following list summarizes each of the planning phases with key descriptors:

Preplanning: Visualizing, sequencing, mental processing, cognitive monitoring and questioning, self-probing, and decision making

Active planning: Preparation, content focus, teaching strategies, and room and material organization

Ongoing planning: During instruction, in-flight corrections, transitions, and checking for prior understanding

Postplanning: Lesson analysis, immediate and future planning, written notes, and planning journals (see Figures 2.2 and 2.3)

CONSIDERATIONS FOR PLANNING

The four phases of planning (preplanning, active planning, ongoing planning, and postplanning) present a workable structure for thinking through the design and implementation of a lesson. The lesson, however, is a template that must match the learner, content, and context of the teaching situation. Designing a lesson that ignores the needs and previous learnings of the students or that poorly integrates the content with the strategies is doomed to failure. Additionally, a lesson that does not consider the context or environment in which the lesson will be taught will make the learning condition that much more difficult for both the teacher and students. We will examine the roles that the learner, content, and context play in planning for instruction.

SOURCES OF INFORMATION FOR PLANNING

Learner

In third-world countries where schooling is not universal, schools have a significant effect on the learner, when compared with those individuals who have not attended school. In industrialized countries like England, Japan, France, and the United States, where schooling is compulsory, the family tends to have a greater impact on the learner (Rutter, Maughan, Mortimore, Ouston, & Smith, 1979). All things being equal and regardless of one's race or ethnic heritage, a family that provides books, discussion, a range of learning experiences, and support for school, including assistance with homework (Paschal, Weinstein, & Walberg, 1983), will give its children an advantage. Children and youth who come to school lacking these experiences and support arrive with a disadvantage. This disadvantage takes the form of prior knowledge.

For example, two first-grade children, Charles and Brian, live in the city and have never seen or touched cows, pigs, or sheep. Both students were asked to identify a picture of a cow. Their choices for answers included a dog, a deer, a cow, and a bear. Charles circled the word *cow* as his answer, but Brian circled *dog* for his answer. Brian had never been exposed to four-legged animals other than the dog, cat, and rodents that he had seen in his neighborhood.

Charles's parents read to him each evening before bed. The stories are about animals, the zoo, letters, numbers, and exciting adventures. Brian only has a few books in his house and they are rarely read to him. When both children entered kindergarten, Charles was ready for the world of words, numbers, and discussion. Through the use of storybooks, Charles was introduced to words, ideas, and concepts he would meet again in school. Both children have equal potential for success in school; however, they will not succeed at the same rate or level. What is familiar to one student may seem like nonsense to another.

Entry Characteristics

Students bring to class what Benjamin Bloom (1976) calls a range of "entry characteristics," which Bloom divides into affective and cognitive behaviors. Affective characteristics incorporate the students' motivation to learn, and cognitive characteristics include the students' prior learnings. According to Bloom, the context of the learning environment and the quality of instruction will determine the learning outcomes. These outcomes embody the level and type of achievement, rate of learning, and affective outcomes (p. 11). See Figure 2.4 for Bloom's theory of school learning.

FIGURE 2.4 *Major Variables in the Theory of School Learning*

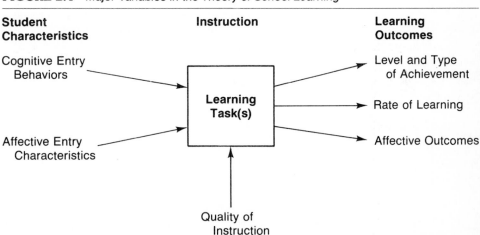

Source: Synthesis of entry characteristics identified by Bloom, B. (1982). *Human characteristics and school learning.* New York: McGraw-Hill. Reprinted with permission from McGraw-Hill, Inc.

FIGURE 2.5   *Entry Characteristics*

Affective Characteristics	Cognitive Characteristics
Motivation	Prior Learnings
Personal Self-Concept	Achievement Level
Content Related Affect	Intelligence Level
School Related Affect	Reading Comprehension

Source: Synthesis of entry characteristics identified by Bloom, B. (1982). *Human characteristics and school learning.* New York: McGraw-Hill. Reprinted with permission from McGraw-Hill, Inc.

Learner characteristics are summarized in Figure 2.5. Affective behaviors include the level of motivation and student self-concept. The motivation to learn and personal self-concept begin in the home prior to formal schooling. The values of the parents for learning and the opportunity to learn prior to school play important roles in the formation of affective characteristics. School- and content-related affect result from a students' prior experiences with schooling and subject matter.

Cognitive characteristics include the prior learnings that a student brings to the classroom. Bloom (1976) indicates that a good predictor of reading success at the first-grade level is the extent of the vocabulary a child brings to school. The same is true for mathematics. A child who knows his or her numbers prior to school will be at an advantage.

The intelligence level of a student is another entry characteristic. General intelligence, as measured by IQ tests, are perhaps a means of determining the academic potential of a student. In recent years the use of IQ tests have been considered a less valid means of measuring academic potential. Educators have been concerned that the scores will be used to establish lower expectations for some students, and the issue of test bias for minority students has also raised serious questions about its use as a predictor for academic success.

Achievement levels, as measured by teacher-made tests, report card grades, and standardized tests, form another entry characteristic. In planning for instruction, the entry characteristics identified by Bloom should be used as a starting point rather than as a justification for student academic failure. Knowing the students in the classroom and designing instruction that responds to their needs is an important first step.

Knowing the Student

Creating a positive yet realistic image of the students and the total class may require going outside the usual sources of data (previous standardized test scores, grades, and other tearchers' comments). These data sources could be used for some diagnostic purposes, but they may also reflect stereotypes built over the years that are perpetuated from teacher to teacher. A few examples of other sources of data that could be used by the teacher to assist in the planning process are described below. The examples are designed to be illustrative rather than exhaustive.

The research literature is consistent on the importance of knowing students in class as early in the school year as possible (Emmer, 1987; Doyle, 1986). Planning activities to get to know the students' names and something about their academic and personal interests will provide an avenue for being more effective in planning your instruction.

   • *Class Photographs.* It is an arduous process to get to know 150 students if you teach at the secondary level. Although the task is difficult, the rewards will be great if the students sense that you care enough to know them by name during the first week of school. Many secondary teachers take photographs of their students on the first day or two of school and have the film processed at a one-hour photo lab.

   • *Home Calls.* Many elementary teachers call each of the 30 parents of their students the first few weeks of school to introduce themselves and discuss any rules, procedures, homework schedules, or activities that will be occurring in the class. The tone is always positive, and most parents are pleasantly surprised that a teacher is calling when something isn't *wrong.* Teachers report that these calls made at the beginning of the year before academic or discipline problems arise are helpful in planning for the class. They also report that the telephone conversations with a parent or guardian increase their background knowledge of the students and provide an understanding of the home environment. A sample format for home telephone calls is provided in the Sample and Examples section at the end of this chapter.

   Some school districts provide secondary teachers with a day off as compensation for calling all the parents in the evenings or on weekends. One high-school mathematics teacher who was required to call parents was initially annoyed at the imposition on her time. However, she later reported that the telephone calls to parents, guardians, and in some cases to older brothers and sisters made a real difference in both the behavior of the students and academic learning. She described it as the best year she had in teaching.

   • *Autobiographies.* Some teachers ask the students the first day of school to write on a 4 × 6 card or a sheet of paper their name, address, home telephone, and work telephone (for secondary students). On the reverse side of the paper or card the students are asked the following questions:

   What do you feel are your strengths in this subject?
   What do you feel are your weaknesses in this subject?
   What do you expect to learn this semester from this class?
   What could I do to make this class your best learning experience?
   What could you do to make this class your best learning experience?

   As teachers, we naturally get to know the children who are behavior problems or academically gifted. Those students who sit quietly and rarely interact become anonymous faces. It is these students whom we must make an extra effort to know.

Content

Content is another name for the curriculum or those learning experiences that are provided to students in school. The curriculum also incorporates the plans that teachers use to guide students through those learning experiences (Glatthorn, 1987). The curriculum is derived from the values of the society. A democratic society like the United States, which values an informed and educated public, includes reading, literacy, and citizenship in the school curriculum. The study of the Constitution, Bill of Rights, and the steps leading to independence, for example, are weighted heavily in the curriculum. In most states, the part of American history that emphasizes democratic principles is taught several times in both elementary and secondary classrooms.

Written Curriculum

The curriculum is available to teachers in a written form, which becomes the main source of content for teaching. These written sources primarily include published textbooks, state and local curriculum guides, teacher editions of textbooks, and workbooks. The curriculum may also be found in packaged materials, including textbooks, workbooks, videotapes, slide tapes, and film materials.

Many states have specific books they purchase and provide to school districts free of charge on the condition that local districts select their textbooks from a state-approved list. Districts who choose to select their own books face considerable expense in providing texts for all its students. The states are able to control the curriculum and provide continuity from district to district through the use of state-adopted textbook purchases. States also provide state curriculum guides to supplement the textbooks. In Texas, for example, the state has identified "essential elements" that reflect minimal levels of content to be taught in all schools in Texas. These so-called essential elements are later assessed through a state-mandated test given to students each year. Students who fail to pass the state test may be held back from advancing to the next grade.

In planning a lesson or mapping out the course of study for an entire year, the teacher must be aware of state, district, and school building requirements and the resources that are provided by each of the levels to support instruction. Current educational reforms of the teaching profession by state legislatures and state education agencies have given greater attention to the standardization of the curriculum between and within school districts. The written curriculum reflects one level of the school curriculum. A second level—the unwritten curriculum—exists in most schools.

Unwritten Curriculum

The unwritten or hidden curriculum (Posner, 1985) is part of most school environments. The hidden curriculum reflects the values of the community that supports the schools, the administrators and teachers who manage and teach in the schools, and the beliefs and values of the larger society. The hidden curriculum sends a variety of messages to students about their behavior, work habits, and home culture.

Students begin to learn about the hidden curriculum as they observe the reactions of teachers and administrators to specific events that occur each day in school. Students are expected to be in class on time, bring all their materials, respect adults, and attend school regularly. There are rules for functioning in the school that are rarely taught but are usually enforced. The hidden curriculum reflects many of the same virtues required to function later in the world of work. It is only recently that the rules for behavior and academic expectations are being taught in the classroom.

Many students and some teachers are not sensitive to this hidden curriculum. This lack of sensitivity or awareness may be due to their being new to the school or not understanding the norms and values that are part of the hidden curriculum. Teachers who are new to a school may want to find a veteran teacher to be a guide in understanding this phenomenon. Students who enter after the school year has begun may need to be paired with a peer who can help the student understand the new environment.

In many instances, the written curriculum is a given. Printed and/or published materials provided by the state, district, or school present the teacher with a framework or, in some instances, a mandate for what is to be taught. Decisions about specifics for individual lessons, however, require considerable judgment and numerous compromises on the part of the teacher to translate the volumes of written materials to a manageable level for students (Glatthorn, 1987). Teachers who consider only the content when planning a lesson miss the complete picture. The student and the context in which the lesson is to be taught should also be considered in planning instruction.

Textbooks and Other Guides

The content of the lesson is usually considered first in the preplanning stage. In a study by McCutcheon (1980), between 85 and 95 percent of the reading and mathematics instruction in 12 elementary classrooms was based on textbooks and other published instructional material. From our discussion with secondary teachers and after reviewing their written plans, the same level of textbook use is also evident in middle- and high-school classrooms.

The teacher's edition of a textbook and the curriculum guide provide a framework for the lesson. There is a tendency for beginning teachers to use these guides as scripts for each lesson. Expert teachers realize that these resource materials are designed to be a starting point for learning rather than an end point. McCutcheon (1980) found in his ethnographic study of 12 experienced elementary teachers that changes in the recommendations of their teacher's guides were based on the following critria:

1. *Do these children need to learn this or do they already know it?*
2. *Will this activity fit into the amount of time I have?*
3. *Could I ask better questions than the ones in the teacher's guide?*
4. *How can I relate it to what they already know or experience in their daily lives and to other things they are doing?*

5. *Could I do part of this activity as boardwork for the group to do while I work with another group?*
6. *Are the children likely to be able to do it?*
7. *Are there problems with the lesson, errors in the book? (p. 10)*

When we asked secondary teachers to determine their use of teacher's guides, they reported many of the same criteria as listed above. Criteria number 5 was not identified since most secondary teachers use whole-group interactions and rarely teach one group while another is doing seatwork.

It is important for the teacher to move beyond the textbook and enrich the lesson with additional examples from the teacher or other sources. Building a repertoire of supporting and enriching activities is an important part of teaching and learning. The repertoire of ideas and activities for the lesson require a building process for cataloguing supporting resources for instruction. Experienced teachers face similar problems of building a new repertoire when new textbook series are adopted by their districts. Considerations of content need to be explored at both the preplanning and active planning phases of designing a lesson, and during the postplanning stage to evaluate needed changes for future lessons. The learner, content, and context are important considerations at all four levels of the planning process. The next consideration in planning is the context or environment in which the lesson will be taught.

Context

The context or environment in which you will teach is an important element in planning. The classroom context includes, for example: (1) the physical arrangement of the classroom (including open space, self-contained environments); (2) desks, chairs, tables, and other furnishings; (3) time of day; (4) class size; (5) other classes or activities that precede or follow the class; (6) class location (e.g., Will the drill team be practicing outside the window?); (7) audiovisual equipment (video, overhead projector, tape player, slide projector); and (8) duplicators, including copiers and ditto machines. The classroom context, which includes colors in the classroom, noise levels within and around the room, chalkboards, wall space, lighting, toys, comfort levels, storage space, and cleanliness, are additional examples of conditions that affect the planning of a lesson.

Beyond Teacher Control

Many context variables are beyond your individual control but must be considered when planning a lesson. Collectively, through their professional organizations, teachers have tried with some success to affect context variables through collective bargaining of teacher contracts. In general, however, a teacher has little direct effect on most of the following: the number of students in class, socioeconomic status of the students, availability of materials, physical size of the classroom, heating and cooling, physical condition of the school, district requirements for curriculum, standardized testing requirements, teacher evaluation, school administrative policies and procedures, parental involvement, community support, and district tax bases.

FIGURE 2.6 *Seating Diagram Showing the Action Zone*

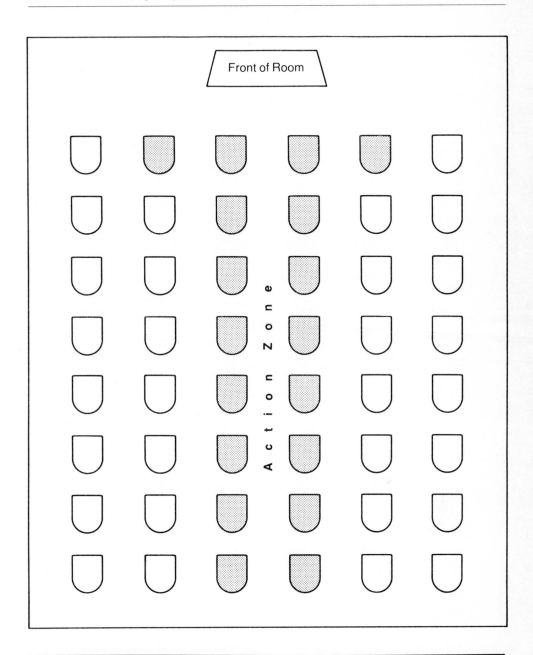

Source: Saur, R. E., Popp, M. J., & Isaacs, M. (1984). Action zone theory and the hearing impaired student in the mainstreamed classroom. *Journal of Classroom Interaction*, 19(2), 22. Reprinted with permission. Based on the work of Adams, R. S., & Biddle, B. J. (1970). *Realities of teaching, explorations with videotape*. New York: Holt, Rinehart and Winston, Inc.

Within Teacher Control

The teacher *does* have immediate control over many context variables. Room arrangement, for example, should be determined by the teacher. Placing student desks in a circle, in rows, or in the shape of a horseshoe will change the patterns of interaction in the classroom. There have been several studies of the patterns of interaction with student desks placed in rows. Figure 2.6 shows that most of the "action zone" interaction takes place in the front part of the room and down the middle, forming an inverted T. The lack of interaction with the students outside the T significantly reduces the contact the teacher has with these students. Changing the seating arrangement to a circle or a horseshoe, or placing the desks in rows but at angles to each other to form a series of Vs, will improve interaction. However, some teachers feel very comfortable with the students seated in rows, and move around the classroom to reduce the effects of the T seating arrangement.

SUMMARY

The following 14 functions of planning provide a strong rationale for planning:

_____ Gives an overview of instruction
_____ Facilitates good management and instruction
_____ Makes learning purposeful
_____ Provides for sequencing and pacing
_____ Ties classroom instructional events with community resources
_____ Reduces the impact of intrusions
_____ Provides for economy of time
_____ Makes learner success more measureable, which assists in reteaching
_____ Provides for a variety of instructional activities
_____ Creates the opportunity for higher-level questioning
_____ Assists in ordering supplies
_____ Guides substitute teachers
_____ Provides documentation of instruction
_____ Establishes a repertoire of instructional strategies

We have seen that planning proceeds through four distinct phases: preplanning, active planning, ongoing planning, and postplanning. Teachers use these four phases to draw on their experiences with the learner, content, and context to develop meaningful instructional plans for both teacher and student. Effective planners are able to visualize future lessons, build from past experiences, and fine-tune lessons while in the midst of instruction. Teachers may improve their planning effectiveness by monitoring their thinking (cognitive monitoring) during and after instruction.

Considerations for planning include the learner, content, and context. Knowing the students in class is an important starting point in planning for instruction. The effective planner will look at both affective and cognitive traits of the learner before making final determinations about how the content should be taught. The teacher who goes beyond the written curriculum and adds something from himself or herself will enrich the learning experience of students. Given the daily press for content coverage, this enrichment must be a planned part of instruction. Planning enables you to challenge the students and broaden your universe of ideas and activities. Although much of the context of the classroom is a given, you have the opportunity to make changes that will benefit everyone.

REFERENCES

Bloom, B. S. (1976). *Human characteristics and school learning*. New York: McGraw-Hill.

Dillon, J. T. (1984). Research on questioning and discussion. *Educational Leadership, 42*(3), 50–56.

Doyle, W. (1986). Classroom organization and management. In M. C. Wittrock (Ed.), *Handbook of research on teaching*. New York: Macmillan.

Emmer, E. (1987). Classroom management and discipline. In V. R. Koehler (Ed.), *Educators' handbook: A research perspective*. New York: Longman.

Glatthorn, A. A. (1987). *Curriculum leadership*. Glenview, IL: Scott, Foresman.

Henak, R. M. (1980). *Lesson planning for meaningful variety in teaching*. Washington, DC: National Education Association.

Manning, B. H. (1984). Self-communication structure for learning mathematics. *School Science and Mathematics, 84*(1), 43–51.

McCutcheon, G. (1980). How do elementary school teachers plan? The nature of planning and influences on it. *The Elementary School Journal, 81*, 4–23.

McNair, K. (1978–1979). Capturing inflight decisions: Thought while teaching. *Educational Research Quarterly, 3*(4), 26–42.

Neely, A. (1986). Planning and problem solving in teacher education. *Journal of Teacher Education, 37*(3), 29–33.

Paschal, R. A., Weinstein, T., & Walberg, H. H. (1983, April). The effects of homework on learning. A quantitative synthesis. Paper presented at the annual meeting of the American Educational Research Association, Montreal, Canada.

Posner, G. (1985). *Field experience: A guide to reflective teaching*. New York: Longman.

Rutter, M., Maughan, B., Mortimore, P., Ouston, J., & Smith, A. (1979). *Fifteen thousand hours: Secondary schools and their effects on children*. Cambridge, MA: Harvard University Press.

Saur, R. E., Popp, M. J., & Isaacs, M. (1984). Action zone theory and the learning impaired student in the mainstreamed classroom. *Journal of Classroom Interaction, 19*(2), 22.

Snyder, M. (1988). *Habitat: A game of chance*. Unpublished lesson plan and teaching analysis.

Wittrock, M. (Ed.). (1986). *Handbook of research on teaching* (3rd ed.). New York: Macmillan.

Yinger, R. J. (1980). A study of teaching planning. *The Elementary School Journal, 80*, 107–127.

Zahorik, J. A. (1970). The effect of planning on teaching. *The Elementary School Journal, 71*, 143–151.

SAMPLES AND EXAMPLES

This Samples and Examples section includes the following:

- A Year at a Glance shows how a teacher looks at important dates to have a broad view of the instructional year.
- A weekly calendar and syllabus are included as examples of planning for both teacher and students.
- Home Calls script to assist with parent contacts.
- Elementary and Secondary Substitute Teacher Letters

SCHOOL YEAR AT A GLANCE

Every month — PTO and departmental unit planning
Every 6 weeks (halfway between report cards) — Progress reviews

AUGUST	SEPTEMBER	OCTOBER
Mark major events on calendar (end of 6 weeks, Open House, fairs and festivals, holidays, homecoming, tests, papers) Set up room In-service—Find out your extra duties. Find out all you can about students you will have. Fire drill	Get acquainted with students Establish rules Diagnostic tests	Halloween activities Homecoming activities Six-week exams Open House Teacher observations Progress reports
NOVEMBER	**DECEMBER**	**JANUARY**
Thanksgiving activities Homecoming Community projects Locker clean-up Career Week programs Guest speaker	Holiday program preparation Progress reports	Midterm tests, papers, grade reports In-service Teacher observations Preplanning for spring
FEBRUARY	**MARCH**	**APRIL**
Black History Month activities History Fair	Fairs, festivals Science Fair Spring break	Standardized tests Order materials for next year Teacher observations PTA Spring break
MAY	**JUNE**	**JULY**
Cinco de Mayo activities Final tests, papers, grades Recommend kids for summer school, retention, promotion In-service Requisitions & inventories Meet with parents about standardized test results Summer school sign-up	Closing procedures Book returns	Summer workshops

A WEEKLY CALENDAR

HERE'S WHAT'S HAPPENING

FOR THE WEEK OF _____

DAY	PLANS*	WHAT TO BRING
MONDAY		
TUESDAY		
WEDNESDAY		
THURSDAY		
FRIDAY		

*PLANS ARE SUBJECT TO CHANGE

CHILD'S NAME _____

SYLLABUS

ASSIGNMENT SHEET

February 27–March 3

MATERIALS: textbook, notebook, pen, pencil, drawing equipment

Monday	Written assignment from Chapter 9.
Tuesday	SIX-WEEKS EXAM.
Wednesday	Begin discussion of Chapter 9 notes. Answer questions 1–12 in genetics notebook.
Thursday	Go over homework. Learn how to do a monohybrid cross. (Do not miss this lecture.) Answer questions 13–24 in genetics notebook.
Friday	Do Monohybrid Worksheet in class in small groups.

March 6–10

Monday	Continue group work on monohybrid problems.
Tuesday	Go over monohybrid problems. Discuss the concept of incomplete dominance. Answer questions 35–40 in genetics notebook.
Wednesday	Learn how to do dihybrid crosses. (Do not even consider missing this lecture.) Do questions 25–34 from genetics notebook.
Thursday	Continue work on dihybrids. Do dihybrid worksheet from notebook.
Friday	LAB: "How can Inheritance Be Predicted?"

March 13–17

Monday	Complete work on lab. Turn in at end of the period.
Tuesday	Do review sheet on Chapter 9 from genetics notebook.
Wednesday	EXAM OVER CHAPTER 9.
Thursday	Read Chapter 10. Do Chapter 10 worksheet.
Friday	Discuss sex determination, mutations, and nondisjunction.

March 20–23

Monday	LAB: "Let's Look at Chromosomes."
Tuesday	Discuss sex-linked inheritance from notebook. Do practice problems from genetics notebook.
Wednesday	Check homework from overhead. Do second set of sex-linked problems.
Thursday	Check homework. LAB: "Human Genetics Lab." PROGRESS REPORTS.
Friday	SPRING VACATION STARTS

POP TESTS FOR THESE 4 WEEKS ARE UNANNOUNCED. HINT: YOU WILL USUALLY HAVE ONE THE DAY AFTER A LECTURE OR DISCUSSION.

HOME CALLS

Hello. I am Jerome Freiberg, Johnny's teacher. I am calling at the beginning of the school year to introduce myself and to give you an idea of the types of activities we will be including during the first few weeks of school. (Total call time: 5 minutes or less.)

1. Portrait of the day: Describe a typical day in your class.

2. Discuss any specific items (e.g., absence packet).

3. Give a sense of the amount of homework and the days upon which it is due.

4. Support the parents in getting their child to school on time: "*I know how difficult it is to get children to school on time, but I would really appreciate your support in having Johnny arrive to school by X o'clock.*"

5. If the conversation is positive, you may want to discuss the possibility of the parent becoming a classroom assistant.

6. End the conversation with a note that you hope you can contact the parent at another time and if he or she has any questions to call the school during your planning time or leave a message and you will call back later that day. It is better *not* to leave your home telephone number.

SUBSTITUTE TEACHER LESSON PLAN

Elementary

Dear Substitute,

Thank you for teaching my students today. I believe that every day my students attend school is important, therefore your job is very important. Please ask Sarah or Jose to assist you with the role. They will show you, using the pocket chart on the front wall, how to collect the lunch money or give tickets for students on free and reduced lunch. They will also help you determine which students will be eating a hot lunch or have a lunch sack.

Please leave me a list of students who have been helpful in class. I have talked with them about the importance of assisting a substitute teacher. I have a homework folder in the right top drawer of my desk. Gladys will collect the homework for you.

My lesson plan is beneath the homework folder and should be followed if possible. Please leave a note describing your day and the content you accomplished. Thank you.

Mrs. Eva Johnson

Secondary

Welcome to Earth Science! Each of my classes has students who will assist you in your organization at the beginning and end of each period. A list of all the student assistants for each period is located in the Substitute Teacher Packet, which is kept in my top drawer. In the packet you will find a picture seating chart for each class, a list of student assistants, and my lesson plan for the day. Please leave me a note about the content you covered in each class. Thank you for being in my shoes while I am out.

Mr. Joseph Evans

CHAPTER 3

Designing Effective Instruction: Creating a Blueprint

CHAPTER OUTCOMES

At the conclusion of this chapter you will be able to:

1. Describe the elements of an instructional design.
2. Develop a lesson plan using an instructional design format.
3. Develop a unit plan using elements of instructional design.
4. Write instructional objectives for three learning domains.
5. Develop effective beginnings and endings for lessons.
6. Modify an instructional design for your needs, priorities, and beliefs.

KEY TERMS
AND CONCEPTS

Elements of Instructional Design
Goals
Objectives
Teaching and Learning Strategies
Materials
Feedback
Assessment
Models of Instructional Design
"Instructional Events" Model
"Lesson Cycle" Model
"Instructional Functions" Model
Unit Designs
Daily Designs
Weekly Designs
Lesson Beginnings
Set Induction
Advance Organizers
"Sponge" Activities
Lesson Endings
Closure
Learning Domains
Cognitive Domain
Psychomotor Domain
Affective Domain

INTRODUCTION

Planning and Designing

In the last chapter we compared the process of planning for a trip with planning for teaching. Stop and ask yourself: "How do I plan for a trip?" One of your authors uses a calendar with spaces for each day leading up to the departure date, and lists the necessary preparations in a sequence of when they need to be done. The other author leaves a trail of "Post-it" notes around the house with reminders to "stop the newspaper," "pack the tennis rackets," and "have the car serviced." A friend of ours has extensive "to do" lists and marks each task off as she completes them. Some people use itineraries prepared by professionals in the travel business, who also provide the necessary reminders in a checklist. And we also know people who use no visible means of planning—but they must have the necessary mental lists, because they travel as smoothly as those of us who put it all on paper.

You will find the same variation in the way teachers design instruction. Planning and designing instruction are opposite sides of the same coin. *Planning* is a mental process—the visualizing that takes place before teaching. During the planning process, we try to match the needs of the learner with specific content for our particular context. *Designing* is the process of putting our mental plans into a blueprint. When we design instruction, we note specific elements of our planning. Developing a blueprint for teaching provides a focus for instruction and promotes systematic and efficient planning.

In this chapter we provide models taken from expert designs, somewhat like the expert travel plans from an agency. We suggest considerations of *context, content,* and *learner* for the design process. And we suggest that you modify your designs as you gain teaching experience.

Considerations in the Design Process

When you plan for travel, you must consider your destination, time of year, distance, length of time, number of travelers, and your goals for the trip. Then you begin to focus your plans. When you plan for instruction, you must consider the *context* of your teaching, the *content* you intend to teach, and the *learners* who will be taught. You must also consider *yourself.* Then you begin to focus your plans—you design instruction.

Consider the Context of Your Teaching

To help you decide on a format for your design, ask yourself questions about the context in which you will be teaching:

- Is the setting formal or informal (rows of desks or clusters of tables and chairs)?
- Is it the beginning, middle, or end of the school year? The school day? The class period?
- Is this a group of 8? 12? 20? 30?
- What kind of management routines are established?

Your context concerns must include elements within and outside your classroom. Consider noise levels, potential behavior problems, and movement that affects your teaching and the teaching of those nearby. Note other schedules, such as library period, lunch break, and recess, which may follow or precede your instruction. Remember, too, that there are often administrative pressures imposed on your design process. You may be required to submit teaching plans to administrators, to use a particular format, or to follow a particular schedule.

Consider the Content of Your Teaching
Again, to help you decide on a format for your design, ask yourself questions about the content you will teach:

- Is there a textbook?
- Is the curriculum unstructured and open ended (e.g., curriculum for creative writing)?
- Is there a big idea or concept to be understood (e.g., relationship between societal discontent and politics)?
- Are there skills to be practiced (e.g., map reading)?
- Are there attitudes to be experienced (appreciation of masterpieces of art)?
- Are there school district objectives to be met?

Content is a major focus for most teachers when designing instruction. In addition to curriculum guides, textbooks, and teacher manuals, teachers' individual interests and areas of expertise become important sources of content. In Chapter 7, which discusses the lecture strategy, you will see how a teacher's travel experience influences the content of her geography instruction.

Consider the Learners to Be Taught
These questions will guide your decision about a format for your instructional design. Ask yourself questions about your learners:

- What kind of learning activities have they experienced? What kind of life experiences? Travel experiences? Activities outside of school?
- Do these learners work well in groups? Do they know how to work in groups?
- What strategies/activities are developmentally appropriate for these learners (e.g., young children need manipulatives for understanding math concepts)?
- Can these learners work independently?
- Have the learners shown interest in the topic? What is their motivation level?
- Is the content relevant to their lives?
- What are the needs of the learners?

Teachers describe the ability level of their students as the most important consideration when designing instruction. You will need to be sensitive to the social interactions of your learners and the patterns of class participation, which could affect many of the teaching strategies and learning activities you might plan.

Consider Yourself

In a study by Clark and Yinger (1979), teachers reported that planning relieved anxiety and uncertainty for them, and that they felt mentally and physically better prepared for teaching. You need to ask yourself: "How can my planning help my readiness for teaching?" Or maybe you need a detailed instructional design to build confidence.

If you are a person who plans in great detail for a trip, and is most comfortable with details written down, you will probably use a similar format to design your teaching. If you are a person who plans with a few major items and who processes details in your head, you will probably design your teaching with a similar focus. Stop and consider how you plan for the other things you do, so that you consider yourself before designing instruction.

Once you have considered the context and content of your teaching, the learners to be taught, and yourself, think about the basic parts or elements of design that you will need for your teaching.

Elements of Instructional Design

There are some universal elements you will find in most lesson designs, whether they are written in a detailed format or in mental form. A description of each will assist your understanding of the design models that follow in the next section.

Goals

Educational goals provide overall direction for teaching and learning in broad terms. On a universal level, a goal may be: All students will develop a love of learning. On a district level, a goal may be: Students will become problem solvers. On a class level, a goal may be: Students will become successful in math computation, or Students will become literary critics. Notice the broad, general quality of the outcomes, and the need for long-range development.

Objectives

Educational objectives specify the learning outcomes in measurable or observable terms. To develop objectives, you must analyze your goals into behaviors that indicate that students are reaching the goal. You may also specify the minimum level of performance necessary for each student that would indicate that the objective and part of the goal are being reached. To be specific, an objective for the goal of math computation (in preceding paragraph) might be: Students will add 10 sets of 3-digit numbers and get 80 percent of them correct. Objectives for the goal of literary critics (in preceding paragraph) could be: Students identify the main characters, plot, and setting of five literary selections, or Students describe the literary strategies used by authors to build suspense, create a setting, and divert attention.

Teaching and Learning Strategies

Teaching and learning strategies provide the vehicle or means by which facts, ideas, concepts, skills, and attitudes transfer to the thinking and actions of the learner. Depending on the strategy in use, this transfer may occur through a variety of media, including the teacher, other students, textbooks, videos, or computers. The question of how to transfer learning may be answered with teacher-directed strategies of lecture, questioning, and demonstration, or with student-directed strategies of cooperative grouping, discovery, and roleplay. They are the "how" of your instructional design, and the core of this book.

Materials

This is a broad category of tools, equipment, and resources, including anything used by you or your learner in the teaching and learning process. Materials can be simply pencils and pens, paper, and textbooks, or more involved audiovisual stimuli such as films and transparencies. Including materials in your design for teaching contributes to your preparedness.

Feedback

All of us need feedback that recognizes our work, our efforts, our progress, and so on. You may provide feedback to students through individual comments on their papers or through verbal responses to their discussions. Students may provide feedback to each other through peer critiques, checking each other's work, and reading to each other. Students may also provide feedback to themselves by checking an answer sheet, or critiquing work with a set of criteria, or through journal writing.

Assessment

This is the means of determining whether students have met the objectives. You can assess as an ongoing process all through the lesson, as well as at the end of the lesson. You may also use assessment at the beginning of a lesson to see what students already know, before you teach. Short-term assessment includes questions, quizzes, and observations of student work. Long-term assessment includes exams, projects, and research papers. Assessment provides information that will be useful for your next lesson design.

Goals, objectives, teaching and learning strategies, materials, feedback, and assessment are threads that run through the most widely used design models. Other models of instruction elaborate from this universal framework. We present three formal design formats for you to use as you begin teaching or as you expand your teaching experiences. They are appropriate for using in their entirety or in parts, after you consider content, context, learners, and yourself.

MODELS OF INSTRUCTIONAL DESIGN

The Instructional Event Model

Gagne, Briggs, and Wagner (1988) described nine instructional events in their design model. We display them in Figure 3.1, and Ms. Rennie follows the design sequence in the following Snapshot.

FIGURE 3.1 *Instructional Events Design Model*

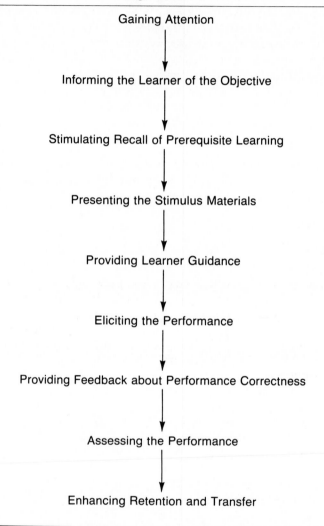

Gaining Attention

↓

Informing the Learner of the Objective

↓

Stimulating Recall of Prerequisite Learning

↓

Presenting the Stimulus Materials

↓

Providing Learner Guidance

↓

Eliciting the Performance

↓

Providing Feedback about Performance Correctness

↓

Assessing the Performance

↓

Enhancing Retention and Transfer

SNAPSHOT: *Elementary Classroom*

On the chalkboard at the side of her second-grade classroom, Ms. Rennie has hung a colorful pizza poster to *gain attention*. "Class, take a look at these pizzas. If you have five people in your family, which pizza would you choose? If you have eight friends over to spend the night, which pizza would you choose? Why?" The students mention the number of slices, or pieces, of pizza as reasons for their choices, and Ms. Rennie continues, "Yes, these pizzas have been cut into different pieces." She writes the word *fractions* on the board, and points to the pizza slices, "These pieces are fractions of the whole pizza. We're going to learn about fractions today, and you'll see why we need them in our lives" (*informs the learner of the objective*).

For several minutes, the class reviews what whole numbers are and talks about some examples to *stimulate recall of prerequisite learning*. Ms. Rennie connects whole numbers to fractions, and together she and the class develop several definitions of fractions. Ms. Rennie writes examples of fractions on the board. "Now class, I've put lots of things on these trays (*presents stimulus materials*) for you to use in your math teams. Look carefully at these things and find as many fractions as you can." (On the trays are newspapers, ads, measuring spoons and cups, pictures of baked goods cut into pieces, and so on.) "Look at the examples on the board to help you remember what fractions are like. You will have 10 minutes to find as many fractions as you can."

While student teams work, Ms. Rennie moves about, commenting to the groups on their efforts and *providing learner guidance*. After 10 minutes, each team reports on the fractions they found (*eliciting performance*). They hear feedback: "You found six sale ads that said prices would be one half off." Ms. Rennie also summarizes a team's findings with, "You found fractions used in ads, cooking, measuring distances, and shoe sizes (*providing feedback about performance correctness*). Why are fractions useful in our world?"

The students return to their individual places and are asked to draw one example of a fraction. Ms. Rennie moves about the desks and asks individual students, "What is a fraction?" and "Tell me about your fraction." When drawings are completed and turned in to Ms. Rennie (*assessing the performance*), the students are given an assignment to do at home: "Find two examples of fractions at home, and copy or draw or bring them in tomorrow" (*enhancing retention and transfer*). The students write the assignment on a sheet labeled "To Do at Home."

Refer to the instructional events listed in Figure 3.1 and be sure that you can identify each one in Ms. Rennie's lesson. Notice how she *gained attention* with the pizza poster and her questions, then *informed learners of the objectives* (learning about fractions and being able to talk about how we use fractions). She *stimulated* their *recall of prerequisite learning* with a review of whole numbers and examples of fractions. She *presented stimulus materials* with the prepared trays of fraction examples, then moved about the teams at work, finding the examples to *provide learner guidance*.

After the teams had worked for 10 minutes, Ms. Rennie *elicited the performance* when she asked for team reports, and *provided feedback about performance correctness* with her comments about the examples. She collected student drawings and asked questions of individuals to *assess the performance*. Her homework assignment was designed to *enhance retention and transfer*.

As we move to the next model, you will see a similar sequence of teaching and learning. You will also notice as you watch teachers that the sequence can be varied to fit a specific topic or objective, or specific learner needs. Although Gagne and other instructional designers propose a particular sequence and format, these can be modified to match the learner, context, and content.

FIGURE 3.2   *Lesson Cycle Design Model*

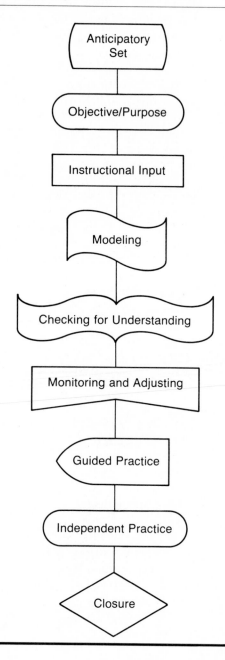

The Lesson Cycle Model

Hunter's (1976) lesson cycle model is widely used in public schools (Stallings & Stipek, 1986). The model contains nine levels, presented in Figure 3.2. In the following Snapshot, Mr. Malter uses the lesson cycle levels in his middle-school math class.

SNAPSHOT: Middle-School Classroom

Mr. Malter begins with newspaper clippings of the recent marathon event in the students' community. On the chalkboard are headlines about the winners and their respective times (*anticipatory set*). "We know that the marathon covered 26 miles, and each of these runners completed the race in the times I have written next to their names. What else would you be interested in knowing about the runners?" The students suggest age of runner, race experience, amount of training, and rate of speed. Mr. Malter writes the suggestions on the board. "Most of these questions would have to be answered by interviewing the runners, but we could answer this one ourselves," Mr. Malter says as he points to rate of speed. "Today we are going to learn how to compute rate of speed, and practice the computation for a number of race examples" (*objective or purpose*).

Mr. Malter reminds the students of the film *Chariots of Fire* and how the runners used the clock tower chimes to determine their speed. "Our formula is a simple way to determine speed," he states. He focuses on the formula: Distance/Time = Rate or Speed (instructional input).

Using the marathon distance and each runner's time, Mr. Malter demonstrates the use of the formula for rate (*modeling*). After three examples, he asks, "What information am I using each time I figure a rate of speed for a runner?" (*checking for understanding*). When students suggest distance and time, he writes them on the board. "That's correct, now what did I do with distance and time?" (*checking for understanding*). With the formula written on the board, he instructs the students to tell him how to compute the next runner's rate. Using the overhead projector, Mr. Malter displays a news clip about an auto race, and asks how to figure the rate of speed of the winning drivers. Individual students suggest using the distance and time information with the formula. Two students come up to the board to compute the rate of speed, while others practice on paper at their desks. Those at the board explain what they did to compute the rate of speed (*monitoring and adjusting*).

On the overhead, Mr. Malter displays another problem, this time in pictorial form. Again, students work the problem at the board and at their desks. After discussing the computation process again, students are asked to work three problems at their desks (*guided practice*). Mr. Malter moves about the room, looking at student work, asking questions, and commenting on computation: "How did you get this answer?" and "Tell me how you did this computations," and "You are using the formula correctly," and "It looks like you

know how to use the formula." He checks the final answers for the three problems and comments, "You all used the formula correctly to compute the rate of
speed." He assigns 10 problems to be done as *independent practice*: "These
examples will give you practice in computing rates of speed so that you can be
fast and sure."

At the end of the seatwork practice, Mr. Malter calls for attention and
asks, "Class, if you were to tell someone what you learned in math today, what
would you say?" (*closure*). After the students describe the process and formula,
they are asked, "What information do you need to do this?" Students are told
that they can finish their problems at home and are assigned one more task—
to "make up a rate of speed problem of your own."

Look at the lesson cycle sequence (Figure 3.2) and identify the levels of the
model as Mr. Malter teaches about computing rate of speed. He used the marathon
news clips as an *anticipatory set* to direct the students' attention and to prepare them
for instruction. He *expressed the objective* directly to the students after creating a need
with students' suggestions of other information of interest.

You saw his *instructional input* and *modeling* as he presented a mini-lecture and
demonstrated several examples on the board. Students began *guided practice* as they
worked the examples displayed on the overhead, and Mr. Malter was able to *check
for understanding*. The guided practice continued when students worked on three
problems at their desks, and Mr. Malter continued to check for understanding as he
moved about, asking for explanations and commenting on work. During this time
and during the previous examples, he was *monitoring* (that is, observing to determine student understanding). If he had noticed student difficulty or misunderstanding, he could have *adjusted* (that is, retaught the computation, reworded the
process, or asked other students to explain the process again).

The assignment of 10 problems and the homework task comprised *independent
practice* (that is, activities without assistance). At the end of the math class, Mr.
Malter brought about *closure* by asking students to review what they had learned
in class.

You now have two design models with similarities and differences. Continue
comparing as we describe a third.

The Instructional Functions Model

When Rosenshine and Stevens (1986) reviewed studies in which teachers increased
student achievement, they found a consistent pattern of instructional functions.
They noted that these functions are appropriate and effective when used to teach
well-structured subjects. Their model is displayed in Figure 3.3 and observed in the
following Snapshot of a high-school geometry class. Again, notice that the sequence
can be adjusted. Make the sequence meet your needs and those of your students, but
include all of the model's elements in your plan to ensure consistency.

FIGURE 3.3 *Instructional Functions Model*

1. *Daily Review*	Check previous day's work
	Check homework
	Reteach when necessary
2. *Teach New Content*	Give an overview
	Give detailed explanations
	Present in small parts
	Maintain a rapid pace
	Relate new content with previously learned content
3. *Student Practice*	Observable practice tasks
	Frequent question/answer
	Frequent feedback
	Monitor practice
	Check for understanding
4. *Feedback/Corrections*	Frequent feedback
	Notice student errors
	Explain and review
	Reteach
5. *Independent Practice*	Seatwork
	Monitoring
6. *Reviews*	Regular schedule (weekly, monthly)
	Reteach

SNAPSHOT: *Secondary Classroom*

Ms. Lasley begins her geometry class with, "OK, class, we have been using *deductive reasoning* and developing *conditionals* and *proofs*," as she points to the terms on the bulletin board. She asks for definitions of each, and describes how the students are using all three in their lives (*daily review*). "I want to check your assignment from yesterday to be sure you understand the work we have been doing. Then, we will move on to using conditionals and proofs in more complex examples." The assignment is checked and a brief review of writing hypotheses is conducted. Ms. Lasley says, "We have a theorem that states that if a point is not on a line, then the point and the line determine exactly one plane. If you need to write a hypothesis for the theorem, how do you begin?" She reteaches the process when she notices confusion. She provides another theorem example and moves around the room, observing student answers and looking for evidence of confidence. "It looks like you are more clear about writing a hypothesis, so we will move on to today's work."

Ms. Lasley reminds the class that they are going to be working on more complex examples—"writing two-column proofs" (*presents new content*). She turns on the overhead projector and displays the example:

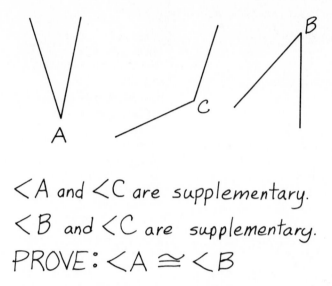

<A and <C are supplementary.
<B and <C are supplementary.
PROVE: <A ≅ <B

Figure from *HBJ Geometry* by James Ulrich, copyright © 1984 by Harcourt Brace Jovanovich, Inc., reprinted by permission of the publisher.

"Notice that we have more givens and when you look at the example, it looks more complex than the proofs we have been doing" (*new skills phased in with old skills*).

Ms. Lasley completes the proof by directing the sequence of steps and using student input. She reviews the entire proof when they finish. "Now, let's try another and work it together," she says, as she reveals a second example on the overhead. When the second example has been completed, she assigns a third example to be worked on, and asks five students (one from each row) to do it at the chalkboard. She observes their work and, as they finish, encourages them to check the work of students in their row. This process is followed three more times at a fast pace (*initial student practice*).

"OK, it looks like you understand how to do these problems quite well (*feedback*). Here are three more to figure out while I check everyone's work. If you feel uncertain, raise your hand and I will come to you."

After 10 minutes, everyone appears finished. "Let's look at these two different conclusions and reasons given for the second problem. Lorianne gave this reason, and Roy gave this one. Lorianne, where did you get your reason? Roy, where did you get yours?" Ms. Lasley makes certain that the class members understand that the figure can provide some conclusions and reasons (*correctives*).

The students are assigned five examples from their textbooks to be worked on during the last few minutes of class and for homework (*independent practice*): "I will continue to check your work and am available if you have questions."

Ms. Lasley followed the instructional functions model for her lesson on two-column proofs, beginning with a *review*, which checked the previous day's work, and a quick reteaching of hypothesis writing. She gave students and overview with her description of using the previous steps of givens and proofs to work with more complex examples. She *presented the new content on the overhead projector and repeated the process of writing two-column proofs three times*. Students *practiced* the proofs throughout most of the lesson and were given *feedback*. When Ms. Lasley discovered a discrepancy between Roy and Lorianne's answers and realized potential problems for students with the particular examples, she clarified for all students. When most class members understood how to write the proofs, she assigned *independent practice*. In the weeks to come, Ms. Lasley will conduct periodic *reviews* and reteach if necessary.

DESIGNS FOR VARIED TIME PERIODS

The design formats you have seen thus far are appropriate for short-term teaching—one or two lessons. When Clark and Yinger (1979) interviewed teachers about planning, they asked them to describe the "three most important types of planning that they did during the school year." Unit designs are most often identified as the most important type, followed by weekly and daily designs.

Unit Designs

Just like lesson designs, unit designs enable you to teach with a sense of direction, knowing what you expect to do, what you will need, and what you expect will happen. Unit designs have been described as a way of organizing materials and activities, relating learning activities to each other, and designing experiences around a central theme or purpose. Unit designs consist of general goals or purposes, specific objectives, activities, resources, and assessment. They may also include an outline of content as well as background information or knowledge, and they may be aligned with a textbook.

The following Teacher Talk discusses a unit design for the study of weather for two first-grade classes. We have included part of their unit design for you to see the activities and materials that are organized around a central purpose.

TEACHER TALK

We wanted students to know a lot about weather—the different kinds of weather, how it affects our lives, and the changes that occur in the four seasons. We also wanted them to appreciate weather. It's also important to us that students learn some skills related to weather. We don't have a textbook for first grade, so we had to use a lot of library sources. We decided to spend three weeks on this unit and to incorporate science and social studies goals. We'll also integrate language arts activities, some math practice, and art and music projects.

WEATHER UNIT

Goals: Understanding of weather and how it influences people

Objectives

Students will:

1. Identify and describe different kinds of weather conditions.
2. Predict daily weather and explain reasons for predictions.
3. Describe some of the changes that can occur in weather conditions.
4. Match appropriate clothing and activities with different kinds of weather conditions.
5. List characteristics of each season and describe the associated weather changes.
6. Discuss safety precautions for different weather.
7. Observe, measure, and record weather.
8. Read a weather thermometer.
9. Create a weather report using the unit's concepts and skills.
10. Describe the advantages and disadvantages of seasons and different weather conditions.

Vocabulary

rainy	blizzard	calendar	fall
forecast	meteorologist	snowy	graph
hurricane	temperature	seasons	cloudy

Teaching/Learning Activities

1. Student groups of four will prepare bulletin boards of different weather conditions.
2. Student group construction of "Fog in a Bottle."
3. Teacher demonstration of varied materials for protection in rainy weather (rubber, plastic, wool, cotton, paper).
4. Class discussion of videotaped weather forecast.
5. Class construction of a weather calendar using symbols to indicate conditions.
6. Student independent use of flannel board cutouts of weather symbols and clothing in matching exercises.
7. Students make season collages, write season poems, and pantomime seasons.

Materials

The Snowy Day. Ezra Jack Keats. New York: Scholastic.
What Happens in Autumn. Suzanne Venino. National Geographic Society.
The Day the Sun Danced. Edith Hurd. New York: Harper & Row.

Films: *Farm Families in Autumn*
Thermometers and How We Use Them
Thunderstorms
Spring Comes to the Forest

Cloud Charts from P.O. Box 1122, Glen Allen, VA 23060.

People: meteorologist, farmer, construction worker.

Picture File: seasons, weather, clothing.

Assessment
1. Student notebooks with weather recording, matching worksheets, poems, drawings, and picture categorizations.
2. Student weather stories and calendars.
3. Checklists of thermometer use and graphing weather conditions.
4. Picture/symbol matching test of weather vocabulary.

The two teachers had planned a total of 30 teaching and learning activities, some for students' independent work, some for whole-class instruction, and some for use at learning centers. Some of the activities were brief and simple, and some were complex and demanded large time blocks. They planned more activities than they actually needed for three weeks, just in case they needed to reteach, enrich, or extend student learning.

Weekly Designs

Yinger (1980) notes that teachers use weekly blueprints to "lay out the week's activities, adjust schedule for interruptions and special needs, and to maintain continuity and regularity of activities." Most weekly plan formats are scheduling tools, often with nothing more than the times and names of activities. They do contribute to preparation in that they are useful for listing materials and other resources. Look at an example from a secondary teacher in Figure 3.4 and notice the abbreviated format and coding scheme.

In Figure 3.5 you see a week-long design from an elementary teacher. This is an especially good example of the kind of plan that would be appreciated by a substitute teacher. It is difficult to teach unknown content to an unknown group of learners in a unknown context, but a detailed plan makes the task more manageable.

In sum, no matter which format you use to design your lesson or plan your day or week, doing so provides a way for you to feel prepared. We remind you to *consider yourself* as you design instruction, and be sure that your blueprint enables you to feel confidence and readiness.

Daily Designs

Teachers use blueprints of a day to "set up and arrange their classrooms, specify activity components, fitting the daily schedule to last-minute intrusions, and prepare students for the day's activities" (Yinger, 1980). They often display the daily plan for students, and use them as a kind of checklist for getting materials ready and

FIGURE 3.4 *Weekly Plan from a Secondary Teacher*

NAME _G. Rutledge_
SUBJECT _English 2B_ PERIOD(S) _1,2,5_
Objectives ¿ Letter writing
SCHOOL _Scarborough H.S._
WEEK OF _March 16-20_

DAY	ELO	INSTRUCTIONAL OBJECTIVES	RELATED ACTIVITIES	RESOURCE/MATERIALS	T.T. CODES	ASSIGNMENTS
MONDAY	16	The student will compare a request letter using the model on p. 27	1. Letter of request 2. Model - p. 27 3. Complete practice 4 - p. 275	English Writing & Skills pp. 274-275	01 02 04 05 07 09	Use evening to work on competition
TUESDAY	17	The student will order a product by mail	1. Letter to order something 2. Model-p. 277 3. Complete practice 5 - p. 278 4. Test	English Writing & Skills pp. 276-278	01 02 04 05 07 10	Oral or written UIL next week
WEDNESDAY	18	The student will explain correction in an order by mail	1. Letter of adjustment 2. Model - p. 279 3. Writing practice 6 - p. 280	English Writing & Skills p. 278-280	01 02 04 05 07	Practice for UIL or polish written contest entry
THURSDAY	19	The student will write a letter of appreciation to be mailed	1. Letter of appreciation 2. Model - p. 281 3. Complete practice 7	English Writing & Skills p. 280-282	01 02 04 05 07	Post final copy of essay contest for mailing
FRIDAY	20	The student will apply in letter for a position	1. Letter of application 2. Model - p. 283 3. Complete practice 8	English Writing & Skills pp. 282-283	01 02 04 05 07	

LEARNING ACTIVITIES/TEACHING TECHNIQUES + CODES 01-10

Independent Study—01 Group Work—03 Supervised Study—05 Illustration—07 Review—09
Question & Answers—02 Discussion—04 Demonstration—06 Lecture—08 Evaluation—10

HOUSTON INDEPENDENT SCHOOL DISTRICT
SECONDARY LESSON PLAN SHEET

Source: Gwen Rutledge, G. C. Scarborough Senior High School, Houston, Texas.

FIGURE 3.5 Weekly Plan—Elementary

Sept. GRADE OR CLASS __First (Robin)__   WEEK BEGINNING _____

Day	Before Sch.	Enter / Arrival (reg) 8:40–9	9–9:30	Whole Group 9:30–10	Recess 10–10:15	Literacy Centers 10:15–11:15	Clean / Inspect 11:15 11:25	Lunch 11:30–12	Quiet Reading 12–12:30	Story book 12:20 to 12:30	Math 12:30–1	Learning Centers 1–1:40	Recess 1:50–2	Gathering 2:05–2:20
MONDAY 18	Ann. room (before PSW) New Jobs (Robert, Tess, Brad)	Journals	New Jobs / Calendar / Zeros / Bobby / Read: Just this Bear	Writing (review use of writers' workshop boxes)		Finish spelling assess.			Theme tubs Beavers & Squirrels		Discovery time Ask kid rules (review) +Q+Q! write down "Math Ideas" (on easel chart?)			Read: Buzzy Bear or the Garden / Take home Zero ditto!
TUESDAY 19	Pam here	→	Calendar / Shoe patterns / 8 rules / Read: Blueberry Bear	↓	Library	Lit. Centers 10:45–11:15 Label room "other clan" Recess 10:30 to 10:45 Diana 10:50–11:10		→	Roombooks Beavers & Squirrels		Pattern papers (little brown books) (First to up real bears open)	Redo Math Assess		Read: Ernest & Celestine discuss care of records
WEDNESDAY 20		→	Calendar / Dot chart patterns / Read: Break-fast time	→	P.E.	Literacy Centers 10:30–11:15 (no recess on gym day a.m.) Label room "Squirrel Clan"	Pam here	→	Theme tubs otters & Raccoons Magazines to each clan		Discovery time see Mon.	↓		Read: Ernest & Celestine Take home Bear note!
THURSDAY 21	get math books for ?	→	Calendar / Dot chart patterns / Read:	Make an award for your bear Write about your bear (use blank bear ditto)	Music	Lit. Centers 10:45–11:15 Meeting note, Meagan and Matt Rewriting time expectations Recess 10:30 to 10:45	Cindy here		Textbooks to each clan in color tubs (New-show how to)		Bear Measuring stations unifix cubes scale string make booklet	early up clean up do Math Assess		Computer 2–2:23 (no recess and recess from comp. hab. room)
FRIDAY 22	Math! papers	→	Calendar / Dot chart patterns / Read: who will be my friend?	→	Recess 10–10:15	Lit. Centers 10:15–10:50 Meeting Carita, Mario, Jesus, ABC cards Clean time 10:50 Entertainment time 11–11:25			Library books otters & Raccoons Theme tubs Beavers & Squirrels		Math books pp. 1–16	Math Assess		Outside w/ Bears (Recess & stories)

Across Learning Centers / Recess block: clean up & inspection 1:40–1:50 → ready to go home → clean & inspect

FIGURE 3.6 *Daily Schedule for Elementary Schools*

General Instructions
1. Please type or use black ink to complete this schedule.
2. Please allow a minimum of 315 minutes daily for primary instructions and a minimum of 330 minutes daily for intermediate instruction.
3. Each teacher assigned should submit schedule (regular classroom teacher, band, reading, etc.).
4. Submit one copy of this schedule to the County Office at close of first school month, and retain one copy for your files.

School _Jones Elementary_ Grade(s) _1_ Teacher _Ms. Johnson_

Time Allotment Daily and Weekly

Daily Time	Monday	Tuesday	Wednesday	Thursday	Friday
8:00 - 8:15	Opening				
8:15 - 9:45	Language Arts				
9:45 - 10:30	P.E.	Music	P.E.	Art	P.E.
10:30 - 11:00	Guidance	Creative Writing (C.W.)		Band	C.W.
11:00 - 11:20	Storytime				
11:30 - 12:00	Lunch				
12:00 - 1:00	Writing to Read				
1:00 - 1:45	Math				
1:45 - 2:00	Recess				
2:00 - 2:20	Language Arts				
2:20 - 2:50	S. Studies	Art	Science	Health	Science
2:50 - 3:00	Clean Up & Go Around				
3:00	Walkers Leave				
3:02	Bus Students Leave				

FIGURE 3.7 *Daily Plan from a Secondary Teacher*

	Monday	Tuesday	Wednesday
7:50– 8:50	Health IIa film "Diet" (volunteer) critique sheets Discussion leaders: Dan, Cody, Alice, Stan, Bea		
9:00– 10:00	Health IIa film "Diet" (volunteer) critique sheets Discussion leaders: Ignatius, Allan, Bo Melissa, Suzanne		
10:05– 11:05	Health IIb overhead "Virus" Lecture reminders: note taking Rdg. pp. 59-90		
11:10– 11:45	Homeroom Journals A-B Sharing (yearbook orders)		
11:45– 12:25	Lunch Meet with team Rm 43 (review materials)		
12:25– 1:25	Stress Mainten. feedback forms Practice relax. techniques – partners		
1:30– 2:30	Sociology Cooperative Learn. groups – demog. concepts Assign – interviews		
2:40–	Call Bo's parents Preview census data Grade stress feedback forms 3:10 Coach soccer		

for accomplishing the day's intentions. We have observed teachers reviewing the daily plan with their classes and assigning students to check off the activities on the day's agenda as they are completed.

In Figures 3.6 and 3.7 we provide one-day designs from an elementary teacher and a secondary teacher. As you can see, these plans look quite different in focus and detail.

LESSON BEGINNINGS AND ENDINGS

As you observed the three models in action, did you notice how important it was to begin the lesson effectively—that is, to gain attention, or to set some anticipation, or to diagnose what students know? Did you also notice how the lessons ended with a sense of closure, or a feeling of completion?

Think about what it is like for you to be in a class that begins in an interesting way, in which the instructor immediately gets you thinking about the subject or arouses your curiosity. Most of us attend well, stay involved, feel positive about the class, and even learn more in those situations. The next time you attend a class, check the ending and see what effect it has on what you remember from the class. Endings generally influence our impression of a class or lesson, and our memory. For those reasons, we want to develop strategies for your lesson beginnings and endings. We begin with three beginning strategies: set induction, advanced organizers, and sponges.

Set Induction

A set is a mental state of readiness, and an induction brings it on, so a *set induction* gets learners thinking and ready for the lesson. Set inductions can provide a reference point between what the student knows and new material, thus creating a link from one lesson or class to the next (Schuck, 1985).

Facilitation Sets
These sets are used to summarize information presented in previous lessons and/or information that will occur. The intent is to bring the students' attention to the current lesson. You may use an outline on the board or on a transparency, or verbally present a short summary of key points. Ask your learners to summarize what they have learned from previous lessons.

Research has shown that set inductions make a difference in the effectiveness of a lesson. The following vignette describes the effect on short- and long-term learning gains.

Motivating Sets
Whereas a facilitation set emphasizes the cognitive aspects of a new lesson by reviewing or summarizing previous learning, a motivating set is intended to catch

Secondary Research Vignette

INTRODUCTION

Schuck (1985) studied the strategies of set induction used alone, set induction used with systematic questioning, and systematic questioning used alone to determine the impact on short- and long-term student achievement.

STUDY DESIGN

Schuck selected 120 ninth-graders from three schools and randomly assigned them to 12 groups. Veteran biology teachers (average of 7.3 years' teaching experience) were also randomly assigned to one of the 12 classes. Classes were then assigned to four groups: Group I received training in questioning strategies, Group II received training in set induction, Group III received training in set induction and questioning, and Group IV received no training. The training included an overview and examples of the strategies, teacher demonstrations, and critiques in two 3-hour sessions.

A 60-item biology test was designed to test the content taught by the teachers. Students were tested immediately after each unit of instruction, 10 weeks later, and 7 months later.

STUDY RESULTS

Teachers trained in set induction had students who scored significantly better (at the $p < .01$ level) and retained their knowledge better than students of teachers who were not trained in any strategies, and students of teachers who were trained in both strategies. (Group III teachers needed to incorporate two new strategies into their lessons, whereas Group II teachers could concentrate on one strategy.)

Teachers trained in set induction had students who achieved and retained their biology content longer than teachers who received training only in questioning strategies.

DISCUSSION AND IMPLICATIONS FOR PRACTICE

The results of this study support the use of a set for linking what students know and what is to be taught. They also support what most of us have experienced as students and as teachers—you need to gain students' attention before you can really teach.

TEACHER TALK

Class, on the left side of the board are key terms related to our unit on the Civil War (*abolition, slavery, states' rights, national unity,* and so on). I want you to define them, using the information we have been studying, before we proceed to the new set of terms on the right.

6th-Grade History Teacher

I will be showing you slides of the different rocks formations studied in our last three classes. Write down the names of each formation as you see it on the screen, then we will examine some specimens of each for other characteristics.

7th-Grade Science Teacher

I am going to hold up some things we find in our classroom and at home. I want you to name the sense that will help you the most to identify this item. Let's try one. (Holds up an onion) Which sense would you use?

Science Lesson Kindergarten Teacher

the students' attention. It arouses curiosity, poses interesting questions, uses dramatic appeal, and creates a need or interest. It induces an affective or emotional response from the learners.

TEACHER TALK

I want you to watch something on videotape. After enjoying Phil Collins's music video, "One More Night," students were intrigued. "Where did people of those times get their entertainment?" After a discussion of minstrels and balladeers, the teacher picked up her guitar and proceeded to sing "Greensleeves." Upon completion, she said, "This type of song is called a ballad, and today we are going to learn the characteristics of a ballad."

10th-Grade English Teacher

With a colorful quilt displayed at the front of the classroom, students were asked to find as many shapes as they could. In time, the teacher said, "Yes, there are polygons, and today we are going to learn to identify various polygons and describe their critical attributes."

5th-Grade Math Teacher

Children were directed to a clock with some numbers and one hand missing: "Look at this clock for a minute—does it look funny or odd to you? Now compare it with our clock on the wall. What is missing?" The children talked about the missing numbers and hand. "That's right, important parts of the clock are missing and today we are going to learn about why we need them to tell time."

1st-Grade Math Teacher

As you might have guessed, it is ideal to provide both motivating and facilitating sets in your set induction. The first-grade teacher above could have begun her sets with, "What do you remember about clocks?" followed by, "Now, look at this clock—does it look funny or odd to you?" The fifth-grade teacher could have reviewed various triangles and their critical attributes to show a similarity with the information about polygons.

Advanced Organizers

Ausubel (1968), who developed this strategy for beginning a lesson, came up with two types of advanced organizers. One of these he called the *expository organizer*, which provides students with an overview of the subject. He called the second type the *comparative organizer*, and it provides a link between what the students already know and what they will be learning.

Expository Organizers

These are appropriate for lessons or classes when the information is new to students. For example, to begin a unit on democracy, you might introduce the issues of freedom and choice by showing photos of Chinese student demonstrations and by discussing protest issues. By using these expository organizers, you will be encouraging your students to think about the "big picture" of democracy as you start the unit.

Advanced organizers help learners begin the lesson or unit with a frame of reference. For a unit of study, it is ideal to have each new advanced organizer build on previous advanced organizers. Students either begin with the broad abstract concept and fill in the details, or begin with the specific, concrete facts and understandings and build the broad overview.

Comparative Organizers

These are appropriate when information is already familiar to students. You build upon the known in order to develop the unknown. For example, if your students have studied about water pollution, you use their knowledge of water pollution to begin a study of air pollution. If your students know about squares, you use their understanding of squares to begin studying about rectangles.

Sometimes, advanced organizers take the form of *setting an agenda* for the class or lesson, such as: "Today we will be studying the parts of a microscope. We will begin by discussing its uses, then look at diagrams of the parts of the microscope. We will work in groups to get to know the equipment, to handle it and find the parts. You will have plenty of time to work with the microscope. We will end by going back to our diagrams and see how many parts you can remember and identify by name." The value of this kind of advanced organizer is that learners know what to expect, know the direction and sequence of the lesson, and know what is expected of them during the lesson.

"Sponge" Activities

The *sponge* is a term used by Hunter (1985, p. 93) to describe activities that "sop up" waiting time at the beginning of a lesson or during the lesson. Sponges take the form of a review or extension of previous learnings, a set or mental readiness for the learning that is to come, or an attention-getting technique to eliminate distractions or behavior that would disturb teaching and learning. They help you maintain the smoothness we describe in Chapter 6.

There are often necessary management routines that need to occur at the beginning of a lesson: getting books out of desks, moving into groups, or settling into the room. Routines can also occur during a lesson: passing out materials or papers, moving to look at a demonstration, or changing from whole-class teaching to group work. Many of those routines are called *transitions*, and we provide suggestions for handling them smoothly in Chapter 6. Sponge activities are designed to keep students thinking about the lesson or class focus during those routines or transitions. As you begin a lesson on geometric shapes or as you pass out colored paper in the middle of the lesson, you may say to the students, "Look around the room and see if you can find any triangles, or squares, or . . . ." As students move to their groups during your lesson on using the microscope, you may suggest, "As you move to your table, see if you can come up with what part of the microscope begins with *l*." You will find lists of sponge ideas from elementary and secondary teachers in the Samples and Examples section at the end of this chapter.

Summary of Beginnings

Set inductions, advanced organizers, and sponges are an important part of your lesson design. They help focus and direct both the planning and the teaching. Your introductions or beginnings can accomplish multiple tasks: gain attention, focus on the subject, create interest and need, stimulate readiness, eliminate distractions, and develop positive affect for a subject. Lesson beginnings represent a brief sliver of instructional time and a small section of your overall design, but they have a major impact on the entire design and the actual instruction.

Ending a Lesson

The last thing you do in teaching a lesson is often what students remember. Unfortunately, we often end lessons or classes with a bell ringing to indicate change of classes, or with, "Time is up. We have to go to lunch. Put your things away and line up at the door." Instead, we suggest using a closure strategy to end a lesson. Closure means to close or to pull together. You provide closure for students when you *review, summarize,* and *repeat your overview* from the beginning of your lesson.

You, the teacher, can provide closure, in verbal or written form, or you may involve students in the process.

TEACHER TALK

The focus of our lesson today was using the microscope. We looked at the parts and studied the names of each. You handled the microscope, found each of its parts, and then we reviewed the names using our diagram to check what we learned.

7th-Grade Science Teacher

We looked at and talked about rectangles today. What do you remember about rectangles?

2nd-Grade Teacher

On your 3 × 5 card, write five terms from our class today that were important to you. Now, compare your terms with a partner, then hand in your cards before leaving for your next class. I will post my terms at the door for you to see as you leave.

7th-Grade Civics Teacher

Depending on the lesson taught, the time available, the size of the class, and your preferences, you can use a variety of closure strategies to accomplish the functions of review and summary. What is most difficult for most teachers is leaving enough time for closure. One of us uses reminders, written in big letters on lesson plans. Some teachers ask a student to signal them to indicate that there are five minutes left in the period. Some teachers use a timer to cue them to begin closure.

INSTRUCTIONAL OBJECTIVES

In the models presented earlier in the chapter, you may have noticed that objectives directed all other elements of the design. Objectives also affected beginnings and endings. As we defined them earlier, *instructional objectives* are descriptions of the intended outcomes of teaching:

1. Objectives may describe the *information* that you intend *for students to know or use.*
2. Objectives may describe the *skill* that you intend *for students to perform or demonstrate.*
3. Objectives may describe the *value* or *feeling* that you intend *for students to experience.*

Think of them as a description of the learner following your instruction.

Criteria of Instructional Objectives

In order to accomplish what you intend by writing them, instructional objectives need to meet three criteria: describe *outcomes* for the student, describe the *conditions for learning*, and state the degree or *level of mastery* you intend. The three elements of an instructional objective are displayed in Figure 3.8.

Instructional objectives also need to be specific and to be measurable or observable. Look at another example:

"Students will list the 50 states of the United States with 80 percent accuracy." Your outcome is for students to be able to list the 50 states, and you can measure or observe whether they can do it. The degree or level of mastery is 80 percent accuracy. This is a specific objective, in contrast to "Students will learn the 50 states" or "Students will know the 50 states."

FIGURE 3.8 *Instructional Objective Criteria*

Objectives State:	Examples (Information Level):
1. What will the student learn?	The names of the 50 states in the United States
2. Under what conditions?	By listing the 50 states
3. What degree of mastery?	80 percent of the states correctly listed
Completed Instructional Objective:	The student will list the 50 states of the United States with 80 percent accuracy.

"Hi, Dr. Brewster. Finished looking at my lesson plans yet?"

To guide your development of instructional objectives, we turn your attention to three frameworks of learner outcomes. These taxonomies classify the learning possibilities of your teaching.

Taxonomies of Learning Domains

Taxonomies are classification systems of the learning hierarchy. They progress from simple to complex. The first and most widely used taxonomy was developed for the *cognitive* domain by Bloom and associates (1956). Shortly after the development, the *affective* domain was classified into a taxonomy by Krathwohl and associates (1964). A taxonomy was also developed for the *psychomotor* domain (Harlow, 1972). We describe each domain and provide specific outcome vocabulary for you to use in writing objectives.

Cognitive Domain

This domain includes thinking outcomes that range from simple to complex:

1. *Knowledge*, the lowest level, asks your learners to remember previously learned material or to make a factual observation. When you want learners to tell when, how many, who, or where, they are using knowledge.
2. *Comprehension* asks your learners to grasp the meaning of information, to

interpret ideas, and to predict using knowledge. They are asked to translate knowledge into their own words. When learners are asked why, or to explain, or to summarize, they are using comprehension.

3. *Application* asks your learners to use previously learned knowledge in new and concrete situations, to use information, and to do something with knowledge.

4. *Analysis* requires your learners to break something into its constituent parts. They are asked to organize, to clarify, to conclude, or to make inferences. The process of analysis helps learners understand "big ideas" and the relationship of parts.

5. *Synthesis* requires your learners to put elements together. They are asked to create, that is, to form a whole or combination that is unique for the learner. Synthesis involves abstract relationships.

6. *Evaluation* requires a judgment. Your learners must give defensible opinions with criteria for their judgment. This level of functioning requires all the other cognitive levels—knowledge, comprehension, application, analysis, and synthesis—in order to be achieved (Houston, Clift, Freiberg, & Warner, 1988).

Notice in our descriptions of the levels of the cognitive domain and in the vocabulary in Figure 3.9, that levels of appropriate questions emerge along with

FIGURE 3.9 *Cognitive Domain Levels and Learner Outcomes*

Knowledge	defines, repeats, lists, names, labels, asks, observes, memorizes, records, recalls, fills in, listens, identifies, matches, recites, selects, draws
Comprehension	restates, describes, explains, tells, identifies, discusses, recognizes, reviews, expresses, locates, reports, estimates, distinguishes, paraphrases, documents, defends, generalizes
Application	changes, computes, demonstrates, shows, operates, uses, solves, sequences, tests, classifies, translates, employs, constructs, dramatizes, illustrates, draws, interprets, manipulates, writes
Analysis	dissects, distinguishes, differentiates, calculates, tests, contrasts, debates, solves, surveys, appraises, experiments, diagrams, inventories, relates, maps, categorizes, subdivides, defends
Synthesis	composes, proposes, formulates, sets up, assembles, constructs, manages, invents, produces, hypothesizes, plans, designs, creates, organizes, prepares, speculates
Evaluation	compares, concludes, contrasts, criticizes, justifies, supports, states, appraises, discriminates, summarizes, recommends, rates, decides, selects

levels of objectives. You will find them helpful as you plan your teaching and learning strategies, and when you develop the assessment strategies described in Chapter 14.

Affective Domain

This domain is also arranged in a hierarchy, from a simple level to a complex level:

1. *Receiving* requires your learners simply to attend—to listen, to notice, to observe—in order to receive.
2. *Responding* asks your learners to discuss, argue, or agree/disagree in response to what is heard or observed.
3. *Valuing* requires your learners to consider what was received, to use it to make decisions about its importance, to regard it as priority, and to place a value on it.
4. *Organizing* requires your learners to place values in relationship with other values, to organize judgments and choices, and to be influenced by the value.
5. *Characterizing*, the highest level, requires that your learners' values become organized to the point of being internalized, or become a part of the learners' life.

There is serious controversy about the role of schools in teaching the affective domain, and yet curriculum about drugs and alcohol, sexuality, and value clarification are the responsibility of teachers in most districts. When writing objectives for such curriculum, the levels of the affective domain will guide your planning. You may intend for learners to listen to information (receive) and discuss the importance of avoiding drugs (respond). Or you may intend for learners to act upon the information (valuing) and avoid situations where drugs are present (organization). Or you may intend for learners to work actively against drugs and to influence others (characterization).

Regardless of your stand on current affective curriculum, we hope that you intend for students to achieve Mager's (1984) minimal affective objective—that they should like your subject matter no less than when they came to your class (Houston et al., 1988, pp. 162–163). Today's district goals often reflect the outcomes of "lifelong learners," "love for reading," "responsible citizens," and "humanitarian living," all of which require teaching and learning in the affective domain.

Writing objectives for this domain is often difficult because the outcomes are personal, not often observable or measurable. We recommend that you describe indicators, or behaviors, that may indicate that students *appreciate, value, care about, feel,* and so on. An objective for appreciation of classical music may take the form of "Students will choose a classical record for listening during free time," or "Students will describe a selection of classical music." You have no certainty that students appreciate the music, but their behaviors indicate the possibility.

Psychomotor Domain

There are a number of physical and movement activities in school curriculum, probably not enough from the standpoint of students. Again, you have a hierarchy of simple to complex abilities:

1. *Reflex movements* are actions that occur involuntarily in response to some stimulus, such as stretching, blinking, and posture adjustments.
2. *Basic fundamental movements* are those innate movement patterns formed from a combination of reflex movements, such as running, walking, jumping, pushing, and pulling.
3. *Perceptual abilities* require the translation of stimuli through the senses into appropriate movements, such as following verbal instructions, dodging a moving ball, maintaining balance, and jumping rope.
4. *Physical abilities* combine basic movement and perceptual abilities into skilled movements, such as distance running, toe touching, basic ballet exercises, and weight lifting.
5. *Skilled movements* are more complex movements requiring a certain degree of efficiency, such as those used in dance, sports, music, and art.
6. *Nondiscursive* (nonverbal) communication is the ability to communicate through body movement, such as gestures, choreographed dance, and pantomime.

For each curriculum area, there are psychomotor objectives to be met. In science, you may intend for your learners to "prepare slides of specimens" or "dissect a frog." In language arts, you may intend for your learners to "pantomime the feeling expressed by a main character" or "use calligraphy to display a haiku." In music, you may intend for your learners to "play a simple melody on the tone flute" or "clap six measures of 4/4 rhythm." In geography, you may intend for your learners to "construct a relief map" or "measure rainfall."

The unit design on weather, which we described earlier, was directed to cognitive, affective, and psychomotor objectives. Go back to those objectives and see if you can differentiate between the three domains. It is also possible to achieve such combinations in an individual lesson or class. Think back to the Snapshots of this chapter. When Ms. Rennie taught her class about fractions, her objective was for students "to talk about all the ways fractions are used." She was working on a cognitive objective at the knowledge level. At the same time, she wanted students to appreciate the usefulness of fractions, an affective objective at the responding and/ or valuing level. When Mr. Malter taught his math lesson, he had several cognitive objectives. At the knowledge level, students were expected to know a formula and to describe the necessary information. At the application level, students were expected to use the formula and perform computations, and at the synthesis level, to create a problem of their own. Performing the computations required psychomotor skills of perceptual abilities. As you watched the lesson, you sensed that Mr. Malter intended for his students to feel enthusiastic about math and confident in their ability to perform the computations. Those are affective objectives.

Reflecting on Objectives

The process of developing and writing objectives is a reflective one. As you reflect, thoughts of your *learners* surface and you try to include their needs and interests in the directions you plan. You consider the abilities, the achievements, the previous experiences, and the developmental level of your learners as you decide objectives for your next lesson or week. As you reflect, the *context* of your teaching also influences the parameters of what you hope to achieve. The arrangement of your classroom, seasonal constraints, special programs, and the emotional climate you have established work to open or set limits on what you intend for your teaching. If there is a holiday approaching or if standardized tests have just been given, you may keep your objectives simple. At other times, you may attempt more ambitious objectives for your teaching and learning. Finally, the *content* of your teaching directly affects your reflection on objectives. You must ask yourself questions about the cognitive level appropriate for your learners. Or are you working toward psychomotor skills? Do you intend for students to achieve affective outcomes? Writing objectives is a comprehensive, reflective process—a major decision-making step in planning to teach.

PERSONALIZING YOUR DESIGN

By now you have noticed the variety of designs used by teachers. Perhaps you are wondering: "Which is the best?" You are the source of the answer. Many districts and schools specify a particular format as a starting point, but from there, experienced teachers personalize the format and the way they use it. To get you started in the process of personalizing, we suggest an awareness of your needs, priorities, and beliefs about teaching and learning. We also suggest attention to efficiency.

Meeting Your Needs and Priorities

Just as individuals plan trips differently based on their needs and priorities, so do teachers plan differently based on their needs and priorities. There is a wide variety of possibilities when we talk about needs and priorities. Again, only *you* have the right answer. We provide two format examples, each with an accompanying Teacher Talk.

TEACHER TALK

I developed this lesson plan to help organize myself daily, as my instruction varies. I feel the need to manage my administrative duties more carefully.
I am on the discipline committee and run the drill team, as well as teach four freshman English classes. It is quite a load but it can be handled with good planning. This format is tailored to my needs for organization. I allowed an extra Friday box to start with, so that at the beginning of the new week, I can easily check where we left off on Friday of the prior week. This helps my memory.

Secondary English Teacher

Lesson Plan

Teacher ___R. Swenson___

Subject(s) ___Eng. & Dance___

School ___Jefferson___

ENGLISH IB—1st–4th Periods

		Admin. (To Do)
Fri.	Objective: Homework:	
Mon.	Objective: Homework:	
Tues.	Objective: Homework:	
Wed.	Objective: Homework:	
Thurs.	Objective: Homework:	
Fri.	Objective: Homework:	

TIGERETTES—6th period		
Mon.	Tues.	Wed.
Thurs.	Fri.	Mon.

The next example comes from an experienced teacher who participated in in-service workshops and reflected on her teaching. She personalized her planning format to meet her needs and priorities.

TEACHER TALK

I have been teaching for a lot of years and it was getting secondhand, that is, I didn't think a lot about what was important in the individual lessons other than getting supplies ready. With art classes, that preparation often takes dominance. I also realized that I was focusing on skills and a few concepts, but ignoring the richness possible in what I was teaching. I had been to a conference on art appreciation and decided that I wanted to expand my classes to include more background. That's when I developed this format. To tell you the truth, I usually run out of time and have this awful rush of cleaning up at the end of my classes. I wanted to get better at planning within my time period so that my classes would end on a calmer note. So, I put the time column on this format to help me think through the minutes available.

Lesson Plan

Process _____   Topic _____

Grade Level _____   Duration _____

Materials

Teacher Aids	Student Supplies

Purpose/Objective	Essential Elements:

Vocabulary-Artist-Culture

Focus/Set

Time	Instructional Activity

Evaluation

Incorporating Your Beliefs

As you teach, your philosophy about teaching and learning may change, depending on your experiences. Your beliefs are also influenced by readings, classes and workshops, and your colleagues. The change is often incorporated in a planning format, as you see in Figure 3.10. This teacher had studied Hunter's lesson cycles and was enthusiastically modifying her teaching to include the elements. She developed her plan, and talked about how and why she incorporated the particular elements into her teaching. You can see her priorities and beliefs when you read her descriptions.

FIGURE 3.10 *Lesson Planning Format*

Teacher _____   Grade _____

Date _____   Subject _____

	Mon.	Tue.	Wed.	Thur.	Fri.
Focus	This is my "gotcha" part of the lesson. I want the students to begin thinking about social studies as they walk in the door.				
Objective	I ask myself what new ideas, concepts, knowledge, or skills will my students learn.				
Explanation	I provide information, demonstrate, and give examples. I provide a link between prior knowledge and the objective for today.				
Check for Understanding	This is where I use questioning, discussion, mini-chalkboards, yes/no cards, and simulations to check for understanding.				
Guided Practice	A problem is placed on the board and we work it together. I check to see if each student knows the solution.				
Individual Practice	I give several other problems for the students to work on individually. Some of the problems the students work on in groups.				
Closure	I use several types of closure. The students will tell me one idea/skill they learned today. The students or I will summarize the lesson.				

Designing for Efficiency

In the weekly design sample from an English teacher (Figure 3.4), you saw a coding system used for teaching and learning activities. Using codes is a way to be efficient about your planning. We suggest that you consider codes for your materials and equipment, assignments, directions, and groups of students. In another chapter, we suggest that you use a color coding scheme to check your plans for variety (easy–challenging work; whole group–individual activities; quiet–noisy).

Including a margin space along the side of your plans as you have seen in some of the formats in this chapter promotes efficiency when you use the space for reminders, "to-do" lists, evaluative comments for future planning, and individualized strategies for specific learners.

Another efficient strategy used by teachers is the development of a card file of teaching/learning activities, often with the activity coded by subject or curriculum area. Then, on the daily or weekly format, a simple code, such as SC-Air-Rev, might appear to indicate a *Science* activity on *Air*, which is appropriate for *Review*. Initially, developing the file takes time, but once you have developed a repertoire of strategies, activities, and resources, you can plan for exciting and varied teaching in an efficient manner. The card file also encourages you to gather ideas from your colleagues in an efficient and organized way.

So, the answer to the question, Which is the best format for designing a teaching plan? is one that changes with your experiences, philosophy, and your needs. The important idea here is to be aware of these influences and make your design format work for you.

SUMMARY

The process of designing instruction is a comprehensive one. It begins as you consider your content, context, and learner for information that helps you make planning decisions. From there, consider yourself to determine how much detail and what kind of design will help you feel comfortable and confident as you face teaching. You will probably include the basic elements of any instructional design: goals, objectives, teaching/learning activities, materials, feedback, and assessment.

Three design models are available to guide your efforts: the lesson cycle model, the instructional events model, and the instructional functions model. Each offers variations of the basic design elements in a format for a single lesson. There are also designs for longer-term teaching: unit designs, as well as daily and weekly designs. You will probably use all three to design instruction.

No matter which design you use, it will be important to begin and end your teaching effectively. Lesson beginnings need to capture student interest, promote a mental readiness, and describe the direction that the lesson will take. You have strategies available to do that: set inductions, advanced organizers, and sponges. As for lesson endings, it is important to bring closure—review and summarize—to what has been taught.

Regardless of the design format you use, it is also important to write objectives for your teaching. They direct all the other elements of instructional design. The taxonomies of the three learning domains—cognitive, affective, and psychomotor—provide levels of complexity in each domain to guide your objective writing. You will want to represent the three domains in your teaching so that you attend to the *whole* learner.

Finally, we encourage you to personalize whatever design format you use to meet your needs and priorities, to incorporate your beliefs, and to be efficient. You might begin with a model, and as you gain experience, personalize it. What is important is to be sure that your design does what teachers have described:

- "To provide a feeling of confidence and preparedness"
- "To organize materials, time, and activity flow"
- "For comfort and knowledge of subject matter"
- " To provide a framework for instruction and evaluation" (McCutcheon, 1980; Clark & Yinger, 1979).

REFERENCES

Ausubel, D. P. (1968). *Educational psychology: A cognitive view.* New York: Holt, Rinehart and Winston.

Bloom, B., Englehart, M., Furst, E., Hill, W., & Krathwohl, D. (1956). *Taxonomy of educational objectives: The classification of educational goals Handbook I, Cognitive domain.* New York: McKay.

Clark, C., & Yinger, R. (1979). Teachers' thinking. In P. L. Peterson & H. L. Walberg (Eds.), *Research on teaching.* Berkeley, CA: McCutchan.

Gagne, R. M., Briggs, L. J., & Wagner, W. W. (1988). *Principles of instruction* (3rd ed.). New York: Holt, Rinehart and Winston.

Harlow, A. (1972). *Taxonomy of the psychomotor domain.* New York: McKay.

Houston, W. R., Clift, R., Freiberg, H. J., & Warner, A. R. (1988). *Touch the future: Teach.* St. Paul: West.

Hunter, M. (1976). *Improved instruction.* El Segundo, CA: TIP Publications.

Hunter, M. (1985). *Mastery teaching: Increasing instructional effectiveness in secondary school, college and universities.* El Segundo, CA: TIP Publications.

Krathwohl, D., Bloom, B., & Masia, B. (1964). *Taxonomy of educational objectives: The classification of educational goals, Handbook II, Affective domain.* New York: McKay.

Mager, R. F. (1984). *Preparing instructional objectives* (rev. ed.). Belmont, CA: Fearon.

McCutcheon, G. (1980). How do elementary school teachers plan? The nature of planning and influences on it. *Elementary School Journal, 81,* 4–23.

Rosenshine, B., & Stevens, R. (1986). Teaching functions. In M. Wittrock (Ed.), *Handbook of research on teaching* (3rd ed.) New York: Macmillan.

Schuck, R. F. (1985). An empirical analysis of the power of set induction and systematic questioning as instructional strategies. *Journal of Teacher Education, 36*(2), 38–43.

Stallings, J. A., & Stipek, D. (1986). Research on early childhood and elementary school teaching programs. In M. Wittrock (Ed.), *Handbook of research on teaching* (3rd ed.). New York: Macmillan.

Yinger, R. J. (1980). A study of teaching planning. *Elementary School Journal, 80,* 107–127.

SAMPLES AND EXAMPLES

This Samples and Examples section includes lists of sponges, or beginning activities, that may be used at the primary, elementary, and secondary school levels.

- Primary Grade Sponges
- Elementary Grade Sponges
- Secondary Grade Sponges

EXAMPLES OF PRIMARY-GRADE SPONGES

1. Be ready to tell one playground rule.
2. Be ready to tell the names of the students in our class which begin with the letter _____.
3. Be ready to draw something that is only drawn with circles.
4. Be ready to tell a good health habit.
5. Have a color written on the board. Have students draw something that color.
6. Have students write the number that comes between a pair of numbers (e.g., 31 and 33; 45 and 47; etc.).
7. Have students write what numbers come before and/or after other numbers (e.g., 46, 52, 13, etc.).
8. Have a word written on the board. Have students make a list of words that rhyme with that word.
9. Have a word written on the board. Have students list words with the same long or short vowel sound.
10. Have students write words listed on the board in alphabetical order.
11. Have students count on paper to 100 by 2's, 5's, 10's, etc.
12. Have students draw animals that live on a farm, in the jungle, in water, etc.
13. Have students list or draw different fruits, vegetables, meats, etc.
14. Have students list things you can touch, things you can smell, big things, small things, etc.
15. Have students list the colors of the clothes they are wearing.
16. "I Spy"—have students write or be ready to name something in the room that begins with the letter _____.
17. Have students list or draw something in the room that has the sound of short *a*, long *a*, etc.
18. Have students write the days of the week, the months of the year.
19. Have students write or be ready to tell what day it is, what month it is, what is the date, what is the year, how many months are there in a year, how many days in a week, etc.
20. Have students draw or write the names of objects in the room that are in the shape of a triangle, circle, square, etc.
21. Have students write a word that begins or ends with certain consonants, blends, etc.
22. Have students write the name, or draw an object that begins with the letter _____.
23. Have students write what they will remember to bring/to do tomorrow.

EXAMPLES OF UPPER-ELEMENTARY SPONGES

1. List the continents of the world.
2. Make up three names for rock groups.
3. List as many kinds of windstorms as you can.
4. Choose a number. Write on a piece of paper. Now make a face out of it.
5. List as many gems or precious stones as you can.
6. Write the names of all the girls/boys in the class.
7. List as many teachers at this school as you can.
8. List as many states as you can.
9. List as many state capitals as you can.
10. Write: (a) an abbreviation, (b) a Roman numeral, (c) a trademark, (d) a proper name (biographical), (e) a proper name (geographical).
11. List as many countries and their capitals as you can.
12. List as many baseball teams as you can.
13. Write down as many cartoon characters as you can.
14. List as many kinds of flowers as you can.
15. Turn to your neighbor. One of you tell the other about an interesting experience you have had. The listener must be prepared to retell the story to the class.
16. List all the things in your living room.
17. Write what you would do if you saw an elephant in your backyard.
18. List as many kinds of ice cream as you can.
19. List five parts of the body above the neck that have three letters.
20. Practice with nouns by listing as many objects in the room as you can.
21. List one manufactured item for each letter of the alphabet.
22. List the mountain ranges of the U.S.
23. Write the 12 months of the year correctly.
24. Make a list of five things you do after school.
25. List one proper noun for each letter of the alphabet.
26. Write one kind of food beginning with each letter of the alphabet.
27. Name as many holidays as you can.
28. Write in increments of 6 as high as you can.
29. Name as many balls as you can that are used in sports games.
30. List as many U.S. presidents as you can.
31. List as many work tools as you can.
32. List as many types or models of cars as you can.
33. List all the colors you know.
34. How many parts of an automobile can you list?
35. How many animals can you list that begin with vowels?
36. List as many kinds of trees as you can.
37. List as many personal pronouns as you can.
38. List as many kinds of transportation as you can.
39. How many different kinds of languages can you name?
40. Write as many homonyms as you can.
41. Pretend you have 5 children. Make up their five names.
42. List as many things as you can that are made of cloth.
43. List as many things as you can that you can wear on your head.

44. List as many movie stars as you can (not TV personalities/stars).
45. List all the musical instruments that begin with the letter _____.
46. List as many TV game shows as you can.
47. List as many politicians as you can.
48. Scramble five spelling words, trade with someone, and unscramble them.

EXAMPLES OF SECONDARY SPONGES

1. List as many states as you can.
2. Write: (a) an abbreviation, (b) a Roman numeral, (c) a trademark, (d) a proper name (biographical), (e) a proper name (geographical).
3. How many countries and their capitals can you list?
4. How many baseball teams can you list?
5. Turn to your neighbor. One of you tell the other about an interesting experience you have had. The listener must be prepared to retell the story to the class.
6. List all the things in your living room.
7. List as many kinds of ice cream as you can.
8. List five parts of the body above the neck that have three letters.
9. List one manufactured item for each letter of the alphabet.
10. List one proper noun for each letter of the alphabet.
11. Write one kind of food beginning with each letter of the alphabet.
12. List as many holidays as you can.
13. List as many U.S. presidents as you can.
14. List as many models of cars as you can.
15. How many parts of an automobile can you list?
16. List as many countries of the world as you can.
17. List as many personal pronouns as you can.
18. List as many kinds of transportation as you can.
19. Write as many homonyms as you can.
20. List as many movie stars as you can (not TV personalities/stars).
21. List as many politicians as you can.
22. List all the places you find sand.
23. List as many breakfast cereals as you can.
24. Make a list of the 10 largest things you know.
25. List as many planets as you can.
26. List all the sports you can think of.
27. List foods that have sugar in them.
28. List foods that have milk in them.
29. List as many musical groups as you can that begin with the letters A–F.
30. List as many teachers at this school as you can.
31. List models of General Motors cars.
32. List all of the parts of speech and give an example of each.
33. Write why these dates are important: 1492, 1606, 1776, 1812, etc.
34. Find rivers, countries, etc., on a map in the textbook.
35. Which TV series can you list that have high school-aged characters as regulars?
36. List as many airlines as you can.
37. List the different sections of the newspaper.
38. List as many islands as you can.

39. List as many musical instruments as you can.
40. List all the foods you can think of that contain protein.
41. List as many kinds of fish as you can.
42. List all the words you can that begin with the prefix *in*.
43. List as many of the album titles of records by (list of artists).
44. List all the countries you know that have the letter *e* in them.
45. List as many animals as you can which cause harm to man.
46. List five books you've read recently that you really enjoyed.
47. Write the name of a movie you saw recently that you did *not* enjoy. Tell why.
48. List as many places as you can remember where you and your family have spent vacations.

Note: Try to select or make up sponges that relate to the content of the lesson that is to follow.

Source: Stallings, J. (1986). *Effective Use of Time Program*. Houston: University of Houston. Used by permission.

CHAPTER 4

The Effective Use of Time: Doing More with Less

CHAPTER OUTCOMES

At the conclusion of this chapter you will be able to:

1. Decide how to use time effectively for teaching and learning.
2. Use time effectively to accommodate district, school, and classroom contexts, content, and the learners.
3. Identify and reduce time losses and wasters.
4. Describe and use strategies for effective use of time.

KEY TERMS AND CONCEPTS

Time
Individual Learners
Model of School Learning
Student Aptitude
Student Perseverance
Opportunity to Learn
Academic Learning Time
Allocated Time
Student Engaged Time
Student Success Rate
Team Teaching or Teacher Teams
Modular Scheduling
Time Savers
Time Losses
Time Wasters
Clarity
Productive Activities
Paperwork

INTRODUCTION

We recently worked with a group of teachers as they returned to school after summer break. We posed a question: If you could be the best teacher ever, or the teacher you pictured when you decided to teach, what would you need? Of the 28 teachers, 25 said *time.* They described a range of wishes—more time for planning, more time for individual students, more time for teaching. Not a surprising response!

Better use of time is often a theme of educational reform (Fisher & Berliner, 1985). As we study teachers, we are learning more about how to be efficient with the commodity of time in classrooms. When Berliner (1982) talked about teachers as "executives" in the "workplaces" of classrooms and schools, he identified "scheduling time" as an extremely important decision. That is new thinking for education. You probably would not have found this chapter in a textbook on teaching 20 years ago.

THINKING ABOUT TIME FOR TEACHING AND LEARNING

As a teacher, you are responsible for extensive curriculum, meeting student needs and differences, and professional contributions outside the classroom. None of your responsibilities acknowledge a need for a personal life. Many young students are surprised to find that their teacher has a home and a life outside the classroom. The growing demands of teaching seem marked with the same naiveté; that is, they leave little time in the day for you. Many teachers experience fatigue, burnout, and disillusionment with the profession for these reasons. Since we do not foresee a significant increase in this commodity of time, we want to help you make the best possible use of what is available.

TEACHER TALK

If I don't lock myself in the art office—isolate myself—everyone stops by—students, other teachers—and then I don't get anything done. I want to talk with people, but I don't have enough time to do everything.

Secondary Art Teacher

Theory and Research Related to Time

As you think about time for teaching and learning in your classroom, both theory and research offer a framework for your thoughts. John B. Carroll (1985) described a theoretical model for school learning with three factors to consider when you make decisions about time in your classroom.

First, keep in mind *student aptitude*—"the amount of time that a student would need to learn something" (pp. 31–32). There are students who "catch on" in the first few minutes of explanation, and those who struggle for days before understanding the same idea. These aptitude differences are important considerations for your teaching schedule.

The second factor is *perseverance*—the amount of time that a student is willing to continue or persist. There are students who give up easily or quit after one or two tries, and those who will persist for a long time. These perseverance differences are important considerations for your teaching schedule.

The third factor is *opportunity to learn*—the amount of time available to learn. One teacher may provide generous amounts of time for a subject, and another teacher may provide a minimum amount of time for the same subject. Some teachers spend much more time teaching one topic or subject than they spend on another. When teachers record how they spend their day or an individual class or period, they learn about differences in their provision of opportunity to learn. We encourage such recording to make decisions about time for teaching.

When researchers examined the difference between effective and ineffective teachers in the Beginning Teacher Evaluation Study (Fisher, Filby, Marliave, Cahen, Dishaw, Moore, & Berliner, 1978), they identified the concept of Academic Learning Time (ALT). Three components of ALT will be useful for your thinking about time for teaching and learning.

The first component is *allocated time*—the period of time you allocate or plan for teaching a specific content area. If you schedule a geography lesson from 2:15 to 3:00 PM, your allocated time is 45 minutes. That time period is affected by your efficiency and preparation. The time you take to find materials, to check on what you are doing, or to pause with, "Now before we begin, are there any questions?" reduces the amount of time you actually have for instruction.

The second component is *student engagement rate*—the amount of time students are engaged in learning. When your students are paying attention, working on tasks, discussing curriculum topics, thinking about ideas, and practicing skills, they are engaged. When they are daydreaming, social talking, or abusing materials, they are not engaged.

The third component is *student success rate*—the rate at which your students perform tasks correctly, answer questions accurately, and solve problems successfully. When curriculum and activities are too difficult for students, the rate is low. When curriculum and activities are too easy for students, work becomes boring and repetitive, and the rate is low.

You may be thinking: How can I promote high levels of Academic Learning Time in my classroom? Research findings show both contextual differences and content adjustments influence ALT (Fisher et al., 1978). Carroll's model reminds us of learner differences, so we direct your thinking about time for teaching and learning to *context, content,* and *learner.*

Context

Time for teaching and learning is influenced by society's expanse as well as the confines of a school district. In your classroom context, you may have time wasters and regularly occurring losses (e.g., special programs, announcements, and taking lunch count), as well as productive activity. We will look at each level of context to direct your thinking about time for teaching and learning.

Societal Demands

As our society becomes more complex, demands on your teaching expand, but the amount of time available stays the same. You will find yourself making frequent decisions about what to teach and how to teach on the basis of efficiency. Effective teachers demonstrate efficiency as they blend curriculum. A secondary English literature teacher may decide to use time wisely by blending a study of women authors and poets and a study of feminist issues with a required set of literature. A second-grade teacher may blend a focus on women in nontraditional roles with the traditional curriculum on community helpers to meet societal demands.

The question of how to teach is a more difficult one—it becomes an issue of educational economics, one of *more* or *less*:

- When more time is spent with individual students, there is less time for the total group.
- When more time is spent on one curriculum area, there is less time for another curriculum area.
- When more time is spent socializing with students, there is less time for instruction.
- When more time is spent in discussions with other teachers, there is less time for paperwork or grading during school hours.

These economic decisions about time are pushed by societal demands, but they are also influenced by the school district context.

School District Demands

As you make decisions about time, you will feel the effect of school district demands in the form of priorities, expectations, and schedules. There will be variation from district to district, depending on size, philosophy, goals, funding, and administrative structure.

To become aware of district demands, begin by reading the priorities described in curriculum guides, often in the form of goals and objectives, textbook pages, and suggested schedules. You will also need to read the expectations of your district as you examine the forms of evaluation used to measure student learning. District schedules must also be reviewed for information on holidays, transportation, in-service days, special programs or events, and early dismissals.

What can you do? There are no simple responses to the demands. Our best answer is for you to be aware of their existence and their constraints on your teaching time. We have seen teachers struggling and thinking, "It must be me . . . if only I . . . maybe my teaching isn't . . . ." Teaching can be very difficult if you do not recognize the demands and constraints. However, a school district can give some provisions.

School District Provisions

Districts are aware of and have responded to the time shortages with variations in instructional and scheduling arrangements. *Team teaching*, or *teacher teams*, is an example of an instructional arrangement. With the arrangement, team members divide curricular responsibilities and make use of an individual teacher's interests and expertise. Districts often contribute to this arrangement with time for planning, resources, and reimbursements for related responsibilities.

In studies at the elementary level (Little, 1981) and at the junior-high level (Bird & Little, 1985), teachers have pointed to achievement gains, improvements in student behavior, and positive student attitudes as payoffs for team work for shared planning and preparation. Examples are less frequent at the high-school level, but there are descriptions of highly cohesive departments or small groups working together (Ball & Lacey, 1984) with similar success.

You may like the team approach for its efficiency. You can focus your preparation and teaching on one curricular area and enjoy interacting with different groups of students each day. Or you may see these advantages differently, and miss preparing for a variety of subject areas and interacting with a more limited number of students.

Some examples of scheduling arrangements are modular scheduling and variations of the year-round school. *Modular scheduling* offers an alternative to the traditional scheduling format of secondary schools. Modules are short, 20 to 25 minutes each, and teachers have flexibility in using them. For example, on Tuesday, the French teacher meets with students for only one module of lecture presentation, but on Wednesday and Friday, he has three modules in which to conduct conversations, play vocabulary games, continue long-term projects, and read literature.

Year-round school has been tried with variations in when students and teachers take a break, and with variations in the components (quarters, fifths, etc.). The plan makes year-round use of school facilities and accommodates varied family schedules.

At this time, there is not enough evaluated use of year-round school or modular scheduling to tell us whether they work. What is encouraging is that districts are aware of the scarcity of time and are developing arrangements to support your teaching time. From there, you must look into your own classroom context as you think about time for teaching.

Classroom Demands

Within the classroom are numerous demands on your time. We call some of them *time losses* and some of them *time wasters*.

Time losses are situations that are out of your control, such as fire drills, assembly programs, school cancellations (weather), health checks, student illness or accident in class, recesses, lunch, and announcements on the intercom.

Our best advice for these losses is to anticipate them and plan accordingly. If you know that an assembly is planned, try to connect your curriculum to the program. Give students specific directions about what to do after the assembly when they return to the classroom. Have a plan of action, well understood by students, for any absences. For example, when a student is absent, an absence packet containing handouts and assignments is placed on his or her desk. Develop a list of activities that will work well during those time losses when students are pulled out of class.

Time wasters are those situations over which you have some control, such as calling roll, socializing during a lesson, teaching unprepared lessons, beginning a lesson when students aren't ready, helping students after an absence, looking for lost materials, late students, and equipment failures. Rather than allowing these to become routine, you can minimize or eliminate them with some of the ideas that follow:

> **EXAMPLE:** Roll must be taken and recorded each day, so students can check themselves off the daily list as they enter the classroom. A student attendance monitor could scan the room and record absences each day.

> **EXAMPLE:** Students who miss school need information, missed assignments, handouts, and class notes. Students can select partners at the beginning of the year, and be responsible whenever a partner is absent to collect assignments and handouts, copy notes, and provide missed information.

TEACHER TALK

I have a box of carbon paper and students use it for note taking when a "partner" is absent. Each student has a folder for notes, assignments, and handouts. If a "partner" is absent, the folder is used to collect the day's work. I used to hate spending time on the previous day's information.

A final suggestion for handling the classroom demands is to maintain *productive activity*. You can hear and feel productive activity when you enter some classrooms—it has a sound or a buzz. There is work being done and there is an attitude of seriousness. You hear, "This is an important study . . . this practice will make a difference in your . . . this is significant information." To maintain productive activity, you will need to provide the following supports:

- *Pace Changers*. After an intense and fast-paced math drill, students stand in place and stretch to music.
- *Student Input*. Before beginning a new unit of study, the topic is displayed on a small bulletin board. Students are asked to contribute "what we already know," "what we are curious about," and "how we want to learn."
- *Evaluation and Feedback*. Students regularly hear, "You have followed all the steps correctly," or "Your work needs more reference material to support your idea."

So you see that you must balance the demands of your classroom with the demands of your district and society to find as much time as possible for instruction. From there, look to *content* and continue your thinking about time for teaching.

Content

Berliner (1982) reminds us that the "final arbiter of what is taught in classrooms is the teacher." As you make your first decision about what to teach, you will be directed by your commitments to content goals and by your attitudes about content. As you make your decision about how to teach, you can make time management a part of your content by the way you teach. Part of what you learned in school indirectly is how to use time. Rather than rely on it happening casually, you can plan for it to occur.

Commitments to Content

Robin, a first-grade teacher who works in an inner-city racially mixed neighborhood, describes independence as a major goal for her students. Her commitment to the goal directs the way she uses her teaching time. Robin is careful to meet district goals but her decisions about what to teach are influenced by her commitment to independence.

Robin begins by analyzing the components of independence into appropriate skills for first grade: problem solving, decision making, recognition of one's own competence, and communication for help and resources. Notice how specific she is with the components of independence. This is an important first step.

With the skills in mind, Robin plans teaching and management strategies. Time is scarce, so she integrates her goal of independence with other parts of her curriculum:

1. Most of the assignments in her class involve choices, so her students constantly make decisions about materials, tasks, and scheduling their work.
2. When her students write in journals or in group stories, there is an emphasis on expressing "what I can do" or "what I have learned."

3. All the materials and equipment in the room are presented with instruction on how and when to use them during the first month of school. From there, students use the classroom independently.
4. Students are taught and even rehearsed in requesting help or attention from volunteers, parents, and visitors. If you enter the room, you can plan on being asked, "Would you listen to me read?" or "I need you to hold this side of my building while I staple it."

In addition, Robin purposefully assesses student achievement of independence. The measurement is informal and usually includes observations of students, student self-reports, and samples of student work. When parents come in for conferences, she asks, "Can Sam do anything new for himself?" She also screens the student journals to see if they can express confidence or new learning.

Robin gains great satisfaction from seeing independence in her students. That is one of the joys of teaching we don't want you to miss. Commitment means finding time and ways to teach with efficiency. Your attitudes and values have a similar influence.

Attitudes about Content

Most of us would admit that we value or like some curriculum area more than others, or care about some topics more than others. If you had a choice, what would you prefer to teach? Why?

Differences in curricular preferences are fine, but awareness is important. Researchers have noted that teachers plan differently for subject matter that they like (Schwille, Porter, Belli, Floden, Freeman, Knappen, Kuhs, & Schmidt, 1983). Differences in your planning may affect student engaged time, motivation, and your enthusiasm—all of which are acceptable. When you believe certain work is interesting or important, you shape similar beliefs in your students. They hear you say, "We are beginning an exciting unit in economics today" with both verbal and nonverbal messages. You are a source of attitudes and your students model and learn accordingly.

What about the work you do not find interesting and enjoyable due to a lack of interest or knowledge? We asked experienced teachers how to compensate for this attitude and they suggested taking courses and workshops in those curricular areas. Our own experience has shown if we put extra planning into those subjects, we have better organized lessons, interesting activities, and enthusiasm for teaching. With a few successful experiences, you may discover new preferences.

Time Management as Content

When you consider time as part of your curriculum or content, you may find that student efficiency can be taught through your own management of time. Begin with goal setting, add some time structures, and plan for environmental supports.

As early as possible, students need to learn *goal setting*. You can model by sharing some of your own goals. You may need to define the word *goal* and illustrate it with examples. Students could interview parents for examples. Then students can set goals for themselves. Initially, they can begin with short-term goals like, "Today I will have a neat desk" or "Today I will be helpful." Later they may learn to set long-term goals.

Once students develop some skill, you can integrate goal setting with other curricular goals. For example, given an overview of a unit on forests and an outline of topics, students can set goals for themselves related to the unit.

At the same time that you are developing goal setting, you can be teaching *time structures* simply by thinking aloud so that students can hear: "We have only 20 minutes left to finish this work," or "Only 15 minutes before the bell rings." Young students learn structures with, "When the second hand is on six, we need to have everything cleaned." They gradually develop a sense of time and how to use it. More mature students need practice in estimating and predicting time structures with, "How much time do you think we need for the lab work today?" or "How many minutes do you think it will take to prepare the room for our group projects?"

Just as you need to identify time losses and wasters, students need the same experience. Class discussions of least favorite times of day, times of boredom, reasons why work doesn't get completed, and reasons for success will prompt awareness. Those losses and wasters that students identify for themselves will be meaningful for them and they will be more likely to take action and become efficient.

To establish *environmental supports*, you will need to instruct students in the use of classroom materials. Teach detailed lessons on using the tape recorder or the stapler. Once taught, provide written instructions for location, use, and storage of many of the classroom materials available during the year. Figure 4.1 provides examples of such instructions for young or nonreading students, as well as mature students. Students can make (or decorate) sets of instructions and hang them in appropriate locations. You may want to encourage students to evaluate the directions or to make suggestions for better use. When students know how to use the environment independently, you have environmental supports for your teaching time.

Along with the what and how of teaching, you will need to consider the learner in your thinking about time for teaching.

Learner Differences

Within most classrooms is a range of differences, including ability and developmental differences. Time looks especially limited when you think about accommodating those differences and meeting individual needs.

Ability Differences

When thinking about *ability differences*, teachers often wish for more time to give attention to a low-ability student or wish for extra time to challenge a high-ability student. We encourage you to consider the use of peer tutors, volunteers, and aides, or some of the cooperative learning strategies described in Chapter 10 to help you meet different ability levels. You will see that these arrangements are not only efficient but appropriate for student learning.

FIGURE 4.1   *Instructions for Independent Classroom Use*

Using Class References & Materials

Item	Where to use...	How to use...
Encyclopedias	in classroom	Find on back shelf - alphabetical order - return.
Periodicals	in classroom at home	Locate in card file, sign out, return to box.
Filmstrips	in classroom study hall	Locate in card file, sign out, rewind or replace.
Games	at back tables	Locate on side shelf (labeled), return to shelf.

Comments: Fill out a comment slip on needs, lost items, etc.

Using the Tape Recorder

1. Check the classroom — listen

2. Check the plug

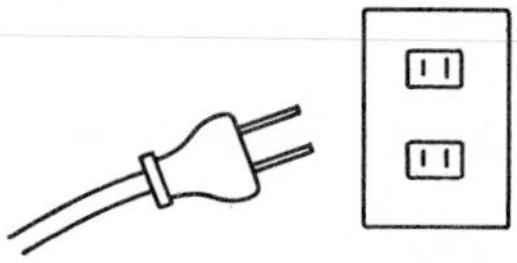

3. Put in the tape

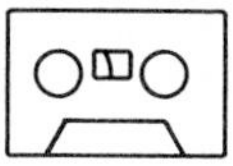

4. Push 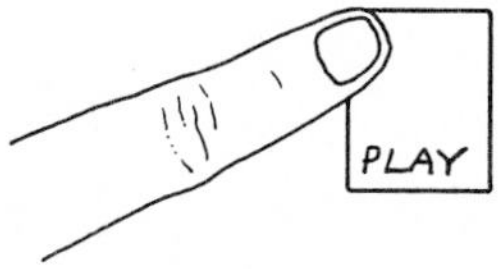 _____ PLAY _____ Play

5. When finished, push _____ REW _____ Rewind

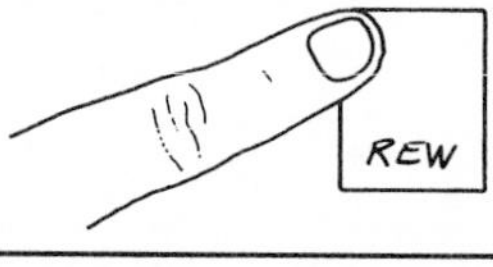

Source: Driscoll, A., & Peterson, K. (1988). *Classroom management course materials.* Unpublished materials, Portland State University. Used by permission.

Another approach to accommodate ability differences is through monitoring, a strategy that checks student understanding of an idea or competence in a skill during the learning process. This strategy will help you determine, before much time passes, who is learning and who is not. Monitoring can be done in a number of ways—questioning, checking student work, observing facial expressions, and reviewing previous learning. Some examples of teacher monitoring will help you see how it saves time:

EXAMPLE: An eighth-grade algebra teacher instructs students in the use of a new formula, then assigns five problems. She immediately moves about the room, looks at each student's work, and determines who is able to use the formula and who isn't. She asks individual students, "Tell me how you do this problem," and monitors understanding.

EXAMPLE: After giving a lecture on osmosis, Ms. Nagel asks fast-paced questions of the class for about five minutes to determine whether the science content was understood. When one of his questions leads to confused looks and few answers, he knows that some information needs explanation or clarification.

EXAMPLE: While young students practice sequencing pictures of story sets, Mr. Hernandez moves about the room and watches them. He watches for confusion or frustrations. He stops and asks often, "Why is this picture last?" or "Why is this picture in the middle?" He can tell from the explanations whether the correct sequence is random or due to student understanding.

Monitoring tells you whether learners understand, whether to slow down or speed up, whether to reteach or go on, or whether to spend some time reviewing. In the end, monitoring will save you time and help you accommodate ability differences in your learners.

Developmental Differences

Two developmental differences have significant influence on your use of time in classrooms: attention span differences and differences in conceptual understanding of time. Young students need brief instructional periods (10 to 20 minutes), but older students can attend for longer periods (15 to 45 minutes). As the school year progresses, the length of the students' *attention span* increases. Holidays, weather, and special events can adversely influence attention span and must be considered in your scheduling plans.

The second difference is student understanding of the *concept of time*. Young students need a great deal of the time structures we previously described, such as, "You have 5 more minutes to work in centers before clean-up time." Older students can conceptualize and plan for longer time periods. You can assist by encouraging them to use schedules or calendars (see Samples and Examples in Chapter 2) to plan their own time structures.

We have been encouraging you to think about time for teaching and directed your attention to the context, content, and learners. Now you are ready for some *time savers* to use in your classroom.

TIME SAVERS

Our time savers are generic because they apply to everyday situations, in and out of school, so you can try them out whether you are currently teaching or preparing to teach. We start with *goal setting*, then focus on your *clarity*. From there, we develop some strategies for *handling paperwork efficiently*, and end with *delegating* as a time saver. In spite of time limits on your teaching, there are ways to increase minutes and hours with these time savers.

Goal Setting

Johnson and Johnson's *The One Minute Teacher* (1986) offers a brief and efficient approach to goal setting. The foundation of their approach is simple and has immediate use.

TEACHER TALK

I was disappointed when I first read *The One Minute Teacher*. I wanted some help with saving time. "One minute goal setting" seemed silly; not very realistic. But as time went by, I thought about it. Then I tried it out. Now I'm using it. I guess it's because it's so simple. It really works.

Begin by thinking quietly about what you want to learn, what you want to accomplish, and what you want to be. Write your goal(s) in the first person, present tense, with a date set for achieving them. Reread your goal often, and when you do, imagine how you feel when you are achieving it.

An example of a goal is: I am preparing my classroom and all my teaching materials for the next day each afternoon before I leave to go home. When you reread this goal, you might think: It feels so good to go home knowing that my room is ready for tomorrow. This creates a self-fulfilling prophecy and the process supports a positive attitude. We know that we lose a lot of time when we have negative feelings, so attitude can be a time saver. While you are using one minute goal setting, it is important to reflect on your time for teaching and how you use it.

A strategy for such reflection is using a time journal, which is a simple record of how you use your time each day. The sixth-grade teacher in the following Snapshot kept a running record of his day. See if your impressions of his day match his. Using a journal will yield information about how you spend your time, which will then direct your goal setting.

SNAPSHOT: *Elementary Classroom*

7:32 AM Arrival: lights, shades, windows. Reviewed lesson plans for equipment and materials needed. Checked the overhead projector, jars for science, and soil samples. Hung colored sheets of directions for group work; stacked newspapers below each sheet.

8:00 AM Recorded grades from two sets of work from previous day.

8:25 AM Coffee in faculty lounge; read announcements.

8:30 AM Greeted students at door.

8:40 AM Current events discussion.

8:55 AM Student journal writing. Wrote in my journal about field trip ideas for next month.

9:05 AM Math review of previous day's lesson, 2 problems on overhead with class participation, 3 problems for independent work.

9:18 AM Taught new strategy; student demonstrations.

9:37 AM Directions for practice assignment (part in class, part for homework); monitored work.

10:05 AM Assigned students to groups for language arts by passing out colored squares as students put away math books and journals. Called attention to direction sheets in six locations of the room and groups moved to locations.

10:20 AM After group work began, wrote words on board for spelling lesson; then moved about, listening to groups.

10:39 AM Gave directions to groups to rotate.

10:59 AM Called students back to places; group leaders placed work in IN basket.

11:03 AM Class left for library period.

11:05 AM Met with sixth-grade teachers to plan field trip.

11:32 AM Students returned; taught spelling lesson.

11:48 AM Prepared to go to lunch.

11:54 AM Took tray to faculty lounge; continued planning field trip with other sixth-grade teachers.

12:24 PM Returned to class; reviewed notes for afternoon science and social studies activities.

12:30 PM Class returned; began lecture on soil, readings in text; row leaders pick up soil samples.

12:57 PM Students began soil analysis activity with worksheets; monitored.

1:13 PM Students reported analysis results to partner.

1:17 PM Reports and samples collected by row leaders.

1:20 PM Student groups continued working on historical skits begun earlier in week. Taught small group about leaders of the revolution.

1:33 PM Taught second small group.

1:49 PM Preparation for recess.

1:51 PM Supervised recess.

2:06 PM Returned to room, practiced songs for history program.

2:20 PM Silent reading—historical novels; small group work on reading skills.

3:05 PM Student choice time (homework, ad game, chess, estimation table, library visit).

3:30 PM Dismissal.

3:36 PM Review and grade student work.

4:16 PM Lights off; went to office to check mail.

4:31 PM Went home after reading mail and writing replies.

This sixth-grade teacher commented that this was one of his better days but a tiring one. He felt that it reflected his efforts to be more organized and to accelerate his transitions or changes in the day. He lamented his lateness for library and recess because "my colleagues are affected by those few minutes."

In the Samples and Examples and the end of this chapter, we provide forms for keeping track of the time you spend in organizing and for recording classroom interruptions. Using reflection strategies will also help you evaluate whether you are achieving your goals. It will be important to check yourself occasionally so that you continue to make progress.

At this point, Johnson and Johnson recommend self-praising (one minute's worth), and teachers deserve this more than anyone. When you stop and review your goal(s), recognize what you have accomplished. You may even want to do it in writing. "One minute" strategies don't use up much of your time. Those who use them tell us that they save time and bring real satisfaction. In the next section, we describe how to achieve clarity in your teaching as a time saver. You may want to make it one of your first goals.

Clarity in Teaching

Clarity in your teaching is efficient because students understand better, work more accurately, and are more successful (Gephart, Strother, & Duckett, 1981). When you are not clear, you may have to repeat directions, reteach a concept, undo a misunderstanding, and so on. We have all had occasions in our lives when our lack of clarity had time-consuming and sometimes disastrous results. To keep it from happening in your teaching, we suggest watching Ms. Daugherty (in the following Snapshot). She demonstrates five behaviors that provide clarity in her teaching: stating the topic or focus, providing an outline to the students, giving many examples and illustrations, connecting to the students' experiences, and repeating the main points several times in the lesson.

SNAPSHOT: Middle-School Classroom—5th Period

1:38 PM Students pick up a study sheet as they arrive. The sheet lists types of landforms, space for examples and definitions, and a reference list.

1:40 PM "Take a look at our topic for today. Be ready to begin in one minute."

1:41 PM "The topic for today is landforms. We will be working on definitions and examples on your sheets. Tomorrow we will do map work with landforms. First, look at the list of landform types and see if you see any that exist where we live."

1:43 PM Students begin raising hands to respond with examples of landforms in the community. "Now, think of your travels and see if you have seen any other landforms listed on your sheet." Again, students respond with examples from vacations and former homes.

1:46 PM Bring out large photographs and ask the class to identify the landforms in the pictures. The class answers in unison as the photos are shown. "Now that you've seen and heard about examples of landforms, let's define what they are." Record students' ideas on an overhead transparency and work toward a common definition: "Landforms are features of the earth's surface that result from natural causes."

1:50 PM Instruct students to complete the definitions and examples of each landform on their sheets: "Remember, landforms are. . . . Be sure to describe the feature and the cause." Underline the terms in the definition. Students practice aloud with several examples.

1:55 PM "It sounds like you are ready to begin defining. When you finish, check the reference list on your study sheet and see if you can find another new example of landform. You're welcome to come up and write it on the transparency."

Did you notice in the Snapshot that the topic was stated? An outline was provided? Examples and illustrations were used? The topic was connected to students' experiences? The main point was repeated? Ms. Daugherty modeled clarity for you in her instruction. Figure 4.2 is a checklist that will also help you to check your clarity. It can be used by you, as a student or as a teacher, to develop awareness of behaviors that promote *clarity in teaching.*

In the Samples and Examples at the end of this chapter is a list of statements for you to assess for clarity. It will help you listen to yourself as you work on this time saver.

FIGURE 4.2 *Instructional Clarity Checklist*

Directions: Below are thirty-two items describing instructional behaviors that contribute to instructional clarity. To the right of these items is a scale. For each item, put a check mark at the location that best describes how often you as a teacher perform the instructional behaviors. The scale is as follows:

4	All of the time	1	Never
3	Most of the time	0	Does not apply
2	Some of the time		

	4	3	2	1	0
1. Explains the work to be done and how to do it	( )	( )	( )	( )	( )
2. Asks students if they know what to do and how to do it	( )	( )	( )	( )	( )
3. Explains something, then stops so student can think about it	( )	( )	( )	( )	( )
4. Takes time when explaining	( )	( )	( )	( )	( )
5. Orients and prepares students for what is to follow	( )	( )	( )	( )	( )
6. Provides students with standards and rules for satisfactory performance	( )	( )	( )	( )	( )
7. Specifies content and shares overall structure for the lectures with students	( )	( )	( )	( )	( )
8. Helps students to organize materials in a meaningful way	( )	( )	( )	( )	( )
9. Repeats questions and explanations if students don't understand	( )	( )	( )	( )	( )
10. Repeats and stresses directions and difficult points	( )	( )	( )	( )	( )
11. Encourages and lets students ask questions	( )	( )	( )	( )	( )
12. Answers students' questions	( )	( )	( )	( )	( )
13. Provides practice time	( )	( )	( )	( )	( )
14. Synthesizes ideas and demonstrates real-world relevancy	( )	( )	( )	( )	( )
15. Adjusts teaching to the learner and the topic	( )	( )	( )	( )	( )
16. Teaches at a pace appropriate to the topic and students	( )	( )	( )	( )	( )
17. Personalizes instruction by using many teaching strategies	( )	( )	( )	( )	( )
18. Continuously monitors student learning and adjusts instructional strategy to the needs of the learner	( )	( )	( )	( )	( )
19. Teaches in a related, step-by-step manner	( )	( )	( )	( )	( )
20. Uses demonstrations	( )	( )	( )	( )	( )
21. Uses a variety of teaching materials	( )	( )	( )	( )	( )
22. Provides illustrations and examples	( )	( )	( )	( )	( )
23. Emphasizes the key terms/ideas to be learned	( )	( )	( )	( )	( )
24. Consistently reviews work as it is completed and provides students with feedback or knowledge of results	( )	( )	( )	( )	( )
25. Insures that students have an environment in which they are encouraged to process what they are learning	( )	( )	( )	( )	( )
26. Makes clear transitions	( )	( )	( )	( )	( )

(continued)

FIGURE 4.2 *(Continued)*

	4	3	2	1	0
27. Reduces mazes	( )	( )	( )	( )	( )
28. Avoids vague terms	( )	( )	( )	( )	( )
29. Avoids fillers (uh, ah, um)	( )	( )	( )	( )	( )
30. Reduces nonessential content	( )	( )	( )	( )	( )
31. Communicates so that all students can understand	( )	( )	( )	( )	( )
32. Demonstrates a high degree of verbal fluency	( )	( )	( )	( )	( )

Source: Gephart, W. J., Strother, D. B., & Duckett, W. E. (1981). *Practical applications of research, newsletter.* Phi Delta Kappa Center on Evaluation, Development, and Research, *3*(3). Used by permission.

Handling Paperwork

When we talk with teachers about reasons for being a teacher, they never mention paperwork. The vignette describes the realities of this time-consuming responsibility.

Paperwork is a reality, so we urge an efficient approach. Become familiar with the seven types of paperwork identified in the study and we will suggest time savers for each type.

• *Type 1: Classwork Paperwork*. Some examples from teachers included, "prepared math worksheet for seatwork," "typed library information ditto," and "collated sheets."

Three suggestions come to mind for this top time consumer: (1) share materials with other teachers, (2) save successful materials from year to year, and (3) get assistance with collating, stapling, and copying. Because this form of paperwork has no easy solution, we encourage you to seek alternatives to doing it yourself. Have students work in groups to prepare their own study guides. Use transparencies instead of individual copies of seatwork. Use student-made flash cards for drill and practice instead of worksheets. Have students develop their own lists of questions to answer.

• *Type 2: Evaluation and Grading Paperwork*. Teachers described these tasks as, "grading chapter tests," "writing comments on papers," and "filling out grade logs."

Collins (1987) shares hints from experienced teachers for grading papers:
—"As you walk around the room checking student work, mark those problems which you check with a red pencil. When you later collect the papers to evaluate, you will have part of your work already done."
—"Ask students to tell you or to tell another student one new idea or an example of a concept at the end of the day or class period."
—"Don't feel compelled to grade every single question or problem, or even every worksheet. Check enough to determine student understanding."
—"Have students themselves, or student monitors, or volunteers grade and check papers."

Research Vignette

INTRODUCTION

In a national as well as a preliminary study conducted in the state of Delaware (1987), paperwork was cited by teachers as the second least satisfying element of teaching. In addition, 72 percent of the teachers indicated that reducing paperwork would contribute significantly to teacher retention and recruitment. Since little descriptive information about the paperwork burden was available, the Delaware State Department of Public Instruction conducted a survey of teacher paperwork.

STUDY DESIGN

Teachers recorded their paperwork activities both during and after the normal school day for 17 days. In a log designed for the study, 58 volunteer teachers (elementary and secondary) coded 3,893 paperwork entries into 16 categories according to the nature of the work.

The paperwork was analyzed to determine: (1) the nature of the various types of paperwork and the length of time it took to complete, (2) the source of paperwork, (3) the level of difficulty of types of paperwork, and (4) the type of school in relation to quantity and type of paperwork.

RESULTS

Teachers in the study reported a total of 1,660 hours of paperwork, and average of 8 hours and 6 minutes a week per teacher. Paperwork related to instruction, such as evaluation/grading, homework, and classwork, accounted for 4 hours and 30 minutes a week per teacher.

Teacher-originated paperwork, such as developing study guides, was the most time-consuming type, with an average of 5 hours and 46 minutes a week. Paperwork that originated within the school, district, or parents accounted for 2 hours and 20 minutes a week. It was found that time spent on paperwork was evenly divided between the school day and outside the school day. Approximately 40 percent of paperwork time during the normal school day was spent on routine or clerical paperwork. In the evenings or weekends, only one quarter of the time was on routine or clerical paperwork.

The most difficult paperwork cited was "responding to parents" and discipline within school. The least difficult included student passes, correspondence within school, and requests.

The table displays the differences in paperwork time and difficulty by school types.

Discussion and Implications for Practice. The research has confirmed that there is a paperwork burden on teachers, but it provides no answers or strategies. We do have an insight from the data, however; we noticed that the majority of paperwork is directly associated with teaching. It originates from within the classroom. We urge you to consider classroom paperwork with questions such as: Does this paperwork contribute to my teaching? To student learning? Could it be accomplished in better or more efficient ways?

Paperwork Time and Difficulty by School Type

School Type	Average Hrs./Wk/Teacher	Percent of Time	
		Less Difficult (Clerical)	*More Difficult* (Professional)
Elementary School	8 Hrs. 52 Min.	35.2%	64.8%
Middle School	7 Hrs. 55 Min.	21.5%	78.5%
High School	7 Hrs. 19 Min.	32.3%	67.7%
Total	8 Hrs. 6 Min.		

Source: Delaware State Department of Public Instruction. (1987). *Teacher paperwork study: Type, time, and difficulty.* Dover: Delaware State Department of Public Instruction. Used by permission.

• *Type 3: Homework Paperwork.* Teachers described this paperwork as preparing, grading, and recording homework.

Some of the ideas for streamlining classwork and evaluation/grading apply here. In addition, we suggest that you organize specific places and routines for homework distribution and collection (e.g., an IN and OUT box, folders or envelopes for student work). Consider providing answer keys or samples for students to grade their own work, or involve parents in the review and checking of homework once or twice a week. Many teachers take a few minutes at the beginning of class to allow student partners to check homework and to record completion and grade.

• *Type 4: Report Card Paperwork.* Teachers listed several tasks for this type: "averaging grades," "recording grades," and "writing comments on report cards."

There are some generic time savers for any kind of reports due at regular intervals like report cards. First, establish sound procedures for recording and storing data such as test grades, samples of students' work, and commentaries. A good filing system or a computer software program will save you time all year. At report card time, organize your data and materials at a work space that will not be disturbed for the time needed to complete your work. Have plenty of space for spreading out. An important suggestion is that you plan for 50 minutes to one hour of work at a time. If you get too tired, you become inefficient and possibly inaccurate. When you stop, straighten and organize your materials for the next work session.

Because of the nature of this paperwork, this is probably an ideal context in which to use the one minute goal setting: "I have a positive attitude about this task," or "I have completed one third of my report cards today," or "I have written thoughtful comments on 10 report cards today."

• *Type 5: Special Projects Paperwork.* This seems to be a catchall category with familiar sounding tasks such as, "prepared form for promotion committee," "licked cafeteria award stickers," and "wrote suggestions for student essay contest."

This is probably the best type of paperwork to which you say *no.* Teachers are conditioned not to refuse requests related to professional work. Drawbaugh (1984) suggests that you consider saying *no* if you have uncertainties about the request, if it will cause you stress, or if it will keep you from or delay your own goals. You should definitely refuse if you are overcommitted or if you just don't want to do it.

Once you have decided, you may have to learn or practice saying *no.* It is important to be pleasant and tactful, but at the same time be persistent and avoid excuses. Get a friend to help you practice so that you can be successful when the situation occurs. Then you can choose those tasks or requests that you really want to do. You will experience real professional satisfaction and increased efficiency with this strategy.

• *Type 6: Test-Development Paperwork.* Even if you have never done this, you can guess the kinds of tasks teachers do: "composed multiple-choice items," or "typed test."

The list goes on for every subject area and for every teacher. Three sound strategies are suggested. First, maintain a test question bank with items from previous tests, other teachers, and commercial materials. With computers, an item bank will be easily achieved, and you can add to the bank on an ongoing basis. Consider involving students in test development. An effective study and review strategy is to have students write test items. You can learn from their ideas and you may have some usable items.

Second, use answer sheets or other resources for scoring objective tests. Third, pay attention to yourself in this task. Look at your time constraints and teaching conditions. What is your schedule like? How large is your class? Be realistic when you plan your tests.

• *Type 7: Correspondence within School.* The diversity of paperwork that falls in this category is unbelievable, but a few samples from teachers included "sent memos to team leaders," "completed report for principal," and "wrote congratulatory note to student of the month."

The strategies for streamlining this type of paperwork apply to all kinds of correspondence, at home and at work. The best advice is to avoid rereading. When you go to the mailroom, take small notes, envelopes, and a pen with you, and jot replies immediately after reading; sometimes, you can reply right on the letter. Throw away those that do not need a reply. Take your calendar with you and you can record scheduling information at the same time. You will no longer have piles of this kind of paperwork on your desk staring at you.

There was also a category called *Correspondence Out of School*, which teachers rated as difficult paperwork, but not as time consuming as the types we reported. Many teachers keep a file of sample correspondence for this purpose. In the Samples and Examples at the end of this chapter, you will find a form for corresponding with parents about work missed due to absence. It's a time saver.

There is hope for the paperwork burden. It is a professional responsibility that we can approach with a few purposeful strategies. We have begun a process for you—that of collecting ideas for saving time. From here, talk to other teachers. They are the best source of time savers.

Delegating

Our final strategy for saving time is delegating. It is a difficult skill to learn, and teachers seem to struggle more than most professionals. Most of us feel some guilt when we delegate, as if we are avoiding our responsibilities. Instead, we need to think of delegating as a competent and professional skill. Learning how to delegate is difficult, but we can get you started. From there, you will need to read, discuss, set goals, practice, and check yourself regularly.

Conditions for Delegating

For delegation to work, there must be a high level of trust between you and your students, between you and other teachers, between you and your administration, and between you and your volunteers or aides. Your classroom climate must be positive, and communication must be open. Another necessary condition is your recognition of the limitations of delegating. It will not solve all your schedule problems, and it may not even produce more time for you. What it *can* do is allow you to do some of those "extras" that you wish you had time for. Carolyn, the teacher in the following Snapshot, demonstrates some other conditions for delegating.

SNAPSHOT: Middle-School Classroom

Carolyn, a sixth-grade teacher, convinced most of the parents of her students to volunteer, so that each would only be scheduled once every two weeks. She conducted several half-day training sessions on classroom routines, teaching strategies, and management. During one session, parents spent time determining which tasks would be satisfying, and where each would be comfortable working. The parents also had choices about the schedule of days for working in the classroom.

Carolyn also scheduled free time each morning and afternoon, during which she moved about the room supervising both parents and students. She scheduled conference times during lunch so that parents could discuss their classroom experiences, problems, and successes, and get feedback or ideas.

Notice the conditions for Carolyn's successful delegation to parent volunteers. She made sure that they were trained and knew how to do the work, and she provided some choices of work. She also supervised and made sure that there were enough people to handle the work. Needless to say, Carolyn didn't have more time. She may have been busier, but she was teaching the way she intended, fitting in all those "extras" that she hadn't had time for previously.

Resources for Delegating

As you observed in the last Snapshot, parents are resources, as well as aides and other volunteers. Your most available source of help is students. You will need to observe the same conditions when delegating to students; that is, they will need instruction, alternatives, supervision, and enough of them to divide tasks. Be sure to identify those tasks that are appropriate for student responsibility. As we describe management routines and using audiovisuals in the chapters that follow, we will recommend and describe procedures for using student help.

Be ready to let go and trust that others will do the work as well as you would. Maybe they will do it differently or maybe they will do it better.

SUMMARY

To help you achieve effective use of time and doing more with less, we set out to direct your thinking as you make decisions on use of time for teaching and learning. Consider society's demands and those of your school district. What are the priorities, expectations, constraints, and provisions? Reflect on your own classroom. How do you handle time losses and time wasters? How much productive activity goes on? Look at your content, and be aware of your commitments to goals and attitudes toward curriculum. Look at the "what" and "how" of teaching, and see how you can include time management as content for your teaching.

When you think of your students, consider ways to accommodate both ability and developmental differences. Be certain that you are monitoring learning, and adjusting the learning time to the differences.

Finally, reconsider the time-saver strategies of this chapter. We have described goal setting, clarity in teaching, handling paperwork, and delegation. Our advice is to work on only one or two strategies at a time. It would be inefficient to try them all at once. Reflect on your use of time, and choose the time saver that will benefit you the most at this time.

As you work on making effective use of time and doing more with less, collect strategies from your own experiences and those of other teachers. Become an expert!

REFERENCES

Ball, S. J., & Lacey, C. (1984). Subject disciplines as the application for group action: A measured critique of subject sub-cultures. In A. Hargreaves & P. Woods (Eds.), *Classrooms and staffrooms: The sociology of teachers and teaching*. Milton Keyes, England: Open University Press.

Berliner, D. (1982). *The executive functions of teaching*. Paper presented at the Wingspread Conference, Racine, WI.

Bird, T., & Little, J. (1985). *Instructional leadership in eight secondary schools* (Final report to the National Institute of Education). Boulder, CO: Center for Action Research.

Carroll, J. B. (1985). The model of school learning: Progress of an idea. In C. Fisher & D. Berliner (Eds.), *Perspectives on instructional time*. New York: Longman.

Collins, C. (1987). *Time management for teachers*. West Nyack, NY: Parker Publishing.

Delaware State Department of Public Instruction. (1987). *Teacher paperwork study: Type, time, and difficulty*. Dover: Delaware State Department of Public Instruction.

Drawbaugh, C. C. (1984). *Time and its use*. New York: Teachers College Press.

Fisher, C., & Berliner, D. (1985). *Perspectives on instructional time*. New York: Longman.

Fisher, C., Filby, N., Marliave, R., Cahen, L., Dishaw, M., Moore, J., & Berliner, D. (1978). *Teaching behaviors, academic learning time, and student achievement: Final report of Phase III-B, Beginning Teacher Evaluation Study*. San Francisco, CA: Far West Laboratory for Educational Research and Development.

Gephart, W. J., Strother, D. B., & Duckett, W. E. (1981). Practical applications of research, newsletter. *Phi Delta Kappa Center on Evaluation, Development, and Research, 3*(3).

Johnson, S., & Johnson, C. (1986). *The one minute teacher*. New York: William Morrow and Company.

Little, J. (1981). *School success and staff development: The role of staff development in urban desegregated schools*. Boulder, CO: Center for Action Research.

Schwille, J., Porter, A., Belli, G., Floden, R., Freeman, D., Knappen, L., Kuhs, T., & Schmidt, W. (1983). Teachers as policy brokers in the content of elementary school mathematics. In L. S. Schulman & G. Sykes (Eds.), *Handbook of teaching and policy*. New York: Longman.

_____ *SAMPLES AND EXAMPLES* _____

There are four Samples and Examples in this section. The first two give you additional information about using your time effectively. The third provides an activity on clarity of directions, and the fourth is an absence packet for students who miss class.

- Time Spent On Organizing has two parts. The first chart is a sample of how a teacher spends her time during a 55-minute period. This chart could be completed by another person or you could tape-record your class and use a stopwatch or clock to determine how much time is being spent on organizing and management activities. The second form is a blank that may be used by you or a colleague.
- The third Sample and Example is a Checking for Clarity activity that highlights the time that can be wasted by giving unclear directions. The first statement is unclear because the type of work is not identified. The third statement is clear because it gives the needed information. When you complete the list, identify the difference between clear and unclear statements. Also notice the length of the statements and the type of information provided in each statement.
- The absence packet is designed to save time when students return from an illness and ask, "Have I missed anything?" The packet is placed on the absent student's desk by a designated student. All written materials would be included in the packet. Also, a student would be asked to take notes using carbon paper and place assignments and other information into the packet.

TIME SPENT ORGANIZING

NAME _____

Time Spent Organizing	Time	
	Started	*Stopped*
Taking Attendance	8:30	4:40
Collecting Lunch Money	8:30	8:50
Collecting Homework or Seatwork	8:30	8:40
Making Assignments for Seatwork	8:50	8:55
Making Assignments for Homework	9:25	9:30
Distributing Books and Materials	8:35	8:45
Explaining Activities and Procedure	8:50	8:55
Organizing Groups	8:50	8:55
Shifting from One Activity to Another	8:55	8:57
Disciplining Students	8:35, 8:47, 9:10, 9:17, 9:25	

continued

NAME _____

	Time	
Time Spent Organizing	*Started*	*Stopped*
Taking Attendance		
Collecting Lunch Money		
Collecting Homework or Seatwork		
Making Assignments for Seatwork		
Making Assignments for Homework		
Distributing Books and Materials		
Explaining Activities and Procedures		
Organizing Groups		
Shifting from One Activity to Another		
Disciplining Students		

Observations of Classroom Interruptions

Students Enter Late
Students Leave Early
Parents Enter
Administrator Enters
Other Visitors Enter
Loud Speaker Announcements
Special Sales
School Events
Outside Noise

Source: Stallings, J. (1980). *Effective use of time training program*. Unpublished manuscript, University of Houston. Used by permission.

CHECKING FOR CLARITY

Circle the statements that have the greatest clarity:

1. Get back to work.

2. Stop that.

3. You need to keep working on the multiplication worksheet until you have finished.

4. What are you doing?

5. Put your pencil in your desk and return to your reading.

6. Sit down.

7. Pay attention.

8. Shhhhh.

9. Sit in your desk and finish your language assignment in the workbook on page 52.

10. Pick up the activity sheet, find a seat at the table, and get to work.

11. Are you listening?

12. Listen.

13. Check your work.

14. John, you need to listen to the directions for your spelling test.

15. Open your book.

16. Listen to me now so you will know what to do when the fire bell rings.

17. Find something constructive to do.

18. When you finish writing your paragraph, check it for spelling errors and raise your hand to show that you have finished.

Source: Rodriguez, C., & Freiberg, H. J. (1985). *Consistency management instructional materials.* Unpublished materials. Used by permission.

ABSENCE PACKET

Inside this folder are _____ papers for the week. Please take time to review and discuss them with your child. Then date and initial this form and have your child return the completed work as soon as possible. (One day of make-up is allowed for each day missed.)

Thank you,

Mrs. Hawley

Date	Parent Signature	Comments
_____	_____	_____
_____	_____	_____
_____	_____	_____
_____	_____	_____
_____	_____	_____
_____	_____	_____
_____	_____	_____

Source: Hawley, L. (1989). *Instructional materials.* Unpublished materials, Creekwood Middle School, Kingwood, Texas. Used by permission.

CHAPTER 5

Classroom Management: Advancework

CHAPTER OUTCOMES

At the conclusion of this chapter you will be able to:

1. Conduct advancework on the context, content, and learner to gather information.
2. Use advancework information about the context, content, and learner to make classroom management decisions.

KEY TERMS AND CONCEPTS

Advancework
Context
Climate
Significant Individuals in Schools
Class Size
Equipment and Materials
Room Arrangement
Use of Space
Location in the School
Content Advancework
Management Messages
Materials' Cues
Content Relevance
Learner Advancework
Physically Active Learning
Mentally Active Learning
Emotionally Safe Environment
Physically Safe Environment
Herding
Transitions

INTRODUCTION

What Is Advancework?

A major computer company prepares to build new facilities in a large urban area, a move involving the transfer of hundreds of employees and equipment. The company sends a group ahead to survey housing costs and availability, schools, shopping, and leisure and recreational facilities with which to develop an information base on the new location. Several company representatives may interview people in some of the neighborhoods to extend the information.

A travel agent takes a cruise on a new ship and records the comments of her shipmates, keeps a tally of expenses, notes the services offered, and critically evaluates the comfort, recreation, entertainment, and food. While enjoying the trip, she develops a detailed description of the cruise.

Both the travel agent and the computer company representatives are conducting *advancework*. Both examples point out the importance of environment, or the context. Both use people as valuable sources of information. For both examples, the advancework content is a range of details and facts to be used in making decisions: whether to recommend the cruise, or where to purchase housing.

Advancework is equally important for you, the teacher, in making classroom management decisions. Your context is complex—a classroom, a school district, and a community. Your content is curriculum—ideas, knowledge, skills, and attitudes. The important people in your advancework are the learners and those in their lives.

Why Conduct Advancework?

Today's classrooms are complex and dynamic. Teachers are expected to manage with an awareness described as "with-it-ness," the ability to be aware of and manage the continuous interaction in the classroom (Kounin, 1970). As a teacher, you are responsible for "efficient use of instructional time and producing high levels of student involvement in learning activities" (Emmer & Evertson, 1981) while "building a relationship with students in order to maintain an orderly work environment with rules and routines" (Doyle, 1980). The strategy of advancework can help you develop a classroom management system to meet the expectations described by Kounin, Doyle, and Emmer and by Evertson—expectations that reflect elements of effective teaching.

In the sections that follow, we will suggest both thinking and action for advancework. Thinking takes the form of questions to ask, information to consider, and awareness to maintain. Action takes the form of examples and models of how advancework is done.

CONTEXT ADVANCEWORK

The context of classroom management has several distinct levels to consider in conducting advancework: the surrounding community, the school and district environments, and the classroom itself. Before teaching, you are an "advance person," surveying each of the levels for information to use in management decision making.

Community Environment

Gathering information about the community context has many advantages for you: an understanding of your students, support for your management decisions, sources of relevant curriculum, and assistance and resources for your classroom. Your best advancework strategy here is to survey the neighborhood and gather information in an organized way for later use.

Surveying the Neighborhood

When you are new to teaching or to a specific school, begin with the neighborhood. A drive or a walk with a teacher who is established at the school might be your starting point. What kind of information could you gather if you traveled through your school's neighborhood at 7 PM? At 10:30 AM? Many communities have local papers or calendars of events. What kind of information would you find? Look for the local library, park, community center, daycare facility, and shopping center. A visit to the library will tell you about how often it is used, who uses it and when, what resources are available and used, and a little about the neighborhood lifestyle. Experienced teachers have told us that they regularly check community bulletin boards for information such as scheduling of community events, parenting programs, guest speakers, and other teaching resources.

Gathering Information

When surveying the neighborhood of your school, it is a good idea to record the information. A Community Checklist is provided in Figure 5.1 to help you record such information. Notice that it organizes what you see and hear so that you can anticipate problems as well as develop sensitivities.

School Environment

Similar information gathering may be conducted with a simple walk around the inside and outside of your school. Note those features that are going to help your management and those features that have potential for disruption.

School Climate

Many experienced teachers and administrators say that they can feel the climate of a school while walking through the halls, listening to students and teachers, stopping in the cafeteria and teachers' lounge, and noting the condition of the building. The climate of a school is related to the behavior of students in the school and has important implications for your management. It is essential advancework information.

FIGURE 5.1 *Community Context Checklist*

Demographics

    Population _____

    Size in Square Miles _____

    Socioeconomic Range _____

    Cultural Representations _____

Community Resources	*Description**	*Management Potential†*
Playground(s)		
Community Center		
Newspaper		
Industry(s)		
Civic Organizations		
Medical Facilities		
Mental Health Agencies		
Scout Organizations		
Programs for the Elderly		
Animal Shelter		
Chamber of Commerce		
Public Transportation		
Daycare Center(s)		
Shopping Center(s)		

*Description can include location, size, use, and condition.

†Management Potential can include influence on or by students and resources for teaching (materials, speakers, field trips).

Significant Individuals

Within the school context are individuals with significant influence on your classroom management. You will be wise to make contact with a range of school personnel: custodian, nurse, bus drivers, secretaries, specialists, and cafeteria staff. They can support your management decisions.

    For example, most custodians welcome the chance to respond to, "How do you want me to leave my classroom at the end of the day?" or "What kind of problems do you want me to handle, and for what kind do you want me to check with you?" When these questions are posed with sincere intent to listen and cooperate, you will gain support for numerous management situations. When you do not create such cooperation, you may operate in deference to custodial concerns and expectations. You are liable to be left stranded to cope with spilled paint, broken chairs or desks, frayed carpet, or other ordinary management problems. You may not get much support.

Similar contacts with other school personnel will help build supportive relationships. We strongly recommend that you consult with your administrator early in the school year about management expectations, plans, and concerns. It has been our experience that most principals welcome being asked to describe their expectations, being consulted about management decisions, and being informed about management problems. The bottom line is that you will have a difficult time without their support for your classroom management.

Other teachers serve as valuable consultants to your classroom management. Their wealth of experiences, routines, practices, successes, and failures are likely to be your most useful resources for management thinking and decision making. Ignoring other teachers' experiences and preferences has the potential to put you at odds with them in your expectations for student behavior, building use, and routines.

As you can see, school advancework also works to generate information and support for your classroom management. Figure 5.2 provides a School Context Checklist for recording and organizing your advancework information. You may want to develop your own list specific to your school.

Classroom Environment

Variation in classrooms is almost without limits. You may teach in cramped conditions, noisy locations, and windowless rooms, and have outdated equipment. You may also enjoy bright carpeted, quiet rooms, well equipped with state-of-the-art materials and furnishings (the eternal optimist in us). To do advancework in your classroom, focus on class size and its effects, equipment and materials, room arrangement, use of space, and your location within the school. You will need to collect information and use it to make management decisions.

Class Size

Many of your management responsibilities are influenced by the number of students placed in your classroom. Simple routines, such as passing out papers, changing activities, leaving the room, grading assignments, and making up missed assignments, are complicated when class size is large. Any routine is smoother and easier with 20 students than with 30 students. Adjustments in routines to accommodate class size are not necessarily difficult, but they require careful thinking and preparation. Some examples of adjustments in large classes are:

1. Dismiss half of the class at a time, regularly alternating which half leaves first.
2. Have stacks of papers located in four corners of the room for distribution by student helpers.
3. Stagger transition time for students to change activities; for example, "Rows

FIGURE 5.2 *School Context Checklist*

School Description

    Location _____

    Enrollment _____

    Grades _____

    Student Population _____

Considerations	*Description**	*Management Potential †*
Building Condition		
Office(s)		
Library		
Cafeteria		
Auditorium		
Gymnasium		
Hallways		
Outside Area		
Surrounding Property		
Entrances/Exits		
Audiovisual Supports		
Computer Technology		
Counseling Support		
Parent Organization(s)		
Student Organization(s)		
Newspaper/Newsletter		
Other		

*Description could include noise, traffic, safety hazards, crowding, and special considerations.

†Management Potential could include influence on or by students, support for management, and resources.

1 and 4 move to the reference shelf area." One minute later, "Rows 2 and 5 move to centers."

The suggestions for grading and recording paperwork in Chapter 4 will be especially helpful if you have a large class. Even your room arrangement will be affected by class size. You may need to eliminate all unnecessary furniture, sometimes your desk, and cluster desks rather than place in rows. Keep class size in mind as you read about equipment and materials.

Equipment and Materials

The kinds of equipment and materials you have to work with will determine a number of your management decisions. Begin by listing what is available and ask yourself if everything on the list is necessary for your teaching. Some teachers have a tendency to store everything available, from fear of not having enough. Ask yourself: Are there potential problems with this equipment? and Where is the best location? Anticipating problems or consequences of use and location is advancework. In the following Snapshot, a fourth-grade teacher demonstrates what can happen without such anticipation.

SNAPSHOT: *Elementary Classroom*

Pam Rossio is preparing for a silent reading time scheduled for the afternoon. She gathers a large selection of books for her students, keeping in mind their interests and varying reading levels. She decides to place the books on a cart so that she can move it to a convenient spot for use, then store it in the back of the room.

That afternoon, Pam describes procedures for the activity and reminds students to preview books before making selections. She shows them the cart of books, assuring them that there are plenty of different selections. "For the next 25 minutes you will be able to select a book and begin silent reading." At least 20 students rush toward the cart, causing an uproar. Above the confusion, Pam directs students to return to their desks. She laughs a bit uncomfortably and says, "I guess we will have to take turns selecting books." She thinks to herself, "I must find another way to distribute the books."

That was Pam Rossio's first year of teaching. If you were to watch her now, you would see book stations in various locations around her classroom. What a difference advancework awareness makes! Here are other examples in which advancework will help you anticipate problems or limitations:

1. You want to use an overhead projector, which is on a permanent stand, but three students in the front corner of the room can't see the image.
2. You have five science kits for a class of 29 students.

To solve the problems or work within the limitations, there are three guidelines. First, consider *smoothness*. How can you handle the situation with the least disruption? Second, *promote student involvement*. Students have great ideas for how to solve typical classroom problems. After a few years of school, they have experience with many situations, so involve them in decisions. And third, *be prepared*. Be prepared for anything. With classroom materials, being prepared means having enough, having them organized, and doing it ahead of time.

To illustrate the three guidelines, we will return to those situations we described and suggest responses:

1. In the case of the overhead projector, work out a movement strategy and places to sit for those students who can't see the image. Whenever the projector is to be used, you can give a signal that tells those students to move to their assigned places.
2. In the case of the five science kits and your class of 29 students, several possibilities exist. Students can use the kits in pairs or threes, with two or three time periods a week set aside for their use. One or two alternative science activities are planned for those students who are not using the kits.

Remember to ask students for solutions and to consult with other teachers. Both are also good sources for advancework ideas for room arrangement and use of space.

Room Arrangement and Use of Space

The way you arrange your classroom communicates management messages about your expectations of how to use the room. Evertson, Emmer, Clements, Sanford, and Worsham (1984) provide advancework questions for room arrangement from their observations of effective classroom managers:

1. *Are high traffic areas free of congestion?*
2. *Can students be easily seen by teachers?*
3. *Are frequently used materials and supplies readily accessible?*
4. *Can students easily see instructional presentations and displays?*

In addition, we suggest that you separate areas of quiet and noisy or active work. Look at the room arrangements in Figures 5.3 and 5.4 and assess them using advancework. Try to have a sensitivity of what it is like to be a student in those rooms. The same awareness is important as you visit real classrooms and as you consider the next topic, location in the school.

Location in the School

Where your room or rooms are located in the school will have advantages as well as disadvantages. The only room at the end of a hallway isolated from general school traffic can be very appealing to some teachers and loathsome to others. Much depends on your personality and teaching style. There are those who shudder when entering the "no wall" arrangements in schools and those who start thinking excitedly about teaching there. Begin with an awareness of personal preference.

Next, assess your location for its advantages and disadvantages. Consider noise, distractions, traffic, and the kinds of activities conducted in nearby areas:

1. What distractions will we experience here?
2. When will this room be most quiet? Noisiest?

must work with our instruction, not interfere, so we describe some subtle management messages to listen for as you teach.

Listen to Your Management Messages

Begin this advancework with your personal preferences about noise, space, and interactions with students. You might consider how you would like someone to describe your classroom. Listen to a tape recording of part of your day, and examine the messages you are sending to students. When teachers' statements were studied for such messages, there was an emphasis on orderliness, following directions, and working quietly (Buckley & Cooper, 1978). Is that how you sound? Is that your intent? With or without your intent, those messages are informal content of your teaching. You will find procedures for analyzing your teaching using audiotapes described in Chapter 15. From there, consider how students interpret your messages.

Listen to Student Interpretations

Part of the content for students comes from the way they interpret our management messages. King (1983) found that students concentrate as much on how to do work and what behaviors to display as they do on actual subject matter. If, in a 20-minute lesson, you spend a great deal of time giving directions, you are probably encouraging students to focus on procedures. The vignette describes how students interpret your management messages. Stevens and Anderson (1987) provide a look at what teachers do and say, and how the environment looks, sounds, and feels to students.

In addition to the messages you send and the interpretations students give, your classroom materials are sources of content.

Listen to Your Materials' Cues

Kounin and Gump (1974) noticed that materials act as signals to students. Different materials signal different behaviors, levels of involvement, and the continuity of a lesson. Watch students as they interact with some of the following:

musical instruments	computers
cuisinaire rods	worksheets
magnets	microscopes
photographs	maps

As you plan for students to use materials, stop and think whether the materials will keep the lesson going, bring it to a halt, or interfere with the learning. We recently observed the use of a very exciting set of materials that pulled students completely away from the intended outcome. Instruction was focused on sequencing. Groups of students were given a set of clue cards to solve a mystery, with a process similar to the game of "Clue." The intent was for groups to sequence the clues or information items in order to see the process of building and connecting information. The sequencing process was ignored in the excitement of solving the mystery.

Elementary Research Vignette

INTRODUCTION

Socialization in school is the process by which students learn how to fulfill the student role successfully. An important aspect of this process is how the student perceives his or her control over what happens in school.

STUDY PROCEDURES

To study student perceptions of control in school, Stevens and Anderson (1987) gathered narratives (descriptive recordings) in 13 third- and fourth-grade classrooms. The narratives were collected by trained observers who focused on what kind of socializing messages students heard and how the classroom social environment was established and maintained. The researchers also gathered student scores on various self-perception measures.

STUDY RESULTS

With the initial data, Stevens and Anderson (1987) identified classrooms with distinctly different patterns of student self-perceptions of control, and three related dimensions of classroom environments. The dimensions were: (1) respect for and sensitivity to individual needs and growth, (2) predictability and structuring of information about the environment, and (3) opportunities for self-regulation.

When classrooms were high on these dimensions, students felt high levels of control over school life. In contrast, low levels of control were felt in classrooms with little evidence of the dimensions. Stevens and Anderson provided a look at the teachers in their study with examples of what they did and how their classroom environments looked, sounded, and felt as they described the three dimensions.

Dimension 1: Respect for and Sensitivity to Individual Needs and Growth. This dimension meant that individual interests, needs, and concerns were respected in consistent communications to students. The environment was emotionally safe for students to take risks and express needs with routines and communications:

"Your talking interrupted me and I'm sure that it interrupted others, too."
"We all make mistakes—even I make mistakes." (p. 17)

The rules in these classrooms were about being respectful of others and self. One teacher had "courtesy cards," which recorded student treatment of others. Procedures supported the worth of students with job systems for student responsibility of classroom maintenance, sometimes requiring two students to work together. There were environmental reminders, such as posters reinforcing concern for others, and quotes encouraging kindness and respect.

Dimension 2: Predictability and Structuring of Environmental Information. In classrooms high on this dimension, students could predict certain aspects of classroom life. Evidence of predictability included:

A regular schedule was posted and followed. Students were prepared beforehand of changes in schedules and routines.
A set of standards for classroom behavior was enforced consistently.

This dimension also referred to how information about the classroom was provided to students. The researchers saw organization and heard reasons for routines and procedures:

"We pass in papers this way because it goes faster, and that gives us time for more important things." (p. 21)
"If you do not turn in your work to the right basket, then I will not be able to read it and give you feedback." (p. 21)

Dimension 3: Opportunities for Students to Practice Self-Regulation. The researchers determined that self-regulation for these students meant that they could pace themselves, assess their progress, evaluate their work, and make decisions regarding their work. They observed:

Students used checklists to assess progress or to record work completion.

Students had choices about which assignment to do or what to do after completion of assignments.

Students received feedback about their decisions (such as, "That's a good idea to use this time to finish your math") (p. 24).

Teachers provided cues such as, "There are three minutes left in the math period" or pointing to a poster of class rules when a student became noisy (p. 23)

The contrast in classrooms low on this dimension was evident just in sounds. There was a lot of "shhhh-ing" by teachers, and bickering and quarreling between students. There was a great deal

of free time for students, and no evidence of student self-checking, self-evaluating, or self-monitoring.

CONCLUSIONS AND IMPLICATIONS FOR PRACTICE

This look at classrooms by Stevens and Anderson tells us that our teaching and management strategies and our classroom environments are related to student perceptions of control. When students feel like they control their school life, they are successfully socialized; that is, they have the skills, knowledge, and attitudes to live and work in schools.

Heated discussions of "whodunit" led to the need for management. The noise level and behavior got out of control with the excitement. At first glance, the clue cards looked potentially appropriate and effective, yet they failed miserably. A simple "What will students be likely to do in this activity?" may have predicted the consequences beforehand.

In addition to your informal content with its management messages, student interpretations, and cues from your materials, it will be important to listen to your content for relevance.

Relevance in Content

When subjects or curriculum appear to have little bearing on students' immediate lives, they struggle with inattention, lack of motivation, and distracting or disruptive behavior. When students do find relevance, their interest and learning increases. Begin your advancework by listening to content with these questions:

1. Can students connect this knowledge or skill to their daily lives now or in the future?
2. Are there societal trends or examples that parallel this information that I am going to present?
3. Is there an alternative to this learning activity that will be more interesting or engaging?
4. Have any of the students had a similar experience? Listen to relevance in the Teacher Talk that follows.

TEACHER TALK

Find examples of sentence structures and highlight them in the newspaper articles you have brought for current events.

Middle-School English Teacher

> Breaking up a whole number into fractions is like slicing a pizza into pieces.
>
> *3rd-Grade Teacher*
>
> Two people in our class, Tahisha and Sam, have experienced a move like the one we will read about in our story today.
>
> *5th-Grade Teacher*
>
> In some ways, the Boston Tea Party was like the demonstrations you have been reading about in our country today.
>
> *Secondary Civics Teacher*

Your advancework for content must listen to the content itself as well as how you present it. When students find meaning and use in curriculum, you will see "high levels of student involvement, minimal amounts of interference, and efficient use of instructional time" (Emmer & Evertson, 1981), as we described at the beginning of this chapter. That is definitely a goal of your management.

LEARNER ADVANCEWORK

Much of what we know about how students learn has implications for managing classrooms. As we suggest advancework questions to pose about your learners, we will use that knowledge.

Students Are Active Learners

Active learners move about physically and intellectually to discover, manipulate, experiment, explore, make mistakes, discuss, and problem solve. Physical movement requires you to ask when, where, how, and how much.

Intellectual movement requires you to ask about learner differences, needs. and interests.

Physically Active Learning

The way you structure learning activities can encourage movement or inhibit movement. Look at the following examples and determine whether learning can be active:

"As you work on your individual reports during this time, use your social studies textbooks and materials from home. Work quietly at your desk."

"As you work on your group research reports during this time, consider using reference materials on the back shelves, the magazines in the reading center, or fill out a pass and go to the library."

"You can do your morning seatwork at your desks, at the work table in the back, or on cushions on the floor. When you finish, you may read books, work puzzles, or listen to story tapes."

FIGURE 5.4   *Secondary Room Arrangements*

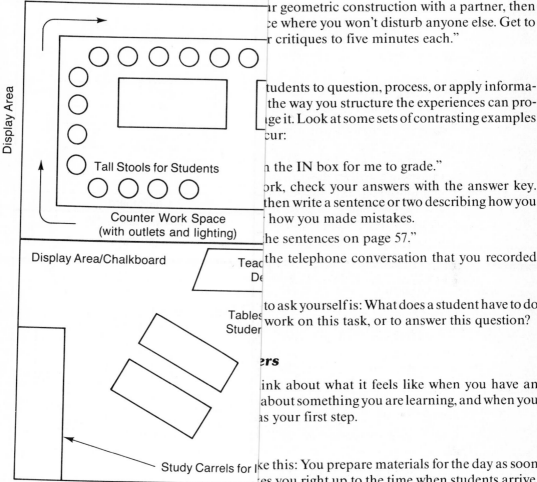

Middle-School S[c]

Display Area

Tall Stools for Students

Counter Work Space
(with outlets and lighting)

Display Area/Chalkboard

Tea[cher] De[sk]

Tables
Studen[ts]

Study Carrels for [...]

High-School En[trance]

...courage physical movement during learning? ...need to understand how to move about, appro- ...nt. Listen again to a structure:

...ur geometric construction with a partner, then ...ce where you won't disturb anyone else. Get to ...r critiques to five minutes each."

...tudents to question, process, or apply informa- ...the way you structure the experiences can pro- ...ge it. Look at some sets of contrasting examples ...cur:

...n the IN box for me to grade."

...ork, check your answers with the answer key. ...then write a sentence or two describing how you ...how you made mistakes.

...he sentences on page 57."

...the telephone conversation that you recorded

...to ask yourself is: What does a student have to do ...work on this task, or to answer this question?

...*ers*

...ink about what it feels like when you have an ...about something you are learning, and when you ...s your first step.

...ke this: You prepare materials for the day as soon ...es you right up to the time when students arrive. ...traighten your desk. You eat lunch at your desk so ...e for your class that night. After school, it is your

...on a day like this: You have a quick cup of coffee ...ts arrive. You listen as a colleague describes a new ...ath. On your break, you ask the librarian to help ...r the drug and alcohol unit you are preparing. At ...the coming tax vote. After school, the teacher next ...terized record-keeping system for your classes. ...ke during and at the end of the two days. Use your

CONTENT ADVANCEWORK

Checking Your Management C[...]

Advancework with content will help [...] management. The complexity of today[...] utility. We will talk about how to condu[...] curriculum is relevant and useful. Do[y...]

awareness to put yourself in the students' place. Then work to provide social opportunities in your teaching.

Providing Social Opportunities

Learning can be exciting when ideas and concepts are discussed and shared. Listen to the following structures that provide social opportunities for students:

> "Ask the person next to you to check your sentences while you check his or hers."

> "Describe an argument for the new trade law to your partner. When you finish, your partner is to describe an argument against the law."

> "Turn to the person behind you and describe one new idea from our class today."

The learning activities that result from these structures support social interactions, communication, and relationships. Those are the qualities we described in the definitions of effective management at the beginning of the chapter. Students would be happy to have those opportunities, as you will see in the Research Vignette describing social needs of secondary students.

Students Are Confident Learners

Students of all ages learn better if they feel confident and if they experience success while learning. You can use your management routines to communicate to students that they are capable, that you trust them, and that they are responsible. These messages promote confidence. Without awareness, however, you may communicate an opposite message. Here's how that message sounds:

> "When you have a problem with the computer, always check with me before working on it."

> "If you can't get work done in your clean-up groups, let me know and I'll help."

> "If you can't figure out how to put your folder together, see me."

Those messages say that it would be best if students didn't try, and that you alone are capable of handling the situations. Try changing those messages by turning them into questions. You will express confidence to your students. Listen to the changes:

> "What are some things you could check on the computer before coming to me with problems?"

> "If you can't get your work done in your clean-up groups, what can you do about it?"

> "When you are putting your folder together, who could you get to help you?"

Secondary Research Vignette

INTRODUCTION
A research study was conducted by James D. Allen (1986) to look at classroom management from a high-school student's perspective.

STUDY DESIGN
This study was conducted in four classes: Agriculture I, Spanish I, Health Education, and English, with observations of classes and interviews of 100 ninth-grade students.

STUDY RESULTS
Through observations and interviews, the researcher discovered two common goals of students: (1) to pass courses and (2) to socialize. Students were observed using six strategies to achieve the goals: (1) figuring out the teacher (usually at the beginning of the semester), (2) having fun, (3) giving the teacher what he or she wants, (4) minimizing work, (5) reducing boredom, and (6) staying out of trouble.

Strategies 2, 3, and 4 were used during the daily events of the class. The fifth strategy was used in response to a boring class. The student would find ways to make it more interesting. This included talking, playing "football," passing notes, and other off-task activities. When the teacher would communicate that students' grades would be affected if they did not stop socializing, they would usually respond with the sixth strategy.

Allen described three class scenarios to demonstrate the interactive effects of students' agendas and classroom contexts on classroom management:

1. When presented with limited academic demands by teachers, students focus on their socializing goal. Their agenda includes having fun and reducing boredom. Although students may receive an easy A or B for the course, students expressed that "they learned very little, and that academically, it was a waste of time" (p. 456).
2. In a high-academic demand course, the students focused on passing the course and providing what was required. However, the students in the study did not enjoy the learning experience because "it was an individual non-social experience" (p. 456).
3. Teachers who provide social experiences in class along with demands for passing the course are identified by students as providing the best learning experiences.

CONCLUSIONS AND IMPLICATIONS FOR PRACTICE
Although one research study does not make a trend, this one was carefully conducted and the findings match most of our own experiences as teachers and students. The issue of socializing presents management problems if socializing is considered an off-task behavior. However, students from this study viewed socializing while performing an academic task as meeting the need to socialize.

As students respond, they get involved, make decisions, and usually take care of the work of your classroom. An advancework strategy we suggest here is to survey your management responsibilities. Some possibilities include:

Recording lunch count
Greeting visitors
Distributing materials
Storing materials and equipment
Controlling room temperature
Maintaining safety

Record keeping
Collecting work
Returning work
Caring for plants
Cleaning
Taking roll

Now, ask yourself: Which of these responsibilities could students safely and successfully handle? An example of an appropriate responsibility and how to delegate it to students is seen in the Teacher Talk from a secondary classroom.

TEACHER TALK

I was fed up with interruptions to my teaching, but I was also trying to put students in charge of our room. Students volunteered to be "door greeters" who welcome visitors in a quiet voice and tell them that "Mr. Peterson is busy teaching." Visitors are asked if they would like to sit and observe until class is finished.

Secondary Biology Teacher

Your advancework begins with listing your responsibilities, deciding which ones students can handle successfully, and communicating that expectation to them.

Students Are Intrinsically Motivated to Learn

In order for students to develop an intrinsic (internal) motivation to learn, they must be able to make some decisions about their learning. They must be able to assess their own learning and acknowledge their own progress or success. You saw examples of how teachers foster these opportunities in the Elementary Research Vignette. Chapter 9 also helps you support intrinsic motivation in your students.

Begin your advancework questions with, "Who is making these decisions?" followed by, "Could students do so?" You can do the same with, "Who is assessing . . . ?" and "Who is providing feedback . . . ?"

A few more examples will give you an idea of how to support intrinsic motivation.

Before beginning a new unit of study, a middle-school geography teacher previews a content outline with students. Then the students list what information they already know about the subject, what information makes them curious, and what information is missing.

A third-grade teacher regularly checks on class routine and rules from the student perspective with a bulletin board write-in spot for individuals to comment on "what's working" and "what's not working." Student comments often result in a class discussion to make changes.

Senior high-school science students in a nearby school regularly complete their lab assignments with a critique of procedures, an assessment of their own understanding, and a rating of their progress.

Students Need to Feel Safe When Learning

Finally, it is essential to provide for emotional safety if learning is to occur. Your advancework must consider basic human needs and find ways to meet them while teaching students.

Providing Emotional Safety

Maslow (1970) represented human needs in a hierarchy with physical needs and safety as essential before others can be met. When children come to school hungry or frightened about a situation on the way to school, they won't be able to learn. If the classroom is an unpredictable, unsafe place where students can be ridiculed, they will be more concerned with protecting themselves than with studying or participating in learning activities.

Many schools and/or individual teachers have adopted the concept of students' rights. You will see an example of those rights in Figure 5.5. They are meant to protect and support the student right to learn by guaranteeing safety from physical and emotional dangers. Emotionally safe classrooms are those in which students can take risks with creative answers, alternative assignments, or asking a so-called dumb question.

FIGURE 5.5 *Students' Rights*

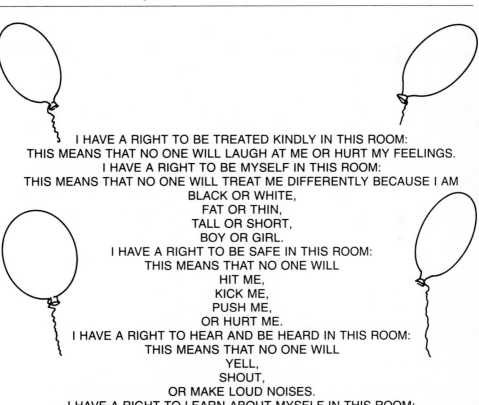

I HAVE A RIGHT TO BE TREATED KINDLY IN THIS ROOM:
THIS MEANS THAT NO ONE WILL LAUGH AT ME OR HURT MY FEELINGS.
I HAVE A RIGHT TO BE MYSELF IN THIS ROOM:
THIS MEANS THAT NO ONE WILL TREAT ME DIFFERENTLY BECAUSE I AM
BLACK OR WHITE,
FAT OR THIN,
TALL OR SHORT,
BOY OR GIRL.
I HAVE A RIGHT TO BE SAFE IN THIS ROOM:
THIS MEANS THAT NO ONE WILL
HIT ME,
KICK ME,
PUSH ME,
OR HURT ME.
I HAVE A RIGHT TO HEAR AND BE HEARD IN THIS ROOM:
THIS MEANS THAT NO ONE WILL
YELL,
SHOUT,
OR MAKE LOUD NOISES.
I HAVE A RIGHT TO LEARN ABOUT MYSELF IN THIS ROOM:
THIS MEANS THAT I WILL BE FREE TO EXPRESS MY FEELINGS AND
OPINIONS WITHOUT BEING INTERRUPTED OR RIDICULED.

Providing a Sense of Belonging

Once safety and survival needs are met, Maslow pointed to the need for a sense of belonging. In your classroom, it is important for students to feel part of a group, to be included in group activities, and to be valued by others. There is evidence that friendships and peer relationships enhance learning activities (Schmuck & Schmuck, 1974). Begin your advancework in this area by asking yourself some questions: Do my routines, comments, and activities encourage competition? Do my routines foster relationships and communication? Can students take risks or try out alternatives?

Listen to the Teacher Talk that follows and decide for yourself if students are going to feel a sense of belonging.

TEACHER TALK

Work carefully on your project, put in lots of effort, and see if you can make yours the best display in the class.

5th-Grade Teacher

You will be working in teams of four on your projects. First, meet to determine each person's strengths and interests, then plan your display and divide the work.

Secondary Health Teacher

When your partner is absent from school, be sure to take notes, record assignments, and collect an extra copy of everything that is distributed to put in her or his folder. Then welcome him or her back.

Middle-School Homeroom Teacher

We are going to be working on environmental collages at the end of the week. I have begun a collection of materials in these bins. We need more. See if you can come up with more materials by Friday.

3rd-Grade Teacher

Providing Physical Safety

The learners' sense of being physically safe will influence their emotional safety. Begin with some questions for students: When and where do you feel safe in our classroom? and When and where do you not feel safe in our classroom? When you work on room arrangement, keep this information in mind.

A second check on students' sense of being physically safe is a look at the transitions that occur in your classroom. A *transition* is a time of change—a change from one place to another, from one activity to another. A common teacher behavior during transitions has been described by Kounin (1970) as "herding." When a fourth-grade teacher directs students to line up at the door to go to the cafeteria, she is herding students. There is potential for physical danger as well as behavior problems.

Consider an alternative to the herding described above. The fourth-grade teacher asks students in row 3 to line up at the door, then row 5, and on through the rows. A second-grade teacher suggests that everyone who had tortillas for breakfast line up, then everyone who had pancakes, then everyone who had toast, and so on. Besides worrying about herding, consider how much interest you could bring to a dull routine.

Many upper-elementary and middle-school teachers have students come up with their own categories for transition routines. We've heard fifth-graders suggest birthdays, favorite pizza ingredients, TV shows, and clothing labels. There doesn't seem to be much worry about transitions in high school, yet there are plenty of adolescents who would welcome a less hassled and gentler move to their next class. Our best advice is to discuss transitions with students and ask for suggestions. In the next chapter, we describe other transition strategies for keeping your classroom running smoothly.

In sum, the learner is an important target for your advancework awareness. That advancework must be maintained for a continual check of the effect of your management on learners.

SUMMARY

Our main objective for this chapter was for you to be able to conduct advancework to gather information to make management decisions. We described your context advancework encompassing the community, the school, and your own classroom.

You will need to survey the community and your school, recording the information for those decisions that follow. Remember to make contact with those important people in you school, and notice the climate. Check your own room for the influence of class size, equipment and materials, room arrangement and use of space, and location in the school for advancework information.

To conduct content advancework, we encouraged you to listen for the messages of your room, your materials, and your routines. Notice, too, the relevance of your curriculum to students' lives.

Learner advancework considered the qualities that promote learning: active students, social students, confident and successful students, intrinsically motivated students, and emotionally and physically safe students. We described structures that promote those qualities, and gave you glimpses of structures that could inhibit them. The most important advice we can offer here is to do advancework. Without advancework, management in classrooms is often characterized by repetition, isolation, and lack of joy.

Although some repetition is necessary for learning, our experience tells us that repetition gets boring for you and your students. Without information gathering, many of your management decisions will be made spontaneously. They may not result in clear information for students, or the intended outcomes. When this occurs, you will have to rethink the decision, or rephrase it to students, or remind them of it—repetition.

Classroom management without support or contacts may mean that you work in isolation. Without advancework, we have seen teachers facing difficult management problems completely alone. Those problems seem larger or more horrible when faced alone day after day.

When problems can be shared with colleagues, they are often met with, "I remember when I was struggling with a student with temper tantrums and thought I would not survive the year." Knowing that you are not the only one helps you see the situation as less personal, and you can be more effective in your problem solving.

TEACHER TALK

A few years ago I had a student who "smart mouthed" me when I would call on her or try to get her to pay attention. She was quite loud, used profanity, and I was embarrassed in front of the other students. I tried everything, but I didn't want other teachers hearing it, so I started closing my door. I was close to tears when I finally went to the school counselor for help. I wish I hadn't waited so long.

It took a while but the student and I both made changes. By the end of the year, we were working together.

Middle-School History Teacher

A management system developed without advancework has more potential for behavior problems and, eventually, discipline. A friend of ours says that when discipline is frequent, "teachers get hurt or they get hard." Instead, we wish you the joy of a smooth-running classroom, exciting content, and involved learners. Advancework can help you experience that joy. In the next chapter, we will guide you from advancework to management strategies which extend beyond discipline to effective teaching.

REFERENCES

Allen, J. D. (1986). Classroom management: Students' perspectives, goals and strategies. *American Educational Research Journal, 23*(3), 437–459.

Buckley, P., & Cooper, J. (1978). *An ethnographic study of an elementary school teacher's establishment and maintenance of group norms.* Paper presented at the annual meeting of the American Educational Research Association.

Doyle, W. (1980). *Classroom management.* West Lafayette, IN: Kappa Delta Pi.

Doyle, W. (1986). Classroom organization and management. In M. C. Wittrock (Ed.), *Third handbook of research on teaching.* New York: Macmillan.

Emmer, E. T., & Evertson, C. M. (1981). Synthesis of research on classroom management. *Educational Leadership, 38*(4), 342–347.

Emmer, E. T., Evertson, C. M., Sanford, J. P., Clements, B. S., & Worsham, M. E. (1984). *Classroom management for secondary teachers.* Englewood Cliffs, NJ: Prentice-Hall.

Evertson, C. M., Emmer, E. T., Clements, B. S., Sanford, J. P., & Worsham, M. E. (1984). *Class-room management for elementary teachers.* Englewood Cliffs, NJ: Prentice-Hall.

King, L. H. (1983). Pupil classroom perceptions and expectancy effect. *South Pacific Journal of Teacher Education, 11*(1), 54–70.

Kounin, J. (1970). *Discipline and group management in classrooms.* New York: Holt, Rinehart, & Winston.

Kounin, J., & Gump, P. (1974). Signal systems of lesson settings and the task related behavior of preschool children. *Journal of Educational Psychology, 66,* 554–562.

Maslow, A. H. (1970). *Motivation and personality* (2nd ed.). New York: Harper and Row.

Schmuck, R., & Schmuck, P. (1974). *A humanistic psychology of education: Making the school everybody's house.* Palo Alto, CA: National Press Books.

Stevens, D., & Anderson, L. (1987). *Classroom socialization and student perceptions of control.* Paper presented at the annual meeting of the American Educational Research Association, Washington, DC.

SAMPLES AND EXAMPLES

There are two Samples and Examples in this section. The first is a Student Need Assessment Questionnaire designed to give you feedback about the climate of the classroom. The second is a brief questionnaire to give you feedback on the difficulty level of the material, effectiveness of the presentation, and the student's participation in class.

- Student Need Assessment Questionnaire (Jones & Jones, 1981) will give you a sense of student thoughts about the affect or climate of your class.
- The second feedback form is designed to give you feedback in three areas: difficulty of material, pace of the presentation, and class participation.

STUDENT NEEDS ASSESSMENT QUESTIONNAIRE

Check the appropriate box.

Your Thoughts about Our Class	Always	Most of the Time	Sometimes	Seldom	Never
Physiological Needs					
1. Do you eat a good breakfast each morning?					
2. Does your teacher touch you enough?					
3. Can you see the blackboard and screen from where you are sitting?					
4. Do I talk loud and clear enough for you to hear?					
5. Do you have time to relax during the day?					
6. Do you have enough time to complete your assignments?					
7. Do we go slow enough in class?					
8. Do you need a study period at the end of the day?					
9. Is the room a quiet place to work?					
Safety and Security					
10. Are your grades fair?					
11. Does each day in this class seem organized?					
12. Do you follow the school and classroom rules?					
13. Is the discipline used in this classroom fair?					
14. Can you say what you'd like to in this class?					
15. Do you feel free enough to ask me questions?					
16. Can you trust your teacher?					
17. Can you get help when you need it?					
18. Are you calm when you take your report card home?					

Your Thoughts about Our Class	Always	Most of the Time	Sometimes	Seldom	Never
Love and Belonging					
19. Is the room a happy place to be?					
20. Do you think that the students in this class like you?					
21. Am I friendly and do I smile at you?					
22. Do I take time with you each day?					
23. Does your teacher show that she likes you?					
24. Do you feel that I listen to you when you have a problem?					
25. Do I praise you when you deserve it?					
26. Do other students respect your property?					
27. Do people praise you when you do well?					
28. Do I listen to your suggestions?					
Self-Esteem					
29. Do you feel involved in this class?					
30. Do you feel proud when you share a project with the class?					
31. Do you take part in class discussions?					
32. What subject area do you feel most successful at? _____					
33. What subject area could you improve in? _____					
Self-Actualization					
34. Are you able to study things that interest you?					

Source: From Vernon F. Jones & Louise S. Jones, *Comprehensive Classroom Management: Motivating and Managing Students,* 3rd. ed., copyright © 1990 by Allyn and Bacon. Reprinted with permission.

FEEDBACK FORM

(No Name) Period _____

Date _____

Rate the material learned today in class:

1	2	3
difficult		easy
1	2	3
interesting		not interesting

Rate today's presentation:

1	2	3
clear		not clear
1	2	3
too slow		too fast
1	2	3
energetic		dull

Rate your participation in class today:

1	2	3
involved		not involved
1	2	3
comfortable asking questions		uncomfortable asking questions

Do you have any suggestions for this class? _____

_____

_____

_____

Source: Driscoll, A. (1988). *Cooperative Professional Education Program training materials.* Portland, OR: Portland State University. Used by permission.

CHAPTER 6

Classroom Management: Beyond Discipline

CHAPTER OUTCOMES

At the conclusion of the chapter you will be able to:

1. Use management strategies to promote instruction.
2. Plan management strategies to begin the school year, handle interruptions and transitions, respond to classroom crises and behavior problems, and communicate with parents and students.
3. Use ideas and information from advancework and management models to make decisions.

KEY TERMS AND CONCEPTS

Classroom Management Models
Reinforcement
Contracts
Class Meetings
Facilitation
I Messages
Active Listening
Logical Consequences
Encouragement
Meta-Analysis
Smoothness
Momentum
Variety
Teacher Mobility
Beginning of the School Year
Interruptions
Transitions
Classroom Crises
Student Behavior Problems
Communicating with Parents
Problem Solving with Parents

INTRODUCTION

When you first thought about teaching, you probably said to yourself, "I'd like to be like Mr. Eliot who taught literature in ninth grade" or "I still remember what it was like in third grade with Mrs. May." What do you remember about your favorite teachers? Take a few minutes and think about those teachers. Write what you remember, or compare memories with someone to see what you have in common.

Those models in your memories influence your decisions as you prepare to teach or as you manage your classroom. Some of the models help you decide how you want to do things, and some help you decide how you don't want to do things. Both are important to your decision making. In this chapter, our intent is to add other models to your thinking.

MODELS OF CLASSROOM MANAGEMENT

Go back to those expert definitions in Chapter 5. They focus *beyond discipline* and we are working for the kind of classrooms they describe. We begin by describing common classroom management models. Some are based on sound theoretical knowledge, and others are developed and supported by classroom research.

- Behavior Modification (from the work of B. F. Skinner [1968, 1971], with comtemporary modifications)
- Reality Therapy (an extension of William Glasser's [1987] Control Theory for treatment of behavior problems in classrooms)
- Teacher Effectiveness Training (a model from Thomas Gordon's [1974] successful parent training)
- Assertive Discipline (a widely used approach of the 1970s from the work of Lee and Marlene Canter [1979])
- The Adlerian Model or Dreikurs' Approach (a model emphasizing reasons for behavior [Dreikur, 1968, 1971])

For each model, we will take you to classrooms via a Snapshot so you can see it in action, and hear the Teacher Talk.

Behavior Modification

In the Snapshot that follows, you will see a middle-school physical education teacher using a modified form of the Behavior Modification model. The group of students, male and female, has been difficult to teach, so their teacher is using a number of strategies from the model.

SNAPSHOT: *Middle-School Classroom*

The rules and routines in Mr. Proust's physical education class are clear and well understood by the students. Students are aware that they make the choice to follow or not follow the rules. As the class begins, students check themselves off a sheet to indicate presence, appropriate attire, and equipment readiness. They go immediately into a well-rehearsed exercise routine.

From there, Mr. Proust demonstrates a new skill—a tennis serve. Several students are asked to try the skill in front of the class, with explanations from the teacher. Students then work in pairs and practice the skill with comments from a partner. Mr. Proust moves through the group, commenting on individual performances, "You moved your arm correctly," or "Your follow-through was just right." He will continue this practice until the skill is well learned.

At the end of class, Amanda approaches with a contract regarding her behavior in class. Mr. Proust comments on her participation, effort, and cooperation with her partner, and checks off spaces on her contract. He waits for Dennis to come out of the locker room and talks to him out of earshot of his classmates. Only Dennis hears the recognition of his class participation.

Within the first month of class, Mr. Proust identified those students who followed the rules and those students who didn't. Dennis was generally cooperative and participated in class activities within the rules and routines; Amanda didn't. Mr. Proust reinforces Dennis's behavior and the behavior of classmates like him, to support the behavior, increasing the likelihood that it will continue. He also uses *reinforcement* in his teaching so that students will continue performing skills accurately.

Amanda's behavior in class became more and more of a problem, so Mr. Proust developed a *contract* with her. It specifies expectations, timelines, and reinforcers, in this case, free-choice gym activities once a month.

When you use Behavior Modification, you analyze the behaviors you observe in your students and design ways to change or maintain them. Your role in a behavior management system is to control or shape behavior. This is accomplished through reinforcing desired behaviors by using rewards and extinguishing undesirable behavior by ignoring or punishing.

Reality Therapy (Control Theory)

William Glasser's (1987) approach focuses on the here and now of classroom life and helping children understand that what they do in classrooms is their choice. Look at the Snapshot of Ms. Hathaway's fifth-grade class and see what Reality Therapy looks and sounds like.

SNAPSHOT: Elementary Classroom

During the first two months of the school year, Ms. Hathaway worked on developing relationships and a kind of classroom community. Opportunity for communication was built into most of the learning activities.

On this particular day, students are working on social studies projects in groups, using maps, art supplies, magazines, bulletin boards, and so on. Ms. Hathaway overhears Jana argue with a classmate about a mess on the storage shelf. When Jana comes to her to complain, she responds with, "What could you do about those feelings?" "What could you say to your classmate?" "Is there a routine we could set up for class that would help with this problem?"

Another student comes to Ms. Hathaway, describing his inability to finish his project because "it won't work" and "everyone is working on something else." Ms. Hathaway responds with, "It sounds like you regret your choice. You really can't blame it on your group, because you had a chance to look at all the possibilities. I hope that you will carry on with your best work until the project is finished."

Later that day, we see Omar approaching Ms. Hathaway with a problem and saying, "Oh, never mind. I'll bring it up at a class meeting." A week earlier, some of the students came up with the idea of a class store, and the topic became a top priority on the class meeting agenda. As a result of the discussion, four students are currently working on some details of having a store. The same thing happened when special art materials were needed for a project but were unavailable through the usual school supplier.

That afternoon, Omar brought up a problem of fighting and other behavior on the playground. Other students chimed in with comments about boredom: "not enough balls," "it's too crowded," "they always jump off the platform right in the middle of our game," and so on. Then they brainstormed some solutions: "a schedule for each section of the playground," "learn some new games," "some kids can't use the platform," "assign playground monitors," and others. The meeting ended with a plan for playground time. Students agreed to work in committees for the next week to draw a large playground map, schedule activities for various areas, and read about some new games. Once the committees finished and changes were made, Ms. Hathaway checked back regularly with, "How are things going on the playground?"

Did you notice that *student responsibility* is the emphasis? Student control rather than teacher control goes along with it. Those class meetings are regularly scheduled, and one important rule is that classmates will take turns talking. The teacher's role in this model is that of a facilitator. *Facilitation* is the act of making something (learning, change, and so on) easier. You will facilitate by teaching problem solving and decision making, reviewing choices, asking questions, challenging satisfaction with choices, and accepting no excuses for poor choices.

Teacher Effectiveness Training (TET)

Thomas Gordon's model (1974) requires you to commit several years of practice to develop understanding and competence in using the model, but you will be able to use it in many life experiences. As you watch and listen to Mr. Hernandez's classroom, you will again hear extensive communication, regular class meetings, and time spent on problem solving, conflict resolution, decision making, and negotiation.

SNAPSHOT: *Secondary Classroom*

In the corner of Mr. Hernandez's history classroom are several soft chairs, large floor pillows, and a magazine rack. Several students are discussing an article in *Time* magazine, while others are planning a bulletin board on the Viet Nam War. Jesse approaches Mr. Hernandez with a plea for another day to work on his history assignment. His teacher responds with, "It sounds like you are not satisfied with your report and think that another day to spend researching would make you feel better about your assignment." Jesse agrees, and Mr. Hernandez negotiates with him about his request.

On another day, in another situation, Jesse may have heard Mr. Hernandez say, "It makes me uncomfortable to change the deadline for an assignment because I can't have grades ready on time."

During the work period being observed, Mr. Hernandez has scheduled individual student conferences to discuss subject matter, learning activities, student progress, attitudes, and class routines. Students have a chance to express opinions, do self-evaluation, and make some scheduling decisions.

In this Snapshot, you heard *active listening*, a process in which the listener accepts the feelings and ideas of another, then communicates an understanding back ("It sounds like you are not satisfied with your report and think that another day to spend researching would make you feel better about your assignment"). You also heard *I messages*, simple expressions of a problem and its effect on a speaker ("It makes me uncomfortable to change the deadline for an assignment because I can't have grades ready on time"). They are not intended to solve the problem but to express it from the perspective of and with the feelings of the speaker. I messages and active listening are important strategies in the Teacher Effectiveness Training model.

Assertive Discipline

This model appeared during the student rights' movement amidst pro-student court decisions, when teachers were frustrated by disruptive behavior and feeling powerless. Canter and Canter (1979) stated, "Problems or no problems, no child should be allowed to engage in behavior that is self-destructive or violates the rights of his peers or teacher" (p. 56). Watch how that occurs in the next Snapshot.

SNAPSHOT: *Elementary Classroom*

Mr. Alter's third-grade class has well-established limits about behavior during small group instruction so that distractions and interruptions are kept to a minimum. He uses that instructional time to focus on individual learning needs and paces his teaching accordingly. The behavior limits during this time require quiet work and limited movement around the classroom.

On one of the front boards is a sign that says:

NAME ON BOARD	1st misbehavior
CHECK (✔) NEXT TO NAME	2nd misbehavior
TWO CHECKS (✔✔) NEXT TO NAME	3rd misbehavior
THREE CHECKS (✔✔✔) NEXT TO NAME	4th misbehavior

CONSEQUENCES

NAME ON BOARD	Discussion with me
CHECK NEXT TO NAME	5 less minutes of recess
TWO CHECKS	Visit principal's office
THREE CHECKS	Parent conference

During the day, Mr. Alter writes one or two names on the board as he continues his teaching. When Nicola talks continuously during quiet reading, he places a check next to her name.

There is also a list of Our Goals on the front board, listing such items as working together, getting work completed, and listening. Occasionally, Mr. Alter places a check in the box beneath the goal list, commenting, "Everyone really listened to the directions that time." When the number of checks reaches 50, the class will have a popcorn party.

Mr. Alter doesn't have to stop his teaching to respond to Nicola's behavior. Notice that he reinforces the desired behavior for the entire class. It was important that he had established clear limits of behavior beforehand and followed through with the consequences of not minding the limits. Teachers using the Assertive Discipline model make sure that students know and understand the rules and limits. Notice the similarity between this model and the Behavior Modification model with reinforcement strategies.

Adlerian Model (Dreikurs' Approach)

Dreikurs' ideas (1972), used for parenting and classroom management, are based on two assumptions: Our behavior is goal-directed and we learn best through concrete experiences. With those assumptions in mind, look at this Snapshot in which the Adlerian model guides Ms. Conley-Trombley.

SNAPSHOT: Middle-School Classroom

There is a climate of conversation in this room—problems are being discussed, questions are posed, effort is urged, and ideas are suggested. The schedule is affected by the time used for conversation; it has large blocks of time for group discussions, individual conferences, and class meetings.

Ms. Conley-Trombley has developed the class rules and limits with her sixth-grade students. Gradually they have also worked out together the consequences for not following the rules. She guides these discussions to logical consequences with, "What is a logical consequence for leaving a mess in the printing center?" When "staying in the room during recess" is suggested, she asks if it is logical. Gradually, students get the idea, and suggest cleaning up the printing shelves and scrubbing equipment in the area as a logical consequence.

When students have problems, Ms. Conley-Trombley works toward the understanding of behavior and its effects with those students involved. When Bill approaches her with a problem that he had at the drawing table, she asks, "What would the others say happened at the table?" and "How did your behavior affect them?" She encouraged Bill to describe his behavior and the problem from different perspectives.

Ms. Conley-Trombley often holds back and lets experience teach her students. When she observes Kerry using one of the pens incorrectly, she waits. Eventually, Kerry realizes that her sketch isn't going to be acceptable for printing. The logical consequence is that she will start over, this time using the pen correctly. Later she talks with her teacher and classmates about what she learned.

In this middle-school classroom, students hear feedback frequently, generally in the form of encouragement. They hear, "You have carefully followed the steps of the process," and "You paid a lot of attention to detail in that sketch," and "Did you notice how clear your print came out?"

Notice how much students are learning from their experiences, from trial and error, and from talking about problems. The intention is that they will confident and competent problem solvers who are responsible for their own behavior. That is Ms. Conley-Trombley's goal as she follows the Adlerian model.

Summary

The five models described are the major ones in use; however, others are available for your study, practice, and use. As part of your continuing advancework, look at *Systematic Management Plan for School Discipline* (SMPSD) (Duke & Meckel, 1980), *Social Literacy Training* (Alschuler, 1980), and *Consistency Management* (Freiberg,

Elementary Research Vignette

INTRODUCTION

The review of classroom management models is unlike the other vignettes in this text because the authors, Emmer and Aussiker (1987), used a technique called *meta-analysis*. They examined the results of many individual studies to look for patterns or trends to answer a specific question, in this review: How effective are the classroom management models?

STUDY DESIGN

Emmer and Aussiker studied the research on Teacher Effectiveness Training, Assertive Discipline, Reality Therapy, and Dreikurs' Approach (Adlerian Model), and looked specifically for effects on student learning, student attitudes, and reduction of behavior problems and discipline. They probed articles, reports, dissertations, and evaluation studies of the four models.

STUDY RESULTS

The researchers found that all models, except Dreikurs', reduced the number of disciplinary actions. All models, except Assertive Discipline, showed improved student attitudes toward school. None of the models achieved reduced disciplinary referrals, and only TET and Dreikurs showed a relationship with improved student achievement.

DISCUSSION AND IMPLICATION FOR PRACTICE

The results do not provide any clear-cut answers. Instead, they probably raise more questions. That is because classroom management is not a simple process with a few right answers. The data also make a case for studying the effects yourself as you make decisions about your own classroom management.

1983; Freiberg, Prokosch, Treister, & Stern, 1990). Models provide alternatives, and you can vary them to accommodate your context, content, and learner. As you will see in the above vignette, one model may not be the answer.

Research Model

With so much descriptive information available about what effective teachers do to manage their classrooms, we felt compelled to combine the observations into a model. As you look at the following Snapshot, watch for the qualities of smoothness and momentum described by Kounin (1970). *Smoothness* refers to the way the classroom happenings appear to be in order, the way changes happen easily, the way routines are established, and the way materials are ready beforehand. *Momentum* refers to the flow of activities and the pace of teaching and learning.

SNAPSHOT: Secondary School Classroom

When the 8:15 AM bell rings, Ms. Holloway reminds students, "We will be correcting homework in 30 seconds. Trade your assignment with your partner and have a folder and a clean sheet of paper ready on your desk." As students get ready, their teacher marks an attendance list.

"Ready, class? The following are the answers for the homework problems: #1—265 feet, #2—39 inches, . . . (and so on)." After the answers are read, students are seen returning each other's assignments, recording numbers in a folder, and passing assignments to the front. Two students take their papers to a box that has a big red question mark on it (used for assignments with question or confusion about answers).

"Today we are going to review the formulas for area and we'll practice using them. At your places, draw the shapes for which you can compute the area—just draw them." Ms. Holloway waits 30 seconds as students draw triangles, rectangles, circles, and squares. She flips on the overhead projector with a list of shapes and points to each, saying, "How many of you drew a circle? A square?" and so on.

"Now let's see how many of the formulas you can remember. Next to your circle, write the formula for the area of a circle. Raise your hands when you have it." Within 15 seconds, she calls on Yolanda for the formula and writes it on the transparency, saying, "Check that you have this formula written correctly on your sheet." She proceeds through the shapes with the same process.

"Now we are going to use the formulas. I will assign each of your work groups a shape. You are to find at least three examples of that shape in our classroom and measure them for information to use in your formulas. Then figure out the areas. Group 1, here is a yardstick; your assignment is rectangles. Group 2, here is a ruler; your assignment is triangles. Group 3, here is a tape measure; your assignment is circles."

Groups of four and five students move about the room and measure items. Some students return to their desks and figure the areas. Others remain near objects and measure.

"You have one minute to finish," Ms. Holloway says. "Now we need one person from each group to go to the board and show us one example from the items that you measured. While they are doing so, see if you can compute the area of the parallelogram I have drawn on the overhead."

Notice the following about this Snapshot:

- The lesson began smoothly and the class began with a fast pace.
- Routines for problems had been preestablished so that the pace can keep moving.
- The teaching strategies maintain involvement of students and a fast pace.
- There was obvious preparation for this lesson.
- There was change of pace with the group activity.
- Change occurs easily and involvement is maintained.

You didn't hear Ms. Holloway attending to behavior problems. If you were to continue to watch this classroom, you would hear explicit rules and directions; that is, students know exactly what to do and how to do it. They are "ritualized," so well taught that they seem to be automatic. That's why Ms. Holloway doesn't spend much time on them anymore.

Secondary Research Vignette

INTRODUCTION

To probe the effects of teacher mobility and physical location in the classroom, researchers in the Science/Mathematics Education Program at the University of Texas collected 10 years of observational data (Fifer, 1986).

STUDY DESIGN

An initial set of findings led to systematic observation of daily routines in secondary science and mathematics classrooms of 55 student teachers, 28 beginning teachers (2 to 5 years' experience), and 27 career teachers (6 or more years' experience). Observational data were collected using classroom diagrams to plot teacher mobility, identify teacher location, record and locate student misbehavior, and code and tally classroom interactions.

STUDY RESULTS

The data show that student behavioral problems "tended to be located in an ever-widening triangle with the point toward the teacher and increasing in both the number of students involved and frequency of occurrence the farther the students were from the teacher (toward the base of the triangle)" (Fifer, 1986, p. 404). The reverse was

true for classroom interaction. The base was toward the teacher and the narrow part and point were away from the teacher. Figure 1* shows the pattern for student misbehavior and for classroom interaction.

In the study, both beginning and career teachers spent 75 to 100 percent of their instructional time at the front of the classroom. Student teachers had been advised to spend at least 50 percent of each class period physically located somewhere other than the front of the room. When they followed this advice, the number and frequency of behavioral problems were reduced or eliminated, and interactions with students increased in both number and individuals involved. When the same advice was followed by beginning and career teachers, similar results were recorded. Figure 2* shows the interaction differences observed for teacher mobility in one eighth-grade classroom.

DISCUSSION AND IMPLICATIONS FOR PRACTICE

This study's author, F. L. Fifer, Jr., recommends that you design lessons with movement around the classroom. Varying your physical location in the classroom is a simple management strategy with comprehensive effects.

FIGURE 1   *Observational Format, Teacher-Mobility, Classroom Behavior, and Classroom Interaction*

Teacher Mobility	Classroom Behavior	Classroom Interaction

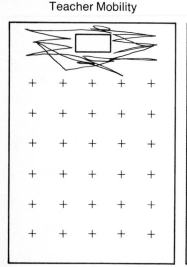
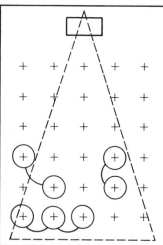
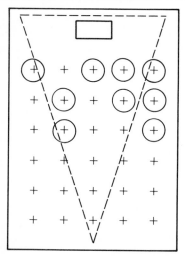

FIGURE 2 *Interactions Observed Relative to Teacher Mobility*

Teacher Mobility—100% Front

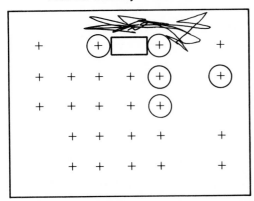

Interactions—5

Teacher Mobility—50% Front

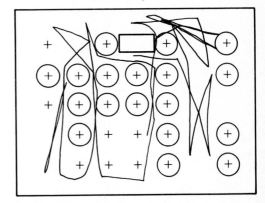

Interactions—18

Source: "Effective Classroom Management" by F. L. Fifer, Jr., 1986, *Academic Therapy, 21*(4), pp. 401–410. Copyright 1986 by PRO-ED, Inc. Reprinted by permission.

There is one last quality to Ms. Holloway's teaching and it is one that is found in all effective classrooms: variety. Vary the way you teach with different instructional strategies from your repertoire. The vignette on page 156 shows you what happens when you vary something as simple as your location in the room.

The complexity of classroom life can be staggering, and you will need the wisdom of many management models. Once you have collected advancework information and gathered ideas from models, you will be ready to make decisions and use classroom management strategies.

CLASSROOM MANAGEMENT STRATEGIES

There are recurring situations that demand your management: beginning of the school year, classroom interruptions, transitions, crises, and student behavior problems. Each requires you to use some advancework information; that is, what you know about your students, the context, and your curriculum. From there, use strategies to stay focused on teaching and to manage beyond discipline.

Beginning of the School Year

Studies of effective teachers show that management is well established in the first few weeks of school. Common sense tells you this is important, but the studies actually describe what teachers do. When researchers Emmer, Evertson, and Anderson (1980) observed effective teachers at the beginning of the school year, they saw them establish rules and procedures, observe students, and begin with energy and enthusiasm. From their observations, Emmer, Evertson, and Anderson offer advice for beginning the school year.

Establishing Rules and Procedures

To be effective in this process, you will need to follow three steps repeatedly during the first weeks of school: (1) teach the rules and procedures with explanations, modeling, and discussions; (2) practice the rules and procedures with students; and (3) provide feedback to students about whether they are following the rules correctly or incorrectly.

In the following Snapshot, this sequence is used to establish procedures for using reference materials.

SNAPSHOT: *Elementary Classroom*

Mr. Silva begins the afternoon with, "I want everyone to turn to the back of the room and look at the shelves of materials." He moves to the back and gestures toward the shelves, "Here we have all kinds of materials you can use when you write reports, prepare your presentations, or just look up information. We have old textbooks, paperbacks, and other nonfiction books, magazines, and pamphlets. It's going to be important to use these carefully and return them correctly so that everyone will have the resources they need.

"Let's pick a topic and I'll show you how to use these materials and how to return them. Let's say your topic is dinosaurs and you want to read about them. First, pick the subject area where you think you'll find dinosaurs." Mr. Silva points to a poster list of subject areas and asks for ideas. Tony says, "Science," and Cecilia says, "History." Mr. Silva responds with, "You may both be correct. Lots of topics could be found in more than one subject area."

Mr. Silva then demonstrates how to look in the science area for textbooks, paperbacks, magazines, and pamphlets. He finds two magazines and a book about dinosaurs. "Now watch this part. First, sign this sheet with your name and the titles of what you have found. Then you may take these to your desk, or work table, or home.

"To return these materials, watch as I put the book in the bin labeled 'Books,' and the magazines in the bin labeled 'Publications.' Then I put a check next to my name here on the list to show that I returned them" (demonstrates on the list). Mr. Silva then asks questions about the procedures.

"Now let's see if Cecilia was correct and look in the history area for information on dinosaurs. Matthew, come up and show us how you would look." As he looks through the book list, Mr. Silva comments, "Yes, that's correct to begin with the book list." Other students are called on to show how to find magazines, how to put away books, and where to use the materials. They also hear, "That's correct, you can use those at the work table," or "No, you need to put those in the bin labeled 'Books.' "

During the next month, students hear, "I noticed you checked your name when you returned the materials," and "You followed the procedures correctly when you used the pamphlets," or "You forgot to complete the information on the list."

The students received feedback about whether their procedures were correct or incorrect. Did you also note that Mr. Silva spent enough time describing and practicing the procedures? Reference materials are going to be used all year, so it is important to spend time establishing procedures well. When this does not happen, and you are still reminding students how to check out books or how to put them away in April, how will you feel?

In the Samples and Examples at the back of this chapter, we provide a First Week Checklist to help you remember important routines and procedures.

Observing Students

During the first month of school, effective teachers plan activities and time schedules that free them to observe students (e.g., an independent practice activity). They are able to see work habits, social interactions, learning preferences, and signs of attitudes toward curriculum and school. You can usually observe students during independent work activities, small group projects, and whole class discussions. It will help if you observe them in different learning situations. You may want simply to record what is happening during these observations or you may want to have a checklist of what you are looking for. (Chapter 14 provides several samples appropriate for using to observe students, and the Learner Profile in Chapter 7 offers another form for gathering information on students.)

Some of your observational time may be spent in one-to-one interactions with students, such as interviews, conferences, or just "getting acquainted" conversations. Such interactions begin a relationship and also allow you to observe students.

Being an Enthusiastic Teacher

Years of teaching prompt our advice: Spend the month before school resting, eating well, exercising, and relaxing. Start the school year with lots of energy, both for planning and teaching. Students are impressed and influenced by high-energy teaching.

TEACHER TALK

I put everything I've got into those first few weeks—my best activities, all my energy, and even a few tricks. I want kids to think that I'm the best teacher they've ever seen or heard. Once I get them on my side, then I can ease up a little and we're ready to work together for the year.

5th-Grade Teacher

Students generally arrive at school after a summer break with high expectations as well as high energy and enthusiasm. They don't want to be disappointed. If you can communicate that you care about them and about your curriculum, that you are ready to teach with energy and enthusiasm, they will be positive too.

Interruptions

Interruptions are regular occurrences in classrooms much to the dismay and frustration of teachers and students. Your advancework with administrators, office staff, and parents can ward off some interruptions. Ideally, a time can be set aside each day for announcements and messages, so that you are interrupted only for emergencies. When school life is less than ideal, begin by prioritizing your interruptions and responding to them in ways that discourage or regulate them.

Prioritizing Interruptions

Start by categorizing your time for interruptions with advancework questions:

- What times of day will interruptions seriously interfere with instruction?
- What times of day will interrruptions cause minimal interference with instruction?
- What times of day are you free to respond to messages, questions, and requests?
- Do you need to stop teaching each time a visitor comes to the door, a message arrives, or someone has a question?

From there, identify high-priority or emergency-type interruptions and low-priority or nonemergency-type interruptions that you can anticipate. An example of a high-priority (emergency) interruption occurs when a third-grader announces that his friend is ill, or a tenth-grader informs you that her friend may be in trouble with a dangerous drug reaction. These call for an immediate response. An example of a low-priority (nonemergency) interruption occurs when a parent or another student brings in a forgotten lunch or a note from the library. These do not call for an immediate response.

Responding to Interruptions

Once you identify instructional times that should not be interrupted and categorize anticipated interruptions, you have some options. Depending on school policy, you can request that messages be held for a later time, hang a "Do Not Disturb—Prime-Time Teaching" sign on your door, or assign students to greet and take messsages. Such procedures communicate an important message—that teaching and learning are too important to be interrupted.

Much of what happens with interruptions in your class will be determined by the way you respond early in the school year. Emmer, Evertson, and Anderson (1980) observed numerous interruptions occurring in the first few days of school. They saw parent requests, administrative questions, visitors, clerical concerns, and late-arriving students. They also noticed that effective teachers did not allow such interruptions to interfere with their work and with the attention being given to students. Effective teachers simply would not be distracted until they had students involved in an activity. These teachers rarely left the room; if necessary, they conversed with parents or faculty inside the room. New students arriving late were assisted by student helpers.

A unique kind of interruption is caused by events that disturb the normal flow or routines of the day. Such events include holidays, special programs, extreme weather conditions, or national events. Kounin (1970) observed teachers trying to proceed with all the normal routines and instruction as if these events didn't exist. He called this "fighting windmills." Teachers are usually unsuccessful and exhausted when they fight windmills.

For example, when school children in southern California witness a snow storm, or when high-school seniors hear that a popular athlete suffered a broken leg, teachers are fighting windmills if they ignore the events and try to proceed as usual. Your alternative is to acknowledge the event, provide time to discuss it, and, if possible, integrate it with your teaching. Stop and experience it with your students, then include it in your teaching. Write poems about the snow or compose a news story about the athlete.

Transitions

Research tells us that the smoothness of your classroom can be predicted by the way you handle transitions (Arlin, 1979). Remember the *herding* behavior we described in the last chapter? It usually occurs during transitions from one place to another. Other transitions include changes from one activity to another, from one subject area to another, and even from the beginning of a lesson to the end of a lesson. Transitions occur regularly each day and in each class period.

When Arlin (1979) observed student teachers at the elementary and junior high-school levels, he found that student off-task behaviors and disruptions were twice as frequent during transitions than during other instruction times. Thus, planning for transitions is essential.

Anticipating and Planning for Transitions

Begin by reviewing your daily plan or class schedule and predict times when change or waiting is inevitable. Visualize what your students will need during those times or what could occur. From there, you can plan as these teachers have done:

EXAMPLE: A kindergarten teacher who anticipates that the librarian might not be ready for her class at exactly 10:00 has three quiet fingerplays ready for the wait.

EXAMPLE: A fourth-grade teacher who looks at his afternoon schedule notices that an intense 40-minute math period is followed by a quiet social studies research activity. He plans a three-minute conversation time for his students to stand near their desks and visit with each other before beginning the research activity.

EXAMPLE: The middle-school history teacher knows that her students have a health class before coming to her room. To make the transition to their history topic, she asks, "Which of today's health problems could have existed during the Civil War?"

Establishing Routines for Transitions

The times when students first arrive, before and after lunch, or at the end of the day are often characterized as ragged, nonproductive, and unpleasant by teachers and students. These transition times occur everyday and are appropriate for well-established routines. These routines should be taught with the same practice and feedback we suggested for the beginning of the year. During the year, add some variety to make them interesting, and adjust them to changes. We see classrooms with interesting routines for transitions in these examples:

EXAMPLE: Second-graders know that from 8:00 to 8:10 AM (when children are arriving) they are to check the Classroom Chore List for assignments. If they don't have a chore, they can read quietly or work on puzzles.

EXAMPLE: Sixth-grade students check the list of materials written in a box on the chalkboard as soon as they arrive in the classroom after lunch. They know that the materials must be organized on their desks by 12:55, when the afternoon class begins.

EXAMPLE: During the last six minutes of a twelfth-grade composition class, students complete a self-evaluation of the day's work and write a plan for their work the next day.

Ending a class on a positive note or starting the day with a smooth beginning is worth the effort you make with these transitions.

Avoiding Student Waiting

Notice in the transition examples that students didn't have to wait. Students feel frustrated, resentful, distrusting, and disappointed when you have to search for the paint or writing paper, when you have to read through the teacher's guide to see what's next, or when you struggle to decide how to do the history projects.

To avoid student waiting, prepare materials, equipment, and procedures beforehand. Involve students. They are quite competent at setting up and adjusting the overhead projector, counting out and arranging stacks of art paper, distributing materials for math, and even writing the agenda on the board. Your responsibility is a planning one, essential to being ready and involving students. Planning conserves time for teaching and learning, and helps you avoid spending time on discipline.

Classroom Crises

Classroom life is subject to a wide variety of crises at any time. Some are regular occurrences, and some are infrequent. What is important, even if a certain crisis never happens, is that you are ready for it.

Anticipating Potential Crises

Again, begin by anticipating what could happen. When groups of elementary and secondary teachers were surveyed for potential and experienced crises, their responses included:

Fire and fire drill	Serious fights
Earthquakes, tornadoes	Student "high" (drugs)
Bomb scares and alerts	Kidnapping of student
Serious injury	Wet pants
Bees, insects, snakes in classroom	Lost student
Visits by angry, violent parents	Broken glass
Spilled paint	Gas leak
Power failure	Student illness

The list could go on. The impact varies but no classroom is free of crises.

TEACHER TALK

You want to hear about crises? One of our worst is when there are bears on the playgrounds and we can't have recess.

Elementary Classroom Teacher (in Alaska)

Preparing for Crises

Our best advice is to prepare. Most schools have specific procedures for some crises, so your first step is to be informed. From there, predict a list of possibilities like the one we just reviewed, and develop a response plan for each. Other teachers and administrators are ideal consultants when you are planning ahead. You don't have to have a detailed written plan; a simple plan composed in your head will do.

An example of a mental plan for a crisis such as serious student injury would have the following steps:

1. Move students out of the area of the injured student.
2. Make the injured student comfortable and secure.
3. Seek assistance (student to office).
4. Get supplies or equipment.
5. Keep everyone calm.

Crises will feel different when they have been anticipated, discussed, and rehearsed. They can also be excellent learning opportunities, so think about how to involve students in your plans. Students gain security from information and practice.

Student Behavior Problems

Student behavior problems have the potential to interfere with teaching and learning. Since the early 1960s, survey research has indicated that student behavior problems are a major concern for teachers, administrators, parents, and community members (Moles, 1987). Even with the best management system, you may have behavior problems. Get ready to work with such behavior by *identifying problems, considering the causes and effects, and developing responses.*

Identifying Student Behavior Problems

Your starting point is one of defining and identifying *problem behavior.* It may mean something different for individual students, for different settings. The important question is: Does the behavior interfere with teaching and learning? The answer is yes when behavior ruins the classroom climate with tension or blocks your teaching with noises or movement.

Remember to use the advancework we urged in Chapter 5 to get others' perspectives as well as make you "supportable." Consider the usual causes of behavior problems:

1. *Teacher-student value conflicts*
2. *Physical, mental, and social status of students*
3. *Lack of teacher preparation*
4. *Negative influence of home and community*
5. *Teacher inexperience in coping with problems*
6. *Differences between teachers' expectations and students' responses*
7. *Lack of communication or miscommunication in classroom (Swick, 1977).*

"Now about our school's number-one problem: discipline. . ."

A profile of teaching in urban schools describes everyday classroom life as characterized by all seven of the major causes (*Education Week*, 1988), so your starting point is to assess your classroom and yourself.

Developing Responses to Student Behavior Problems

Before deciding how you will respond to behavior problems, distinguish between minor and major problems. Just like interruptions, you don't want to respond to all of them in the same way. *Minor* problems are one-time occurrences, irritations, or distractions. *Major* problems are recurring interferences that bring with them tension and other problems. For minor problems, you need responses that do not interfere with your teaching and that are quick and easy to use:

1. *Signals.* Teachers use a hand signal or small body motion (like a 3rd-base baseball coach) to communicate, "Stop what you are doing." Effective teachers can point a finger or nod their heads at a disturbing student without ever stopping their teaching. Students generally know that the message means to stop.
2. *Eye Contact.* Teachers simply pause and make eye contact with a student and send the message to pay attention.
3. *Proximity.* Teachers move closer to the student to stop or control the behavior. When students are whispering instead of listening, a teacher walks toward them while continuing a presentation.

For major problems, you will need a more comprehensive approach. Start with the student. Talk in private about the behavior and possible causes. In addition to the student's ideas and feelings, check the following:

1. School records for possible medical or psychological causes
2. Social interactions and peer relationships
3. Classroom for lighting, temperature, room arrangement, furniture condition, comfort, and location of student
4. Your teaching and curriculum for appropriateness to student ability, need, and relevance to student

Anticipate what you may find out when you begin this approach. When you ask your student what is happening or why a problem exists, you may hear, "Your class if boring," or "My parents are getting a divorce," or "I work a night shift at McDonald's and I'm tired," or "I'm hungry." Be ready for the possibilities. You may need the assistance of counselors or other personnel. If you have done your advancework, you know what kind of support you will have.

School records can help with specific information and a look at homelife to understand what you are seeing in the classroom. Students often reflect what is happening at home, or use school to release feelings and tensions from home.

We know that there is a significant relationship between disruptive behavior and the degree to which a student is accepted socially by peers. One way to check on interactions and relationships is to use a sociogram to survey students' preferences among peers. Figure 6.1 shows the type of information you can get from a sociogram. For students like Keenan and Priscilla, who haven't been chosen, you may want to observe their social interactions. If they are having difficulty, you may need to assist them or structure classroom situations so that they experience social acceptance.

The fourth check is based on the influence of physical conditions of an environment. For example, overcrowding is known to have a direct effect on student behavior, causing restlessness, inattention, and agressiveness. Try putting yourself in the students' place and see how it feels.

The last suggestion asks you to check your own teaching and curriculum. Review the advice of Carroll in Chapter 4 and your advancework on students and content in Chapter 5. Listen to your communication and management messages and watch how you interact with students. Be assured that you or the curriculum are not the cause of the behavior problem.

You may have a great deal of information when you complete the five steps sug-

FIGURE 6.1 *Sociogram Information for a Middle-School Homeroom Class*

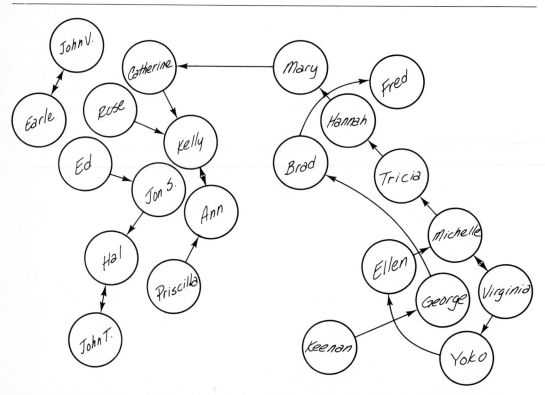

gested, but you still have a problem. An important next step in this comprehensive process is to communicate with the student's parents.

Communicating with Parents

Communication with parents can result in information sharing, agreement and support, and consistency between home and school, all of which are especially important when behavior problems exist.

Advancework for Communicating with Parents

Begin with a recognition of the importance and power of parents. They are teaching the student how to express needs and feelings, to cooperate, and to respond to situations. Whether or not you agree with their teaching, recognizing parents' importance is essential to effective communication.

From there, establish informal communication, ideally before a problem exists. This can be done with handwritten notes, brief phone calls, or conversation after school. The tone is positive and the message is, "I want to work with you," or "I'm glad to have your daughter in my class," or "Your son is involved in our projects." If this advancework is done, a problem-solving session will be part of ongoing communication.

Conferencing with Parents

Think of this step as a two-way process. Each of you has important information for the other. If you have done your advancework, parents will feel secure about asking and answering questions. They can learn about class routines, goals, curriculum, expectations, and their child's behavior. You can learn about the student's experiences, interests, expectations, and behavior at home.

In addition to advancework for conferences, it will be important to keep your talk free from educational jargon. Buskin (1975) found that jargon is a serious barrier to communication with parents. Parents find it meaningless, frustrating, offensive, and insulting. Tape a practice conference and listen carefully to your choice of words. Develop your questions at this time to assure clear wording, non-threatening quality, and specificity of information you are seeking.

Continue your preparation by establishing an agenda, developing important questions in advance, and gathering and organizing data to share. A conference agenda should be simple and, if possible, the topic to be discussed should be shared in advance. An example of a way to encourage parent input is provided at the end of this chapter in the Samples and Examples section.

When you use actual samples or data in conferences, parents can assess the situation. When they look at a set of unfinished work, or a sociogram, or a destroyed desk, they can see the problem for themselves.

Finally, we suggest a summary at the end of the conference to clarify the discussion, emphasize a decision, or extend the communication. Listen to a middle-school science teacher summarize a conference with Jeff's parents in the following Teacher Talk.

TEACHER TALK

It sounds like we agree that Jeff is enthusiastic and puts effort into his work for this class. We definitely want to encourage his attitude, but his socializing in lab does keep him from the quality of work of which he is capable. We will keep a check on lab work and report writing. Your idea of special social activities with his school friends on Friday nights is great. Let's talk again in three weeks to see how Jeff is doing. I'll call you.

In the Samples and Examples at the end of this chapter, you will find a form to use for parents to provide input about the success of a conference. It continues the two-way communication after the conference has ended.

Problem Solving with Parents

When student behavior problems are major, a problem-solving approach may be needed in the communication with parents. Rutherford and Edgar (1979, p. 20) recommend a process that is universal for use in other settings. We urge you to follow the steps and develop some skill with the process:

1. Set goals by agreeing on the problem, listing desired outcomes, and deciding how to evaluate the outcomes.
2. Select the solution by discussing alternatives and determining a mutually agreeable solution.
3. Put the plan into action and provide each side with feedback.
4. Evaluate and share results by checking the outcomes and the process.

The first step is best done with some evidence of the problem's existence. Some of Jeff's lab reports, half finished, along with some test scores, and a seating chart of the lab were appropriate for the conference with his parents. Identification of the problem was best done with positive language such as, "Jeff needs to use all of his lab time for experiments and reports," instead of "Jeff needs to stop socializing during lab."

The second problem-solving step requires true collaboration; that is, both parents and Jeff's teacher should suggest solutions and agree on the final decision. When Jeff's teacher wanted to move him from his friends in the lab, his parents suggested a Friday night social as an alternative to socializing in lab. Jeff's parents expressed a wish to have him learn how to control his social behavior in school settings, and his teacher agreed.

Jeff's parents took the lead in implementing the plan, and his teacher followed with a conversation at school. After the first week, his teacher phoned his parents to assure them of his agreement and his already improved work.

It has been our experience that many problem-solving efforts in classroom management stop short of the fourth step—evaluation. Two months after the conference, Jeff's teacher and parents will meet again to look at his lab work, discuss his behavior, hear about the Friday night socials, and generally decide if the solution was effective.

This problem-solving process supports the kind of relationship you seek with parents and students. You saw it used earlier (page 150) in the class meeting in Ms. Hathaway's third grade to solve problems on the playground. We encourage you to practice and use problem solving for other aspects of classroom life.

SUMMARY

We began by urging you to consider both personal and professional models of classroom management, those teachers you remember, and the models of Behavior Modification, Reality Therapy, Teacher Effectiveness Training, Assertive Discipline, and Dreikurs' Approach. We looked at effective teachers for an additional model of managing a classroom with smoothness and momentum.

The theme for handling the recurring situations of beginning the school year, interruptions, transitions, crises, and student behavior problems was *preparation*. Anticipate and plan your responses to these situations. With student behavior problems, you may need simple responses or a comprehensive approach. Part of your more complex response is communication with parents. Check your attitudes and language for effective communication and practice problem solving to work successfully with parents on behavior that interferes with your teaching. A foundation for all of your management responses is advancework for information and support as you handle situations.

A conclusion of this chapter and of our experiences with classroom management is that it requires lifelong learning. Just about the time you think that you have mastered all of the competencies you need to manage a classroom, you have a student or a class that baffles you. Just about the time we think we have all the answers for management problems, a student in one of our classes poses one for which we say, "Hmmmm, I'll have to think about that one."

Be ready to keep learning—read about classroom management, attend workshops, talk about management with other teachers. Most importantly, watch those who are effective. Just as the researchers in this chapter did, you can get the best information from their practices. What you will notice is that their focus is on teaching and learning. Their management goes beyond discipline.

REFERENCES

Alschuler, A. S. (1980). *School discipline: A socially literate solution*. New York: McGraw-Hill.

Arlin, M. (1979). Teacher transitions can disrupt time flow in classrooms. *American Educational Research Journal, 16*, 42–56.

Buskin, M. (1975). *Parent power: A candid handbook for dealing with your child's school*. New York: Walker and Company.

Canter, L., & Canter, M. (1979). *Assertive discipline*. Los Angeles: Canter and Associates.

Doyle, W. (1986). Classroom organization and management. In M. C. Wittrock (Ed.), *Handbook of research on teaching* (3rd ed.). New York: Macmillan.

Dreikurs, R. (1968). *Psychology in the classroom*. New York: Harper and Row.

Dreikurs, R., Grunwald, B., & Pepper, F. (1971). *Maintaining sanity in the classroom.* New York: Harper & Row.

Dreikurs, R., & Cassel, P. (1972). *Discipline without tears.* New York: Hawthorn.

Duke, D., & Meckel, A. M. (1980). *Managing student behavior problems.* New York: Teachers College Press.

Education Week. (1988). A bold step from the ivory tower. *Education Week, 7*(39), 21–31.

Emmer, E. T., & Aussiker, A. (1987). *School and classroom discipline programs: How well do they work?* Paper presented at the annual meeting of the American Educational Research Association, Washington, DC.

Emmer, E., Evertson, C. M., & Anderson, L. M. (1980). Effective classroom management at the beginning of the school year. *The Elementary School Journal, 80*(5), 219–231.

Fifer, F. L. (1986). Effective classroom management. *Academic Therapy, 21*(4), 401–410.

Freiberg, H. J. (1983). Consistency: The key to classroom management. *Journal of Education for Teaching, 9*(1), 1–15.

Freiberg, H. J., Prokosch, N., Treister, E., & Stein, T. (1990). Turning around five at-risk elementary schools. *Journal of School Effectiveness and Improvement, 1*(1), 5–25.

Glasser, W. (1969). *Schools without failure.* New York: Harper & Row.

Glasser, W. (1987). *Control theory in the classroom.* New York: Harper & Row.

Gordon, T. (1974). *Teacher effectiveness training.* New York: David McKay.

Kounin, J. (1970). *Discipline and group management in classrooms.* New York: Holt, Rinehart & Winston.

Moles, O. C. (1987). *Trends in student misconduct: The 70s and 80s.* Paper presented at the annual meeting of the American Educational Research Association, Washington, DC.

Rutherford, Jr., R., & Edgar, E. (1979). *Teachers and parents: A guide to interaction and cooperation.* Boston: Allyn and Bacon.

Skinner, B. F. (1968). *The technology of teaching.* New York: Appleton-Century-Crofts.

Skinner, B. F. (1971). *Beyond freedom and dignity.* New York: Knopf.

Swick, K. J. (1977). *Maintaining productive student behavior.* Washington, DC: National Education Association.

SAMPLES AND EXAMPLES

There are four Samples and Examples in this section. Sample student management contracts are provided, along with a First-Week Checklist and two Parent Conference forms.

- Student management contracts are based on a behavior management model of discipline.
- The First-Week Checklist is designed for you to review prior to the opening of school.
- The two parent conference forms reflect two sources of data about teacher/parent interactions. The first form is a needs assessment about the topic(s) for the meeting, which would be completed by the parent prior to the meeting. The second form is a feedback form about the meeting. Both forms will facilitate communication between teachers and parents.

SAMPLE STUDENT MANAGEMENT CONTRACTS

For Pupils Who Can Read

Contract

What I Do	My Count	What Happens
	1 2 3 4 5 6 7 8 9 10 11 12 13 14 15 16 17 18 19 20	5 = ☆ ☆ ☆ ☆ ☆ ☆

Teacher: _____
Student: _____
Dates: _____

For pupils who are not yet readers ⟶

Contract

What I Do	My Count	What Happens
	1 2 3 4 5 6 7 8 9 10 11 12 13 14 15 16 17 18 19 20	Each day get 00000 Lose 0 for each talk out End of day 00 = help teacher

Teacher: _____
Student: _____
Dates: _____

For Pupils Who Are Not Yet Readers

Contract   Date ____

I will earn checks ✓ each day for:

   ✓ raising my hand to speak
   ✓✓✓ helping others
   ✓✓ working at centers

I will lose checks ✓ each day by:

   ✓ talking out
   ✓✓✓ fighting
   ✓✓ not working

At the end of the week, I may earn:

   ✓✓✓✓✓ Extra recess time
   ✓✓✓✓ Extra art time
   ✓✓✓✓ Lunch with teacher

Teacher: _____
Student: _____
   M T W Th F M T W Th F

FIRST-WEEK CHECKLIST

Have You:

_____   Learned your students' names?

_____   Greeted students by name on arrival?

_____   Learned information about students' interests, goals, likes and dislikes?

_____   Made procedures, standards, and limits clear and public knowledge?

_____   Consistently reinforced the procedures and standards you have set up?

_____   Given students overviews prior to an activity to let them know what to expect?

_____   Given students responsibility on a graduated basis?

_____   Used visual aids?

_____   Recorded, distributed, and introduced textbooks?

_____   Set up place and system for keeping records, forms?

_____   Made calendar notes of dates, questions, ideas?

_____   Become familiar with facilities, faculty?

_____   Asked questions of other teachers, principal?

_____   Reviewed and used curriculum guides?

_____   Planned for next week?

_____   Given yourself a pat on the back?

Source: Freiberg, H. J., & McFaul, S. (1980). *Project Entry Teacher Corps Instructional Booklets.* Houston: University of Houston—University Park. Used by permission.

PARENT CONFERENCE FORMS

Dear _____,

A parent-teacher conference will soon be scheduled for you. In order for me to plan a useful and informative conference, it is important to ask for your ideas and areas of concern. Please answer the following questions and return one of the copies to me by the end of the week. The other copy is for you to keep and bring to the conference.

1. What are your child's feelings about school? What does he or she say? What does he or she like or dislike about school?

2. Does your child have any "special friends" or talk about other children in class?

3. What kind of changes have you noticed, if any, since your child started school?

4. Are there any problems for you or your child that I can help with?

Please check 3 topics related to your child's school experiences that you would like to discuss during the conference.

_____	Following directions	_____	Friendships
_____	Self-confidence	_____	Self-control
_____	Getting along with others	_____	Work habits
_____	Working with a group	_____	Language
_____	Listening, attending	_____	Other

Any other thoughts about the conference?

_____
Parent signature

PARENT CONFERENCES

Would you please take a moment to evaluate our conference? This will help me as I plan for future conferences.

Was there an area which you especially appreciated my sharing or that was helpful?

Was there an area which we neglected to discuss that you feel I should have brought up?

Do you have any other comments to share?

Do you feel the conference time was adequate in length?

Source: Driscoll, A., & Newmann, A. (1989). Materials for communication with parents. Portland, OR: Portland State University and West Linn School District Cooperative Program. Used by permission.

CHAPTER 7

Lecture: From Passive to Active Learning

CHAPTER OUTCOMES

At the conclusion of this chapter you will be able to:

1. Describe the role of the learner, content, and context in providing effective lectures.
2. Describe three goals of lecture, including information, motivation, and reflective, critical thinking presentations.
3. Identify guidelines from research that may increase interactive opportunities of lecture.
4. Describe the benefits and limitations of lecture.
5. Describe six variations of the lecture approach.

KEY TERMS AND CONCEPTS

Style Without Substance
Learner Profile
Information
Motivation
Critical Thinking
Teacher Control
Scope and Pace
Stimulus Variation
Cuing
Pausing
Media
Enthusiasm
Variability
Guided Note Taking

*Lek' cher, n. (French lecture, from the LATIN Lectura, a
reading.) A disclosure on some subject read or delivered before
an audience; a formal or methodological discourse intended
for instruction.*
Webster, 1972, p. 485.

INTRODUCTION

The lecture method is both generic across subjects and grade levels, and ancient in
its roots. Lecturing can be found in a seventh-grade English class as well as in a
college freshman mathematics classroom. It is universal to all content areas and
most grade levels, and is the predominant teaching method in secondary and
college classrooms. It is ancient in that its roots can be traced back to Greek civilization with the writings and discussions of Socrates, Plato, Aristotle, and Demosthenes.
The lecture is well documented as a strategy for communicating ideas to others; it
also has been known in Greek folklore that many a listener has been put to sleep by
an uninspired and long-winded presenter.

The lecture method has survived over 2,000 years because it is both efficient and
familiar. In this century, particularly in the late 60s and early 70s, the lecture
approach received a great deal of criticism for misuses and unskilled applications.
This criticism is also evident in the commission reports of the 90s. A study conducted by the National Assessment of Educational Progress (Mullis, Owen, &
Phillips, 1990) of achievement for nine million students since 1970 states, "Across
the past 20 years, little seems to have changed in how students are taught. Despite
much research suggesting better alternatives, classrooms still appear to be dominated by textbooks, teacher lectures and short-answer activity sheets" (p. 10). A 1984
film documentary based on the Carnegie Commission Report shows unenthused
teachers lecturing to glassy-eyed students.

The research on effective teaching (see Wittrock, 1986) has promoted a direct
instruction approach at the elementary and secondary level, often characterized by
the use of lecture or presentation strategies. The research (Rosenshine, 1983)
includes excellent guidelines for providing interest, clarity, audience considerations, and organization in response to NAEP or Carnegie-type criticism. Lecturing, without regard for learner, content, and/or context, however, provides the
dull and tedious schooling episodes that most of us would like to forget.

There are perhaps two sources for the problems identified by critics of the lecture method. The first may be a lack of teacher motivation. The second possibility is
that teachers are simply unaware of the range of possible options in the lecture
method due to a lack of effective role models in high school and college classrooms.
Regardless of the reasons, the lecture method is not always seen as a dynamic tool
for teaching and learning. In order to understand the potential of the lecture
method, this chapter provides an analysis of the benefits and limitations as a teaching tool. Additionally, suggestions for maximizing its effectiveness as a teaching
method are presented generically as well as specifically for elementary and secondary settings.

STYLE WITHOUT SUBSTANCE

A contrast to the boredom of many lecture memories are the "entertainers" we have encountered in education. Is the following Snapshot a familiar one?

SNAPSHOT: *Secondary Classroom*

It is the beginning of September and George Washington High School is about to open its doors for the new school year. The students file into the school and head for their 8:30 AM classes. Mr. Johnson, a social studies teacher, is a new member of the faculty. Many of the students are eager to see the new teacher. They have heard through the grapevine that Mr. Johnson is great. His students are not disappointed by his first lecture. He uses great amounts of humor, enthusiasm, movement, and vocal inflection to embellish his presentation. After a few weeks, the students come to idolize Mr. Johnson, except for Tom, who complains the presentations are entertaining but lack depth or substance. His peers call Tom an egg-head and dismiss the objections.

The above situation is hypothetical but relates to a series of studies conducted on the effects of lecture on both medical professions and undergraduate college students (Williams & Ware, 1977). The researchers hired a *Hollywood actor* to teach six different types of lectures, varying from high, medium, and low levels of content to high, medium, and low levels of expressiveness. The expressive manner of the "teacher" is reflected in humor, enthusiasm, movement, and vocal inflection (p. 450). The students' ratings of the instructor were not sensitive to the fact that little substance was being presented in a very entertaining manner. The phenomemon has been called the *Dr. Fox Effect* because, in the first study, students thought the lecturer was a professor of medicine.

The point of the story and research is that form without substance is meaningless. Although the expressive manner of the teacher is a very important motivating factor, without knowledge and wisdom the learning experience becomes shallow. Our experiences have demonstrated that mature and committed students are resentful and discouraged by entertainment without relevant content. Many a student has assessed an instructor with, "Sure, it was a fun class but I didn't get what I needed from it. We just listened to stories." We've observed elementary students obviously enjoying an engaging activity or game, and later frustrated with questions or assignments for which they had inadequate preparation.

So we return to the teaching model of our text and examine the lecture strategy with respect to the learner, the content, and the context.

Learner

Knowing about the learner will assist you in making decisions about the type of lecture and the content to be incorporated into the lecture. Although you do not have control over the experiences of the students prior to their entry into your classroom, you should have some knowledge about both the characteristics of the group and the individuals who make up the group. For example, what is the academic background of the students? Have they already mastered some of the information you will present? Do they need a prerequisite set of skills and knowledge level before they can comprehend the information or ideas presented in the lecture? Do the students have an average or less than average attention span (as determined by developmental levels)? Do they have the ability to operate at a formal operational or concrete operational stage of development? Can you rely on symbols or will you need concrete examples?

You want to challenge the students but you do not want to frustrate them. This will interfere with their ability to learn and your ability to be effective. The teacher needs to know if the students are effective in taking notes or if some are having difficulty in synthesizing the information presented during the lecture. The teacher may decide to provide content outlines for the entire class or provide specific training for those students who have poor outlining skills. In either case, the teacher uses data about the students to improve the conditions for learning in the classroom.

Information about the learner can be gained from direct observations of the students, classroom discussions, quizzes or pre-tests, student interest inventories, standardized test scores, class and homework assignments, and other lecture experiences. Research (Slavin, 1987, 1988) indicates that effective teachers adapt instructional strategies and materials to the ability level of the students. The process of knowing your students should begin on the first day and continue throughout the year. Knowledge about the students will assist in planning both the content and the format of the lecture.

Knowing your students should not be a justification for lowering expectations or watering down the curriculum. Knowing something about your students will provide you information to create meaningful examples and provide opportunities to build on prior knowledge and experiences. The Learner Profile in Figure 7.1 provides some important information about the interests, work habits, philosophy, and learning styles of your students in grades 3 through 12. For younger students, the questions are read aloud and the students respond orally. Complete the profile and compare your responses with other members of your class.

Ultimately, effective teachers need to put themselves in the place of the student, to maintain an awareness of the learner, to ask: What would I learn from this lecture? Would I find this material interesting? What am I communicating by my style, my choice of words, my nonverbal language?

One characteristic of teaching that appeals to learners of all ages and that is especially important when using the lecture strategy is enthusiasm. Although enthusiasm is difficult to measure and nearly impossible to teach, we all know it when we see it.

Enthusiasm

Charles Pine, professor of physics at Rutgers University for 36 years, received a national outstanding college teacher award in 1984 (Heller, 1984). He is an

FIGURE 7.1 *Learner Profile*

1. List five things you like to do:

   a. _____

   b. _____

   c. _____

   d. _____

   e. _____

2. What was the title of the last book you read? _____

3. What is your favorite TV show? _____

4. How much time do you spend watching TV each day? _____

5. What is the first thing you do when you come home from school? _____

6. Where do you do your homework? _____

7. What is your favorite school subject? _____

8. What do you think is the purpose of school? _____

9. What do you think is the purpose of homework? _____

The following list contains 10 interest areas. Rank each area from 1 (I like the best) to 10 (I like the least) in the space provided.

_____ Listening to teacher give information

_____ Working in centers

_____ Working in groups

_____ Solving problems in groups

_____ Doing worksheets

_____ Working alone

_____ Seeing films

_____ Doing projects in the classroom

_____ Doing projects outside the classroom

_____ Reading

excellent example of how a teacher can combine form and substance to the benefit of both teacher and student. The summer he received his award for teaching excellence, he shared his teaching methods with (high school) math teachers from over 16 public school districts in New Jersey. A student who nominated Mr. Pine for the award noted:

> *He can transpose his classes into the realm of the subject he is discussing, whether it be climbing into an atom to observe the interaction of atomic forces, standing on a revolving turntable to get the feel for rotating and relative coordinate systems, or venture inside a balloon to observe how the individual air particles contribute to the total pressure. . . .*
> *"You've got to give of yourself," Mr. Pine explains. "In the end, the most important factor, I think, is enthusiasm. Even after all these years, I think it's fun going into a classroom."*
> (p. 28)

You, as a teacher, must ask yourself questions to determine the presence or absence of enthusiasm. Check for attitude toward subject matter, students, the school setting, and self; check physical factors (fatigue and enthusiasm don't combine well) and preparation (it's hard to be enthusiastic when you're not sure what comes next). Look at your own learner profile: What characteristics on your profile will contribute to teaching enthusiasm? What characteristics will limit your enthusiasm?

In contrast to the examples of quality lectures found in secondary and higher education, many elementary teachers avoid the lecture strategy. Armed with child-development principles that identify the short attention span of young children, and sold on the advantages of activities and discovery learning, novice elementary teachers plan every possible teaching strategy except lecturing. The common scene in elementary classrooms is a very brief explanation of new material, an abundance of directions, and students doing seatwork for most of the instructional time. In an attempt to be sensitive to young learners and to heed the advice that children learn by doing, elementary teachers have generally ignored lecturing.

As with all of the strategies described in this book, lecturing is appropriate for some curriculum content and for certain learning objectives, just as discovery learning is appropriate for some curriculum content and for certain learning objectives. However, even kindergarten students can and will attend to a brief (5 to 6 minutes) lecture presentation. Although it is important for any lecturer to attend to organization, pacing, focus, clarity, and audience, it is especially critical for elementary teachers to assess these aspects of a lecture. The management and organization of lecture—or as many classify it in the elementary grades, presentation skills—require specific planning and implementation strategies. The following summary of the research provides a framework for the use of lecture with elementary school students.

Research Summary
Rosenshine (1983) summarized ideas from the research on effective instruction and some studies of teacher clarity to provide suggestions for effective presentation specifically in a lecture format. His guidelines* reflect a sensitivity to the learner of

any age, including middle and high-school students, but are especially important for the young learner.

1. *Content material should be presented in small steps.* A first-grade teacher is presenting the concepts of maps to his class. Each of the concepts (scale, representation, etc.) is taught in individual lessons and is broken down further into parts for a lecture. *Scale* is first defined, then its purpose is presented, then variations of scale are described, and finally examples of scale are provided. Within the lecture on scale, each of the understandings is developed completely before the teacher continues to the next aspect of the concept.

2. *Presentations should focus on one thought (point, direction) at a time.* When the first-grade teacher is trying to develop the concept of scale, the time would not be appropriate to introduce students to the different kinds of maps, such as aerial maps, topographical maps, and so on.

3. *Digressions should be avoided during presentations.* Young children are notorious for sidetracking presentations, and elementary teachers often yield to the digressions. A discussion of maps is likely to initiate students' recall of map use on vacations, and discussions can quickly turn to lengthy descriptions of various rides at Disneyland. Elementary teachers need to be especially smooth and skillful in guiding student input to contribute to the subject focus.

4. *When possible or appropriate, modeling should accompany the lecture.* A fifth-grade teacher has been teaching a unit on decision making. When she presents the steps to decision making, she models each step in a scenario from classroom life and demonstrates how to proceed through each step.

5. *Lectures are best accompanied by many varied and specific examples.* During an initial overview lecture on the concept of farms, the kindergarten teacher introduces a wide variety of replicas of farms. These include photographs, dioramas, models, slides, songs, art prints, literature, and so on.

6. *Effective lectures are characterized by detailed and redundant explanations for difficult points.* Many concepts provide difficulty for young children. When teaching the purpose of advertising to first-graders, explanations need to be redundant in order to overcome the students' misconceptions about advertising, then to establish new knowledge about advertising. Such concepts may take several lectures.

7. *Before proceeding to the next point in a lecture, checks for student understanding should be conducted.* As the second grade teacher presents the process of observation through the sense of vision, he will be covering the characteristics of an object observed through the eye. Before proceeding to the characteristics that can be observed through the tactile sense, begin with, "Before going on, let's list all the things we know about the artichoke by using our eyes."

8. *Student progress should be monitored through the lecture by means of questions.* With the same presentations on observation through the sense of sight, the second-

*Rosenshine, B. (1983). Teaching functions in instructional programs. *The Elementary School Journal*, *83*(4). © by The University of Chicago Press. All rights reserved.

grade teacher may ask, "Can we tell that the artichoke is soft with our eyes? Can we tell that the artichoke is green with our eyes? Can we tell that the artichoke is sour with our eyes?"

9. *Lecturers should stay with the topic, repeating material until students understand.* Again, with the level of difficulty that young students encounter with complex concepts, a lecture on a new and/or abstract concept may extend over a period of several days or a week. The information may be best presented with different examples, continued questioning, and some redundant lecturing over time to accomplish student understanding.

The major obstacles to the success of the lecture strategy at all levels are not student attention span or the inappropriateness of the strategy but a lack of clarity and organization. Additionally, there may be a lack of sufficient explanations and examples, teachers assuming that everyone knows *without checking for understanding*, and the introduction of more complex material before students master the prior material. These failings reflect a lack of awareness of the learner. Effective lecturing then requires consideration of the learner during the planning phase and during the implementation (the actual doing).

Application Activity
Return to your student profile for review. Which of your own characteristics would influence planning decisions? Which characteristics would influence the actual teaching process? Consider the lecturing in this course. What characteristics of the lecturing match your learning characteristics? What is not matching and interfering with your learning? (See the Samples and Examples section at the end of this chapter for additional activities.)

Content

The content is the substance of the lesson. The content in the lecture includes facts, skills, ideas, rules, principles, concepts, and generalizations. The teacher must have a mastery level of the content to be able to translate the information effectively to the students. Teaching strategies, motivational techniques, and effective planning cannot substitute for depth in the content area to be taught. Additionally, content knowledge is a prerequisite for the development of goals and objectives of the lesson—a first step in the planning and organization discussed in Chapter 2.

Planning the Lecture
What are your goals for the lesson? Is your intent *to provide information, to motivate the students*, or *to provide a critical thinking, reflective presentation.* All three goals individually, or collectively, could be an instructional outcome of the lesson. Once the goal(s) is(are) determined, then objectives for the lesson need to be developed based on the learner, content, and context. Ask yourself: What do I expect the students to learn from the lesson? The answers to this question lead you to a decision about the strategy or strategies to be used to deliver the lesson. If the lecture method

seems to be the most effective strategy for the lesson, then some preliminary organization of the content is necessary.

For an *informational* presentation, the content information is analyzed into concepts and subconcepts followed by a sequencing process. For example, if you wanted to teach a lesson on tunnelling and underground excavation, you could develop the following outline beginning with the history and concluding with the future of tunnelling (Encyclopaedia Britannica, 1981, p. 750):

Tunnelling*

I. History
    Ancient tunnels
    From the Middle Ages to the present
        Canal and railroad tunnels
        Subaqueous tunnels
        Machine-mined tunnels
II. Tunnelling techniques
    Basic tunnelling system
        Geological investigation
        Excavation and materials handling
        Ground support
        Environmental control
    Modern soft-ground tunnelling
        Settlement damage and lost ground
        Hard-mined tunnels
        Shield tunnels
        Water control
        Soft-ground moles
        Pipe jacking
    Modern rock tunnelling
        Nature of the rock mass
        Conventional blasting
        Rock support
        Concrete lining
        Rock bolts
        Shotcrete
        Preserving rock strength
        Water inflows
        Heavy ground
        Unlined tunnels
III. Underground excavations and structures
    Rock chambers
        Rock-mechanics investigation

*Reprinted with permission from "Tunnelling and Underground Excavation" in *Encyclopaedia Britannica,* 15th ed., © 1981 by Encyclopaedia Britannica, Inc.

Chamber excavation and support
Sound-wall blasting
Shafts
Shaft sinking and drilling
Shaft raising
Immersed-tube tunnels
Development of method
Modern practice
IV. Future trends in underground construction
Environmental and economic factors
Improvement of surface environment
Scope of the tunnelling market
Potential applications
Improved technology

What are some ways you could vary the stimuli for a lecture on the topic of tunnelling? What other approaches could you use to develop the lecture? Can you think of another way to analyze the content? Other concepts?

The *sequencing* of information may follow a time line of events (e.g., events and corresponding dates leading up to the Civil War) or a classification system similar to those used extensively in the sciences to describe the relationships among organisms in a hierarchical system. A simple classification system of trees could be started using the following outlining format:

Trees

I. Kinds
  A. Hardwoods
    1. Oaks
      a. Live Oaks
      b. Water Oaks
      c. Red Oaks
    2. Maples
  B. Softwoods
    1. Pines
      a. Yellow Pines
      b. Southern Pines
    2. Cedars

The above classification system allows the lecturer to plan the lesson around common characteristics or trees. Knowing where you are going in the lesson will maximize the instructional time and provide the students with a greater opportunity to learn.

With younger students, an outline based on concepts to be learned is an appropriate starting point. From the following list of concepts, teachers can then anticipate possible questions, examples, and extensions of the basic concepts.

Farms

1. Definition of *farms*.
2. There are different types of farms.
3. Different kinds of farms provide different kinds of products.
4. Different kinds of farms require different kinds of equipment, work, and people.
5. Farms may be different sizes.
6. In our community, there are dairy farms and fruit/vegetable farms.

Here again, awareness of the learner determines the amount of detail we plug into a basic outline. For the primary-grade student, the concept of different kinds of farms might be planned with an outline as follows:

2. There are different types of farms:
   a. Dairy farms
   b. Fruit/vegetable farms
   c. Poultry farms
   d. Grain farms

However, for an upper elementary-student, the outline may extend to regions of the United States or to individual versus corporation farms. An activity to develop sample outlines around given topics (e.g., our community) is provided in the Samples and Examples section at the end of this chapter.

If your goal is primarily *motivational*, then the planning process should focus on a lesson of high interest to the students. The teacher should incorporate a high level of stimulus variation and enthusiasm. Providing information would be secondary to creating a high level of interest for the general subject area. For example, a high-school English teacher provides a motivating set induction by entering the classroom dressed like the character in a Shakespearean play. The English teacher then presents a soliloquy on teen-age love, using modern-day English for the next five minutes. The students became highly motivated to read about the ancient teen-age love story of Romeo and Juliet.

The elementary teacher can promote motivation for learning about farms by having the fifth-grade students prepare a bulletin board of newspaper and magazine headlines and pictures about the woes of the farmer, federal measures influencing farmers, food price fluctuations, or the route food takes from the farm to the table. A kindergarten teacher may set up a display table of products, such as butter, fruits and vegetables, eggs, cereal, beef, rice, and so on, as a stimulation to learn about the different kinds of farms. With younger students, it is important to precede or follow lectures with experiences. Such combinations involve conscientious planning with much advance preparation for such experiences as field trips, visitors, films, and props (costumes, display items, demonstration equipment, etc.).

SNAPSHOT: *Elementary Classroom*

Mr. Groff instructs the fifth-grade class to get out pencils, a piece of paper, rulers, and math textbooks. "Place all of the items at the corner of your table," he directs the students, "then look at the overhead." On the transparency he had previously written examples of metric and standard measurement. (*Note*: By having the transparency prepared, Mr. Groff saved time and kept the flow of the lesson moving.)

When the students are ready to attend, he reminds them that they have been studying both metric and standard measurement, quickly reviews the equivalents of each, and begins an explanation of the importance of using the appropriate measurement units. "When we choose the appropriate unit of measure, we can accomplish the task efficiently and easily. If we choose an inappropriate unit, we may make errors, or the task may take us a very long time, or we may be unable to carry out the measurement."

Mr. Groff continues, "Let me give you an example of what I mean by an inappropriate unit of measure. Last week I observed first-graders studying measurement. Because they don't understand standard units of measure yet, they were using familiar things as units—their fingers, blocks, their feet, and a crayon. One little girl wanted to measure the length of a wall in the classroom with her finger as a unit of measure. The teacher allowed her to begin measuring so that she and her classmates would learn the idea of appropriate measurement units. Now, if I asked you to measure a block in our neighborhood using your rulers and the unit inch, what would happen?"

Students described the length of time it would take, all the mistakes that would happen, and many potential frustrations. From there, Mr. Groff returned to the list of units on the overhead transparency and asked for appropriate units for measuring the classroom, a building, a book, and so on. He reviewed the standard possibilities for measuring his examples, then reviewed the metric possibilities for measuring his examples. He followed his review with the question, "Who can tell us why it is important to choose the appropriate unit of measure?" He then proceeded to give directions for practice of making appropriate selections from a handout.

Developing motivational strategies for the beginning of a lecture is an important step in focusing the students' attention.

If your goal for the lesson is to encourage *critical and reflective thinking*, the lesson should build on the information, ideas, and concepts developed in previous classes. For example, a class who had been studying genetics in biology was presented a lecture on gene manipulation through selective control of the gene pool. The lecturer developed a scenario for the future of a world in which most major genetic diseases were eliminated. At the conclusion of the 20-minute lecture, the students were asked for their reactions to the ideas presented. The lecture led to a very thought-provoking discussion.

A reflective/critical thinking lecture could include current research and opinions that were not available when the text was written. It could incorporate opposing viewpoints, present critical issues identified by other authors, and identify and present different interpretations and conclusions (McMann, 1979). Nine elements are presented by McMann (1979)* to facilitate higher-level thinking, including:

1. *The lecture should always provide new or supplemental information. Teachers should not abuse the lecture by reciting tedious facts, or chronology, or by restating the obvious material in textbooks.*
2. *Students must be cognizant of the lecture topic and goals, the skills to be learned, and the logical development of the lecture. To achieve this end, a brief outline can be prepared and presented to students.*
3. *Students can be required to analyze the lecture through a developed model similar to the historical model presented [below]. Students' written critiques can also be evaluated by the instructor.*

   Historical Model
   1. *Historical Issue*
   2. *Author and Source*
   3. *Interpretation*
   4. *Supporting Evidence*
   5. *Refuting Evidence*
   6. *Assumptions*
   7. *Logical Consistency*
   8. *Fallacies*
   9. *Questions*
4. *Students should participate by asking questions, clarifying ideas, challenging the evidence, suggesting alternative conclusions and evidence. The lecture is not meant to stifle student response and creativity, and analysis is not meant to be strictly teacher-oriented.*
5. *Questions must be formulated and asked by the instructor during the lecture to emphasize the importance of significant information. Insist that students speculate on questions, clarify values, cite examples, provide arguments, criticize evidence, state assumptions, and cite logical fallacies.*
6. *Facts as facts have an importance secondary to their use as evidence in supporting an interpretation or a point of view. Thus, the students' efforts must be redirected toward the analysis of the facts rather than memorization of the facts.*
7. *Teachers must know their students and the factors which influence their receptivity to a lecture. Such factors might include their academic abilities, physical handicaps, learning disabilities, their interest in social studies (or other subjects) and the specific topic, their understanding of previous material, and the prevalent classroom atmosphere which the students generate.*
8. *Lecture information must not remain in a vacuum. The information must either assist the students in their understanding of the topic or the students must be able to utilize the information in a structured, but creative manner. Conversely, teachers must be creative*

Source: F. McMann, Jr., "In Defense of Lecture," *Social Studies, 70,* pp. 270–274, 1979. Reprinted with permission of the Helen Dwight Reid Educational Foundation. Published by Heldref Publications, 4000 Albemarle St, N.W., Washington, D.C. 20016. Copyright © 1979.

in extending the lecture information to subsequent classroom activities, particularly in the areas of student research.

9. *Teachers must exhibit an enthusiastic attitude toward the lecture as an effective method, its content and the skills demanded. A prophetic sense of boredom and impending doom will surely alienate students and diminish their interest and enthusiasm. (p. 273)*

Again, your awareness of the learner will determine the appropriateness of the lecture strategy for reflective/critical thinking. Recognizing the limits of first-graders' higher-level thinking abilities, the teacher can nevertheless plan for lectures that prompt reflection. A mini-lecture of the typical farmer's day with a transparency and slides of the activities could be followed by questions to promote critical thinking. First-graders could be asked: Is the farmer's life a hard or easy life? Why? Would you like to be a farmer? Why or why not? What's different or alike about your parents' work and the farmer's work?

As demonstrated in our examples, the reflective/critical thinking goal may be achieved if you plan for this type of lecture from the beginning. The foundation could be established with an informational lecture and then build to a reflective/critical thinking presentation. The teacher who moves beyond information to synthesis, analysis, comparison, and evaluation can add a unique dimension to the instructional process. This approach would alleviate, but not eliminate, many of the limitations of the lecture method. If you are unfamiliar with the reflective lecture approach, then begin by focusing several weeks ahead in planning a 15- to 20-minute mini-lecture that would challenge the students' higher-level thinking abilities.

Context

The context refers to the total learning environment (discussed in Chapter 1), which includes three elements: the classroom, the school, and the community. Each of the elements offers opportunities and limitations for the teacher designing a lesson.

Consider the size of the class or group attending the lecture. The use of slide-tape presentations, overhead projector, chalkboard, or other stimuli will depend on the physical layout of the room. Also consider the sound transmission aspects of the room. Will your voice carry to the last student in the classroom? If the area is an open space environment, then the limitations placed on the lecturer are greater than in a four-wall classroom, especially if other instructors are also lecturing.

Since the effectiveness of the lecture depends on the attention of the students, will there be distractions in the room? Will distractions reduce the effectiveness of the lecture by claiming the attention of the students? (For example, having the classroom overlooking the football practice field would be a real distractor in the fall.) Will the students be seated in such a way that you will have the opportunity to have eye contact with each student? Contextual elements may be incorporated into the lesson if the lecturer considers them in the planning process.

Which of the following contextual factors affect this class?

_____ Outside noise levels
_____ Lighting
_____ Types of chairs/desks
_____ Placement of chalkboards
_____ Size of room
_____ Size of class
_____ Time of day
_____ Requirement vs. option
_____ Temperature of the room
_____ Windows
_____ Open arrangement
_____ (Other) _____

Which of the factors checked will influence learning?

Many of the suggestions from Rosenshine (1983) demonstrate the importance of contextual considerations, and many of the following management suggestions will provide adjustments to the context. The Examples and Samples section at the end of this chapter contains four contextual situations that could provide potential opportunities and limitations for teaching.

TEACHER CONTROL

One of the key reasons teachers use lecture as a strategy is the degree of control it provides them over the students. All the attention (or at least most of the attention) is directed toward the teacher. The teacher controls the material, the flow, and the types of questions asked to the students, and monitors the flow of questions from the students. As you will see in the next few pages on the benefits and limitations of the lecture strategy, lecture can be used both to stimulate and stifle learning. If you wish to maximize the use of this strategy, then effective planning and preparation are a must. The organization of ideas and examples must flow from the beginning to the end. The first step, then, is to establish a purpose or goal for your lecture and plan an outline accordingly. Once the sequencing or logical organization has been determined, you should:

1. Identify two or three key concepts to be included in the lecture and support these concepts with examples or illustrations within the lecture.
2. Prepare notes that highlight the key concepts, subconcepts, and points to be made during the presentation.
3. Use analogies, stories, and examples to support your ideas and provide a frame of reference for the students.
4. Close your lecture with a summary of the key points in the presentation by writing these points on the board, using an overhead projector, or having the students summarize them.

Guidelines from Research

When

Lecture should be considered primarily to introduce and explain new concepts, to help incorporate smaller units of information into larger logical structures, to add insight and expand on previously presented concepts, and to review and summarize (Bowman, 1979; Brock, 1977; McMann, 1979). Although its use is typically limited to providing information, this limitation is imposed by the lecturer, not the strategy. Motivational, reflective, and critical thinking lectures are viable elements.

Scope and Pace

Many researchers and teacher educators recommend that a lecture should be limited to three to five concepts (Bowman, 1979; Brock, 1977; Stanton, 1978). At the elementary school level, one concept per lecture would be appropriate. The length of the lecture should be limited to 10- to 15-minute segments interspersed by other strategies (e.g., questioning and discussion) and stimulus variations. It is also important to have a pace that most closely matches the absorption rate of the students (Bowman, 1979). If the teacher talks too slowly, the students will become bored too quickly and they will become frustrated. Audiotaping or videotaping a lesson will assist you in determining the proper pace for a lesson.

Stimulus Variation

There is a consensus among the researchers that stimulus variation is a key element to an effective lecture (Couch, 1973; Kintsch & Bates, 1977; Napell, 1978; Williams & Ware, 1977). Stimulus variation during the lecture includes the following elements:

1. *Humor.* The use of humor to reinforce examples and illustrate concepts in a lecture (Kaplan & Pascoe, 1977) was effective in facilitating long-term retention and comprehension. Other studies have also shown that humor can be an effective means of reinforcing learning (Desberg, Henschal, & Marshall, 1981; Gruner & Freshley, 1979). At the school of education at Tel Aviv University, a course is offered for preservice and in-service teachers in the use of humor in the classroom. Humor, used to reinforce ideas and concepts, can be an effective tool for the lecturer. It should be noted that humor, directed at a student or the class, can interfere with the instructional process by creating a negative climate for learning. Also, sarcasm should never be confused for humor. The students look to the teacher as a role model; sarcasm presents a very negative model for the class.

2. *Cuing.* The lecturer has the advantage of knowing the key ideas and concepts of the presentation. This should be communicated to the students. Key points can be emphasized by:

    a. pausing

    b. verbally highlighting a word or concept by changing voice tone

    c. using gestures (e.g., hand and facial), including physically moving away from the desk to emphasize a point

    d. pointing to the chalkboard.

The instructor needs to communicate to the learner a level of expectation regarding the material presented. The students should be told if they are to *memorize and recall* (e.g., the periodic table of elements or the battles of the Civil War) or *compare and contrast* (e.g., the causes of the French Revolution with the American Civil War). A study conducted by Kintsch and Bates (1977) found that five days after a lecture, verbatim memory was greatly reduced. However, unique elements (e.g., humor, analogies, and anecdotes) were remembered the best when compared to non-unique elements such as general topics or details of the lecture. Cuing the students to the key points of the lecture will facilitate learning.

3. *Pausing*. A very innovative way of stimulating learning during the lecture is provided by Rowe (1976): "If a lecturer pauses at least two times during a lecture for 2 minutes per pause and has students in adjacent seats share notes and comments, more of the content of the lecture will be learned and retained by more students." The sharing by three students will be an effective overlap for the information presented. The process focuses the students on the lecture material and provides the stimulation of on-task student-student interaction.

4. *Media*. The use of slides (especially those taken by the teacher), overhead projector, chalkboard, films, records, video, posters, maps, and computers (with projector screen) are effective means of providing information. This seems particularly true in the age of visual communication. In many cases, materials developed by the instructor have more impact than packaged programs. For example, before a field trip, take slides of the key points to be viewed by the students during the trip. This is important for trips to museums or institutes where the students may become overwhelmed by the amount of information. For example, the use of visual stimuli and computer simulations of molecules had a dramatic impression on the students studying physics.

The media used during the presentation must be heard and seen clearly by all the students in the classroom. Media can provide the linkage between the familiar (concrete) and the unfamiliar (abstract) elements of the lesson. It should be noted that the first law of any technology is that it may not work. Prepare the lesson with this possibility in mind.

5. *Enthusiasm*. According to Brock (1977, p. 4), a "positive relationship exists between the enthusiasm which students perceived that the lecturer exudes and their learning of the course material." The many studies of the Dr. Fox Effect (discussed earlier in this chapter) underscore the impact of a highly expressive presentation on learning as measured by test results (Williams & Ware, 1977, p. 450). It would be difficult to imagine students becoming excited about a topic if the teacher lacked the interest and enthusiasm for the subject. Enthusiasm is not a skill but an attitude that the teacher brings to the class.

As with any instructional element, the use of stimulus variation should be used in moderation. One study (Henson, 1980, p. 117) found that "movement through the class, gesturing and pausing" lowered the effectiveness of lectures to elementary school students. Good judgment in the use of the preceding five elements of stimulus variation will assist you in keeping the interest of the students without distracting them from the focus of the lesson.

Benefits

Every strategy used in the classroom has both benefits and limitations for the teaching-learning process. Three studies, one of which covered 50 years of research, reported by Hillocks (1981), another of which reviewed 91 studies (Henson, 1980), and the third of which encompassed 96 research projects over 40 years (Smith, 1978), found that the lecture approach is no less effective than other teaching methods. Several studies supported the use of lecture "to introduce a unit or build a frame of reference . . . [for] demonstrating and clarifying matters . . . [to] set the atmosphere or focus of students' activities, . . . [and for] introducing and summarizing the major concepts that were presented in a lesson" (Henson, 1980, p. 116).

Some of the benefits of the lecture strategy include the following:

1. The most information may be presented in the shortest period of time.
2. The teacher has a degree of control (pace, content, organization of the material and time) that may not be present with other instructional strategies.
3. It provides an overview of a new concept of unit or learning.
4. It provides the opportunity to sharpen and practice note-taking (psychomotor) and listening skills.
5. The same facts and information are presented to all students, which enables the class and instructor to have a common frame of reference.
6. Facts and information have been preorganized to follow a logical sequence. The sequence may flow from a time line of events or build from ideas to form concepts.

Similarly, the current research on effective instruction supports the use of the lecture strategy. Studies in grades 4 through 8 (Evertson, Emmer, & Brophy, 1980; Good & Grouws, 1979) found that effective mathematics teaching was characterized by twice as much time spent in lecture, demonstration, and discussion than ineffective mathematics teaching. Effective teachers use this additional presentation time to provide redundant explanations, use many examples, provide sufficient instruction so that the students can do the seatwork with minimal difficulty, check for student understanding, and reteach when necessary (Rosenshine, 1983).

Additionally, data from the Beginning Teacher Evaluation Study (BTES) looking at second and fifth grades, reports that students spent about 30 percent of their time in a teacher-directed setting and 70 percent of their time doing seatwork (Fisher, Berliner, Filby, Marliave, Cahen, & Dishaw, 1980). When students were in teacher-led groups, their engagement rate was about 84 percent, whereas during seatwork it was about 70 percent (Rosenshine, 1981). Other studies (Soar, 1973; Stallings & Kaskowitz, 1974; Stallings, Needels, & Stayrook, 1979) found that direct instruction or supervision by a teacher is related to higher engagement of students than students working independently. Gump's (1982) third-grade study found that engagement was higher in whole-class presentations, tests, and teacher presentations (approximately 80 percent) than in supervised study and independent seatwork (approximately 75 percent). These kind of data should cause elementary teachers or those preparing to teach to consider how their teaching time is to be spent. Specifically, their planning may begin to reflect a valuing of the lecture strategy.

Limitations

Research shows that students who are highly motivated and are effective in note taking benefit the most from the lecture approach (Henson, 1980). A study by Frank (1984) indicates that students who are able to synthesize the information presented in a lecture into an outline are at a distinct advantage over students who write down almost every word the teacher says. This note-taking ability translates into high test scores for some students. However, in a study conducted by Maddox and Hoole (1975) with college students, only 52 percent of the key ideas presented in a lecture were evident in the students' notes. Although lower-achieving students benefit the least from the lecture method, they seem to prefer this method over other strategies that require a more active role in the learning process (Couch, 1973).

College students who were preparing to become secondary teachers were asked by their instructor (Birkel, 1973) to express their views about the lecture method. The negative views clearly outnumbered the positive. The students felt the following about lecture method: (1) boring and uninteresting; (2) lacked teacher-student or student-student interaction; (3) poorly organized and presented; (4) content was irrelevant, not current and was accessible elsewhere; (5) focused mainly on the lowest level of cognition; and (6) ignored individual differences.

Although the list was developed in 1973, few teachers or students would argue that this is not an accurate reflection of lecture in classrooms of the 1990s. Often the key of *variability* is missing from the lecture method and this encourages the student to be a passive notetaker, detached from the learning process. Students do not assume a major share of the responsibility for their own learning. Many faculty complain that their students lack "motivation, initiative, responsibility, vision, interest beyond the assigned task, and imagination, but many [faculty] are only dimly aware of the fact that they, with their methods and attitudes, may be creating and perpetuating this condition" (Osterman, 1982).

Some of the limitations of the lecture method cited by educators (Annis, 1981; Frank, 1984; Gage & Berliner, 1975; Henson, 1980; Hoff, 1980; Kintsch & Bates, 1977; Napell, 1978; Oddi, 1983; Osterman, 1982) include the following:

1. The lecture method can be boring if stimulus variations (use of humor, voice modulation, and visuals) are not utilized during the presentation.
2. Student participation is limited to approximately 12 percent of the total interaction in the classroom, thus reducing the opportunity for feedback.

3. The lecture method emphasizes the lower-level cognitive skills of memorization and recall rather than synthesis and evaluation.
4. The lecture approach places students with poor note-taking skills at a disadvantage in the classroom.
5. Students in the lecture class are more passive and take a less active role in their own learning.
6. Due to a lack of interaction, the teacher has difficulty immediately determining the amount of student learning.
7. The lecture method rarely provides the opportunity for the inclusion of the affective learning domain (attitudes, feelings and values) or the psycho-motor domain.
8. Because the lecture approach is directed to large groups of students, individual needs are rarely identified or met.

The limitations of lecture seem to reflect an imbalance between teacher and student interaction. In most lecture situations the teacher is active and the students are passive. This so-called limitation of lecture is more a function of a narrow teacher repertoire. Lecture as a strategy has greater potential than its current use in most middle and high-school classrooms. Expanding the operational definition of lecture to include several variations will move lecture along the continuum from being a teacher-dominated strategy to having greater student involvement.

The two research vignettes that soon follow provide for additional data on the lecture strategy.

Variations

One way of compensating for some of the lecture limitations is to develop an understanding and ability in implementing variations of the strategy. If you were to observe in classrooms of many different grade levels and instruction of varying curriculum content, you would note the available variations. As you review this list of lecture variations, try to visualize your experiences with each:

1. *Pure lecture.* The teacher talks to a group of students for up to an hour or more. They passively listen without interrupting or asking questions. Many students will be taking notes of the lecture.
2. *Chalk talk lecture.* This approach is more common than the pure lecture. The teacher uses the chalkboard to illustrate points or draw conclusions. By writing on the board, the teacher may limit visual contact with the students.
3. *Guided note-taking lecture.* The teacher may provide detailed notes or outlines for students for the day's presentation. In some cases, the teacher will have the students complete worksheets during different parts of the lecture (Broadwell, 1980, p. 13).
4. *Audiovisual lecture.* The teacher uses a range of media to facilitate the lecture. The overhead projector, slide projector, 16mm projector, or video cassette recorder are utilized to provide stimulus variation.

5. *Combination lecture*. The teacher uses questioning and discussion, either during the lecture or at its conclusion, to provide feedback and correction if the students do not understand a particular part of the presentation.

6. *Mini-lecture*. The teacher limits the lecture to 15 minutes and focuses on introducing a new unit, summarizing major concepts, or setting the focus for major activities (Henson, 1980). During the remainder of the instructional time, the teacher incorporates other instructional strategies. The mini-lecture is most frequently used at the upper-elementary and middle-school levels.

Lecture with Other Strategies

The blending of lecture with other universal teaching strategies will add to the variability and effectiveness of the presentation. Combining lecture with discussion and questioning, for example, will increase the degree of students' interaction and involvement (Hillocks, 1981; Rowe, 1976; Yu & Berliner, 1981). Combining lecture with demonstration could reinforce the visual elements of the lesson.

As we move further away from the teacher-centered strategies, the blending process becomes more difficult. Each strategy has its own conditions for effectiveness. The lecture can be conducted with a group of 20 or 200, yet the use of discovery would be limited beyond the range of 30 to 40 students. The learner, context, and content must be considered when planning for one strategy or a combination of strategies. As you master the various strategies presented in this chapter, you will begin to realize the potential of a broad repertoire of instructional options for different teaching situations.

Elementary Research Vignette

INTRODUCTION

The Learning Research and Development Center (LRDC) of the University of Pittsburgh has been closely studying the arithmetic teaching of seven effective elementary school teachers. These teachers have taught from 12 to 25 years and were identified through the combined data sources of standardized tests scores over a five-year period, student growth scores, principal and supervisor nominations, and classroom observations.

STUDY DESIGN

The effective teachers were observed, interviewed, videotaped, and consulted for a period of one to three years.

RESULTS

The teaching of these effective teachers in the content area of mathematics is characterized by clear and accurate presentations that are rich in example and demonstration. They have developed routines that set the stage for the presentation structure and they explain new information well. Gaea Leinhardt (1986) describes content-based agendas (composed of content organizations as a sequence of strategies planned for presentation) of these teachers. Through the interview process, researchers were able to identify these agendas as highly coded note lists, or the steps that teachers intended to follow and possible changes or extras, depending on situations. Leinhardt (1986) includes the agenda of a second-grade math teacher in her description of teaching expertise. Her teacher related:

> First of all I'm going to drill the children on how to add ten to one place numbers . . . then some problems on the board . . . two place subtraction . . . some foolers [problems that surprise their thinking] . . . to warm up . . . then I'm going to show them using stick subtraction without regrouping just to get them used to using sticks again. Then I plan to go to the feltboard . . . a little bit more abstract. Then if we have time, I'm going to show them with the real problem . . . straight to the abstract. (pp. 30–31)

For this expert teacher and others in the study, the presentation of new material includes identifying the goals, building representations of concepts or procedures, demonstrating features or steps, and proving the legitimacy or consistency of the new information or process—the content-based agendas.

CONCLUSIONS AND IMPLICATIONS FOR PRACTICE

The kind of information about effective presentations that is emerging from the University of Pittsburgh's LRDC observations of expert teachers is congruent with the guidelines on lecturing provided by Rosenshine (1983) and elements of lecturing to facilitate higher-level thinking provided by McMann (1979).

TEACHING NOTE TAKING

An aspect of both context and learner is a knowledge of procedures or routines. Research on classroom management (Emmer, Evertson, & Anderson, 1980) advocates the teaching of procedures clearly and completely at the beginning of the school year.

An important procedure that is usually ignored is teaching students how to listen to a lecture or how to take notes during a lecture (see Figure 7.2; Hemler, 1990). A major reason for the lack of success with lectures may be the students' lack of preparation in how to respond to and learn from the lecture strategy. In a classroom management course at the University of Utah, which is characterized by frequent

FIGURE 7.2   *Guided Note Taking for Earth Science*

Name _____

Date _____

Class _____

The Moon
A. Description
    1. Basic description
    2. Gravity
    3. Structure of the moon
       a.
       b.
       c.
    4. Instruments left on the moon

B. Surface Features of the Moon
    1. Moon after it formed (describe)
    2. Craters — (define)
       a. Rays —
       b. Flat bottoms —
       c. Mare—
C. Origin of the Moon — 3 basic theories
    1. Daughter Theory —
    2. Capture Theory —
    3. Sister Theory —

simulations and roleplaying situations, students are taught how to listen to a lecture and practice the strategies. Many university students express the lack of such information in their entire school life, and yet acknowledge the importance of something that sounds so simple.

Teaching is primarily a decision-making process (Shavelson, 1976). Your decisions to use a lecture and to plan and present a lecture involve critical considerations about the learner, the content, and the context. Your decision making is also based on your knowledge about the lecture strategy. You need to be well informed about both the benefits and the limitations of lecturing, variations of the strategy, and research findings on characteristics of its use. What may have seemed to be a simple teaching strategy at the beginning of this chapter should now be appearing as a complex element of teaching, which requires a knowledge base, comprehensive planning, and high levels of awareness. It is a strategy worth the effort, as illustrated in the benefits section of this chapter.

Finally, research has provided numerous additional considerations for teaching with lectures. Guidelines for appropriate times, scope and pace, stimulus variation, and note taking are available for directing your lecture behavior. The research findings and conclusions have been summarized and supplemented with suggestions in this final section of the chapter.

Secondary Research Vignette

INTRODUCTION

The abundance of research regrding the effectiveness of student notes versus outlines versus complete lecture transcripts is beginning to provide teachers with some clear directions on the issue of note taking during the lecture.

STUDY DESIGN

A study conducted by Annis (1981) looked at three approaches to student note taking. The college students in the study were asked for their preference of lecture notes. One group received a complete four-page, single-spaced typed set of lecture notes. The formatting of the complete notes did not provide space for the students to add their own comments. They were also instructed not to write any of their own notes or write on the pages given them.

A second group of students were provided with a partial set of notes with headings and key points distributed over the four pages. The four pages of notes were formatted to provide the opportunity for students to add their own comments on the pages.

A third group of students were given four blank pieces of paper. They were told to use these sheets of paper for their notes of the lecture.

RESULTS

During the students' regular midterm examination two weeks after the lecture, students in the three groups answered both multiple-choice and essay questions. The students who used partial notes and personal notes scored significantly better ($p < .01$) than the group that was provided with a complete transcript of the lecture (p. 181).

The higher test scores of the two groups highlights the importance for the students to translate information provided in the lecture into a meaningful set of ideas. This encoding and decoding process is supported by other studies (Frank, 1984; Petrich & Montague, 1981) conducted on the effectiveness of note taking. Although this study was conducted at the college level, the implications for secondary teachers are important.

CONCLUSIONS AND IMPLICATIONS FOR PRACTICE

Frank (1984) found in an analysis of field-dependent and field-independent students that the former "take wordier and less efficient notes." It seems that field-dependent students approach note taking "as a task of trying to write down as much information as possible" (p. 676). Frank makes the following observations:

The results of the present study provide evidence that the typical classroom procedures in which the teacher lectures and students take notes may favor the performance of field-independent students over field-dependent students. Thus, teachers may want to consider providing students with external organizational aids while lecturing, perhaps through outlines on either an overhead projector, a blackboard, or a handout. By clearly presenting the structure of a lecture, the teacher may be able to help the performance of the field-dependent student without hindering the performance of the field-independent student. An alternative to providing field-dependent students with external organizational aids would be to provide them with explicit training designed to develop note-taking skills (e.g., recognizing superordinate and subordinate relationships, abstracting important ideas, and paraphrasing). The findings of the present study suggest that some combination of teacher-supplied organizational structure and actual training in note-taking skills may help to maximize the learning and cognitive performance of field-dependent individuals. (p. 676)

You are encouraged to try out this approach to note taking in your own instructional setting and assess its effectiveness. You can determine which students need assistance in note taking by presenting a lecture and collecting and analyzing the students' notes for that lecture. The context and learner may cause some variation of the use of note taking, but research provides some clear directions for maximizing its use.

SUMMARY

- Lecture has the longest historical use as a teaching strategy.
- Commission reports of the 80s and 90s are highly critical of teacher-dominated lecture methods.
- Students learn in a variety of ways. Being able to tap several learner strengths through a learner profile or other source will expand the teacher's repertoire.
- Enthusiasm is a starting point for teaching rather than an end point. Depth of content by the teacher is the foundation for teaching. However, enthusiasm draws students into the subject when they see the teacher as a role model of interest.
- The nine steps Rosenshine (1983) highlights for effective lecture improves the opportunity for learning by students of any age.
- The three instructional goals of lecture—information, motivation, and reflective/critical thinking—should be blended to enhance the lecture strategy.
- Contextual variables place constraints and opportunities on any teaching strategy. Because of the verbal (and at times) the visual nature of lecture, physical surroundings play an important role in the success of this strategy.
- Humor, cuing, pausing, media, and enthusiasm play important roles in varying the stimuli for lecture.
- Research indicates that lecture is no less effective than other strategies (Hillocks, 1981; Henson, 1980; Smith, 1978). However, from the teacher and students' perspective, the strategy has advantages and limitations.
- Variations on the lecture theme can encompass pure lecture, chalk talk lecture, audiovisual lecture, combination lecture, and mini-lectures.
- Lecture is neither good or bad; it is the way we use it that determines if students will learn from this strategy.

The key to effective teaching is the ability to match the instructional approach with the learner, content, and context. If the lecture method meets these conditions, then the teacher should consider the benefits and limitations in the planning and implementation of this strategy. Chapter 8 presents questioning and discussion strategies that are most frequently combined with lecture.

The lecture strategy can move the learner from being a passive observer to an active participant. Your ability to use an expanded repertoire of approaches within the lecture strategy and combining this strategy with other strategies will improve your teaching options and student opportunities to learn.

REFERENCES

Annis, L. F. (1981). Effect of preference for assigned lecture notes on student achievement. *The Journal of Educational Research, 74,* 179–181.

Birkel, L. F. (1973, July). The lecture method: Villain or victim? *Peabody Journal of Education,* 298–301.

Bowman, J. S. (1979). The lecture-discussion format revisited. *Improving College and University Teaching, 27,* 25–27.

Broadwell, M. M. (1980). *The lecture method of instruction.* Englewood Cliffs, NJ: Educational Technology Publications.

Brock, S. C. (1977). *Aspects of lecturing: A practical guide of IDEA users.* Manhattan, KS: Kansas State University. (ERIC Document Reproduction Service No. ED 171 218).

Couch, R. (1973). Is lecturing really necessary? *The American Biology Teacher, 10,* 391–395.

Desberg, P, Henschal, D., & Marshall, C. (1981). *The effect of humor on retention of lecture material.* Lubbock, TX: Texas Technical University. (ERIC Document Reproduction Service No. ED 223 118).

Emmer, E., Evertson, C., & Anderson, L. M. (1980). Effective classroom management. *Elementary School Journal, 80,* 219–231.

Encyclopaedia Britannica. (1981). *Tunnelling and underground excacation* (Vol. 18), p. 750.

Evertson, C., Emmer, E., & Brophy, J. E. (1980). Predictors of effective teaching in junior high mathematics classrooms. *Journal of Research in Mathematics Education, 11,* 167–178.

Fisher, C., Berliner, D., Filby, N., Marliave, R., Cahen, L., & Dishaw, M. (1980). Teaching behaviors, academic learning time and student achievement: An overview. In C. Denham & A. Lieberman (Eds.), *Time to learn.* Washington, DC: Department of Education, National Institute of Education.

Frank, B. M. (1984). Effect of field independence-dependence and study technique on learning from a lecture. *American Educational Research Journal, 21*(3), 669–678.

Gage, N. L., & Berliner, D. C. (1975). *Educational psychology.* Chicago: Rand McNally College Publishing.

Good, T. L., & Grouws, D. (1979). The Missouri Mathematics Effectiveness Project: An experimental study in fourth-grade classrooms. *Journal of Educational Psychology, 71,* 355–362.

Gruner, C. R., & Freshley, D. (1979, November). *Retention of lecture items reinforced with humorous and non-humorous exemplary material.* Paper presented at the annual meeting of the Speech communication Association, New York. (ERIC Document Reproduction Service No. Ed 193 725).

Gump, P. V. (1982). School settings and their keeping. In D. Duke (Ed.), *Helping teachers manage classrooms.* Alexandria, VA: Association for Supervision and Curriculum Development.

Heller, S. (1984). For top professor, teaching is a matter of timing. *Chronicle of Higher Education, 29*(2), 23, 28.

Hemler, D. (1990). *Guided note-taking outline.* Unpublished curriculum materials. Bruceton High School, Bruceton, WV.

Henson, K. T. (1980). What's the use of lecturing? *The High School Journal, 64,* 115–119.

Hillocks, G., Jr. (1981). The response of college freshmen to three modes of instruction. *American Journal of Education, 89,* 373–395.

Hoff, D. B. (1980). Participatory lecture. *Journal of College Science Teaching, 9,* 217–220.

Kaplan, R. M., & Pascoe, G. C. (1977). Humorous lecture and humorous examples: Some effects upon comprehension and retention. *Journal of Educational Psychology, 69*(1), 62–65.

Kintsch, W., & Bates, E. (1977). Recognition memory for statements from a classroom lecture. *Journal of Experimental Psychology: Human Learning and Memory, 3,* 150–159.

Leinhardt, G. (1986). Expertise in mathematics teaching. *Educational Leadership, 43*(7), 28–33.

Maddox, H., & Hoole, E. (1975). Performance decrement in the lecture. *Educational Review, 28,* 17–30.

McMann, F., Jr. (1979). In defense of lecture. *Social Studies, 70,* 270–274.

Mullis, I., Owen, E. H., & Phillips, G. (1990). *America's challenge: Accelerating academic achievement, a summary of findings from 20 years of NAEP.* Princeton, NJ: The National Assessment of Educational Progress, Educational Testing Service.

Napell, S. M. (1978). Updating the lecture. *Journal of Teacher Education, 29*(5), 53–56.

Oddi, L. (1983). Lecture: An update on research. *Adult Education Quarterly, 33,* 222–229.

Osterman, D. N. (1982). Classroom lecture management: Increasing individual involvement and learning in the lecture style. *Journal of College Science Teaching, 12,* 22–23.

Rosenshine, B. (1981). How time is spent in elementary classrooms. *Journal of Classroom Interaction, 17*(1), 16–25.

Rosenshine, B. (1983). Teaching functions in instructional programs. *The Elementary School Journal, 83*(4), 335–351.

Rowe, M. B. (1976). The pausing principle— Two invitations to inquiry. *Journal of College Science Teaching, 5*, 258–260.

Shavelson, R. (1976). Teachers' decision-making. In N. L. Gage (Ed.), *The psychology of teaching methods. Seventy-fifth yearbook of the National Society for the Study of Education. Part I.* Chicago: University of Chicago Press.

Slavin, R. E. (1987). Ability grouping and student achievement in elementary schools: A best evidence synthesis. *Review of Educational Research, 57*(3), 293–336.

Slavin, R. E. (1988). Synthesis of research on grouping in elementary and secondary schools. *Educational Leadership, 46*(1), 67–77.

Soar, R. (1973). *Follow-through classroom process measurement and pupil growth.* 1970–71. Final Report. Gainesville, FL: College of Education, University of Florida.

Smith, I. K. (1978). Teaching with discussion: A review. *Educational Technology, 28*(11), 40–45.

Stallings, J., & Kaskowitz, J. (1974). *Follow-through classroom observation evaluation.* 1972–73. SRI Project URU-7370. Menlo Park, CA: Stanford Research Institute.

Stallings, J., Needels, M., & Stayrook, N. (1979). *How to change the process of teaching basic reading skills in secondary schools.* Menlo Park, CA: Stanford Research Institute International.

Stanton, H. E. (1978). Small group teaching in the lecture situation. *Improving College and University Teaching, 26*, 69–70.

Thatcher, V. S. (Ed.). (1972). Definition of lecture. *The New Webster Encyclopedia Dictionary of the English Language*, p. 485.

Williams, R. G., & Ware, J. E., Jr. (1977). An extended visit with Dr. Fox: Validity of student satisfaction with instruction ratings after repeated exposures to a lecturer. *American Educational Research Journal, 14*(4), 449–457.

Wittrock, M. C. (Ed.). (1986). *Handbook of research teaching* (3rd ed.). New York: Macmillan.

Yu, H. K., & Berliner, D. C. (1981). *Encoding and retrieval of information from lecture.* Tucson, AZ: The University of Arizona. (ERIC Document Reproduction Service No. ED 206 738).

SAMPLES AND EXAMPLES

There are three Samples and Examples in this section. The first two ask you to think about different content areas and grade levels and to develop an outline for a lesson. The final activity gives you four different situations and asks you to discuss the opportunities and limitations within the framework of a lesson.

- Actvities #1 and #2 develop outlines for different topics and grade levels.
- Activity #3 presents four situations for you to consider in developing your lessons.

OUTLINING

The following activities ask you to select one or two topic areas and develop an outline for a specific grade or content area.

Activity #1

Work in a small class group and develop an appropriate outline for content for the following topics and learners:

1. Our Community	5-year-olds (kindergarten)
2. Metrics	7-year-olds (second grade)
3. Solar System	10-year-olds (fifth grade)
4. Art Appreciation for the Renaissance Period	12-year-olds (seventh grade)
5. Commodities	14-year-olds (ninth grade)
6. Chinese Cuisine	Adults

Activity #2

Complete the following activity with a class member either during or after class, depending on your professor's instructions.

Return to the content outlines developed in Activity #1, select one outline and brainstorm a list of creative strategies to motivate the intended students to want to focus on the content. Do not limit your ideas—be as creative as possible.

Activity #3

Consider the following scenarios and describe both the opportunity(s) and limitation(s) for your teaching that come from these contexts:

1. You are a middle-school social studies teacher in a small, suburban, blue-collar community. The copper mine located at the edge of the school district has shut down 50 percent of its operations and laid off 180 employees who are parents of your students.

2. The elementary school in which you teach second grade is preparing for a school fair to raise money for computers. The entire school is buzzing with the excitement of the preparations, decorations, and parent involvement.

3. Last night, two students in your high-school senior English class were critically injured in an auto accident after leaving a party where drugs and alcohol were used.

4. You teach fifth grade in an upper-class suburban neighborhood. Most of your students have traveled to other countries; have their own computers; study music, art, and athletics in expensive after-school facilities; and are generally very bright.

Discuss the opportunity(s) and limitation(s) with your peers in class of utilizing the above situations as part of a lesson plan.

Questioning and Discussion: Creating a Dialogue

CHAPTER OUTCOMES

At the conclusion of the chapter you will be able to:

1. Describe the advantages and disadvantages of questioning.
2. Identify and ask a variety of questions.
3. Develop several approaches to asking questions and using discussion in the classroom.
4. Improve wait time for allowing students to respond.

KEY TERMS
AND CONCEPTS

Check for Understanding
Go Around System
Higher-Level Questions
Convergent and Divergent Questions
Values Clarification
Correcting Student Responses
Controlling Questions
Management Focus
Content and Context
Wait Time I & II
Teacher Moves
Discussion

Good Questions are Locks Which Generate Their Own Keys
Maroski, 1987

INTRODUCTION

On the surface, all questions may seem alike. However, the following Snapshot portrays a few elements in the broad spectrum of questions and responses during five minutes in a world history class.

SNAPSHOT

(Teacher) Class, today we are going to discuss the events leading up to World War II in Europe. John, what are you doing? **(J)** I was trying to find a piece of paper. **(M)** Mr. Johnson, may I be excused? **(T)** Why do you need to be excused at the beginning of the period? **(M)** I forgot my book in my locker. **(T)** Share a book for today.

(T) Bill, tell us one event that led to the start of World War II? **(B)** I don't know. **(T)** If I say *economy*, does that bring to mind any conclusions? **(B)** Yes, there was a great depression in Europe. **(T)** Good, can someone add to Bill's point? Sarah? **(S)** The collapse of the Wheinmar Republic in Germany, a worldwide economic depression, and the reparations and humiliation Germany faced after its defeat in World War I were the seeds for another war. **(T)** Excellent answer, Sarah. Jose, can you add to Sarah's answer? **(J)** Germany was ripe for a dictator who offered Germans a better life, the conquest of Europe, and revenge for their loss during the first World War. **(T)** Very good assessment. **(T to the class)** The Germans had a very advanced culture, including art, music, and literature. Why would they start a destructive war as a distraction from their country's economic problems?

All questions are not alike. This chapter will explore the differences in questions and questioning and will discuss the advantages and limitations of this technique. Additionally, rules for effective discussions will be presented and ways in which you can involve all students will be examined.

Before beginning, the following information will be of interest to you.

Did You Know?

- The two most common verbal interactions in the classroom between teachers and students are questioning and discussion.
- Questioning by far is the most dominate teaching strategy after lecture in upper elementary and secondary classrooms (Gall, 1984).
- At the junior, middle, and senior high school level, the teacher talks 70 to 75 percent of the time and students talk about 25 to 30 percent of the time.

- Within student talk, recitations or responses to teacher questions form the majority of the interaction in the classroom.
- The types of questions teachers ask can make a significant difference in student achievement. A review of the research on teacher questioning by Redfield and Rousseau (1981) indicates that higher levels of teacher questioning produce greater student gains on standardized tests. For example, if we compared two students on the same standardized achievement test, the student in the class with lower-level (recall type) questioning would score at the 50th percentile, whereas the student in the class where the teacher asked high-level (synthesis and analysis type) questions would score at the 77th percentile (Berliner, 1987).
- In a study of teacher questions in England of 230 lessons by 36 teachers in five high schools, Kerry (1987) and his colleagues found the following:
  a. Teachers asked 43.7 questions per hour of observed teaching time.
  b. During the professional lifetime of a teacher, nearly one and one half million questions will be asked of students.
  c. Only 3.6 percent of all questions were coded as being high order.
  d. Language teachers in the study asked the most questions, with 76.5 questions per hour.
  e. Geography, history, and religion instructors asked the least questions, with 21 to 24 each hour.
  f. Teachers establish questioning patterns, with the number and types of teacher questions being similar across lessons. (p. 33)

Have You Thought About?

The process of teacher questions and students responses is unique to the classroom. Only in school do those who know the answers—the teachers—ask questions of those who may not know the answers—the students. You can imagine driving up to a gas station and asking the attendant, "I know where 5th and Main Street is, do you?" In everyday life we ask questions to complete missing information and increase our understanding of a situation. Young children (especially 2 to 5 years old) ask what seems to be an endless stream of questions. Children ask questions to provide a context or framework for what is occurring. The parents' acceptance or rejection of a child's questions begins to shape both self-concept and early learning. This becomes evident when children are read stories by their parents and the child feels free to ask numerous questions about the plot, characters, pictures, or for clarity.

Studies of preschoolers document the spontaneity of childrens' questions of their parents when being read stories. In one case study, two children asked 810 questions of their parents while being read stories over a total of 75 hours (Yaden, Smolkin, & Conlon, 1988). The spontaneity of children's questions are also evident in daily situations. The first time a child goes with a parent to the gas station, questions and answers may go like this:

CHILD: What is that thing? (pointing to the gas door opening in the car)

PARENT: It is an opening so I can add gas to the car.

CHILD: What is gas?

PARENT: Gas is the food for the car. It gives it the power to go just like food gives you the power to go.

CHILD: Where does gas come from?

PARENT: From oil in the ground. The oil is made into gasoline.

CHILD: Do we drink gas?

PARENT: No. Gas is only for cars. It would make people very sick. It is a poison for people.

CHILD: Why do you give money to the man?

PARENT: Many people work hard to make the gas for the car and we need to pay them for their time and effort.

The young child is asking questions to provide meaning for what is occurring and to create a frame of reference for future visits to the gas station.

Why Ask Questions?

In the classroom, teachers ask questions for a variety of reasons. The most common include:

1. Checking for student understanding of instruction
2. Evaluating the effectiveness of the lesson
3. Increasing higher-level thinking

In addition to these three primary reasons, teachers also ask questions to control student behavior, manage the pace and direction of the lesson, create a bridge between activities, and increase student participation.

Checking for Student Understanding

A common reason teachers give for asking questions during instruction is to check if students comprehend the information being presented. Questioning allows the teacher to respond immediately to the levels of student comprehension and modify instruction through different examples or instructional strategies. A typical pattern found in many classrooms includes some form of information giving (e.g., lecture, presentation, film, demonstration, etc.) and questioning of the students after the instructional presentation. Questioning may also occur after group activities to determine if the group is on track and using their time effectively. Rosenshine and Stevens (1986) suggest seven steps for checking student understanding. Next to each of the steps is a brief commentary of how each of the steps could be implemented in the classroom.

1. Prepare a large number of oral questions beforehand.
    COMMENTARY: *In the upper-elementary, middle, or secondary classroom,*

writing the questions on a 4 × 6 index card will be useful. This is important in developing a greater variety of questions and in building a bank of higher-order questions.

2. Ask many brief questions on main points, on supplementary points, and on the process being taught.

   COMMENTARY: *Using questions that require short answers are appropriate for lessons where basic skills or facts are the objective. For example, knowing that Pearl Harbor was bombed on December 7, 1942, has tripped up many a student, including at least one presidential candidate (George Bush during his 1988 presidential campaign).*

3. Call on students whose hands aren't raised in addition to those who volunteer.

   COMMENTARY: *It is estimated that 80 percent of the questions in the classroom are answered by 20 percent of the students. As a teacher, it is natural to call on students who have their hands raised and will usually provide the correct answer. Questioning provides intellectual stimulation and all students need this interaction with the teacher. One technique for including all students in question/answer sessions is the Go Around System, which is discussed in detail in the Snapshot that follows.*

4. Ask the students to summarize the rule or process in their own words.

   COMMENTARY: *Students should explain how they arrived at their answer. A wrong answer may not be as important as the steps the students took to arrive at the answer. Students who have poor learning strategies learn from students who have developed good strategies for solving problems.*

5. Have all the students write the answers (on paper or chalkboard) while the teacher circulates.

   COMMENTARY: *The use of small hand-held chalkboards will assist many elementary and middle-school students in writing and computation skills. If the teacher asks a question and the students hold up their boards, only the teacher will see their answers, giving students with incorrect answers some privacy. The chalkboards provide a quick check for the teacher and a mental note can be made for those students who are having difficulty. One-to-one or small group instruction could occur later in the period to provide students further assistance. If a majority of the class is having difficulty, the teacher could stop and reteach the concept or give additional examples.*

6. Have all students write the answers and check them with a neighbor (frequently with older students).

   COMMENTARY: *If the teacher provides an answer sheet or writes the answers on the board, the students could check each other's work. It is not necessary to have an older student do this. Students working in pairs with mixed abilities will meet the need.*

7. At the end of a lecture or discussion (especially with older students) write the main points on the board and have the class meet in groups and summarize the main points to each other (Rosenshine & Stevens, 1986, p. 384).

COMMENTARY: *Groups of two or four could meet at the end of the lesson or class for a few minutes to discuss what they have learned. The teacher should present two or three questions on the board, overhead projector, or a handout for the students to discuss. If there is adequate time, one student from each group could orally give his or her answers to the questions or written responses could be given to the teacher if time is limited.*

SNAPSHOT: Go Around System

We have assisted teachers in utilizing a questioning technique called the *Go Around System* (Freiberg, 1987). The Go Around System has been used in elementary, middle, and high schools in West Virginia, Texas, California, and Missouri. It is a strategy for providing question equity through a fairer distribution of questions. The teacher goes around the room in order and says to each student, "Tell me one idea you learned from yesterday or from today's class without repeating another student's answer."

A student who can't give a response when it's his or her turn can *pass*. Students who pass must raise their hands and give a response before the activity is complete. The teacher recognizes a student who has passed after a peer has finished speaking. The teacher will go back to those students who haven't raised their hand to respond by the end of the activity, which takes 3 to 5 minutes.

The students call this the *fair system* because they all need to respond and have the option to pass if another student repeated their response or they forgot. Students in classes where this procedure is used say it takes the pressure of responding off and places the emphasis on learning. Students who finish responding are actively listening to be sure their response is not repeated by another student.

Teachers who have used the Go Around System have shared some humorous stories. One high-school history teacher in West Virginia told of a student in his class who passed when asked a question. The teacher, however, was *not* using the technique in his classroom. The student explained that he was new to the school and his other teacher allowed students to pass if they didn't know the answer and could raise their hands later with a response. After some deliberation the teacher tried the technique in his class with great success.

A seventh-grade mathematics teacher used the Go Around System with dramatic results. During the first week of use, almost all the students passed. The students were testing the teacher to see if she really meant it. After a week, however, the number of students passing diminished. The teacher was pleased she stayed with the system long enough for it to work.

Questioning techniques like the Go Around System help equalize the opportunity for asking and answering questions. There may be a tendency on our part to ask boys more questions than girls (see Fennema & Peterson, 1987)

> or ask the right side of the room more questions than the left. Having a system to distribute questions fairly will create a healthier climate for learning.

The Go Around System provides a tool for providing greater variability and equity in questioning. Combine this with other procedures (e.g., volunteers, choral responses, calling on students randomly rather than in order) for questioning students in the classroom.

Evaluating Lesson Effectiveness

Questioning enables the teacher to judge the effectiveness of instruction. Many teachers can see confusion in the eyes of the students, but need a better tool for determining student comprehension than student nonverbal clues. Two studies on teacher understanding of student clues for comprehending the lesson conclude that, even after training, teachers are not a good judge of what the students are thinking or understanding during the lesson (Berliner, 1987).

Verbal questioning assists in judging the depth of student comprehension during the lesson. The complexity of your questions determines the ability to measure the level of student understanding. Factual or recall questions will elicit factual responses. The teacher may be willing to limit lesson effectiveness to lower-level factual information but students will not be able to apply, analyze, synthesize, or evaluate information without the opportunity to practice these skills in the classroom. Asking more complex and demanding questions may not always elicit more complex student responses but, given enough practice, students will begin to respond to teacher questions at increasing higher levels.

TYPES OF QUESTIONS

There is a range of questions that are asked in classrooms, including higher level (analytical), lower level (factual), convergent (one answer), divergent (several possible answers), valuing (clarifying student thoughts), and controlling (directing student comments). Each type of question has an important role in stimulating thinking. The literature is very clear, however. In most classrooms teachers ask higher-level questions only 10 to 20 percent of the time (Dillon, 1988; Gall, 1984; Pate & Bremer, 1967). Few questions are in the higher levels, requiring students to synthesize facts, ideas, and concepts for comparison and analysis. Most classroom questions only require a student to recall simple facts. The mental processing needed to respond to a perplexing question in which a single factual answer is not available requires a student to:

- Analyze the question.
- Search through his or her memory (similar to looking in a file cabinet) to find facts relevant to the question.
- Synthesize the facts and reach a conclusion.
- Respond to the question in less than 2 seconds.

Allowing students to experience a range of questions will build their cognitive ability to respond to a more complex world in which simple facts can be recalled from computers, but analysis, synthesis, and evaluation must originate from the individual.

Asking higher-level questions broadens the base of learning and better prepares students for an information society. Asking higher-level questions has numerous stumbling blocks, including the following:

Hurdles to Higher-Level Questions
- The curriculum is driven by textbooks, which until recently emphasized factual information. Teacher editions are just beginning to include higher-level questions.
- Most questioning is spontaneous. It is easier to ask factual questions in the fast-paced dynamics of the classroom.
- Higher-level questions that are clear to the students are more difficult to construct and require greater effort and time on the part of the teacher. Poorly constructed higher-level questions may confuse the students and result in the teacher spending additional time explaining.
- Teachers have rarely experienced higher-level questions in their own learning and have few positive models upon which to draw.
- Higher-level questions require mastery of the content area. In the elementary classroom where the teacher may have 13 different content preparations, achieving mastery in all areas may require years of experience. At the secondary level, it is estimated by the National Educational Association that 20 percent of secondary teachers are teaching in areas they were not originally certified. By the time mastery has been achieved, the pattern of asking lower-level questions may already be ingrained.
- Higher-level questions elicit less predictable responses from the students, requiring more time for student answers and somewhat greater uncertainty for the teacher.
- Lower-level questions do assist students in basic skills learning. It takes time for students accustomed to factual questions to begin to realize the teacher wants more than one-word or short-answer responses.

Although obstacles exist in asking higher-level questions, raising the intellectual climate of the classroom is an important enough goal to seek strategies for implementing a greater range of questions. Building thinking questions is the first step in expanding the range of teacher/student interactions in the classroom.

Using Bloom's Taxonomy of Questions

Bloom's taxonomy (Bloom, Englehart, Furst, Hill, & Krathwohl, 1956), presented in Chapter 3, for designing instruction has also been widely used for distinguishing higher and lower questions. Table 8.1 shows questions at each level of Bloom's taxonomy. The six main headings include Bloom's subheadings and sample questions

TABLE 8.1 *Questioning Strategies in Context with the Cognitive Domain of Learning*

Category	Sample Question
Knowledge	
1–1 Knowledge of specifics	Who discovered the Mississippi River?
1–2 Knowledge of ways and means of dealing with specifics	What word does an adjective modify?
1–3 Knowledge of universals and abstractions in a field	What is the best method for calculating the circumference of a circle?
Comprehension	
2–1 Translation	What do the words *hasta la vista* mean?
2–2 Interpretation	How do the Democrats and Republicans differ in their views of spending?
2–3 Extrapolation	Given the present population birth rate, what will be the world population by the year 2000?
Application	How has the Miranda decision affected civil liberties?
	Given a pie-shaped lot 120 ft. × 110 ft. × 100 ft., and village setback conditions of 15 ft. in all directions, what is the largest size one-story home you can build on this lot?
Analysis	
4–1 Analysis of elements	What are the facts and opinions in the article we read?
4–2 Analysis of relationships	How does Picasso organize colors, shapes, and sizes to produce images?
4–3 Analysis of organizational principles	How does John Steinbeck use his characters to discuss the notion of friendship in *Of Mice and Men*?
Synthesis	
5–1 Production of a unique communication	How would you write a simple melodic line?
5–2 Production of a plan	How would you go about determining the chemical weight of an unknown substance?
5–3 Derivation of a set of abstract relations	What are the common causes for cell breakdown in the case of mutations, cancer, and aging?

continued

TABLE 8.1   *(Continued)*

Category	Sample Question
Evaluation	
6–1 Judgment in terms of internal evidence	What are the fallacies of Hitler's *Mein Kampf?*
6–2 Judgment in terms of external evidence	"Who can judge what is wrong with the architect's design of the plumbing and electricity?" requires the ability to cope with not being right and not always getting approval from the teacher. In general, the pace is slower and there is more opportunity for students to exchange ideas.

Source: Adapted from Ornstein, A. (1988). Questioning: The essence of good teaching. *NASSP Bulletin, 11*(499), 17–19. Used by permission.

for each of the subheadings. There are several other ways of developing higher-level questioning strategies in the classroom. The next types of questions, convergent and divergent, also promote higher levels of thinking.

Convergent and Divergent Questions

Another way of looking at lower-level and higher-level questions is from a convergent or divergent perspective. Convergent questions focus on a correct response. The questions can be factual—Who traveled to the land we now call America in 1492?—to more demanding—Why did Columbus name the people he met Indians? The latter question requires more information than relating a name with a date. To answer the second question, students would need to know that Columbus thought he was traveling to India and assumed that he had landed in India, therefore the people he met were Indians.

Divergent questions tend to be more demanding of a student's thought processes. There may be several correct responses to a divergent question, which asks for student opinion or conjecture. However, you may seek student opinion that is "educated" and draws on factual information established through convergent questioning. Divergent questions tend to be at the upper levels of Bloom's taxonomy (analysis, synthesis, and evaluation), whereas convergent questions tend to be at the lower levels of the taxonomy (knowledge and comprehension). Table 8.2 provides several examples of convergent and divergent questions.

Values Clarification

A third type of questioning was developed by Raths, Harmin, and Simon (1966) to help teachers clarify students' values and focus on the affective elements of learning.

TABLE 8.2 *Sample Convergent and Divergent Questions*

Subject and Grade Level	Convergent Questions	Divergent Questions
Social Studies, 5–7	Where did the Boston Tea Party take place?	Why did the Boston Tea Party take place?
Social Studies, 7–9	What are three products of Argentina?	How does wheat production in Argentina affect wheat export prices in our country?
English, 5–7	What is the verb in the sentence, "The girl told the boy what to do"?	How do we rewrite the present and future tense of the verb in the sentence, "The girl told the boy what to do"?
English, 10–11	Who wrote *A Farewell to Arms*?	How does Hemingway's experience as a news reporter affect the story, *A Farewell to Arms*?
Science, 2–5	Which planet is closest to the sun?	How would you compare living conditions on Mercury with Earth?
	Who was the first American astronaut to travel in space?	What planet, other than Earth, would you prefer to visit if you were an astronaut? Why?
Science, 9–11	What are two elements of water?	How is water purified?
Math, 4–5	What is the definition of a triangle?	How have triangles influenced architecture?
Math, 6–8	What is the shortest distance between two points?	What is the best air route to take from New York City to Moscow? Why?

Source: Ornstein, A. (1988). Questioning: The essence of good teaching. *NASSP Bulletin, 7*(499), 17–19. Used by permission.

Figure 8.1 indicates the seven steps Raths and colleagues believe support the development of a value. The teacher's questions provide examples of questions that could be asked to clarify the students' thinking.

For example, a student may suggest that homework should *not* be a requirement. If a teacher wanted to *clarify* the student's position on homework, then the questioning strategies would be more indirect. Figure 8.2 provides 20 possible teacher responses to a student's statement on homework. Identify those statements listed in Figure 8.2 that clarify the student's position. Check your answers in the Samples and Examples section at the end of this chapter.

"No, it's not a horsey or a doggy. It's two squiggles and two dots!"

FIGURE 8.1 *Questioning Strategies for Clarifying the Valuing Process*

1. *Choosing freely*
   a. Where do you suppose you first got that idea?
   b. How long have you felt that way?
   c. What would people say if you weren't to do what you say you must do?
   d. Are you getting help from anyone? Do you need more help? Can I help?
   e. Are you the only one in your crowd who feels this way?
   f. What do your parents want you to be?
   g. Is there any rebellion in your choice?
   h. How many years will you give to it? What will you do if you're not good enough?
   i. Do you think the idea of having thousands of people cheering when you come out on the field has anything to do with your choice?

2. *Choosing from alternatives*
   a. What else did you consider before you picked this?
   b. How long did you look around before you decided?
   c. Was it a hard decision? What went into the final decision? Who helped? Do you need any further help?
   d. Did you consider another possible alternative?
   e. And there are some reasons behind your choice?
   f. What choices did you reject before you settled on your present idea or action?
   g. What's really good about this choice which makes it stand out from the other possibilities?

3. *Choosing thoughtfully and reflectively*
   a. What would be the consequences of each alternative available?
   b. Have you thought about this very much? How did your thinking go?
   c. This is what I understand you to say . . . [interpret statement].
   d. Are you implying that . . . [distort his statement to see if he is clear enough to correct the distortion]?
   e. What assumptions are involved in your choice. Let's examine them.
   f. Define the terms you use. Give me an example of the kind of job you can get without a high-school diploma.
   g. Now if you do this, what will happen to that . . . ?

FIGURE 8.1 *(Continued)*

h. Is what you say consistent with what you said earlier?
i. Just what is good about this choice?
j. Where will it lead?
k. For whom are you doing this?
l. With these other choices, rank them in order of significance.
m. What will you have to do? What are your first steps? Second steps?
n. Whom else did you talk to?
o. Have you really weighed it fully?

4. *Prizing and cherishing*
   a. Are you glad you feel that way?
   b. How long have you wanted it?
   c. What good is it? What purpose does it serve? Why is it important to you?
   d. Should everyone do it your way?
   e. Is it something you really prize?
   f. In what way would life be different without it?

5. *Affirming*
   a. Would you tell the class the way you feel some time?
   b. Would you be willing to sign a petition supporting that idea?
   c. Are you saying that you believe . . . [repeat the idea]?
   d. You don't mean to say that you believe . . . [repeat the idea]?
   e. Should a person who believes the way you do speak out?
   f. Do people know that you believe that way or that you do that thing?
   g. Are you willing to stand up and be counted for that?

6. *Acting upon choices*
   a. I hear what you are for; now, is there anything you can do about it? Can I help?
   b. What are your first steps, second steps, etc.?
   c. Are you willing to put some of your money behind this idea?
   d. Have you examined the consequences of your act?
   e. Are there any organizations set up for the same purposes? Will you join?
   f. Have you done much reading on the topic? Who has influenced you?
   g. Have you made any plans to do more than you already have done?
   h. Would you want other people to know you feel this way? What if they disagree with you?
   i. Where will this lead you? How far are you willing to go?
   j. How has it already affected your life? How will it affect it in the future?

7. *Repeating*
   a. Have you felt this way for some time?
   b. Have you done anything already? Do you do this often?
   c. What are your plans for doing more of it?
   d. Should you get other people interested and involved?
   e. Has it been worth the time and money?
   f. Are there some other things you can do which are like it?
   g. How long do you think you will continue?
   h. What did you not do when you went to do that? Was that o.k.?
   i. How did you decide which had priority?
   j. Did you run into any difficulty?
   k. Will you do it again?

Source: Louis E. Raths, Merrill Harmin, and Sidney B. Simon, *Values and Teaching*, 2nd ed. (Columbus, OH: Charles E. Merrill, 1966), pp. 63–65. Reprinted by permission of Mildred Raths.

FIGURE 8.2 *Clarifying Responses*

Clarifying responses enable students to identify their own values by using a series of probing or clarifying questions. (*Note*: The answer sheet appears in the Samples and Examples section at the end of this chapter.)

Directions: Circle those questions that you feel clarify the student's position or value.

Value Statement
JIM: I think students should not do homework.

Teacher Responses:
1. Are you making a rationalization because you usually forget to do your homework?
2. Have you considered any alternatives?
3. Why don't you try doing your homework; it may help you in school.
4. Your parents want you to do homework.
5. You will need homework if you go to college.
6. Is this a personal preference or do you think most people believe that?
7. What are your ulterior motives?
8. How long have you felt this way about homework?
9. Have you expressed this belief to other people?
10. The school requires homework.
11. How can I help you do something about the idea?
12. When did you start to feel this way about homework?
13. Doesn't homework help you in school?
14. What are some of the good things about homework?
15. What do you mean by *homework*? Can you define the word?
16. If I didn't give you homework, the other students would be very upset.
17. What would be the effect of no homework?
18. What are your reasons for not wanting homework?
19. Is this (not having homework) very important to you?
20. I don't think this is a good idea.

In addition to asking questions to *check for understanding, evaluate lesson effectiveness,* and develop *higher-level thinking,* questions are also used in nonacademic areas. Controlling student behavior and organizational questions are two of the most common uses.

CAUTIONS AND CONCERNS

Controlling Questions

Using questions to control student behavior may limit the effectiveness of questioning in academic situations. The following exchange occurred in a fourth-grade classroom. The teacher was giving instructions and two students were poking each other at their desks. The teacher turns to one of the students and asks:

> T: John, what's your problem? (tone is negative with the emphasis on "your problem")

J: Nothing.

T: Then there must be a phantom flying around the classroom. (teacher walks toward student and class laughs)

J: (John does not respond)

T: You have to sit next to each other all period. Either you settle it or I'll settle it. (some class members make an "ooh-ooh" sound, others laugh nervously)

J: I will knock his teeth out after school.

T: That's going to solve something—"knocking out teeth"? How would you like someone to knock your teeth out?

J: OK.

T: Come here. (class laughs very nervously)

J: (John looks down)

T: Now class, let's turn to page 36.

The questioning sequence is designed to control John's behavior through intimidation. Latter sequences indicate that John continues to be a problem and any relationship the teacher had with John has deteriorated. The teacher is showing a genuine lack of respect for the student in front of his peers. In a secondary classroom, the verbal escalation could have led to a physical confrontation.

The above interaction is perhaps more extreme than most situations, but asking students questions when they are not paying attention or purposefully asking questions above the academic level of students to show power begins to destroy the interpersonal fabric of the classroom. Creating more equitable questioning patterns (described in this chapter) could prevent the need for controlling questions or intimidation, which is usually at the expense of student self-esteem. In addition to the actual content of a question, the tone of the teacher also conveys a great deal of meaning.

Questioning Tone

The tone of a question generally speaks much louder than any of its words. The question, How did you arrive at that answer? may seem very neutral. The tone of the question, however, may be perceived by a student to be hostile, intimidating, encouraging, or friendly. The tone combined with nonverbal language (e.g., rolled eyes, standing very close to the student, or smiling) may create feelings in the student that are quite separate from the content of the question. When question tone is used as a controlling or intimidating factor, students call these *put-downs*. Because the classroom is a very public place, the use of intimidating tones during questioning has a rippling effect beyond a single student. It may intimidate other students listening to the question and create a more negative classroom climate. Students could withdraw from classroom interaction if they experience consistent teacher put-downs during questioning. It is important to be sensitive to tone of voice and non-verbal movements during questioning. The audiotape analysis presented in Chapter 15 will assist in determining the types of questions and the tone in which they are asked.

Clarity in Questions and in Text

There is a time and place for questions. Throughout teacher training and most of a teacher's professional career we are told to ask questions. But some questions only lead to confusion. Being declarative by making a statement of what is appropriate or expected is, at times, a more appropriate action than asking a question. For example, questions during transitions may not be effective in achieving the objective of moving students from one activity to another.

Unclear directions bring about clarifying or organizational questions from students that may be unnecessary and take time away from instruction. This is the case when teachers ask questions while trying to manage a range of activities. The following provides examples of teacher statements in the classroom. Some are in the form of questions and others are statements of what the student needs to achieve. For example, question number 1 asks, "Will you get back to work?" In some instances, the student could say no. Question number 2 gives the student specific information about what is expected. Review the list and determine how the statements for action differ from the questions.

1. Will you get back to work?
2. You need to keep editing your papers until the bell rings in 10 minutes.
3. Why are you doing that?
4. Ann, take out your reading book and place your story book in your desk.
5. How many times have I asked you to stop that?
6. David, you and Bill seem to be distracting each other from completing your work. Please focus on your own work. Group time will occur in 15 minutes.
7. Do you want me to keep you after school?
8. Work that is not completed during school time will need to be completed at home or after school.
9. You really want to be excused from the field trip, don't you?
10. You will not have enough information about the exhibit if you don't complete your work, which could make the trip a poor learning experience.

Statements 2, 4, 6, 8, and 10 give the students information about the task at hand. They are direct and clear and provide enough information for the students to follow the directions. The other statements (1, 3, 5, 7, and 9) listed in the form of questions are unclear and rhetorical and give the teacher unusable information. For example, question 3, "Why are you doing that?" usually receives the student response, "I don't know." "What are you doing?" is usually answered, "Nothing."

Questions in Any Content

Many teachers in our interviews about questioning indicate that some content areas don't lend themselves to higher-level questions. Earlier in this chapter we saw at least seven reasons why teachers don't use higher-level questions, but with practice and experience higher-level questions can be used with any type of content. A case in point is the nursery rhyme story of the three little pigs. (In brief, each little pig built a house—one of straw, one of sticks, and one of bricks. The wolf was able to blow down the first two houses but not the third.) We asked elementary, middle, and high-school teachers to construct questions using higher- and lower-level questions. Given some prior thought and planning something as basic as a nursery rhyme could lend itself to a range of questions, including higher-level questions. The following is a representative sample of the questions they were able to develop. *L* designates lower-level questions and *H* designates higher-level questions.

1. What material did the first pig use to build his house? (L)
2. Who was the smartest of the three pigs and why? (H)
3. Why is a house important for both pigs and people? (H)
4. Which pig would you rather be? (H)
5. Who was the villain in the story? (L)

The content of a lesson should not be an inhibitor to asking a range of questions. Creating the expectation (for both teacher and student) that higher-level questions will be part of every lesson will eventually make the strategy automatic.

Questions in Context

The type or level of question is context specific. A question that may be considered higher level for a first-grader would be lower level for a fifth-grader. A first-grade class that has studied geometric forms and knows the properties of a right angle would be recalling factual information if the teacher showed a picture of a right triangle and asked the students to identify it. However, the same picture given before any instruction would be at a higher level if the students had to figure or discover what the drawing represented.

Wait Time

The amount of time students have to think during questioning has been an area of concern of educators and researchers for the last 20 years. Rowe (1974) found teachers wait or pause one second or less for students to respond to their questions. She analyzed 900 tapes of teacher wait time and concluded that there are 10 positive effects of teachers waiting 3 to 5 seconds for student responses during questioning:

1. The length of student response increased.
2. Student-initiated and appropriate (related to the topic or subject) responses increased.
3. Student failure to respond to questions reduced.
4. Student confidence in responding (as reflected by confident tone of voice) increased.
5. Student speculative responses increased.
6. Student-to-student interactions increased and teacher-focused instruction decreased.

7. Student evidence to support statements increased.
8. The number of student questions increased.
9. Participation of students who were identified as slower by the teacher increased.
10. The variety of student responses to teacher questions increased.

Wait Time I

There are different opportunities for teachers to pause or wait during questioning. This pausing or waiting allows students time to think. The "bombing" rate, which results from rapid-fire questions directed toward a student, interferes with student thinking. The advantages to student learning are significant (White & Tisher, 1986; Tobin, 1986). The first opportunity for wait time is after a teacher asks a question to the student (Wait Time I). Research suggests that a teacher wait 3 to 5 seconds for students to respond to higher-level questions during this first wait time opportunity. The average interval between teacher question and expected student response is 1 second, but practice and self-assessment will greatly improve your Wait Time I. (See Chapter 15 for extending wait-time strategies.)

Wait Time II

A second opportunity for waiting comes after a student has responded to a question. Many teachers immediately respond with an acknowledgment or elaborate on the student's comments and continue to another student. Pausing after students respond to questions has been associated with increases in achievement (White & Tisher, 1986). Student responses tend to be extended in Wait Time II situations. Wait time techniques will work only if students take advantage of the extra time. Students who do not use the extra wait time may need some cues that extra time is available. Encourage students to clarify, expand, or support their initial responses to your questions without your needing to ask them each time.

The following vignette provides additional evidence that wait time plays an important role in teacher questioning and student learning.

Improving Wait Time

The need for extended wait time becomes more critical for higher-level questioning and more complex concepts. A fast-paced verbal drill that requires simple responses would bog down with a 3- to 5-second wait time. But most other questioning should include a much greater wait time than is presently provided students. The teacher "bombing rate" (where students have one second to think before the next teacher statement), described in early studies of wait time, creates greater pressure on many students and increases the failure rates in the classroom. The lack of success in answering teacher questions causes some students to withdraw from classroom interaction. Improving wait time requires conscious effort and practice.

Writing down higher-level questions and counting silently to three after asking questions are two strategies for improving wait time. Probing student responses rather than mimicking or providing low-level responses (e.g., "ok," "yes," "uh huh") will provide greater opportunities for students to respond and think during questioning. An audiotape analysis provided in Chapter 15 will also provide a concrete

Middle-School Research Vignette

INTRODUCTION

Kenneth Tobin (1986) studied the effects of wait time on student achievement in sixth- and seventh-grade middle-school mathematics and language arts classes. The study of wait time was conducted during whole class instruction. The teacher was presenting information to the entire class and teacher questioning was occurring. The results support the use of wait time from 3 to 5 seconds for improving achievement in mathematics and language arts classes over the control groups classes. Other differences were also noted in classes where teachers waited after asking students questions.

This study was based on previous research on wait time conducted by the author (Tobin, 1980; Tobin & Capie, 1982) and by Mary Bude Rowe (1969). Previous research indicated that teachers allow students less than a second to respond to teacher questions and provide streams of information without pausing to allow students to reflect or to provide any emphasis for importance.

Tobin felt for teacher talk to have any influence on student learning, the rate of information presented to the students should be in balance with the students' abilities to absorb or process the information. The time needed for students to think through complex information should be greater than for simpler verbal information. Tobin emphasized the need for teachers to pause during presentation of information to allow students time to reflect on the information and for teachers to pause after asking questions, particularly complex questions, to allow student time to think about the answers. From the amount of time and pace of presenting information to the time given students to think through questions, the teacher is the controller of time in the classroom.

STUDY DESIGN

Ten sixth- and seventh-grade mathematics teachers received training and seven special lesson plans to improve their wait time to an average of 3 seconds. Additionally, the 10 teachers received feedback on how to improve their wait time. A control group of 10 teachers received feedback

on their organization of the classroom but not on wait time. A one-hour test was given at the conclusion of the experimental unit for all science classes in the study. A similar format was used for 10 sixth- and seventh-grade language arts teachers and a control group of 10 language arts teachers who received placebo feedback. However, a test was not given for the language arts classes.

RESULTS

The differences between the extended wait time teachers and the control group teachers was rather dramatic. The table represents the differences in both mathematics and language arts classes. Some categories have been collapsed for the table on page 222.

CONCLUSIONS AND IMPLICATIONS FOR PRACTICE

The research study by Tobin supports the earlier work by Rowe (1969, 1974) on the positive effects wait time can have in whole class discussion. The areas of difference between those teachers who were trained for extended wait time and those who used their usual practices include:

1. Teacher wait time was significantly greater (beyond 3 seconds) for the teachers who received feedback and training.
2. Achievement on tests for students in the extended wait time classes were significantly greater.
3. The number of teacher statements was reduced.
4. Teacher interruptions of student talk were reduced.
5. Failure of students to respond to teacher questions was reduced.
6. The average length of student statements increased in extended wait time classes.
7. Teacher asked higher-level questions.
8. Teacher had a need to react less after student statements.
9. In the extended wait time classes, teacher responded more with probes or extensions of student thinking rather than lower-

continued

level mimicry or simple repeating of student statements or brief acknowledgments.
10. Students in the extended wait time classes had additional time to think of responses and more opportunities for verbal interactions in the classroom.

The increased wait time from 3 to 5 seconds for both mathematics and language arts classes improved the quality of teacher/student interaction. The additional time teachers gave students was used for thinking and processing of information. This reduced the student failure rates to respond and extended student statements. Teachers asked higher-level questions and probed student responses more, rather than simply mimicking student answers. It would appear that in whole class settings where one student is responding and the class is watching, the interaction is also a learning experience for students not immediately involved in the teacher/student interaction.

Wait Time Differences*

	Wait Time/ Feedback Group Mean		Control Group (No Feedback)	
	Math	*Language Arts*	*Math*	*Language Arts*
1. Teacher wait time in seconds	3.3 sec.	4.5 sec.	0.9 sec.	1.5 sec.
2. Number of teacher statements	43.0	44.6	61.0	76.1
3. Length of teacher statements in seconds	6.0 sec.	Don't know	8.4 sec.	Don't know
4. Length of student statements in seconds	4.7 sec.	7.6 sec.	2.6 sec.	3.4 sec.
5. Student failure to respond to teacher questions	.80	0.1	4.40	6.2
6. Number of teacher interruptions while students are talking	0.00	Don't know	1.70	Don't know
7. Teacher reacting after student talk	0.15	0.12	0.21	0.24
8. Teacher mimics or repeats	0.16	0.03	0.32	0.23
9. Teacher probes after student finishes response to teacher question or student statement	0.46	0.52	0.26	0.18
10. Teacher asks higher-level questions				
a. comprehension	0.12	Don't know	1.31	Don't know
b. application	0.59	0.79	0.29	0.52

*All comparisons were significantly different at the $p = .05$ level or better.

Adapted from Tobin, K. (1986). Effects of teacher wait time on discourse characteristics in mathematics and language arts classes. *American Educational Research Journal, 23*(2), 197–198. Copyright 1986 by the American Educational Research Association. Adapted by permission of the publisher.

method for checking wait time during actual classroom instruction. After the teacher provides appropriate wait time and the student does not know the answer, then the interaction moves to a different level.

Teacher Moves

When the teacher asks a question and the student answers, several options are presented to the teacher. (See Figure 8.3 for a visual display of teacher options when student responses are correct.) For a correct response, the teacher can (1) acknowledge the answer (Good, Sally) or praise the student (Sally, I like the way you brought the facts together to reach a conclusion); (2) extend the answer to achieve greater clarity by asking the student to elaborate, expand, or give an example; (3) probe student thinking by asking another related more demanding or higher-level question of the student; and/or (4) ask a related question to another student to build on the response of the first student. If the student gives an incorrect response or states, "I don't know," the teacher also has several alternatives. Figure 8.4 shows three teacher options for an incorrect student response.

FIGURE 8.3 *Teacher Options after Student Responds Correctly*

Teacher Asks Recall Question: The capital of our nation is named after what president?

Student Responds: George Washington.

	Teacher Options:	
	Same student	New student
Acknowledges or Praises Response "Good, Sally"	or *Extends or Probes; Asks Another Question* "Are there any other places named after presidents?" Student responds: "Our school is named after Abraham Lincoln, and the city library is named for Thomas Jefferson."	*Builds on First Student's Response* "Why do you think we name important public places like schools and libraries and cities after our nation's leaders?"

FIGURE 8.4 *Teacher Options after Incorrect Student Response*

Teacher Asks Recall Question (waits 3 seconds): The capital of our nation is named after what president?

Student Responds: I don't know.

	Teacher Options:	
	Same student	New student
Gives Clues "The capital is named after the first president of the United States."	*Asks Additional Questions* "Who was the first president of the United States?"	*Redirects Question* It is better to restate the question than to say, "Can someone help Sally?"

Why Students Don't Ask Questions

The spontaneity of children's questions becomes drastically reduced as they enter the classroom. Rather than a few children competing for the time of their parents, now 25 or more children are competing for the time of one adult, their teacher. The more socialized to school students become, the fewer questions they ask. The classroom is a very public place; students begin to understand teacher cues about questioning from watching the teacher interact with class members. If one student's question is ignored by the teacher or receives a frown, indicating the student should know the answer, students soon realize that the teacher may not want to hear from them. If the pattern is repeated every day and the teacher provides limited opportunities for student-initiated questions, the message for students regarding their involvement becomes quite clear.

Students learn by first grade that answering teacher questions is good but asking too many questions may show ignorance. This lesson is quite universal. Researchers in Czechoslovakia found minimal student-initiated questions in the classroom. Mars (1984) (citing Fenclova [1978]) indicates that of 30 lessons in grade schools, vocational schools, and grammar schools, only 60 student-initiated questions were recorded. Nearly half the student questions were related to management or organization concerns. Only 2 of 60 recorded student questions dealt with students attempting to "penetrate more deeply into the subject matter" (Mars, 1984, p. 10). Student passivity, which is reflected in classrooms where teacher talk dominates, creates a classroom climate that discourages student questions. "The pupil is afraid of revealing his ignorance when asking, while the teacher does not encourage the pupils enough to ask questions as he is not sure he could always answer" (Mars, 1984, p. 10).

Student involvement is a motivator for learning. Encourage student questions and give students opportunities to formulate questions. One way of increasing student involvement in the classroom is by providing the opportunity for student-initiated questions directed at creating greater understanding of the subject matter. Student-initiated questions require the teacher to establish a climate for exploration and reflection. Students who receive negative feedback after asking content-relevant questions either verbally or nonverbally from the teacher or classmates will quickly learn to remain silent. For example, after completing a text chapter or unit, ask the students to write three questions they feel have not been answered. These questions could then be used as a starting point for class discussion. Several other techniques presented in this chapter for creating fairness in questioning and greater student involvement will aid in creating a climate for student-initiated questions. One way to improve both the frequency and quality of student questions is through discussion.

Advantages of Teacher Questions

Questioning has a number of important advantages for teachers:

1. *Understanding.* It provides an opportunity for the teacher to check for understanding.

2. *Lesson effectiveness.* It gives an indication of the effectiveness of instruction for the whole class.
3. *Higher-level thinking.* The level of dialogue and thinking is raised when higher-level questions (opinion, synthesis, and evaluation) are used in the classroom.
4. *Student participation.* It increases student involvement in learning.
5. *Communication skills.* Combined with discussion, students can improve on their oral and social communication skills.
6. *Self-checks.* It allows students to hear peer responses to the same question and compare answers with their own.
7. *Review.* It provides students with opportunities for review of recently taught information.
8. *Cues.* It cues students about what the teacher feels is important.

The advantages of questioning begin to show how the teacher can begin to shape a learning community in the classroom through dialogue. However, as with all teaching strategies, questioning also has its limitations.

Limitations of Questions

The use of teacher questions also has its limitations. One researcher (Dillon, 1985) concluded that teacher questions inhibit discussion in the classroom. Teachers can misuse questions to limit dialogue by dominating the interaction, or they can use questions for classroom management rather than academic purposes, addressing students who are not paying attention. The following list provides some insight into the limitations of teacher questions. Suggestions are provided in the notes we developed to assist you in modifying the limitations.

1. The teacher may ask the same students most of the questions.

   NOTE: *For elementary students, drawing popsicle sticks from a can with a student's name on each stick allows the teacher to ask questions in a more random fashion. For upper-elementary and secondary classrooms, the teacher can have the students write their name on two 3 × 5 cards. The teacher collects the cards and uses the two decks of cards to draw the students' names. Two decks are used to increase the chance that a student may be called on more than once.*

2. The questions may only be directed at factual recall and ignore higher-level questioning skills.

   NOTE: *Writing the higher-level questions on cards in advance will ensure that higher-level questions are asked during the lesson. Classifying questions according to Bloom's taxonomy helps assure that higher-order questions are included in the discussion.*

3. The students may become bored if the teacher does not try to vary his or her question routine.

   NOTE: *Using a combination of volunteers and teacher-selection of students to answer questions will reduce boredom. (See Go Around System described in the earlier Snapshot.) Be sure to ask the question first; then call out the student's name.*

4. The use of questions can be time consuming if you do not have the questions prepared in advance.

   NOTE: *Incorporating questions into the lesson will provide more time to observe and interact with the class than trying to think about the next question during instruction.*

5. Adequate wait time needs to be provided for the students to answer the questions.

   NOTE: *Rowe (1974) suggests that 3 to 5 seconds between the time the teacher asks a question and the next teacher statement will give students adequate time to respond. This is particularly important for higher-level questions. (Houston, Clift, Freiberg, & Warner, 1988, p. 201)*

CLASSROOM DISCUSSION

Questioning and discussion are different sides of the same coin. Although both strategies attempt to create a measure of student knowledge, questioning is teacher directed, whereas discussion provides greater student input. Discussion is a universal strategy designed to provide students with active participation in the classroom, either through verbal input or from listening to classroom members speak. It also provides the teacher with insight into students' thinking, which is seldom provided through other strategies.

Discussion Defined

Discussion is the interchange of ideas between students and their teacher or among students. Discussion may take place in whole class settings, within groups of students, or between two students. Discussion requires a climate of reflective listening, respect for the speaker's ideas, and noninterference from the teacher.

Setting the Stage

Creating a trusting and positive classroom climate is a necessary prerequisite for discussion. A trusting climate is created together with your students. Take the lead in establishing the direction for positive classroom discussions by employing the following guidelines.

1. *Be sure the goals for discussion are clear for both students and yourself.* You and your students may need to determine what you hope to achieve through discussion. For example, the discussion activity could expand on the viewpoints of the text or create alternative strategies for solving a problem. It is useful for a short discussion of the goals to alleviate concerns of students about "What we are supposed to do?"

2. *Actively listen while students are talking.* This includes positive eye contact with the student talking and avoidance of interjection with other students or organization activity (e.g., shuffling papers on the desk).

3. *Refrain from commenting after each student statement.* Teachers have a tendency to make comments or elaborate on every student statement. This practice inhibits discussion and limits the available time and the number of students who could participate.
4. *Develop discussions from a series of lessons or a unit that would supply students with enough information, ideas, or concepts to allow for a knowledgeable discussion.*
5. *Encourage student-to-student dialogue without going through the teacher.* Most classroom interactions go through the teacher. For example, during higher-level questioning, a typical pattern looks like the following sequence:

Questioning

T: What are some differences and similarities between ancient Greek forms of democracy and our current American democracy?

SUSAN: Both forms had a group of people called a *Senate* that made decisions for all the people.

T: Yes, that is correct.

T: Bill (hand raised), you have something to add?

BILL: Both the U.S. Senate and the Ancient Greek Senate included mostly rich men. (class laughs)

T: Bill has an interesting point. Let's discuss the composition of the two Senates.

The interaction in the classroom stopped at the teacher each time and a pattern of "turn taking" is evident. A discussion on the same topic may look like the following sequence:

Discussion

T: What are some differences and similarities between ancient Greek forms of democracy and our current American democracy?

SUSAN: Both forms had a group of people called a *Senate* that made decisions for all the people.

T: (Remains silent and no one talks for five seconds)

BILL: Both the U.S. Senate and the Ancient Greek senate included mostly rich men. (class laughs)

SALLY: (Looking at Bill) I don't know about the wealth of the Ancient Greek Senate but the U.S. Senate has members who are not rich.

SUSAN: Yeah, but how many?

MELISSA: We need to look at a reference source for this information.

JANE: Mrs. Thomson, what would be a good source to find out about the wealth and perhaps other information on members of the current U.S. and the ancient Greek Senates?

The role of the teacher is very different in the two sequences. The first interaction is highly patterned, with the teacher taking turns with the students. The teacher, however, would be talking 50 percent or more of the time. In the second sequence, the teacher is more of a moderator or facilitator, with students looking to the teacher as a resource.

Foiling Discussion through Questions

Some researchers indicate that teacher questioning during discussion is the primary inhibitor to implementing this strategy successfully. Because most teachers see their role as being the gatekeeper during questioning, it is difficult to change roles for discussion. The discussion may become too teacher dominated, which, in fact, foils discussion in the classroom (Dillon, 1985). In his study of five high-school classrooms using transcriptions of teacher/student interactions, Dillon began to see patterns of how teacher questioning foiled discussion. One could argue that the teacher was trying to keep the students on track. However, the transcripts indicated the teacher questions moved the class discussion away from the original focus. The difficulty of implementing discussion in the classroom relates to the change of roles the teacher must make during this strategy from giver of information to facilitator of interaction. In addition to the change of roles, most teachers have had little or no opportunities to see effective discussion in their own schooling.

Student Responsibilities

Some classrooms are dominated by a few students. The Go Around System, notecards for secondary classes, and the use of popsicle sticks or tongue depressors for calling on students (all discussed earlier) are designed to equalize the interaction and the opportunity for participation. During discussion the most verbal students will tend to dominate the discussion. The teacher is faced with the decision between free flow of ideas and the need to provide the greatest participation. Following are some rules students should agree to prior to classroom discussion.

1. *All students should actively listen while classmates are talking.* Talking or other distracting activities will minimize the effectiveness of the discussion.
2. *Students are not permitted to make "killer statements"* (Raths, Harmin, & Simon, 1966). Killer statements inhibit discussion by putting down the student's comments. Examples from the classroom include: "That's a dumb idea" or "You're not very bright today."
3. *Students need to be prepared for the discussion.* If reading or prior meetings in small groups are required, students are expected to have accomplished these tasks before the discussion. Students who are not prepared could listen but not actively participate.

Teacher Approaches

Dillon (1988) suggests two approaches to discussion: (1) pose a single question for discussion and (2) pose a question for which there is no ready answer. Dillon proposes the following action in creating a tone for discussion.

1. *Prepare the question for discussion.*
   a. *Conceive of just the right one.*
   b. *Formulate it in just the right way.*
   c. *Pose just that one in just that way.*
2. *Ask questions that perplex self.*
   (Do not ask questions that do not perplex self.)
3. *Use alternatives to questioning.*
   a. *Statements—State your selected thought in relation to what the student has just said.*
   b. *Student Questions—Provide that a student asks a question related to what the speaker has just said.*
3. *Signals—Signal your reception of what the student is saying, without yourself taking or holding the floor.*
4. *Silences—Say nothing at all but maintain a deliberate, appreciative silence for three seconds or so, until the original speaker resumes or another student enters in (p. 128).*

Students may need to learn how to discuss. Learning a new strategy takes time and requires a progressive building of expertise. Discussion may be a strategy that develops gradually during the school year rather than trying to implement the strategy the first weeks of school. Like the other universal teaching strategies, discussion should be used in combination with other strategies.

The two strategies of questioning and discussion are interrelated. Teachers who ask higher-level questions, wait before and after student responses, respect student ideas, encourage participation by all students, and create a climate of exploration will expand the opportunities for both meaningful questions and discussion. The need to constantly monitor our use of questioning and discussion strategies becomes evident in the following Teacher Talk, in which five teachers reflect on their uses of questioning and discussion.

TEACHER TALK

I recently read a research study that found that student teachers, in general, planned more evaluation, memory, and convergent types of questions (in that order). In looking at my own lessons, I see this as true—even in myself. I believe this research article has helped me by making me more aware of my own teaching behavior and I will make sure I incorporate more questions based on the other cognitive levels.

Secondary Student Teacher

How should I as a classroom teacher employ the strategy of discussion in teaching literature? I feel strongly that children need to talk about what they have read, and I have used discussion as a teaching tool almost always with literature. After the children have read the Junior Great Books stories, the class is arranged informally in a circle or semi-circle. With the teacher, or sometimes an interested parent, as moderator, the group considers open questions such as "Why do you think that the main character did . . . ?" or "Why do you think that the author has such a character to . . . ?" The students accustomed mostly to questions with definite answers need some time to adjust to this new sort of questioning and for a while will persist in asking,

"Well, what *is* the answer?" When they accept the idea of the no-answer question, they begin to feel more free in discussion and enjoy the experience.

Middle-School English Teacher

My classroom setting is first grade. My reading groups are small—nine students—seated at a table. Since the group is small, it is not necessary for the children to raise their hands or for me to call their names. They have already been shown the eye-contact body signal I use for "calling." The first question I ask of the group is designed to arouse curiosity based on the story we are reading (e.g., What could happen if Sally did not go home after school and went with her friends to the haunted house?). The first question is used for a set induction and to set the purpose for reading. Most of these first questions are based on the students' opinion.

1st-Grade Teacher

I ask questions all the time, that's the way I learn (as a teacher). Yet in my 18 years of teaching experience, in how many situations have I required students to formulate questions? Two, maybe three. The teachers I know sum up a lesson with "Any questions?" and when there's no response, they say, "Good." Perhaps I'd better add to my teaching repertoire the question "What are you wondering?" because I have a suspicion that, although I haven't missed the boat in asking questions, I may be missing one oar.

High-School Mathematics Teacher

As an observer in the classroom, I noticed that the questions used at the elementary classrooms I am observing are only at the literal (information or factual) levels. The teachers mostly ask the students to comprehend things that are straight out of the book. The students do fine in the reading circle, but when they go back to their desks to do seat work, they are lost. They seem to forget what seemed so clear to them in the reading circle. Just because the question is worded differently from the text, or goes deeper than the text's meaning, they do not understand what is going on. My observations and work with these students seem to support the findings that students need different levels of questions in order to better comprehend the material and to move their level of reasoning beyond the literal (factual) level.

Graduate Certification Student

SUMMARY

In a book for the National Education Association, William Wilen (1987) summarized the research on questioning and identified nine key points that are used here to summarize questioning.*

Questioning Skills, for Teachers (2nd ed.). © 1987, National Education Association. Reprinted with permission.

1. Plan key questions to provide lesson structure and direction. *Write them into lesson plans, at least one for each objective—especially higher-level questions. Ask some spontaneous questions based on student responses.*
2. Phrase questions clearly and specifically. *Avoid vague or ambiguous questions such as "What about the heroine of the story?" Ask single questions; avoid run-on questions that lead to student frustration and confusion. Ask one question at a time. Clarity increases probability of accurate responses.*
3. Adapt questions to student ability level. *This enhances understanding and reduces anxiety. For heterogeneous classes, phrase questions in natural, simple language, adjusting vocabulary and sentence structure to students' language and conceptual levels.*
4. Ask questions logically and sequentially. *Avoid questions lacking clear focus and intent. Consider students' intellectual ability, prior understanding of content, topic, and lesson objective(s). Asking questions in a planned sequence will enhance student thinking and learning.*
5. Ask questions at a variety of levels. Use knowledge-level questions to determine basic understandings and to serve as a basis for higher-level thinking. Higher-level questions provide students opportunities to practice higher forms of thought.
6. Follow up student responses. *Develop a response repertoire that encourages students to clarify initial responses, lift thought to higher levels, and support a point of view or opinion. For example, "Can you restate that?" "Could you clarify that further?" "What are some alternatives?" "How can you defend your position?" Encourage students to clarify, expand, or support initial responses to higher-level questions.*
7. Give students time to think when responding. *Increase wait time after asking a question to three to five seconds to increase number and length of student responses and to encourage higher-level thinking. Insisting upon instantaneous responses significantly decreases probability of meaningful interaction with and among students. Allow sufficient wait time before repeating or rephrasing questions to ensure student understanding.*
8. Use questions that encourage wide student participation. *Distribute questions to involve majority of students in learning activities. For example, call on nonvolunteers, using discretion for difficulty level of questions. Be alert for reticent students' verbal and nonverbal cues such as perplexed look or partially raised hand. Encourage student-to-student interaction. Use circular or semicircular seating to create environment conducive to increased student involvement.*
9. Encourage student questions. *This encourages active participation. Student questions at higher cognitive levels stimulate higher levels of thought, essential for inquiry approach. Give students opportunities to formulate questions and carry out follow-up investigations of interest. Facilitate group and independent inquiry with a supportive social-emotional climate, using praise and encouragement, accepting and applying student ideas, responding to student feelings, and actively promoting student involvement in all phases of learning. (Wilen, 1987, pp. 10–11)*

In addition to the nine points for questioning, the following should be added for classroom discussion.

1. Create a positive climate for discussion.
2. Prepare questions for discussion that have no immediate answer.
3. Limit teacher questions and the role of gatekeeper during discussion.

4. Prepare students for their role in discussion.
5. Develop the use of discussion gradually.

Intellectual stimulation and improved student participation are two goals of questioning and discussion. Properly used, these strategies can enhance learning and improve the quality of the teachers' and students' lives in the classroom.

REFERENCES

Berliner, D. C. (1987). But do they understand? In V. R. Koehler (Ed.), *Educator's handbook*. New York: Longman.

Bloom, B. S., Englehart, M. D., Furst, E. J., Hill, W. H., & Krathwohl, D. R. (Eds.). (1956). *Taxonomy of educational objectives: The classification of education goals, handbook I: Cognitive domain*. New York: David McKay.

Cuban, L. (1984). *How teachers taught*. White Plains, NY: Longman.

Dillon, J. T. (1987). Antique questions. *Questioning Exchange, 1*(1), ii.

Dillon, J. T. (1988). *Questioning and teaching*. New York: Teachers College Press.

Fennema, E., & Peterson, P. (1987). Effective teaching for boys and girls: The same or different? In D. C. Berliner & B. V. Rosenshine (Eds.), *Talks to teachers*. New York: Random House.

Freiberg, H. J. (1987). *Generic teaching strategies: School and teaching effectiveness institute*. Preston County Schools, Kingwood, W.V.

Gall, M. (1984). Synthesis of research on teacher's questioning. *Educational Leadership, 42*, 40–47.

Houston, W. R., Clift, R. T., Freiberg, H. J., & Warner, A. R. (1988). *Touch the future: Teach!* St. Paul: West Publishing.

Kerry, T. (1987). Classroom questions in England. *Questioning Exchange, 1*(1), 33.

Maroski, L. (1987). Question quotes. *Questioning Exchange, 1*(1), i.

Mars, J. (1984). Questioning in Czechoslovakia. *Questioning Exchange, 5*, 8–11.

Ornstein, A. (1988). Questioning: The essence of good teaching. *NASSP Bulletin, 11*(499), 17–19.

Pate, R. T., & Bremer, N. H. (1967). Guiding learning through skillful questioning. *Elementary School Journal, 67*, 417–422.

Raths, L. E., Harmin, M., & Simon, S. B. (1966). *Values and teaching* (2nd ed.) (pp. 63–65). Columbus, OH: Charles E. Merrill.

Redfield, D. L., & Rousseau, E. W. (1981). A meta-analysis of experimental research on teacher questioning behavior. *Review of Educational Research, 51*, 237–245.

Rosenshine, B., & Stevens, R. (1986). Teaching functions. In M. C. Whittrock (Ed.), *Handbook of research on teaching* (3rd ed.). New York: Macmillan.

Rowe, M. B. (1969). Science, soul and sanctions. *Science and Children, 6*(6), 11–13.

Rowe, M. B. (1974). Wait time and rewards as instructional variables, their influence in language, logic, and fate control: Part one—Wait time. *Journal of Research in Science Teaching, 11*(2), 81–94.

Tobin, K. G. (1980). The effect of an extended teacher wait-time on science achievement. *Journal of Research in Science Teaching, 17*, 469–475.

Tobin, K. G., & Capie, W. (1982). Relationships between classroom process variables and middle school science achievement. *Journal of Educational Psychology, 14*, 441–454.

Tobin, K. (1986). Effects of teacher wait time on discourse characteristics in mathematics and language arts classes. *American Educational Research Journal, 23*(2), 191–201.

White, R. T., & Tisher, R. P. (1986). Research on natural sciences. In M. C. Whittrock (Ed.), *Handbook of research on teaching* (3rd ed.). New York: Macmillan.

Whittrock, M. C. (Ed.). (1986). *Handbook of research on teaching* (3rd ed.). New York: Macmillan.

Wilen, W. W. (1987). *Questioning skills, for teachers: What research says to the teacher.* Washington, DC: National Education Association.

Yaden, D., Smolkin, L. B., & Conlon, A. (1988). Preschoolers' questions about pictures, print convention, and story text during reading aloud at home. *Reading Research Quarterly,* 24(2), 188–214.

SAMPLES AND EXAMPLES

There is one Sample and Example in this section.

- The Clarifying Responses answer key for Figure 8.2.

TEACHER RESPONSES (ANSWER SHEET)

1. Are you making a rationalization because you usually forget to do your homework?
2. Have you considered any alternatives?
3. Why don't you try doing your homework; it may help you in school.
4. Your parents want you to do homework.
5. You will need homework if you go to college.
6. Is this a personal preference or do you think most people believe that?
7. What are your ulterior motives?
8. How long have you felt this way about homework?
9. Have you expressed this belief to other people?
10. The school requires homework.
11. How can I help you do something about the idea?
12. When did you start to feel this way about homework?
13. Doesn't homework help you in school?
14. What are some of the good things about homework?
15. What do you mean by *homework*? Can you define the word?
16. If I didn't give you homework, the other students would be very upset.
17. What would be the effect of no homework?
18. What are your reasons for not wanting homework?
19. Is this (not having homework) very important to you?
20. I don't think this is a good idea.

◯ = Clarifying Response

CHAPTER 9

Interactive Practice
for Learning: Beyond Drill

CHAPTER OUTCOMES

At the conclusion of this chapter you will be able to:

1. Describe the outcomes of practice.
2. Design practice activities for varied content, contexts, and learners.
3. Design interactive practice activities that promote an active learning role for students and the development of learning strategies.
4. Design and use recitation, review, seatwork, homework, and learning centers for student practice.

KEY TERMS
AND CONCEPTS

Practice
Learning Strategies
Rehearsal Strategies
Elaboration Strategies
Organization Strategies
Comprehension Monitoring
  Strategies
Affective Strategies
Explicit Explanation
Drill
Automaticity
Recitation
Mnemonics
Review
Seatwork
Guided Practice
Independent Practice
Worksheets
Homework
Learning Centers

INTRODUCTION

Did You Know?

- Elementary students spend 70 percent of their instructional time doing independent seatwork assignments.
- Over half (54 percent) of high school students report doing homework for one to two hours per night.
- Of all students in classrooms, 20 percent do not complete their assignments in the allotted time.
- First-graders spend 40 to 60 percent of an average reading lesson doing seatwork.
- One third of all elementary schools have a written homework policy.
- When students are practicing new material, the percentage of correct answers should be 80 percent, whereas when students are reviewing, the percentage should be close to 95 percent.
- When students have contacts with a teacher during seatwork, their engagement rate increases by about 10 percent.

These facts and figures add up to the importance of practice and reasons for conducting practice effectively. They come from a range of studies and surveys of classrooms and schools (Anderson, Evertson, & Brophy, 1979; Brophy, 1980; Fisher, Berliner, Filby, Marliave, Cahen, & Dishaw, 1978; Good, Grouws, & Ebmeier, 1983; Goodlad, 1984; Knorr, 1981; Rosenshine & Stevens, 1986).

Do You Practice?

Before we proceed, take a few moments and reflect on how you use practice in your daily life. How often do you practice something? How does it affect your learning? Do you have any tricks you have developed to learn something quickly?

We asked ourselves and noticed that in our efforts to learn to speak Spanish, we practice lists of vocabulary and common expressions with flash cards twice a day. But we want to be more direct with our colleagues, so we practice assertive responses mostly in our imagination, but sometimes in real life.

Notice that some of your practicing is done almost effortlessly and some demands awareness and intense thinking. Our concept of practice for this chapter has the same range of complexity. Classroom practice was often a drill exercise for many of us as students. It meant little more than repetition. Remember the way you learned the multiplication facts? Or the Gettysburg Address? When you look at the outcomes of student practice in this chapter, you will see that drill is just one kind of practice needed for learning, and that the content of practice has possible variations.

CONTENT

Not only do you use practice strategies for students to learn concepts, information, skills, and attitudes, you also intend that your students experience learning itself.

FIGURE 9.1   *Types of Practice Strategies*

---

1. Practice for Change
   * Skills
   * New behaviors
   * Changes in behavior
   * Confidence
   * Retention of information
2. Practice for Structured Content
   * Structured subject matter
   * Skills
3. Practice for Learning Strategies
   * Rehearsal strategies
   * Elaboration
   * Organization
   * Comprehension monitoring
   * Affective

You may consciously plan some outcomes, and some outcomes may just happen. For example, you plan a practice activity to build confidence in students about a difficult math computation skill. During that same activity, students may also come up with a process that checks the accuracy of their computations. The content of practice has a wide range of possible outcomes and you must consciously plan for as many of them as possible. Within the content there are several types of practice strategies, which are listed in Figure 9.1 and described in this section of the chapter. We begin with practice for change as one category of content.

Practice for Change

When you look at the behavioral view of learning (that is, learning as a change in behavior), you see practice as an important part of the process. Behavioral psychologists Skinner and Thorndike describe it as a conditioning process. When the process is translated into educational programs, behaviors are split into small steps that are practiced. Practice yields outcomes like skills, new behaviors, changes in behavior, and, sometimes, confidence as skills are learned.

A contrasting view of learning is held by cognitive psychologists, Piaget, Bruner, and Ausubel, who see learning as an internal process. The change they describe is in the person's ability to respond or behave. With this view is the need for awareness, motivation, and feelings. Practice, therefore, must be accompanied by thinking or cognitive processing.

So *practice for change* can have both behavioral and cognitive outcomes: skills, behaviors, retention of information, motivation, confidence, and self-awareness.

Practice for Structured Content

When Rosenshine and Stevens (1986) looked for common features of successful teaching of structured subject matter, they found three that stood out: (1) teachers instructed in small steps with student practice after each step, (2) teachers guided students during initial practice, and (3) teachers provided all students with a high level of successful practice (pp. 378–379).

Notice that the features are limited to structured subject matter such as math computation, map reading skills, accounting procedures, and reciting some vocabulary words. Outcomes such as creative writing, reading comprehension, and developing relationships in groups require a more complex form of practice.

Practice for Learning Strategies

The learning strategies described by Weinstein and Mayer (1986) in their review of research can help you provide practice with different levels of complexity. Such practice can help students *learn how to learn*.

Rehearsal Strategies

There are both basic and complex rehearsal strategies. Basic rehearsal is nothing more than repetition of information. You encourage basic rehearsal when you lead your kindergarten students in a singsong repetition of the days of the week. Your middle-school students use basic rehearsal when they recite a conjugation of the verb *to be* in French. You use basic rehearsal when you recite a new phone number over and over to yourself.

There is also complex rehearsal, and you use it when you learn more complicated material or perform a more complex task. Your repetition is combined with more thinking. When fifth-grade students underline adverbs in a sentence, they use complex rehearsal strategies. When you go through your notes from a class and underline the important points, you use complex rehearsal. You think about the information in your notes and decide what's important.

Elaboration Strategies

Elaboration strategies require the learner to develop relationships. Basic elaboration calls for simple relationships, such as the pairing of items, or putting a set of details together into a story or picture. When you have your tenth-grade students match properties with each chemical element, they use basic elaboration. When your sixth-grade students see a list of characteristics (such as angry, defiant, strong, young, and devious) and identify a character in a story, they use basic elaboration.

Complex elaboration is for complicated tasks such as summarizing, paraphrasing, or making comparisons. When your middle-school students relate the information they have learned about drug addiction to other forms of addiction, they use complex elaboration.

Organizational Strategies

Again, you have both basic and complex forms of this type of learning strategy. Organization is an ordering or grouping process that can include sequences, hierarchies, and categories. When your ninth-grade students develop a time line of events surrounding World War II, they use a basic organizational strategy. When second-graders categorize the foods of a menu into the four food groups, they use basic organizational strategies.

The most common use of a complex organizational strategy is one we all use or have used, namely, outlining chapters of our textbooks. When you put the teaching strategies of this text into a lesson you plan to teach, you will be using complex organizational strategies.

Comprehension Monitoring Strategies

These strategies are quite complex. They involve checking yourself to determine what you understand and what you don't understand, being aware of how you are learning, and identifying what you want to know before reading or studying.

Felicia Gomez (secondary teacher in Chapter 1) helps students use this strategy when she directs them to "think about what you might want to learn about Melville from this film." She models this strategy for students by saying, "I will be interested to see if his early life influenced his writing. So I stop and think to myself, 'What do I know about his writing?' I remember that there is a theme of rebellion against life in his work. Then I ask myself, 'What kind of experiences could have caused him to write with that theme?' I begin thinking that I'll look at his family and his school years." To continue teaching comprehension monitoring, Felicia might turn the film off at intervals to check that students are thinking about the influences: "Have you seen anything in Melville's life that explains his writing theme?" As you can see, Felicia's modeling will be important to teach comprehension monitoring.

Affective Strategies

These strategies begin with an awareness of a feeling or an attitude. The strategies are then used to experience motivation, confidence, or positive attitudes, or to change a feeling or attitude. When you are aware and deliberately using strategies to focus attention on a lecture even though you dislike the subject, you are using an affective strategy.

Research studies show that students can learn to cope with various anxieties by using affective strategies. In the studies, students were taught visualization techniques through teacher modeling and student practice. Students identified fears or negative thinking, and practiced positive "self-talk." The results were changes in feelings and attitudes (Goldfried, Linehan, & Smith, 1978). You probably use these strategies to study content that you don't value. Notice how you talk to yourself or develop ways to motivate yourself. You are using affective strategies.

In sum, the content of practice has a potential range from simple change to complex learning strategies. In order for practice to have comprehensive outcomes, the *context* must support an active learning role for students.

CONTEXT

Our goal here is to help you think about and use practice as an interactive process. You provide the context for this process in the way you structure practice activities.

When learning is interactive in your classroom, learners seek information, make decisions about learning, respond to teaching, and even determine how to study and learn. The way you structure practice can reinforce that active quality and empower your students to determine their own learning.

Providing a Description for Practice

A simple way to begin establishing a context for interactive practice is to identify the learning strategies as students use them. Provide a description of what they are doing and why they are doing it. Listen to this Teacher Talk.

TEACHER TALK

Notice that you are alphabetizing lists of words over and over. You are practicing this so you will be able to do it quickly and easily. Then you can use alphabetizing for looking up words in a dictionary or a telephone book.

1st-Grade Teacher

That description helped students see what they were doing and why they were doing it. We asked those students, "What are you doing?" and "Why?" during another alphabetizing practice several days later. Their answers included the idea that practice would make them fast, and they described a number of uses for alphabetizing. There was a note of confidence in their responses. Sometimes you can ask students the reason for practice instead of telling them: "What are we doing when we recite this list of names?" "Why do we want to know these facts so well?" We have heard students come up with insightful reasons for practice.

Providing a Model for Practice

You continue to promote active learning for your students by modeling the learning strategies for them. As you model, you need to think aloud. Watch and listen to a middle-school teacher demonstrating and explaining to students as she models how to outline information and take notes during a lecture.

SNAPSHOT: Middle-School Classroom

Ms. Holtz begins her class on biological science with, "During the year I am going to be lecturing in class regularly. Lecturing is a kind of teaching that you will be experiencing often as you go through school. Have you seen or heard a lecture? What is it?" Students respond with, "It's when the teacher talks to us about something. We have to be quiet and listen." One boy in the back called out, "It's boring." Others took courage and added, "I get sleepy," "I daydream," "I want to talk." Ms. Holtz nods her head.

"You're right about what happens with lectures sometimes. That's why I want to talk about it today. I use lecturing because it's a fast way to present a whole lot of information and sometimes I need to do that. I want to teach you some strategies to help you learn from lectures. We're going to learn how to take notes and how to outline your information. We're going to work on not being bored."

Ms. Holtz flips on the overhead projector and displays the words *Animal Tissues.* "That's our topic for today, so we begin with a title. As I start my lecture, I will tell you that I am going to describe six kinds of tissue: epithelial, supporting, muscle, connective, blood, and nerve. I write those kinds down and leave lots of space in between each one to take notes." She adds the six kinds to the overhead transparency sheet. "I will describe the functions of each kind of tissue, or what the tissue does, and give a few examples." Ms. Holtz asks students if they could suggest some ideas for more entries on their outlines. As they add *function* and *examples*, she lists the words on the overhead. "Now you have an outline to use as you take notes."

"Watch for three minutes as I lecture and take notes." She begins her lecture on animal tissues, and writes notes on the transparency as she talks about the first kind, epithelial tissue. (*Note:* We can see that Ms. Holtz has her outline and notes on a card next to the overhead projector.) After she finishes, she directs students' attention to the notes, to the information under *function* and under *examples.* Then she adds, "Do you notice that this information doesn't seem to fit in any category? But it seemed important, so I wrote it at the end." She asks students if any of them have been using this note-taking process in their other classes. Several describe how they take and use notes.

"Now we'll practice outlining and taking notes as I lecture about the second kind of tissue." She continues her lecture and models the note taking on the overhead. After she finishes the second kind of tissue, she moves about the room and comments on students' notes. She has several write their notes on the chalkboard as examples, and pairs students to compare and critique each other's notes and outlines.

Notice how Ms. Holtz was teaching the learning strategies of organization. Later we see her show students how to apply the strategies to a chapter in their textbooks. A few days later, Ms. Holtz teaches the students how to go back through their notes and underline important ideas, a complex rehearsal strategy. Again, she makes sure that they realize what and why by saying, "Notice that when you underline important words and ideas, you are kind of repeating them. That will help you to remember them."

If you were to watch Ms. Holtz for a few more days, you would see her continue her modeling until she observed that the students were successfully taking notes and outlining from lectures. She stops modeling gradually and she listens to students' thinking as they compare with a partner. She is using reciprocal teaching. The guided note-taking strategies described in Chapter 7 for use with lectures is another way of providing reciprocal teaching. We will now look at one more way to provide a context that supports active learning in practice.

Providing Explanations for Practice

As students practice, your explanations provide a context of verbal assistance. Explanations are especially important when you teach students a new process and then give them a task using the process. You may be teaching a writing process or a learning strategy. When you do, provide explicit explanations, rather than a quick abbreviated version. *Explicit* means free from vagueness and ambiguity, leaving nothing implied.

Research on reading instruction provides helpful advice for using this strategy. You will see an example of explicit and nonexplicit explanations in the vignette.

In the vignette, Teacher A's explanation provided students with a framework for the context clues. Teacher A also defined, by example, what a context clue is and provided additional examples outside the reading lesson for discovering new words. Teacher A used all of the ideas of this section, not just explicit explanation. She identified what skill was being used and why and how to use it. She also modeled the skill for students while giving explanation.

When you use the three strategies, *provide description, model,* and *provide explanation,* you provide a context for active learning and your students learn how to learn. You may find that some learners continue to have problems during practice. Researchers found that student off-task behaviors were most frequent during seat-work or practice activities (Fisher, Berliner, Filby, Marliave, Cahen, & Dishaw, 1978). We noted at the beginning of this chapter that 20 percent of all students do not complete independent assignments, many of which are practice activities. We want to look at the learner to help you with those problems experienced by students in practice.

LEARNER

We have observed a variety of learner problems during practice activities: the student who can't stay focused on her practice activity, the student who doesn't finish most of his practice assignments, the student who distracts everyone around her, and so on. Lack of practice may result in lack of understanding or forgetting, so you may have achievement concerns. We suggest that you observe the learner and check yourself when these problems occur.

Observing the Learner

Mullen (1987) developed a list of factors that could contribute to a student's ability or inability to complete work. The factors provide a framework for observing your students. Figure 9.2 includes the framework and suggested classroom compensations for when you notice one of the factors.

When one of your students continually does not complete practice assignments or makes frequent errors on those assignments, use the factors as a checklist to record your observations for a period of time. If you find that some of the factors exist, try some of the suggested compensations.

Elementary Research Vignette

INTRODUCTION

Duffy, Roehler, and Rackliffe (1985) were interested in the quality of teacher explanations and the effect of training on explicit explanations.

STUDY PROCEDURES

The researchers studied seven fifth-grade teachers who taught in similar schools in a large urban school district. All teachers received five two-hour training sessions on how to incorporate explicit explanations into their reading instructional routine. Researchers observed each teacher teaching a particular skill to a reading group. Teachers administered a test following each lesson to assess student use of the skill, and students were interviewed to assess awareness of what skills were taught, when to use specific skills, and how to use the skills.

STUDY RESULTS

Analysis of the lessons revealed that teachers talked to students in qualitatively different ways during the lessons. The differences took two forms. First, they conveyed different information about what was to be learned, and second, they provided different kinds of verbal assistance.

One teacher (Teacher A) talked more at the beginning of the lesson, providing a step-by-step description of the process that students were learning to use (explicit explanation). Another teacher (Teacher B) began her lesson with a lengthy questioning session, and at no point did she explain how to use the process being taught. This same teacher seldom elaborated on students' answers, in contrast to Teacher A, who commented on appropriate ideas and helped students develop responses.

The following is an excerpt of both teachers' interactions with their respective classes:

Teacher A: "Look for the clues in the context. Remember the context means all the words before the new word or the words after the new word. Sometimes they are words in a different sentence close by the new word. After you look for clues, . . . (continues describing steps). This is a skill you can use any place you read. When you read the newspaper, your social studies book, or your library book. Maybe when you read the cereal package in the morning. Any place where you come to a word that is new to you, you can use this skill" (p. 9).

Teacher B: "The other words in the sentence are called what?" Students respond, "Context clues." "Mary, what is it called? (Pause) Okay, on the board I've listed the strategy. Okay? The first step is to read the sentence. . . . The next thing? . . . The third thing? . . . And then you? . . ." (p. 10). Throughout the lesson, she emphasized memorizing the steps, not how the steps can be used to figure out the meaning of an unknown word.

The student inteviews revealed that, when teachers gave less specific information, students had less specific understandings of what was taught.

CONCLUSIONS AND IMPLICATIONS FOR PRACTICE

This study suggests that noticeable differences in student understanding result if the teacher is unclear rather than explicit. The implication is for teachers to pay more attention to their descriptions, the way they provide information, and the directions they give. All of those communications need to be explicit.

Checking Yourself

When there are learner problems during practice, check on yourself. Look at the practice activities you have planned. Is the practice connected to the outcomes of the

FIGURE 9.2 *Factors for Observing the Learner During Practice*

Physical Factors

1. Fatigue observations
- Seems chronically tired
- Lays head on the desk
- Yawns
- Stretches
- Falls asleep in class
- Moves with effort

Classroom compensations
- Check with the parent concerning student's bedtime and diet
- Refer for physical examination
- Have the student design a contract that specifies how much work he thinks he can accomplish that day
- Set a timer for a certain amount of work to be accomplished
- Give a snack break
- Allow the student to do something he wants to do after he accomplishes a teacher-assigned task

2. Hearing difficulty observations
- Tilts head
- Asks for directions to be repeated
- Reads lips
- When back is turned, does not respond
- Follows instructions incorrectly

Classroom compensations
- Refer for audiological examination
- Seat at the front of the room
- Present directions and materials visually as well as orally
- Face student when speaking
- On a worksheet, complete the first problem with the student to ensure that he understands

3. Visual acuity difficulty observations
- Rubs eyes
- Squints
- Looks closely at book or paper
- Complains about being unable to see the board
- Loses place when reading
- Redness in eyes

Classroom compensations
- Refer for vision examination
- Select proper seating in preferred location
- Present material orally as well as visually
- Provide good lighting

Academic Factors

1. Achievement above grade level observations
- Scores on group and/or individual tests indicate achievement in the upper 5th percentile
- Advanced vocabulary
- Quick mastery of new material
- Exceptional comprehension
- Keen interest and curiosity

Classroom compensations
- Provide curriculum at appropriate level
- Furnish individual instruction
- Assign enrichment projects
- Reduce rote memory and redundant assignments
- Provide assignments that would encourage self-challenge
- Have student design project himself

2. Achievement below grade level observations
- Scores on individual or group standardized tests below the 25th percentile
- Reads in lower group
- Answers to questions are unrelated to question
- Requires much repetition to learn new materials
- Learns better when material is presented concretely

Classroom compensations
- Provide curriculum at appropriate level
- Provide guide sheets for comprehension subjects
- Shorten spelling lists
- Reduce assignments to the essential. Do not assign bonus pages, extra seat work, etc.
- Provide manipulative and concrete materials to assist with assignments

Perceptual Factors

1. Visual perceptual difficulty observations
- Reversals
- Difficulty copying
- Poor handwriting
- Continually looks at the board when copying

Classroom compensations
- Limit copying tasks
- Have a peer copy notes

FIGURE 9.2 *(Continued)*

- Allow student to write the answer rather than copy entire sentences
- Give tests orally

2. *Auditory memory weakness observations*
   - Asks for directions to be repeated
   - Cannot remember names of people or objects
   - Has difficulty with rote sequences (phone numbers, addresses)

   Classroom compensations
   - Give directions visually as well as orally
   - Help the student begin the assignment
   - Provide "over" drill for auditory activities (A peer could be used for this.)
   - Give short, concise oral directions
   - Have the student repeat the instructions

3. *Visual memory weakness observations*
   - Continually refers to the board when copying
   - Has difficulty remembering sight words, spelling words, or what he sees

   Classroom compensations
   - Give directions orally as well as visually
   - Have the student listen to tapes of the lessons
   - Provide access to a dictionary and other reference material

4. *Auditory discrimination difficulty observations*
   - May have a speech impediment
   - May read lips
   - Has difficulty with rhyming words
   - Has difficulty discriminating extraneous and significant sounds
   - Has difficulty differentiating sounds

   Classroom compensations
   - Needs a quiet environment
   - May need ear plugs to block out noises
   - After giving directions, information, etc., have student repeat them
   - Provide information visually as well as orally

Behavioral Factors

1. *Distractible observations*
   - Gazes around room
   - Does not attend to task
   - Attends to insignificant noises or observations

   Classroom compensations
   - Use a carrel
   - Seat in the least distractible area in room
   - See that student's desk is cleared of all material except what is necessary to task
   - Supply worksheets with only a few items on a page
   - Tap student on the shoulder (or give him some other signal) when he is not attending

2. *Fidgitiness observations*
   - Taps hands and feet
   - Moves around in chair
   - Although not out of the seat, is continually moving

   Classroom compensations
   - Allow student to get out of his seat after completing a short task
   - Provide lessons on a computer
   - Seat next to calm, quiet students
   - Give assignments that involve a hands-on approach

3. *Perfectionistic observations*
   - Continually checks and rechecks his responses
   - Erases and rewrites
   - Tries to form letters perfectly

   Classroom compensations
   - Consider possibility of counseling
   - Discuss behavior with the parents
   - Provide a relaxed atmosphere
   - Give praise

Motor Factors

1. *Fine motor difficulty observations*
   - Poor spacing
   - Difficulty forming letters
   - Difficulty staying on the line
   - Incorrect pencil grip

   Classroom compensations
   - Limit written work
   - Have the student tape his answers
   - Use a typewriter or computer
   - Have a peer copy the student's notes

Source: "The Incomplete Assignment" by J. Mullen, 1987, *Academic Therapy, 22*(5), pp. 469–475. Copyright © 1987 by PRO-ED, Inc. Reprinted by permission.

curriculum? Do your students know exactly how to do the practice work and understand why they are doing it?

We suggest that you audiotape record yourself giving directions for practice, describing practice activities, or modeling for practice. You will be able to examine your explanations and directions as researchers did in the preceding vignette and eliminate interferences to student understanding of practice.

As you look at the common forms of practice used in classrooms, you will see the need to vary practice. Variety will be an important quality to observe in your use of practice because learner problems can result from the boredom of using the same approach.

INTERACTIVE PRACTICE STRATEGIES

In our observations of classrooms, we have seen four common strategies for practice and one that is not so common. We will describe some guidelines for using these strategies interactively and suggest some variations.

Recitation

Recitation is the simplest form of practice, often called *drill*. Most of us experienced it early in our schooling. It is a rehearsal strategy appropriate for recall-type learning (remember the taxonomy in Chapter 3).

Outcomes for Recitation

The repetition that students experience in recitation is useful for rehearsing facts, skills, procedures, and specialized vocabulary. If we asked you to recite the days of the week, they would just spill out of your mouth. They have been overlearned through repetition.

Rosenshine and Stevens (1986) talk about practice for automaticity. *Automaticity* is reached when you do something successfully, rapidly, and with "no thinking through" each step. Recitation allows us to do it verbally and with efficiency. This seemingly simple strategy has the potential for dull teaching, so we suggest some guidelines for both effective and interesting use.

Effectively Using Recitation

As we begin this advice, we remind you to identify for students what recitation is and why they are doing it. We also encourage sensitivity to individual students. Occasionally students are extremely shy or fearful, and recitation in front of a class is painful. Consider providing some opportunities for students to recite in private or with a partner. As students are successful, gain confidence, and become part of a group, they can gradually be brought into public recitation.

As you lead a recitation session for the whole class or a group, remember to be prepared so that you can maintain an interesting pace, or the *momentum* we described in Chapter 6. Be sure to call on those students who volunteer as well as those who don't. When a student answers incorrectly, you may correct the answer and move on to maintain the pace. You may also want to consider the options in Figures 8.3 and 8.4 (Chapter 8) provide fast-paced, brief feedback, such as, "That's correct" or "Right." Finally, be sure that you are using recitation for appropriate content.

The last guideline is best explained with some examples:

> **EXAMPLE:** A middle-school math teacher asks students to recite in chorus the names of the different kinds of triangles as she points to them on a bulletin board. Then she calls on those students with hands raised to describe the qualities of each.

> **EXAMPLE:** Seniors in an accounting class take turns by rows defining procedural terms listed on an overhead sheet. They then take a turn describing a step in the procedure.

> **EXAMPLE:** Second-grade students name the parts of a plant as their teacher points to a large diagram. The teacher calls on individual students by using a set of cards with their names to provide everyone a turn.

Those examples demonstrate appropriate content for recitation: facts, vocabulary, procedures, steps, and simple concepts. It will be difficult to follow the other guidelines if you are not working with appropriate content.

Making Recitation Interesting

The first suggestion for making recitation interesting is to vary the way students respond. In the examples just described, you saw students respond in turn, by row, in unison or chorus, randomly but with everyone having a turn, and by a volunteer system with hands raised. That variation adds interest. We also know from research that each of those strategies is effective for different contexts, content, and learners. Ordered turns for responding work well in small groups, especially for reading instruction (Anderson, Evertson, & Brophy, 1982). Call-out responses seem to benefit low-achieving students (Brophy & Evertson, 1976). Choral responses have proved effective for specific educational programs (Becker, 1977; Reid, 1978–82), and have been related to higher engagement rates for students (McKenzie, 1979).

A second way to make recitation more interesting is to teach students some strategies for remembering. We call these strategies *mnemonics*, systematic procedures for remembering. Think about it. How do you remember names and faces? Mnemonics are interesting and effective for all ages (Levin, 1981), and many students delight in their use. Some common mnemonics you may teach students are:

1. Put words to be remembered together in a sentence. For your use in remembering the principles of motivation, May (1990) suggests *Novelty Needs Level Feedback*. It will help you remember that to motivate students, you need novelty, concern with their basic needs, teaching at an appropriate level, and feedback whenever possible.

2. Put words or information into a rhyme. We all know, "Thirty days has September . . ." and probably still use it.
3. Put the first letter of words into an acronym (abbreviation) or use an acronym to remember symbols. We still remember FACE as the names of the spaces of the G clef.

Both research and experience tell us that one person's mnemonics do not necessarily work for another person. An interesting class activity is to have students develop their own, so that they become aware of how they remember.

Recitation is an important practice strategy that you can use effectively and with interest for students. An added bonus to using recitation is that there is no paperwork!

Review

Literally, review means looking again or relooking at something, going back over material. When you use review this way, it's more recitation. Instead, to use review effectively, you must help students apply and transfer their learning, an interactive process.

Outcomes of Review

In an effective review session, your students will be accurately aware of their own learning, or lack of it, and so will you. This means that review is appropriate for concepts and understandings that have been previously developed and learned.

Effectively Using Review

To conduct a review effectively, we suggest some guidelines:

1. Begin with simple, fast-paced questions to get students thinking about the content.
2. Build from the initial questions and recalled information to other concepts and information.
3. Extend the information or concepts to new situations or problems.

Following the guidelines will take planning. It is difficult to structure questions and a review sequence spontaneously. It takes thinking and organizing beforehand.

Making Review Interesting

After students have checked their homework answers to the social studies questions, Mr. Chang asks, "If you lived in the pioneer days, how would you have answered these questions?"

After each group has conducted a brief review of the problem-solving steps taken by members to work on an assigned problem, Mrs. Piazza asks, "What are some problems in your lives that are similar to the problems that your group solved?"

Students finish a quick review of the previous day's information on the circulation system. They are challenged, "Today we are going to study diseases of the system. See if you can predict them with what you already know about circulation."

Not only are these reviews interesting but they extend review to application and transfer for individual learners. Whenever the learner feels an involvement of self in the review, it's more interesting.

In sum, review is a form of practice that requires thoughtful planning for effective use, builds from recall to understanding to application, and is interesting when learners see a relationship between self and content.

Seatwork

Seatwork is probably the most commonly used practice strategy. When Goodlad studied junior and senior high schools (1984), he saw a range of 54 to 61 percent of time spent in seatwork-type activities. As stated in the beginning of this chapter, 70 percent of time in elementary classrooms is spent in seatwork. Those data make this section critical for this book and for your teaching.

Outcomes for Seatwork

Two functions for seatwork are generally given by teachers: instruction and management. Seatwork offers you a way to engage students in practice activities that do not require your attention for a period of time. The activities are usually quiet and of limited physical activity, so that a large number of students can work independently. The quiet, nondisturbing nature of seatwork allows you simultaneously to teach individual students or a group. This outcome is important when you consider the complexities of your classroom and multiple learner differences.

Fortunately, there are descriptions of successful teachers and classrooms in the research literature from which to provide insights for using practice effectively.

Using Seatwork Effectively

We suggest a sequence of practice that begins with guided practice and moves to independent practice. *Guided practice* is practice in which you lead or direct students in their initial practice and provide guidance. For example, when you give a math seatwork assignment, use the first two or three items or problems for guided practice, saying, "See if you can do the first two problems. Then we'll check them together on the overhead." You can then move about checking for problems or questions.

In guided practice, it is important to check that students understand, to look and listen not only to the answers but to the thinking. This allows you to discover errors before they become habits. It is easier to reteach immediately than after lots of practice Rosenshine and Stevens (1986) suggest that you use a large number of brief questions to check for understanding, calling on students who have raised their hands as well as those who have not. Additional questioning techniques are provided in Chapter 8.

In addition to checking for understanding during guided practice, it is important to provide feedback to students. *Feedback* is information about understanding or misunderstanding, progress or lack of progress, accuracy or inaccuracy in student work. Good, Grouws, and Ebmeier (1983) suggest a type of feedback called *process feedback* (sometimes called *academic feedback*) that is helpful to student understanding. Listen as teachers provide process feedback.

TEACHER TALK

"Your steps are done in the correct order."

"You used the criteria of function and characteristics to place each organism in its category."

"Your opening paragraph does two things: It uses a surprise statement to get attention and it tells the reader what topics will be coming."

"I notice that you remember to use quotation marks when someone says or thinks."

Once guided practice is complete (that is, your students are ready to proceed with understanding), they can move to *independent practice*. Much of this practice is done as seatwork. Anderson, Brubaker, Alleman-Brooks, and Duffy (1985) studied how to make seatwork work and, together with the teachers observed in the studies, generated a set of guidelines. They are organized around tasks of using seatwork: selection of seatwork, explanation of seatwork, monitoring seatwork, and evaluating seatwork. They begin with selection, and remind you that it is important to match task and student. They also urge you to consider the quality of your selection, assuring the task will make sense to students.

When Anderson describes explanation of seatwork, you are reminded to include information about *how* to do it and *why* you are doing it. Does that sound familiar? Remember to provide the kind of explicit explanations you hear in the Teacher Talk that follows.

TEACHER TALK

Watch as I transfer the data from a table to a bar graph. I look at the entire list of amounts—25 pounds, 40 pounds, 65 pounds, 35 pounds, and 80 pounds, and think to myself, "I will need to break up the scale by 5s. I will have lines at 5-pound intervals." Label your intervals to the left, and label the bottom of your graph with the names of the workers like this. Then you can graph each worker's amount by drawing a bar up to the amount weighed like this.

Middle-School Math Teacher

After explanation, Anderson and colleagues (1984) recommend monitoring seatwork. For this task, the teachers and researchers were specific.

1. First, do not start another task or instruction immediately after a seatwork assignment is given.

2. Second, take a few minutes to circulate among students in between other tasks or group instruction to check on seatwork progress.

3. Third, establish systems through which students can get help while you are busy teaching others—a buddy system, a "help card" propped on their desks. (p. 28)

Finally, evaluate seatwork. You may check the work in the student's presence immediately after completion, or check it later and return it the next day. Be sure to include more process feedback about errors, accuracy, and understanding.

Making Seatwork Interesting

Although there are no limits to the possibilities of content for seatwork, in reality, the majority of it takes the form of worksheets and textbook questions. Our first suggestion is to provide variety in seatwork content. Our second is to use worksheets and textbook questions in interesting ways.

1. *Worksheets.* Start by determining if it is worth using. Osborne (1981) suggested guidelines for developing worksheets for reading instruction (Figure 9.3) and we find them useful for most worksheet development. Use them to critique commercial worksheets and those that you develop.

Guideline number 6 warrants some discussion. You may be thinking that if you limit your worksheets to a finite number of task forms, or a limited number of types

FIGURE 9.3 *Guidelines for Developing Worksheets*

1. The layout of the pages should combine attractiveness with utility.
2. Instructions to the students should be clear, unambiguous, and easy to follow. Brevity is a virtue.
3. Most student response modes should be consistent from task to task.
4. Student response modes should be the closest possible to reading and writing.
5. When appropriate, tasks should be accompanied by brief explanations of purpose.
6. There should be a finite number of task forms.
7. Workbook tasks should contain enough content so there is a chance students doing the task will learn something and not simply be exposed to something.
8. The instructional design of individual tasks and of task sequences should be carefully planned.
   a. As students become more competent in using a particular skill, their practice tasks should become increasingly more complex.
   b. Individual tasks should be do-able by students.
   c. Responses should indicate whether or not students understood the task.
   d. Tasks should be designed so that their intent is achieved.
9. The skills being practiced should relate to the main reading.

Source: Osborne, J. (1981). *The purposes, uses, and content of worksheets and some guidelines for teachers and publishers* (Reading Education Report 27). Urbana, IL: Center for the Study of Reading, The University of Illinois. Used by permission. Jean Osborn is Associate Director for the Center for the Study of Reading, University of Illinois.

of work, it will get boring. Instead, this limit allows students to focus on the content of the task rather than how to do it. This same advice applies to the "response modes" or ways of answering in guideline number 3. Once students have learned a number of procedures, they can be successful and think about the content.

Another suggestion for making worksheets more interesting will sound familiar. Discuss the purpose with students so that they understand *why*. Scheu, Tanner, and Au (1986) demonstrated that primary-grade students understand worksheet purposes, can explain them, and learn more from practicing with such understanding.

2. *Textbook questions.* Do you remember "Read the chapter and answer the questions"? This assignment often results in boredom and frustration. Those questions and the way that they are assigned have the potential to make this seatwork more interesting if they are used intelligently (Turner, 1989).

Suggestions for intelligent use include giving the assignments in clusters or stages instead of all at once. Students can be overwhelmed because textbooks are generous with questions. Consider clustering the assignment around a single topic or theme. Turner also suggests dividing the work among students. In Chapter 10, we describe cooperative learning strategies in which students work together on a task such as answering textbook questions. Turner also suggests appointing an assignment mentor, someone willing and capable of helping those students who have difficulty.

Most of this advice about seatwork applies to other practice strategies as well, so keep the suggestions in mind as we move to practice through homework.

Homework

You would think that homework means work that you do at home. That was probably the intent; however, homework is often done in a car or bus, at an ice cream parlor or hamburger stand, just outside the school or on a playground. It seems to have taken on the qualities of taste and smell over the years, because dogs and babies frequently chew on it.

Outcomes of Homework

On a serious note, homework is intended to extend teaching and learning outside the classroom. When students are asked, they feel that homework helps them get good grades. Research has demonstrated a positive relationship between homework and achievement. Both educators and parents attribute to homework the development of personal responsibilities, work and study habits, and self-reliance (Knorr, 1981).

Using Homework Effectively

To use this strategy effectively, you will make two important decisions. The first is to determine *how much* homework. Begin with sensitivity for family and personal obligations of your students. From there, consider a developmental guide for appropriateness:

Grades K–3:	Short, informal assignments (10 to 30 minutes).
Grades 4–6:	Thirty to sixty minutes a day.
Grades 7–9:	One to two hours a day.
Grades 10–12:	One to three hours a day.

We remind you that no two students or families are alike and no two teachers are alike. Some teachers don't assign homework on weekend or vacation periods. Sometimes students use those times to complete long-range assignments (like research papers) or to make up work missed.

Your second decision is to determine *what kind* of homework. We could provide a long list of appropriate assignments, but one quality is essential. Unless the homework practice is designed to involve parents, it should be work that can be done independently. Students should have the knowledge and skills to do the assignment and should understand clearly how to do it. Remember your direction giving, checking for understanding, and providing a purpose? Those are important for student homework assignments.

The following categories support appropriate homework assignments:

1. *Rehearsal activities.* Practice through repetition; for example, spelling words or foreign language vocabulary.
2. *Preparation activities.* Practice that gets students ready for new subject matter; for example, reading about a country to be studied and making a list of questions or unfamiliar terms.

"Dot-matrix homework is not acceptable."

3. *Review activities.* Practice that promotes transfer of what was learned to a new situation or application to other situations; for example, using measuring skills used in class to measure items at home.
4. *Integration activities.* Practice that reviews many skills and concepts and requires students to put them together; for example, making a poster about nutrition showing the concepts and skills learned during a two week unit.

Making Homework Interesting

To help you use this strategy in more interesting ways, we urge you to involve family members. There is potential for enthusiasm, new perspectives, and increased support for students when families are involved. Begin with basic suggestions for family members who want to help and be involved. You will find ideas in Figure 9.4.

We suggest further that students set up a notebook in which both in-class assignments and homework assignments are listed. Students can be taught to record information about due dates, directions, page numbers, and points to remember about how assignments are to be done.

As we have suggested with most of your teaching strategies, the support and assistance of parents and other family members enhance the potential for student achievement.

Have you ever seen young children who have just started school? When they first get an assignment, they are thrilled to tell you that they have homework and

---

FIGURE 9.4   *Homework Suggestions*

- Provide a quiet, well-lighted place for the student to do homework.
- Help the student budget his or her time so that a regular schedule for study is set.
- Take an active interest in what the student is doing in school. Ask him or her to explain a particular assignment and tell what is being learned by doing it. Compliment good work or when improvement is shown. Make an occasional constructive suggestion, but avoid severe criticism and undue pressure. A positive attitude by parents will encourage students to do their best.
- Encourage the student to seek additional help from the teacher at school if he or she seems to be having any difficulty with the work.
- Insist upon sufficient rest, proper diet, and periodic check ups to maintain good health.
- Encourage, guide, and, at times, help your child with homework, but under no circumstances do it for him/her.
- Consult your child's teacher as soon as problems arise.

Contact the teacher, counselor or principal:
- If your child worries or frets over homework assignments.
- If you or your child do not understand the assigned work.
- If your child does not understand how to proceed with assignments.
- If you think your child is assigned too much or too little homework.
- If other problems regarding homework exist.

Source: Guidelines Regarding Homework, Beaverton School District 48J, Beaverton, Oregon, 1989. Reprinted with permission.

can't wait to get started. With appropriate assignments, realistic amounts of work, and satisfying involvement of families, we might be able to maintain some of that enthusiasn for homework.

Learning Centers

You may be surprised to find us writing about learning centers in this chapter. We decided to talk about centers here because they help you provide practice in varied forms, interactively, and with a range from simple to complex. Learning centers provide interesting practice in both elementary and secondary classrooms.

Outcomes of Learning Centers

A learning center can be a physical area where a student can work independently or with other students on varied learning activities. It can be a time or a place where students have some choice of activities and can pace themselves. Centers provide an opportunity to practice making decisions, practice following directions, practice new skills, practice using resources and materials, review previously learned information, and enjoy practicing. Centers also provide an opportunity for you to observe students at work, or for you to work undisturbed with a student or small group. You can provide and manage a variety of individualized practice activities with centers.

Using Learning Centers Effectively

The outcomes of learning centers may have overwhelmed you because they make centers sound like a "Super Strategy." It will be important to use them effectively, as you see in Ms. Tannenbaum's classroom.

SNAPSHOT: Elementary Classroom

While teaching about the metric system, Ms. Tannenbaum sets up a learning center for practice in using metric measurement. The activities planned for the center need physical space, so student work tables are shifted to one side of the room. This leaves open floor space along the side of the classroom next to the long counter top where the center will be arranged.

On Monday, Ms. Tannenbaum introduces the learning center to students during math time with, "We will have a week-long set of activities for you to get lots of practice using metrics. I want you to be able to think in metrics when you measure." She walks over to the side of the room and points to a sign, "This is Dr. VonMeter's Laboratory." The students laugh. "In order to use the laboratory, you must be ready to think and work in metrics. At the same time, you will have some fun with measuring."

Ms. Tannenbaum shows students the initial activity, constructing a folder to hold their work records of center activities. Each student has a sheet and she calls attention to it, "Look at the sheet—it's a checklist of the activities at the center. As I show you each activity and explain the directions, check it off on your sheet."

She demonstrates how to do each activity and checks that students understand: "Renee, tell us how to do the Mr. Mouse activity," or "Tomas, what's the first thing to do in the Pacefinder activity?" Each activity has a direction sheet, examples, and an answer key to check when finished.

After directions, Ms. Tannenbaum asks students to look at the checklist again. "Notice that for each activity, I've asked you to indicate how well you did and how well you liked or didn't like the activity. When you finish all of the activities, you earn a metric license." She shows the license and again gets smiles and laughter.

Before students begin trying the activities, Ms. Tannenbaum points to a schedule of group work for the week. Different groups of students will be working with her for 20 minutes each day starting on Tuesday. "On the day that your group works with me, you'll only have 15 minutes in the laboratory."

Ms. Tannenbaum follows some guidelines in her use of learning centers. (1) She places the centers in areas that will not disturb or be disturbed. (2) She ensures easy movement of students in, out, and within the center. (3) She provides space for materials and supplies, finished and unfinished work (the back of a cabinet door, window sills, bulletin board, and even the floor).

In managing the center, Ms. Tannenbaum also followed some guidelines for us. Did you notice that she gave clear and complete directions for the activities? She also provided additional directions in written form (look at them in the Samples and Examples sections at the end of this chapter). If we had continued watching her, we would have seen her use the remainder of the first day of the metric center to observe, watching for potential problems or confusion. She provided a record-keeping strategy for students with the folders, and a few of the activities were autotelic (self-correcting). Everything for Dr. VonMeter's Laboratory was organized in advance.

In scheduling the center, it is best begun as part of a class period. An effective use of time is seen in classrooms where student groups follow a rotating schedule with time to work at centers, time to work with their teacher, and time to work independently at desks on assignments. A word of caution: We have often heard, "When you finish your seatwork, you may go to the centers." Our concerns for this scheduling are the student who has difficulty completing seatwork and may never get to use the centers, and for the message it communicates about "just getting done." Did you notice how Ms. Tannenbaum scheduled the centers so that all students had a chance to use them? She also scheduled small groups of students to work with her during that time period. Her schedule gave ample time for all students to try all activities, ample time for her to do some observing, and ample time for her to instruct small groups.

Some other scheduling arrangements include using a sign-up sheet for students to schedule themselves for daily use, and using a buddy system where students

FIGURE 9.5 *Learning Center Checklist*

_____ 1. Have you planned an introductory learning experience to precede the learning center?

_____ 2. Does the learning center attract through color, design, and novelty?

_____ 3. Does the center challenge, excite, and interest students?

_____ 4. Are there easy and difficult tasks?

_____ 5. Do activities or tasks provide feedback to students?

_____ 6. Are the tasks of activities provided in small, easy to follow sections?

_____ 7. Is there a source of information easily available to students?

_____ 8. Is the center free from inaccuracies, misspellings, and grammatical errors?

_____ 9. Is each activity independent of other activities?

_____ 10. Is there opportunity for independent and cooperative work?

_____ 11. Are directions clear, simple, and complete?

_____ 12. Can the center be used by students independently?

_____ 13. Is the center portable and designed for easy storage?

_____ 14. Are the materials durable?

_____ 15. Do you have a way to determine which students have completed each activity?

_____ 16. Do you have a way of collecting student responses to activities?

_____ 17. Is there a clear procedure for obtaining and storing materials?

_____ 18. Is there a recording system?

Source: May, F. B. (1980). *To help children communicate*. Columbus, OH: Merrill Publishing Company. Used by permission.

use centers in pairs. Our suggestions could go on and on. To capsulate this advice, we offer a checklist for setting up, maintaining, and evaluating your learning centers in Figure 9.5.

Making Learning Centers Interesting

To help you in this task, we suggest student involvement and the assistance of parents, volunteers, or an aide. They can make materials, work with individuals or groups in the center, or observe students as they practice. We encourage student involvement in planning and constructing of centers. Listen to teacher enthusiasm when students are involved.

TEACHER TALK

What more could a teacher ask than to have students ask permission to develop a center on Japanese Haiku while the class is studying a unit on poetry?

High-School English Teacher

We were studying Australia and one objective was for students to name and describe the animals native to the country. The students took over a center and painted a mural of the animals and their habitats. They made puppets of the animals and gathered magazines, stories, and poems. They even made a matching game. To tell you the truth, by the time they had the center set up, they had met the objective.

Middle-School Teacher

I was hesitant to let my students come up with their own ideas for a center but I decided to try it. They wanted a center for wrapping packages. We gathered wrapping paper, old boxes, lots of tape, cards and envelopes, and ribbon. For three months, they practiced wrapping presents and designed and wrote cards. I watched them practice measuring, writing, predicting, and using materials like tape and scissors.

Preschool Teacher

Talk about active learning! Practice can be exciting and relevant to students' lives with learning center activities, especially when students have planning input.

SUMMARY

As you use the practice strategies of recitation, review, seatwork, homework, and learning centers, remind yourself of the importance of complexity in practice content. Provide an interactive context for practice, and spend time observing learners as they work. Follow the guidelines for using practice effectively. By now, you may have reached automaticity with them:

- Provide a purpose or reason for the practice activity.
- Give clear directions and spend enough time for students to understand.
- Check for understanding of both the "how to do" and the content of practice.
- Provide feedback and evaluation about the accuracy, understanding, and content of the practice.
- Be sure that the practice is worth doing, connected to learning, and appropriate and interesting to the learner.

Now that you know the guidelines, check yourself on using them. Tape-record your directions for practice activities. Practice writing and giving process feedback. Schedule time to monitor student practice. Ask yourself the purpose of the practice activities before making assignments. Ask students for feedback about the practice activities.

Make effective practice a priority in your professional development. From there, you will need to be a student yourself and practice, practice, practice.

REFERENCES

Anderson, L., Brubaker, N., Alleman-Brooks, J., & Duffy, G. (1984). *Making seatwork work* (Research series #142). East Lansing, MI: Institute for Research on Teaching, Michigan State University.

Anderson, L., Evertson, C., & Brophy, J. (1979). An experimental study of effective teaching in first grade reading groups. *The Elementary School Journal,79*, 193–222.

Beach, D. M. (1977). *Reaching teenagers: Learning*

centers for the secondary classroom. Santa Monica, CA: Goodyear.

Becker, W. C. (1977). Teaching reading and language to the disadvantaged—What have we learned from field research? *Harvard Educ. Rev, 47,* 518–543.

Brophy, J. (1980). *Recent research on teaching.* East Lansing, MI: Institute for Research on Teaching, Michigan State University.

Brophy, J., & Evertson, C. (1976). *Learning from teaching: A developmental perspective.* Boston: Allyn and Bacon.

Duffy, G., Roehler, L., & Rackliffe, G. (1985). *Qualitative differences in teachers' instructional talk as they influence student awareness of content.* East Lansing, MI: Institute for Research on Teaching, Michigan State University.

Fisher, C., Berliner, D., Filby, N., Marliave, R., Cahen, L., & Dishaw, M. (1978). Teaching behaviors, academic learning time, and student achievement: An overview. In C. Denham & A. Lieberman (Eds.), *Time to learn.* Washington, DC: U.S. Government Printing Office.

Goldfried, M. R., Linehan, M. M., & Smith, J. L. (1978). Reduction of test anxiety through cognitive restructuring. *Journal of Consulting and Clinical Psychology, 46,* 32–39.

Good, T., Grouws, D., & Ebmeier, H. (1983). *Active mathematics teaching.* White Plains, NY: Longman.

Goodlad, J. (1984). *A place called school.* New York: McGraw-Hill.

Knorr, C. L. (1981). *A synthesis of homework research and related literature.* Paper presented to the Kappa Delta Pi conference, Washington, DC.

Levin, J. R. (1981). The mnemonic '80s: Keywords in the classroom. *Educational Psychologist, 16*(2), 65–82.

Lowenberg-Ball, D., & Feiman-Nemser, S. (1986). *Using textbooks and teachers' guides: What beginning elementary teachers learn and what they need to know* (Report #174). East Lansing, MI: Institute for Research on Teching, Michigan State University.

May, F. B. (1980). *To help children communicate.* Columbus, OH: Charles E. Merrill.

May, F. B. (1990). *Reading as communication: An interactive approach.* Columbus, OH: Charles E. Merrill.

McKenzie, G. (1979). Effects of questions and test-like items on achievement and on-task behavior in a classroom concept learning presentation. *Journal of Educational Research, 72,* 348–350.

Mullen, J. (1987). The incomplete assignment. *Academic Therapy, 22*(5), 469–475.

Osborne, J. (1981). *The purposes, uses, and content of workbooks and some guidelines for teachers and publishers* (Reading Education Report 27). Urbana, IL: Center for the Study of Reading, The University of Illinois.

Reid, E. (1978–82). *The reading newsletter.* Salt Lake City, UT: Exemplary Center for Reading Instruction.

Rosenshine, B., & Stevens, R. (1986). Teaching functions. In M. C. Wittrock (Ed.), *Third handbook of research on teaching.* New York: Macmillan.

Scheu, J., Tanner, D., & Au, K. H. (1986). Designing seatwork to improve students reading comprehension ability. *The Reading Teacher, 40*(1).

Turner, T. (1989). Using textbook questions intelligently. *Social Education, 53*(1), 58–60.

Weinstein, C. E., & Mayer, R. E. (1986). The teaching of learning strategies. In M. C. Wittrock (Ed.), *Third handbook of research on teaching.* New York: Macmillan.

SAMPLES AND EXAMPLES

Five learning center Samples and Examples are provided here to give you ideas for starting your own centers:

- Laboratory Checklist
- Measure Up
- Metric License and Metric Measuring License
- Spanish Center
- Use Your Senses

DR. VONMETER'S LABORATORY CHECKLIST

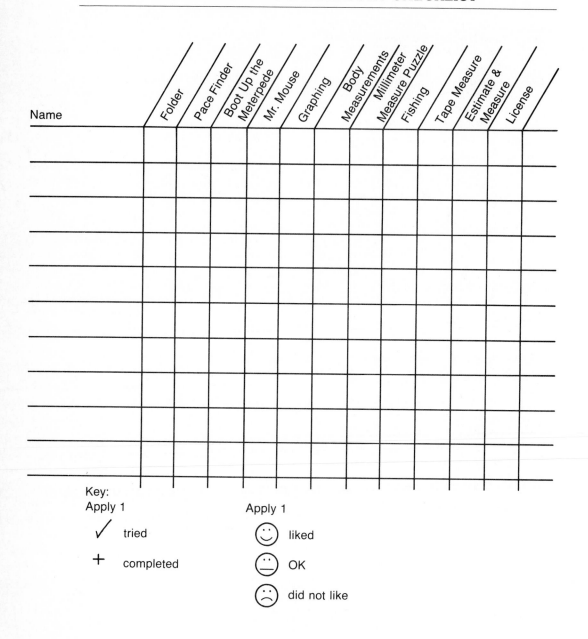

Name	Folder	Pace Finder	Boot Up the Meterpede	Mr. Mouse	Graphing	Body Measurements	Millimeter Measure Puzzle	Fishing	Tape Measure	Estimate & Measure	License	

Key:
Apply 1

✓ tried

+ completed

Apply 1

☺ liked

😐 OK

☹ did not like

Source: C. Holz, Portland State University, 1988. Used with permission.

MEASURE UP

Your Name _____

Partner's Name _____

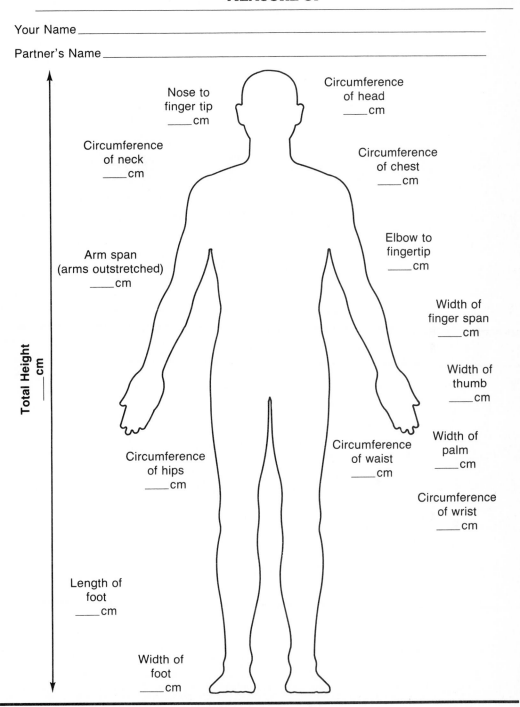

Nose to
finger tip
____cm

Circumference
of head
____cm

Circumference
of neck
____cm

Circumference
of chest
____cm

Elbow to
fingertip
____cm

Arm span
(arms outstretched)
____cm

Width of
finger span
____cm

Width of
thumb
____cm

Total Height
____cm

Circumference
of hips
____cm

Circumference
of waist
____cm

Width of
palm
____cm

Circumference
of wrist
____cm

Length of
foot
____cm

Width of
foot
____cm

Source: C. Holz, Portland State University, 1988. Used with permission.

METRIC LICENSE

Directions: You have already measured all the needed information.
1. Find the information from other activities.
2. Transfer the information correctly onto your license.
3. Make sure to put your name and date on your license.
4. Place your finished sheet in your folder. Congratulations!

Metric Measuring License

This license entitles _____,
upon completion of the form below, to be an OFFICIAL METRIC MEASURER,
authorized to measure, at any time, using any OFFICIAL METRIC UNITS (such as
cm, dm, m, km, g, or kg), ANYTHING that can be measured either with OFFICIAL
MEASURING TOOLS or by ESTIMATION.

For use in estimation:

height ____cm   arm spread ____cm   nose to fingertip ____cm

plain step (pace) ____cm   elbow to fingertip (cubit) ____cm

tip of thumb to tip of little finger with hand widespread (span) ____cm

width of palm (hand) ____cm   width of thumb ____cm

For use in buying clothing and accessories:

circumference of head ____cm   circumference of neck ____cm

circumference of wrist ____cm   foot length ____cm and width ____cm

circumference of chest ____cm   circumference of waist ____cm

circumference of hips ____cm   Date _____

ALL OF THESE MEASUREMENTS WILL CHANGE—
KEEP YOUR METRIC MEASURING LICENSE UP TO DATE

Source: C. Holz, Portland State University, 1988. Used with permission.

Materials Teacher Provides:

The teacher provides the game board with five or more cities in Mexico as the targets in the game. For each city there should be a short narration in Spanish about the city or a filmstrip with written Spanish narration. There should be a deck of question cards for each city with three questions about the city written in Spanish on each card and with the answers on the back of the card. A spinner with moves from 1 to 4 should be included at the game board.

Objective:

Upon completion of the center the student should be able to demonstrate an understanding of Spanish narration, discuss the cultural aspects of cities in Mexico, and show an increased verbal fluency in Spanish.

Directions:

1. Players should select a token. They are going to take a trip in Mexico, and the object is to visit five cities and collect a token from each one.

2. The player spinning the highest number goes first. Players can start at any of the starting points on the game board.

3. Players spin the spinner to determine the number of spaces they can move. Each time they come to or land on a city, they stop and view a filmstrip on one of the cities, with narration written in Spanish, or they listen to a cassette tape recording with the narration in Spanish. To be able to collect a token from the city visited, the player must answer three questions correctly about the city. The questions are written in Spanish, but the player answers in English. Each city has a set of questions with the answers so that each player gets a different set of questions and answers.

4. The other players should check the answers to the questions. If the player gets them right, he gets a token for that city. If he misses one of the questions, he does not get a token and must come back to the city another time for a token. The first player to get five tokens wins.

Source: From Don M. Beach, *Reaching Teenagers: Learning Centers for Secondary Classrooms* (Santa Monica, CA: Goodyear Publishing Co., 1977), pp. 160–161. Reprinted by permission.

USE YOUR SENSES

Objective:
The student will write five sentences using ten sense image words selected from a box.

Directions:
1. Draw ten words out of the box.
2. Using the words that you have drawn that appeal to the senses, write five sentences using any combination of two or more words. You must use all ten words at least once in the five sentences.
3. Underline the sense image words you used.

Materials Teacher Provides:
The teacher should provide a box with thirty to forty words that could be used as sense image words. Include such words as "buzzing," "crackling," "soft," "velvety," "dark," "brilliant," "blazing," "chortling." As a warm-up exercise to the center activity, the teacher could provide a worksheet with directions similar to these:

Imagery is a result of words stimulating our senses of sight, hearing, touch, smell, and taste. We respond in various ways both physically and mentally to the use of sensory-stimulating words, or imagery. Look through your literature books and find two examples each of vague imagery and concrete imagery.

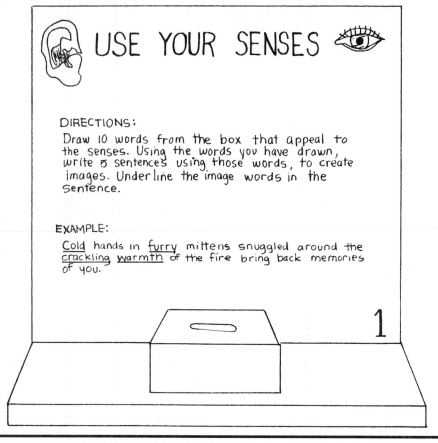

Source: From Don M. Beach, *Reaching Teenagers: Learning Centers for Secondary Classrooms* (Santa Monica, CA: Goodyear Publishing Co., 1977), pp. 30–31. Reprinted by permission.

CHAPTER 10

Grouping for Instruction: Involvement and Interaction

CHAPTER OUTCOMES

At the conclusion of this chapter you will be able to:

1. Examine the context, content, and learner for information to use in making grouping decisions.
2. Use different grouping arrangements to accommodate differences in context, content, and learners.
3. Develop routines and procedures to manage grouping arrangements and to use volunteers and aides.

KEY TERMS AND CONCEPTS

Grouping
Cohesive Environment
Group Norms
Interpersonal Skills
Cooperative Work Habits
Varying Student Roles
Varying Student Involvement
Group Size
Assign to Groups
Within-Class Grouping
Interest Grouping
Ability Grouping
Homogeneous
Regrouped for Selected Subjects
Heterogeneous
Cross-Age and Peer Tutoring
Cooperative Learning Arrangements
Joplin Plan
Staggered or Split Scheduling
Aides and Volunteers

INTRODUCTION

We use *grouping* as a generic term, a way of organizing students for teaching and learning. Many teachers think that grouping helps them individualize or match their teaching to individual learners. Some teachers see grouping as a way of reducing the crowds, that is, allowing them to teach a few students at a time. Many of the first teachers in our country grouped students for the same reasons. We will examine the practice of grouping students as it has progressed in our educational history and see what we have learned.

Grouping—Yesterday and Today

The practice of grouping students for instruction has been with us since the beginning, but it continues to be marked with problems, professional concerns, and legal difficulties. With all of our research and development knowledge, we continue to struggle with effectively teaching all of the different learners in our classrooms, and grouping is our most common response.

Past Practices

In the 1920s, testing came into popular use, and with it came ability grouping. Educators thought that teaching students in homogeneous groups or groups of similar ability would contribute to student achievement. By 1930, studies showed that homogeneous grouping was not effective for achievement and raised questions of effects on student attitudes, self-concept, and educational opportunities (Kelliher, 1931; Mann, 1960; Strauss, 1957).

Ability grouping continued and by the late 1960s, the practice prompted serious equity questions. Some forms of ability grouping were seen as creating racially identifiable classes (McPartland, 1968). Studies of the interactions between teachers and students suggested that ability grouping resulted in low-level expectations expressed by teachers to low-ability students compared to expectations expressed to students of other ability levels (Persell, 1977).

Today's Practices

We continue to study the effects of ability grouping practices, but current conclusions are that the practices are not satisfactory for students of all achievement levels (Slavin, 1987a). We know that for some curriculum areas and for some students, ability grouping can be instructionally effective (Slavin, 1988; Barr & Dreeben, 1983), but our concerns for the side effects of the practice have remained.

Fortunately those concerns have kept educators working on the development of grouping alternatives and improved ability grouping approaches.

We encourage your thoughtful decisions when grouping students for learning. Use the insights from current research and practice. Consider the differences in context, content, and learner. Your decisions will include those related to group size, student assignment, and group configuration. We will describe some common grouping practices, some management routines, and procedures for using volunteers and aides.

IMPLICATIONS FOR GROUPING

When you plan to group students for instruction, begin by looking at the context—the physical environment and the socioemotional environment. Look at the content—your intended outcomes and the outcomes possible with the dynamics of group work. Look at the learner—for varying roles and different types of involvement.

Context

To make grouping decisions without considering the physical and socioemotional context of teaching and learning is like packing a suitcase for a trip without knowing anything about the place where you are going. Let's look at your teaching space and assess its arrangement and climate.

Physical Environment

Self-contained classrooms or classrooms designed for one group of students present simple considerations for grouping. Your arrangement of furniture is influenced by number of students, necessary equipment, and your imagination. Since we seldom (or never) hear a teacher say, "I have too much room," your limit is space. To use grouping arrangements with the usual amount of space, try the following:

1. Leave several empty areas (e.g., corners) where students can bring and arrange chairs or pillows to work together.
2. Cluster tables and chairs or desks to accommodate a small work group.
3. Locate groups where students can be easily seen or supervised by you.
4. Arrange the classroom furniture for flexibility, with several movable sets of furniture.
5. Assign "moving committees" of students who go into action when arrangement is needed.
6. Consider adjoining hallways, patios, and storerooms to extend classroom space.

In Chapter 12, we describe similar ways to prepare the environment for teaching with roleplay, simulation, and drama, often conducted in small groups of students. Consult teachers in adjoining rooms and your administrator to prevent misunderstandings and problems of distraction and schedules.

If you teach in an open-space school or in a classroom without walls, you may have large spaces for grouping but other kinds of concerns. Teachers who work in such spaces insist that discussions between neighboring teachers must:

1. Establish common agreement about standards for student behavior.
2. Establish common agreement on student movement.
3. Identify activities scheduled for minimum noise.
4. Coordinate arrangement and use of furniture, equipment, and supplies.

So, freedom of space for grouping demands responsibility and coordination;

otherwise, chaos and tension will occur. Another suggestion is for students, parents, and aides/volunteers to be well informed of all the agreements, scheduling, and arrangements. Student involvement in the decision is ideal.

Scheduling

Another environmental consideration is time. In your self-contained classrooms, you make decisions about pace and schedule. Grouping is best scheduled in short time periods, with opportunity for movement around the room between activities. Time periods vary with second-grade students (5 to 20 minutes) and high-school juniors (20 to 40 minutes), but there are time limits in terms of attention and comfort for all students. In your open-space classrooms, you are able to have more movement within and between groups, as well as more concurrent group activities, so time is less structured.

Socioemotional Environment

If you were to ask what kind of classroom would best support grouping practices, we would use the word *cohesive*. In a cohesive classroom, students develop socially and emotionally and are able to be group members. Notice the norms of a class to determine its cohesiveness.

Group norms are the "normal" or expected ways of behaving and responding. You initiate norms when you model respect and social relationships. You maintain norms when you prohibit certain behaviors and encourage others. To protect a cohesive environment, prohibit the following:

- Put-downs
- Discrimination in activities (by gender, race, physical differences)
- Negative interactions
- Student rejections

To promote a cohesive environment, encourage the following:

- Focus on errors rather than individuals when correcting mistakes.
- Make help available for those who seek it.
- Accept diverse opinions or ideas.
- Structure work for alternative approaches.
- Respect student needs and differences.

If the norms of your class are to work cooperatively and to enjoy individual group members, it will be easier and more effective to use varied grouping strategies. There must also be frequent opportunities for student interaction. Planned activities and assignments can provide opportunities such as:

- Student committees design and construct bulletin boards and displays.
- Student teams are responsible for discussing and solving class problems.
- Student pairs volunteer for classroom responsibilities.
- Students critique each other's work and assist with revision.

"While we all believe that each child has his or her own learning style, Ms. Perkins, nevertheless. . ."

You have the beginning of group development if students get to know each other. To keep the interaction going, effective teachers offer two suggestions. First, change group membership from time to time (e.g., every three to four weeks). Second, provide an opportunity for students to form friendships with students of differing ability. When we describe some different grouping arrangements, you will get ideas for how to use their advice.

With the physical environment and socioemotional environment in mind, move to the content of teaching. It is the next source of information for making grouping decisions.

Content

Begin by identifying your intended outcomes. They may be knowledge or under-standings, skills, or attitudes. As students learn in groups, they can achieve additional goals related to working in groups.

Knowledge and Understanding Outcomes

Toward these goals, grouping provides opportunity for peer interpretation and shar-ing of experiences and insights. Haven't you struggled with trying to help someone understand an idea, only to have another person be successful by stating the idea differently? The task of explaining is often made difficult by the difference in stu-dent perceptions and experiences. In small groups, students have more opportunity to paraphrase, explain, describe, ask for clarification, and talk about content than whole class interactions provide.

You are often the only adult in your classroom, and there are limits to the experiences and insights you bring. Each student can contribute additional experiences and insights, and in small groups, they have opportunities to do so. Some examples of how you can provide opportunity for both peer interpretation and student sharing of experiences and insights include:

- When you form groups to study a geographic location or a piece of equipment, mix students who have experience with those who have no experience.
- Have students work together to write definitions of abstract or sophisticated concepts.
- Have students describe their impressions of a field trip or observations of a demonstration in groups.
- Have students describe and compare family customs, holiday celebrations, and home responsibilities.
- Have student groups predict what will happen in a story or a play.
- Have student groups paint a mural to interpret a poem, a feeling, or a stereotype.
- Have students work in groups to develop a response to a crisis, a problem, or an award.

You might look at this list and say that these could all take place in a whole class setting. Yes, they could. However, hearing 28 to 31 students describe a response is time consuming and does not happen often. When it is done with a whole class, certain students often do the sharing, and others get bored. In small groups, everyone can express and be listened to in a reasonable amount of time.

Skill Outcomes

Toward these goals, grouping assists the practice and feedback that must accompany your teaching. You can effectively model and describe a new skill to 30 students, but it is difficult to provide feedback to each individual. Grouping of students can provide peer coaches as well as peer motivation.

When students work in small groups to practice a skill, they can coach each other's learning. When a sixth-grade student is struggling with long division problems, there is nothing like a friend standing by saying, "OK, now what do you do next? Right. Now, subtract the number. Yes, 23 is correct." The issue of numbers (that is, 30 students and 1 teacher) is not much of an issue if you divide the class into five groups to practice using the microscope. In each group, students can check each other's procedures and provide feedback. You will find more discussion of the coaching role in Chapter 12.

There is also the advantage of peer motivation when students work in groups. When students participate in a small group, there is a personal quality to their work because others are aware of their efforts, their successes, and even their struggles. Motivation is higher in these situations, especially when group members work on a group task. Complex tasks requiring well developed skills are much better accomplished through group work than individual work (Cotton & Cook, 1982).

The following Snapshot gives you a glimpse of how a group of students can practice skills and receive feedback as they work simultaneously on a complex science project and some problem solving.

SNAPSHOT: Secondary Classroom

First-year biology meets in the lab once a week to follow up information from the lecture classes. Today, as students enter the lab, they hear, "We are going to be working on a new process and some important lab skills. As soon as you get to your table, read the chart of tasks for this period."

Soon all students are reading the chart. There are 35 students arranged around six work stations of equipment, sinks, and storage. Ms. Newcomb begins. "Today we are learning the process of making slides, as well as studying slides of bacteria. First, I have a list of procedures for making slides. Your entire group should review the steps carefully and make sure everyone understands. Each of you is to take a turn making a slide. Have others observe you to check your process. When your slide is complete, look under the microscope and compare it with the image on the overhead projector. If your image is different, you have a problem. After everyone in your group checks their images, the group should work on the problems."

Before students begin their small group activity, Ms. Newcomb asks the students at Table 1, "Tell us how you will do your work today." Three students describe the work procedures accurately. The teacher adds, "Here are some group interaction requirements," pointing to the following three requirements (which she has written on the chalkboard):

Group Interaction Requirements
1. Students will be observed by at least two peers and will get feedback on their work.
2. Students will ask at least one peer to check their work.
3. Students will have the assistance of all group members to solve problems.

Ms. Newcomb then says to the students, "I will be observing your work and expect you to follow the requirements. Remember, we are working on being effective group members."

We see students move around to form small groups of three, with one student beginning the steps to make a slide and two others watching. We hear, "Be careful not to touch the slide," and "Wow, that was fast," and "You forgot the solution," and "That's right." When one student struggles, we see at least two others assisting or encouraging, "Try it again, you will get it."

At Table 4, we hear, "OK, we have two problems here," and "What could be the reasons for the images not matching?" We hear students coming up with several reasons and someone writing them on paper. Then a student asks, "What can we do?" Again, several ideas are expressed and written. Table 4 decides to remake the slides that have problems and to watch the sequence of application carefully. We hear comments of help and encouragement as they begin.

In addition to the illustrations in the Snapshot for grouping students to work on skills, students can help each other edit and rewrite, assess progress, evaluate completed work, set goals, and solve problems. You can move through the groups and listen to the coaching and motivation.

Attitudes and Values Outcomes

The influence of group norms is especially noticed when we work on attitudes with students. Peer pressure is powerful, even for young students. In secondary classrooms, social patterns and group sentiments influence how students respond to an attitude or value that is new or different. To teach content with attitude and value outcomes, it will be necessary to provide opportunity for group discussions so that students can hear different points of view.

To have effective group discussions, everyone must be involved. A group size of 8 to 10 is the absolute maximum. Arrangement is important so that individuals can see everyone in the group. Discussion topics must spark interest. For secondary students, curfews, drug use, ecology, and nuclear power are appropriate topics. Suitable topics for elementary students include allowances, playground rules, and friendships. Students today have quite a bit of savvy and contribute to insightful discussions. With grouping and a small number of students in a group, everyone can be involved. Contrast that possibility with the one in this Teacher Talk.

TEACHER TALK

My class was minimally engaged. I did most of the talking, and three or four of the best students talked the rest of the time.

Elementary Teacher

In situations dominated by you or a few students, few attitudes and values will be developed. One last reason for grouping must be included. We have been told by learners of different ages, "I am more comfortable expressing myself in a small group than in front of the whole class." Grouping is a sensitive approach, an appropriate approach for working on the personal outcomes of attitudes and values.

Outcomes of the Grouping Process

The grouping process works toward the "meta-goals of education" (Napier & Gershenfeld, 1985) or broader goals for students, possibly because they reflect real-life situations better than whole class configurations. Students will eventually work in family groups, on athletic teams, or with a department staff. Working in small groups in classrooms will promote the interpersonal skills, cooperative work habits, and a sense of competence necessary for working in future groups.

Interpersonal Skills

In small groups students have ample opportunity for practice and talking and listening because everyone can be involved. Even young students learn to wait for a turn, to comment on another's ideas, and to be accepting of different opinions if they regularly experience small group interaction.

In groups you model those interpersonal skills, so be sure that your listening and speaking are worth noticing by students. You might say, "When Aaron is talking, I sit still and think about only what Aaron is saying." You might paraphrase a student's expression with, "Aaron said that he thinks that raising the bus fares could cause a hardship for students and elderly people. He is worried about their travel if fares increase." Students hear your acceptance and hear Aaron's ideas repeated.

You also have the authority to insist on appropriate respect for each student's expression. Interruptions or judgments are not allowed if you want students to express ideas freely.

Cooperative Work Habits

Working in a small group demands different work habits than working independently within a class. Students have a chance to experience different work styles and a sense of their own and others' strengths and limitations.

In the preceding Snapshot, students learned about the effects of cooperation, everyone working together. In the process of dividing responsibilities, students also learn negotiation strategies. The give and take of life's situations are experienced in cooperative work groups.

A Sense of Competence

When students participate as a member of a group or team, they have an increased opportunity to succeed or complete tasks or projects. Group assignments do not feel as overwhelming to students as individual assignments may feel. Group members can joke about a task, the deadline, or the possibility of the work, and all it takes is one member who is determined to succeed, and a group gains momentum.

In order to support the success of group work, and ultimately individual success, give attention to how you structure tasks and situations. Some examples are:

- Tenth-grade students evaluate each other's work on the final project and include feedback on cooperation, speaking, listening, dependability, and good humor.
- When each third-grade group completes its display of pioneer scenes, the group convenes to acknowledge one contribution of each member.

Learner

The following Snapshot gives you a glimpse of the diversity of students you will meet. Your learners bring individual differences, especially noticed in their participation and the kind of roles they take in classroom activities.

SNAPSHOT: *Elementary Classroom*

It is 8:20 AM at Raleigh Hills Elementary School and students in a fifth-grade class are already engaged in silent reading. Most of them have a book in front of them and appear to be reading.

In the last row are two girls and three boys. Aletha is the tallest girl in the class, dark skinned with thick hair and glasses. She arrives at school with enthusiasm and can't wait to read. Today she is almost finished with *Johnny Tremaine*. Aletha, to the delight of her teachers, frequently refers to her reading repertoire for information in social studies, science, art, and music. Next to Aletha is Jonathan, who is plump and taller than most of the boys, and is equally enthusiastic about coming to school. His enthusiasm isn't for books, however, it's for his friends. He reads easily, but with regular interruptions to make noises, faces, and quick comments to those around him. *Island of Blue Dolphins* was read by his best friend, so he's giving it a try. He prefers humorous stories and sometimes mysteries.

Camille is sitting with her back to Jonathan. She nods at him with a bit of disgust, often in the direction of her girlfriends in the next row. She is reading *Mrs. Wappinger's Secret* but can't remember what it is about. Yesterday she came to school with her hair all braided into plaits with different colored bands. During silent reading she worried about how she looked and kept her mirror on her desk. Today she can't remember what happened in her story.

Jeff stares at Camille a lot. He wants to read but he keeps noticing things that amuse or interest him. Jeff is short, has short brown hair, and wears glasses. His mother decided to get involved with his reading and asks questions about his book each day. Every few minutes Jeff tries to concentrate on his story, *Homer Price*. He actually read it last summer, often in his bed late at night, so he doesn't have to give it much attention. Jeff says very little in class.

Next to Jeff is Martin, a slim active student. He is rapidly reading *The Egypt Game*, a sophisticated mystery. When Martin recommends a book, others in the class try to read it. His choices are usually those of his older brother, a bright and popular middle-school student. Occasionally his choices are beyond his reading ability, but Martin perseveres anyway. He wants his teacher and classmates to notice his reading and the advanced level of his choices, and spends much of his silent reading time looking for such attention.

In front of this row of fifth-grade students are 23 others. These students are from middle-class homes, a suburban neighborhood with single-family dwellings and a few luxury apartments. About half live with single parents, and all but three have siblings at home.

A look at their reading choices suggests that five of these fifth-graders are struggling with books that are aimed at third-grade readers. Eight of the fifth-graders read at levels of secondary students with ease and enjoyment. Some would read for two hours and never notice the time passing. Others last two minutes and then think of something they want to talk about.

If you were to watch these students all day as they interact in class, work on assignments, and gather at recess, you would see Jeff hesitate to answer when called on and his difficulties with frequent unfinished work. You would see Aletha taking charge of getting a project done for two of her friends, and often looking for something to do. You would see Martin interrupt his teacher to add information, or to disagree, or to volunteer to take care of anything and everything.

If you were hired to teach this fifth-grade class, how would you use this beginning information to group these students? What would you provide for Aletha? For Martin? What would be important to remember as you assign Jeff to a group? Or Camille? We suggest two possibilities that can accommodate the diversity of the fifth-grade class: varying student roles and varying types of involvement.

Varying Student Roles

In a typical class situation, most students perform a listening role (we hope) and a few have a speaking or active role. The level of participation is high for a few and minimal for many.

In traditional group arrangements, students choose or are given leader or follower roles. Some students never experience leadership, some never follow. Cooperative learning strategies offer an alternative with varied roles for different experiences in the same activity. We think that the range of roles can be expanded and can be used in different grouping arrangements. Listen to learner roles:

- *Direction Giver.* Here are the steps we are supposed to follow in our experiment. First, we are to arrange the three beakers in order of size. Then, we are to fill each with 4 ounces of water. . . . Let's get all the things we need first.
- *Summarizer.* Here is what we have done. We said that our problem is the bullying going on around school, especially outside the back door. We made a list of all the worries kids have. Then we thought of 17 different things to do about the problem, but we decided that only two of them were OK. We are going to write a letter to the principal asking for help, and we are going to have a committee to patrol the block around the school.
- *Generator.* Who are some characters who would have lived during this time in history? In a town like Salem, I would expect to find a minister and a shopkeeper. Other ideas?
- *Observer.* I noticed that Ethan and Luanne did most of the talking. Reg took notes all the time and Sharon listened. The only time everyone talked was when we came up with ideas to solve the problem.
- *Record Keeper.* My notes show that we spent 14 minutes trying to agree on the problem. We came up with solutions in 7 minutes but everyone had ideas.
- *Evaluator.* This group did good work today—everyone was quiet and working, the table is clean, and all the equipment is put away.

Add to these roles a Reader, a Time Keeper, an Encourager, a Supply or Resource Person, and a Clarifier, depending on learner maturity and the nature of the learning activity. This variety of roles is appropriate for different grouping arrangements, different content, and definitely different learners. In addition, you can accommodate learner diversity by varying the types of involvement in groups.

Varying Student Involvement

Within different group structures, learners may be involved independently, cooperatively, and competitively. Even with a group task, some learners go about their work in an isolated way. Some work in coordination with other learners. Others compete and work to be best or fastest. The varying types of involvement that follow allow for differences:

- *Sharing Resources or Materials.* Here is my set of colored pencils. They are great for maps.
- *Clarifying an Idea.* Electricity is not really a conductor; it takes the form of a current.
- *Adding Examples.* When I visited a farm, I saw a different kind of fence. It looked like this. . . .
- *Providing Controversy.* I disagree. I don't think that our country should put up with another country taking our people as hostages. I think we should be tough and fight.

Remember the fifth-grade we viewed in the earlier Snapshot? Aletha would be challenged and involved if she clarifies an idea. Martin could provide controversy in a noninterruptive way. Jeff could comfortably share resources until another type of involvement was appropriate. Grouping arrangements assist you in accommodating learner differences with varying student roles and varying types of involvement.

GROUPING FOR TEACHING AND LEARNING

As you use grouping strategies, you will be faced with important decisions: How many students to a group? How to assign students to groups? Which grouping practice to use? Before we describe some "how to group" arrangements, we will discuss your decisions.

Grouping Decisions

Begin with your objective. What do you want group members to learn or do? What outcome is intended for the work? What do you want to happen to members? With your objective in mind, move to a decision about the group size.

Group Size

This factor will affect the outcome of group work, so consider some general principles about group size to guide your decision:

1. The larger the group, the broader the range of experiences, expertise, skills, and interests to contribute to the learning activity.
2. The amount of materials or supplies may direct group size.
3. The amount of time available may direct group size. Smaller groups can be more efficient.
4. The size of the task and the number of component responsibilities may determine group size.
5. Larger groups (more than six) require skills of coordination and collaboration for every individual to be involved.
6. Large groups have the potential for members to be or stay uninvolved or to dominate.

In addition to the principles, look at some common group sizes and see what you can expect from this dimension:

- *Two-person group.* This size promotes a relationship and generally ensures participation. This is a good way to begin with inexperienced "groupies" (students who have not been grouped before). In a pair, students gain experience and skill before working in a complex group arrangement.
- *Three-person group.* This arrangement allows for a changing two-person majority. Participation is very likely because no one wants to be the odd person out. Roles in this size group can be those of speaker, listener, and observer, and learners can experience all three roles in a brief period of time. This size group is appropriate for creating descriptions, organizing data, drawing conclusions, and summarizing ideas.
- *Four-person group.* In a four-person group, there will likely be different perspectives. This size is small enough that each member will have a chance to express himself or herself and can be comfortable doing so. Often this size groups emerges as two pairs when opinions are expressed. A group of four people requires basic communication and cooperation skills, but offers ideal practice for learning group process.
- *Five-person group.* This size group is considered the smallest size for problem solving, with enough diversity of opinions or perspectives. The odd number of members facilitates decision making. This size group provides continued practice in group process, and even in brief time periods every student has an opportunity to express ideas.
- *Six-person group.* This size group is often used to share data or to develop a report on a topic. In a group this size, leadership or a majority may emerge, and may be needed so that everyone is involved.
- *Seven-person group.* This size group of students works well on a major class

assignment or project. In an average class of 30 to 35 students, this means four to five projects or reports to listen to, read, or critique. In this size group, however, subgroups or pairs may develop. There must be enough time for each member to express ideas or to participate. Otherwise, side conversations occur or students become uninvolved.

Group size may have sounded like a simple decision, but it has significant implications. Variance in group size will mean variance in student experience and learning. You will find help with phasing in cooperative groups in the Samples and Examples at the end of this chapter.

TEACHER TALK

I don't usually think about how many students to put in each group. I just start assigning them. I do think about those students with behavior problems, because I can't group certain students in the same group. Once I set up the groups, I usually have to move students around. A group may be too big or too small. Sometimes it goes smoothly, but not often. I keep thinking that I need to plan for it.

10th-Grade Teacher

Assignment of Students to Groups

Again, this decision sounds simple, but it is complex and has significant implications. Your starting point is what you know about your learners. What relationships are possible? What kind of interactions will result? What problems are potential?

Consider the outcomes you intend the groups to achieve, and select needed students. If you intend for groups to develop skits, you probably want one or two creative individuals in each group. If you want groups to prepare study outlines, you may want one very organized student in each group. We want to remind you that one objective of grouping is for students to experience diversity of learners, so do consider diversity in group composition. Examine the following strategies for assigning students to groups:

- *Random assignment.* This is a simple process, appropriate when you have decided that student assignment will not influence the outcome and is not necessary for the process. There are a variety of ways to be random:
  a. Have students count off by the number of desired groups. (For example, if you want four groups, have students count off by four. Then have all the "1s" go to one group, all the "2s" to a group, and so on.)
  b. Place group names or numbers in a basket and have students draw for their group assignment.
  c. Use a naturally occurring classroom phenomenon such as rows of desks, table clusters, or room quadrants.
  d. Hand out materials with a group number or symbol on them and have students find other group numbers.

   e. Use creative matching with puzzle pieces, song titles, book characters, or cities in one state. (For example, "Find the three other people who have characters in your novel.")
       Some of the random assignments begin group process as learners interact to find group members. Some are fun and offer an element of surprise. Some are efficient. Vary your assignment strategies to keep classroom life interesting.

- *Assignment by ability.* You have several options for sources of information with which to group this way: a pretest of new curriculum, current grades, achievement data, and your experience with the learners. You may want to place students of similar ability levels in one group (a strategy called *ability grouping*) or you may want to structure each group with a representation of high ability, low ability, and middle ability (a strategy called *stratified grouping*). When we talk about grouping arrangements, we will describe when and why you would use these structures.

- *Assignment by social criteria.* Begin by assessing social skills and relationships among your learners, then consider grouping to complement or provide diversity. You may use sociogram information or student lists of desired work partners or team members. Mix your introverts and extroverts, leaders and followers. Have students compose groups with, "Choose two people you know well and two people with whom you have never worked." Try out new ways of assigning, then step back and observe. You will gather new information about your learners for future grouping.

- *Assignment by interest.* For this kind of assignment, survey student interests. (Chapters 7 and 12 provide instruments for this purpose.) With groups of students with similar interests, there is usually high motivation and content exploration. When high-school seniors work in groups to study and read favorite authors, those students who enjoy Kurt Vonnegut will work together to study the author with greater depth than in a whole class pursuit. Students enjoy choosing favorite inventions, explorers, countries, kinds of literature, industries, careers, and so on to study in groups. There is nothing more satisfying than observing a group working on a topic in which they are interested, sharing ideas, and working with an exciting momentum.

Before proceeding to a description of common grouping practices or arrangements, we remind you that decisions of group size and assignment of students to groups are not appropriate for "on the spot" thinking.

Common Grouping Practices

Before discussing the grouping practices that you as a classroom teacher will select, we want to address a practice called *between-class ability grouping*. In many elementary schools, students are assigned to self-contained classes on the basis of a general achievement or ability measure. In junior-high or middle schools, students may be assigned by ability to different classes for each subject. Secondary students may also be assigned to a homeroom or a set of classes by ability. These forms of between-class ability grouping are not supported by research evidence of positive effects on students. There is evidence of psychological drawbacks: low expectations for some students, reduced self-esteem, pressure for achievement, and stigmatizing of some student populations. Those outcomes are in contrast to those we have proposed for grouping, so we encourage you to know the research (see our references) and be involved in related schoolwide decisions.

Our list of practices contains the most commonly used grouping practices, some combinations, and some not so common practices. Our descriptions are intended to give you a working knowledge, and a repertoire of choices. Read, participate in workshops, and learn more about grouping practices. In this section, we provide:

1. A description of the arrangement in practice
2. What we know about grouping from research and experience
3. Suggestions for how to use grouping effectively

The research information and classroom examples will assist you in developing grouping practices for your teaching repertoire.

Within-Class Ability Grouping

This arrangement takes the form of teachers assigning students to one of a small number of groups for instruction on the basis of ability level. Groups work with different materials, in different activities, and at rates unique to their need and ability. In practice, the best-known example is the reading group you see in elementary classrooms. Less common is ability grouping in elementary mathematics (Hallinan & Sorenson, 1983). Most teachers limit the number of groups to three in order to provide adequate direct instruction to each.

The abundance of between-class ability grouping and time frame of secondary instruction seems to limit the use of within-class ability grouping. When you find partial ability grouping in high schools, it is usually for skill development, with groups of students with beginning skills, groups with intermediate skills, and so on.

What we know from research is that ability grouping for teaching has mixed effects. In math, all groups benefit, but effects have been more positive for low-achieving students. The number of instructional groups has an effect, and two or three groups have been used for higher achievement effects than four or more groups (Slavin & Karweit, 1985).

Even with the abundance of reading group practice, there is little available research. A comprehensive study by Filby and Barnett (1982) does, however, provide us with some conclusions for both research and teaching. They compared classes grouped for reading instruction and classes with whole group instruction. Their findings included:

1. No strong and consistent effects of grouping patterns exist for students at any ability level.

2. There are significant differences in attention rates for different ability groups, with high-ability students showing higher rates.
3. Oral success rates were higher in grouped classes, and written success rates were higher in classes with whole class instruction.
4. Student perceptions of other students' ability showed high agreement (90 percent) for whole class instruction, and less agreement (75 percent) in grouped classes.
5. Student perception of self data were similar for both grouped and whole class instructional arrangements.

The results reported prompt us to urge your awareness of the complexity of outcomes for ability grouping arrangements.

To use this practice effectively, grouping should be limited to several subjects, generally reading and math in elementary classes. In secondary classes, the limit can be applied to sections or outcomes of the curriculum rather than the whole course.

Student assignment should be made on the basis of the specific skill or curriculum, not on general achievement. To be effective, adapt your level and pace of instruction to meet students' needs in the group (Barr & Dreeben, 1983).

Regrouping for Selected Subjects

A common arrangement in elementary schools involves having students remain in heterogeneous classes (mixed ability) most of the day and regrouped for selected subjects, usually reading and math.

In practice, you will see this arrangement in schoolwide use. You can observe three second-grade classes all scheduled for reading at the same time, and watch students leave their heterogeneous rooms and go to a class with other students of similar ability level in reading, and possibly math. The classes are organized to meet their ability levels. In a junior-high or middle school, students may be grouped this way for math, English, and science.

What we know from research is that this practice can improve student achievement (Slavin, 1987a). What we know from teachers is that the arrangement allows them to focus their planning and instruction on one group or one ability level, and that better instruction and materials can result.

To use this arrangement effectively, limit your grouping to one or two subjects, and adapt your instructional level and pace to student performance level.

Tutoring Groups

This practice takes the form of cross-age tutoring (age differences between tutors and those being tutored) and peer tutoring (same age or grade). The intent of this practice is to provide individual help to students.

In practice, peer tutors are usually those students with high ability in a particular subject area or skill, or partners within same ability levels. For cross-age tutoring, older students of any ability level can tutor younger students. Tutoring is also done by volunteers or aides.

What we know from research of tutoring practices is that tutoring requires preparation and careful procedures. An overview of studies (Klaus, 1975) provides qualities of successful tutoring practices for your application:

1. A respectful relationship between tutor and tutee
2. Well-organized and long-term arrangements
3. Structured tutoring assignments that prescribe content, sequence, and procedures
4. Matching of same-gender students
5. No evaluation by tutors

We have seen positive effects for tutees' general achievement and performance in specific subject matter (Fogarty & Wang, 1982; Hartrup, 1983), and positive effects for tutors (Hartrup, 1983).

We see students informally tutoring all the time, so it makes sense to take their lead and organize. Teachers who use tutoring have described some exciting experiences.

TEACHER TALK

We pair up our sixth-graders with first-grade students for shared writing. The sixth-graders carefully choose the writing that they bring in so that it will be appropriate for reading to young children. First-graders bring in pictures and bits of writing, some invented spelling. They share what they have written, then they respond to each other's writing.

Sometimes we teachers stay and listen. It has been the most thrilling experience of my teaching.

6th-Grade Teacher

To use this technique effectively, tutoring programs need your supervision. You will need to provide some training or preparation for the tutors, schedule the tutoring, check on progress, and provide a liaison between tutors and tutees.

Cooperative Learning Arrangements

These arrangements provide for small, heterogeneous, or mixed ability groups to work toward a common goal. Cooperative learning occurs in three different structures:

1. Assignment of individual students to specific responsibilities within a larger group task or project
2. Assignment of students to work together on a common project or task
3. Assignment of students to groups to study and be responsible for group members' learning (the group goal is the achievement of all group members)

We will describe examples of each structure in practice.

In practice, student heterogeneity (mixed ability or dissimilarity) is a resource for these grouping arrangements. The range of different perspectives, understandings, and skills help individual members in the cooperative learning groups.

The first structure we listed has students working on individual tasks within a large group task, as in jigsaw teaching (Aronson, Blaney, Stephen, Sikes, & Snapp, 1978) or group investigation (Sharon & Sharon, 1976). You see six high-school seniors working on a bid proposal for a contracting job. Each of them is checking on a different aspect of the job for costs, schedules, and potential problems. They will put their estimates together for the bid.

The second structure has students working on a common task or product in groups, as in cooperative learning (Johnson, Johnson, & Holubec, 1986). You see a group of four fifth-graders working together on a salt map of South America.

The third structure has students working as a team to master curriculum, as in Student-Teams-Achievement-Division (STAD) (Slavin, 1987b) or Teams-Games-Tournament (TGT) (DeVries & Slavin, 1978). You see ninth-graders in groups of six studying the classifications of insects and related examples. You see them test each other with a "What Is It?" game and some flash cards.

Some 122 studies of cooperative learning arrangements were reviewed and compared (Johnson & Johnson, 1987) to provide a knowledge base. What we know from these studies is that student achievement is positively affected in a variety of subject areas at grade levels from 3 to 12 when curriculum mastery is the focus. Those results have not been found for arrangements in which a group task or project is the focus.

In addition to academic effects, cooperative learning arrangements have positively influenced attitudes towards subject matter and learning experiences, a continuing motivation to learn more about the subject being studied. Cooperative learning experiences promote liking among students, and encourage interpersonal attraction among students from different ethnic groups, handicapped, and non-handicapped students. More differentiated, dynamic, and less stereotyped views of other students have resulted.

To use cooperative learning arrangements effectively requires organization. You and your students must learn and practice organizational skills with respect to materials and equipment, work space, planning, and scheduling. You may need to teach the skills of cooperative work, communication, and division of labor for the arrangements to be successful.

In sum, the four common practices we have described can be seen in many schools and are effective for specific curriculum and for some learners. As a result of ongoing study of these practices and discontent with findings, we have alternatives. We describe two of them here.

Team Assisted Individualization (TAI)

This arrangement has students working in teams of mixed ability in math, with members working on material appropriate to skill level. Team members help each other and check each other's work. As they work, their teacher instructs small groups of students pulled from the various teams to work on specific concepts or skills from the curriculum.

In practice, you would see in one class of third-graders instruction in fractions and money, division with a remainder, and metrics. Six teams of students are studying together, sometimes with all topics represented in each. The student who has mastered division with a remainder may be helping the student who is still struggling with the process.

What we know about this arrangement is limited, but initial studies show positive achievement effects for students in TAI for math computation (Slavin, 1987b).

To use TAI effectively, student relationships must be considered. Because students must help and encourage each other with work of different difficulty levels, it will be important to develop sensitivity and a cooperative spirit. Again, organization will be essential. For instance, the third-grade example just mentioned required preparation for teaching four different math concepts or skills, providing practice work at the appropriate difficulty levels for all, and monitoring.

Cooperative Integrated Reading and Composition (CIRC)

This arrangement places students to work in mixed ability teams for a series of reading activities.

In practice, you would see students in teams reading aloud to each other, working together to complete activities related to story structure, reading comprehension, vocabulary, and spelling. In writing activities, students critique each other's writing, help each other revise, proof each other's work, and cooperate on editing final copies.

What we know is limited, but initial research has shown positive results: improved ability to read orally, increased understanding, and writing with greater clarity (Stevens, Madden, Slavin, & Farnish, 1987).

To use CIRC effectively, we recommend the same sensitivity and cooperation for your class and the same organization for your teaching that we described for TAI.

It is likely that many teachers are using their own combinations of grouping arrangements. Hopefully, they will be studied, described, and available for your classroom. There are also some grouping practices in use that are not so common. It is important for you to have a working knowledge of these practices for your repertoire.

The Joplin Plan

This plan is generally used for reading, and groups students without regard for grade level. At a specific time of day, all students regroup according to reading ability. One reading group may include four second-graders, nine third-graders, five fourth-graders, and two six-graders. Teachers can focus time and effort on one reading group and not be managing other students. Achievement effects of the Joplin plan have been positive.

Staggered or Split Schedules

This is a scheduling arrangement that results in the reduction of class size for part of the school day. Half of the class arrives at the regular starting time and leaves early in the afternoon, and half of the class arrives late in the morning and stays for the regular departure time.

Teachers in this scheduling arrangement are able to work with smaller numbers of students for a substantial portion of the school day. Although no research results are available, teachers report increased interaction with students and more opportunity for individualized instruction.

Whether you decide to use a common grouping practice or a not so common practice, it will be important to stay flexible. Be ready to change, move students, or abandon groups altogether. It will also be important to manage the grouping arrangements with routines and procedures for student movement, for independent work activities, and for using the assistance of aides and volunteers.

Management of Grouping Arrangements

Depending on the complexity of your grouping arrangement, you will need a set of routines and procedures. We describe management considerations to use with most arrangements. Adapt them to your context, content, and learners.

Student Movement (In and Out of Groups)

Getting students in and out of groups must be done smoothly because the process affects both the behavior of students and the beginnings and endings of learning activities. The transitions we described in Chapter 6 provide ideas for handling these changes. For the transition routines with grouping, you must make some decisions:

- Is there a need for quiet moving in and out of groups?
- Do students need a break in between group work?
- Can two groups move at once?
- Will one part of the classroom be congested?

Teachers often make brief announcements, such as "Group 2, come up to the front now; Group 3, move to the centers," as another group returns to individual desks. Some teachers use a musical signal, a clapping routine, or move quietly from group to group, giving instructions. The latter has the effect of a staggered movement and usually feels less chaotic. For these movement routines to be smooth, they must be taught and practiced. Students can actually rehearse the movement pattern and associated behaviors.

Another effective practice for smooth movement in and out of groups is to provide a description of what is to be done when students get to the location. An example will show what we mean: "When you get to your tables, open your notebooks to the list of equipment necessary for your work and check off each item as you gather equipment," or "When you get to your desk, look up the meaning of *substantive* in your glossary and raise your hand when you find it." These directions influence the pace of movement and efficiency with which students are ready for the next activity.

Effective teachers roam the room between each group activity and check on independent work and student progress. These are pauses of only two or three minutes, but they have positive effects on student achievement and behavior.

Managing Independent Work Activities

If you intend to instruct small groups of students, you will need to be assured that other students are involved in challenging work, have their needs met, and are not disturbing anyone. This is a complex demand and calls for well-developed classroom management. Chapters 5 and 6 provide many strategies, but we will describe additional ways to manage this situation.

A major consideration in the management of independent work activities is the quality of work or activity. Can it be done independently? Do you want it done independently? Take a look at the knowledge and skills needed to do the work and check the difficulty level. Is the work worth doing? Will it interest, challenge, and promote learning?

Once you assess the quality of independent work and plans for appropriate worthwhile tasks or activities, there are effective routines that assist the independent workers:

1. Provide generous amounts of direction complete with examples before moving to independent activities.
2. Have work information (directions, schedule, materials) posted in a prominent location.
3. Have alternatives provided for those who complete work with time remaining.
4. Consider the noise level of the independent work.
5. Have clearly defined behaviors for independent work.
6. If the work period is long, provide a physical and social break midway in the period.

A routine that promotes smoothness when you are coordinating group instruction with supervision of independent work is one for getting help when you need it. As we suggested in Chapter 6, have a student or committee assigned to assist others who have trouble with directions or questions. Make tape-recorded sets of directions or a recipe card format posted on the board. What is most important is that students are completely certain of how to get help. The cooperative learning arrangements that we described include this kind of student assistance.

With all of these responsibilities—movement of groups, supervision of independent work, and instruction of small groups—the assistance of another adult can really ease the management. Coordinating the help of another adult is the focus of the next section.

Using Aides and Volunteers to Assist with Grouping

When teachers and principals were interviewed about concerns in their use of aides and volunteers for grouping, they listed three items: training of assistants, assignment of aides and volunteers, and planning time (Bossert & Barnett, 1981). We describe how they become part of your management.

Training and Preparation of Aides and Volunteers

Depending on the experience of your volunteer or aide, the need for training will vary. Begin by finding out about that experience. You may be comfortable in an informal conversation or you may need a formal set of questions in survey form. Once you have such information, you can plan an outline of essential information for training.

We suggest an orientation session and ongoing training. If you have an experienced assistant, you may want that person to work with the new aide. It will be important for the newcomer to observe you and your students, and the time will be profitable if they know what to observe. An example from a group of secondary teachers offers a guide for observing your class.

> *Classroom Observation Guide*
> 1. Note the time, day, and subject matter.
> 2. Watch how students follow routines (pencil sharpening, using resources, leaving the room).
> 3. Listen for the kinds of help students need frequently.
> 4. Watch what distracts students from work.
> 5. Watch what kind of behavior is acceptable and unacceptable.

Once an aide or volunteer becomes acquainted with your classroom, other training strategies include:

- Modeling of teaching and management strategies
- Written directions or guidelines for work with groups
- Collaborating with other teachers to hold training
- Student helpers who explain routines and procedures

Be sure to check on state and district policy and procedures regarding other adults working in your classroom.

Assignment of Aides and Volunteers

Your assignment decisions must accommodate both your classroom needs and those appropriate to the other person's experience and preferences. A teacher in Portland, Oregon, offers her volunteers a choice of working directly with students or preparing classroom materials, and writes up job forms for both types of work. Volunteers pick up a job description when they arrive and work efficiently and successfully at their choice. Another teacher who relies for help from other adults writes lesson plans for them. This means extra work for her, but she finds better assistance results from her efforts.

Discuss and put in writing your expectations for assistance, and listen to your aide's expectations. With both aides and volunteers, there is a wide variation in work preferences. Some are comfortable doing clerical work, making materials, or grading quizzes. Some enjoy teaching and interacting with students. Some come with real expertise and need to be able to use their skills. If your assignments reflect those preferences and expectations, you can depend on assistance. Planning will also ensure regular or ongoing help.

Planning with Aides and Volunteers

Once again, the limits of time make planning and coordinating with aides and volunteers a major concern. We don't have any secrets for how to find extra time, but there are ways to be efficient with the time available. Preplanning communication ensures that planning time addresses important topics and concerns. A form for volunteers to complete at the end of the day or class may ask for evaluation, needs, concerns, information, and suggestions. You may want to provide written feedback in similar form. An agenda for planning time will also help.

You have few options for when you can meet and plan: during class time, after school, before students arrive, during a break or lunch, or at a monthly Saturday meeting. Some districts have an early dismissal day, and planning is done after students leave. What will be important is a schedule convenient to you and your aide or volunteer.

When you observe a teacher who has prepared, assigned, and coordinated volunteer assistance, you will see exciting teaching. The time spent getting an aide or volunteer ready has definite payoffs. One advantage reported by teachers is the possibility of working with the same volunteer or aide over a long period of time. The Samples and Examples section at the end of this chapter provides ideas for your work with volunteers and aides.

SUMMARY

Most teachers enter the profession with a genuine liking for people. Is that true for you? In the process of instructing large numbers of students with all the necessary management responsibilities, you may forget or lose sight of that enjoyment. Make it your starting point and think of grouping as a way to appreciate all the unique individuals you have the opportunity to meet and teach.

With that appreciation, begin the process of information gathering. Look at your teaching context. What will support grouping? Where are the obstacles? Check the physical environment for furniture arrangement, space, and movement. Coordinate use of physical space with those around you. Remember to assess your socioemotional environment. What are the group norms? What opportunities exist for student interaction?

Review your content. What are your intended outcomes? With knowledge and understandings, use your grouping to provide peer interaction and broadened experiences. With skills, use your grouping to provide peer coaching and motivation. With attitudes and values, use grouping to provide discussion and individual involvement.

Look at your learners. The diversity is exciting. Plan for your learners to experience different learning roles and different types of involvement within your grouping.

With information about your context, content, and learner, be ready to make decisions. Consider group size and assignment of students to groups. Then proceed to your repertoire of common grouping practices, combinations of grouping practices, and not so common grouping practices.

Once your grouping decisions have been made, check your management for routines and procedures for student movement in and out of groups, for independent work activities. Use aides or volunteers to assist your grouping arrangements. Prepare and train them, assign them carefully, and schedule time to plan together.

Reflect on the kind of groups in which your students will work and live in their adult lives. Provide the same opportunities that await them—that is, working with individuals with the same abilities, interests, needs, and goals, or with different abilities, interests, needs, and goals. Use your grouping arrangements to reflect life.

REFERENCES

Aronson, E., Blaney, N., Stephen, C., Sikes, J., & Snapp, M. (1978). *The jigsaw classroom*. Beverly Hills, CA: Sage.

Barr, R., & Dreeben, R. (1983). *How schools work*. Chicago: University of Chicago Press.

Bossert, S., & Barnett, B. (1981). *Grouping arrangements*. San Francisco: Far West Laboratory for Research and Development in Education.

Brophy, J. E. (1987). Synthesis of research on strategies for motivating students to learn. *Educational Leadership, 45*(2), 40–46.

Cotton, R., & Cook, E. (1982). Meta-analysis and the effects of varius reward systems: Some different conclusions from Johnson et al. *Psychological Bulletin, 92*, 176–183.

DeVries, R., & Slavin, R. E. (1978). Team-games-tournaments (TGT): Review of ten classroom experiments. *Journal of Research and Development in Education, 12*(1), 28–38.

Dunkin, M. J., & Biddle, B. J. (1974). *The study of teaching*. New York: Holt, Rinehart and Winston.

Filby, N., & Barnett, B. (1982). *Classroom organization and student learning*. Paper presented at the annual meeting of the American Educational Research Association, New York.

Fogarty, J. L., & Wang, M. C. (1982). An investigation of the cross-age peer tutoring process: Some implications for instructional design and motivation. *Elementary School Journal, 82*, 461–469.

Good, T., & Brophy, J. (1984). *Looking in classrooms*. New York: Harper and Row.

Hallinan, M., & Sorenson, A. (1983). The formation and stability of instructional groups. *American Sociological Review, 48*, 839–851.

Hartrup, W. W. (1983). Peer relations. In P. Mussen (Ed.), *Handbook of child psychology, Vol. 4, Socialization, personality, and social development*. New York: Wiley.

Johnson, D. W., & Johnson, R. T. (1982). *The internal dynamics of cooperative learning groups*. Paper presented at the annual meeting of the American Educational Research Association, New York.

Johnson, D. W., & Johnson, R. T. (1987). *Cooper-

ation and competition. Hillsdale, NJ: Erlbaum.

Johnson, D. W., & Johnson, R. T., & Holubec, E. J. (1986). *Circles of learning: Cooperation in the classroom.* Edina, MN: Interaction Book Company.

Kelliher, A. V. (1931). *A critical study of homogeneous grouping.* New York: Bureau of Publications, Teachers' College, Columbia University, Contribution to Education No. 452.

Klaus, D. J. (1975). *Patterns for peer tutoring.* Paper presented at the annual meeting of the American Educational Research Association, Washington, DC.

Mann, H. (1960). What does ability grouping do to the self-concept? *Childhood Education,* 357–361.

McPartland, J. (1968). *The segregated student in desegregated schools: Sources of influence on Negro secondary students.* Baltimore, MD: Johns Hopkins University, Center for Social Organization of Schools.

Napier, R. W., and Gershenfeld, M. K. (1985). *Groups, theory, and experience.* Boston: Houghton Mifflin.

Persell, C. (1977). *Education and inequality: The roots and results of stratification in America's schools.* New York: Free Press.

Sharon, S., & Sharon, R. (1976). *Small group teaching.* Englewood Cliffs, NJ: Educational Technology Publications.

Slavin, R. E. (1987a). Ability grouping and student achievement in elementary schools: A best evidence synthesis. *Review of Educational Research, 57*(3), 293–336.

Slavin, R. E. (1987b). Combining cooperative learning and individualized instruction. *Arithmetic Teacher, 35*(3), 14–16.

Slavin, R. E., & Karweit, N. (1985). Effects of whole class, ability grouped, and individualized instruction on mathematics achievement. *American Educational Research Journal, 22,* 351–368.

Stevens, R. J., Madden, M. A., Slavin, R. E., & Farnish, A. M. (1987). Cooperative integrated reading and composition: Two field experiments. *Reading Research Quarterly, 22*(4), 433–454.

Strauss, S. (1957). Looking backward on future scientists. *The Science Teacher,* 385–388.

Webb, N. M. (1984). Stability of small group interaction and achievement over time. *Journal of Educational Psychology, 76,* 211–224.

Webb, N. M., & Kenderski, C. M. (1984). Student interaction and learning in small-group and whole-class settings. In P. Peterson, L. C. Wilkinson, & M. Hallinan (Eds.), *The social context of instruction: Group organization and group processes.* Orlando, FL: Academic Press.

SAMPLES AND EXAMPLES

There are three Samples and Examples that give you help in organizing parent volunteers in the classroom and one figure that describes the phasing in of cooperative groups.

- The Parent and Volunteer Survey will help you find out parent schedules and areas of assistance.
- Tasks for Volunteers at Schools and Home is a checklist for volunteers regarding their roles in the classroom and materials that could be created at home for the classroom.
- The Volunteer Worksheet is a feedback sheet from a volunteer to the teacher.
- Phasing in Cooperative Groups is a chart that shows cooperative grouping should be phased in with groups of two for short periods of time. Expand with groups of two with longer time periods before moving to groups of four. If you have problems at one level, move back to the level in which you had prior success.

PARENT VOLUNTEER SURVEY

Parents are the key to an enriched and varied school experience for children. No single adult can educate a class of 25 children over a period of 10 months and provide all the information or challenges they need to grow fully. Together we can make this a special year for your child. I invite you to share yourself in any ways that feel comfortable for you. Thanks from all the kids and me!

I can volunteer to help in the classroom (circle the day and time that is best for you):

Days: Mon.   Tues.   Wed.   Thurs.   Fri.

Times: Mornings   Afternoons   Once in a while

_____ I will help out on field trips.

_____ I can make things at home (playdough, math games, etc.). The teacher will provide easy to follow directions and much gratitude!

_____ I have a skill I can share with children.

_____ I have a hobby I can share with children.

_____ I have a collection I can share with children.

_____ I have a talent I can share with children.

_____ I could share information about another country or culture (photos, clothing, objects for example).

_____ I have a job that I could demonstrate/the place where I work is available for a field trip.

_____ I will be a room parent and attend class celebrations.

_____ I will provide treats for class parties.

_____ Call me for special projects. Phone:

Concerns or comments:

Your name: _____

Your phone: _____

Thank you!

Kindergarten teacher

Source: Tong, S., Erickson, C., & Weber, J. (1988). *Parent volunteer materials*. Unpublished materials. Portland State University, Portland, OR. Used with permission.

TASKS FOR VOLUNTEERS AT SCHOOL

1. Help children learn to play a game.
2. Help a child with an individual need. Example: learn the alphabet, count, skip, etc.
3. Fill paint containers.
4. Make a telephone call. (Phone numbers should not leave the school without written parental permission.)
5. Put up a bulletin board.
6. Prepare material.
7. Read a story.
8. Assist a small group with a task.
9. Assist in woodworking, cooking, gardening, spool knitting, etc.
10. Write children's dictated stories.
11. Correct work with students.
12. Help make or confirm field trip plans.
13. Help with a creative project.

TASKS FOR VOLUNTEERS AT HOME

For parents who cannot help in the classroom, the following is a list of ways to help at home:

- Make classroom games.
- Type stories.
- Collect or prepare art materials for projects.
- Staple books together.
- Make bean bags.
- Make musical instruments.
- Make and mend doll clothes.
- Build or repair cages, bookshelves, doll houses, etc.
- Take pets over vacation.
- Help with bulletin boards.
- Assemble teaching aids—flannel boards, individual pocket charts, chalkboards, etc.

Source: Tong, S., Erickson, C., & Weber, J. (1988). *Parent volunteer materials*. Unpublished materials. Portland State University, Portland, OR. Used with permission.

VOLUNTEER WORKSHEET

Name _____   Date _____

I. Task:
   Materials Needed—

   Instructions—

   Children Involved—

   Time Frame—

II. Feedback from Volunteer: (Things to consider: Does anyone need additional help? Do
    you have some suggestions for improving the lesson? Other . . .

Source: Tong, S., Erickson, C., & Weber, J. (1988). *Parent volunteer materials*. Unpublished materials. Portland State University, Portland, OR. Used with permission.

PHASING IN COOPERATIVE GROUPS

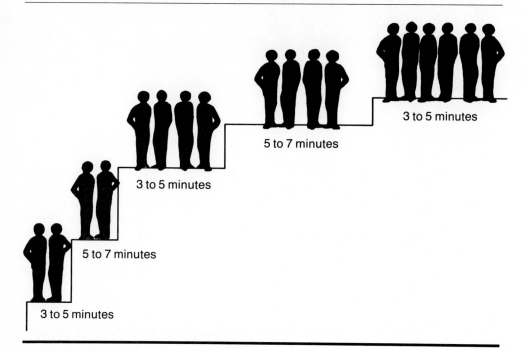

3 to 5 minutes

5 to 7 minutes

3 to 5 minutes

5 to 7 minutes

3 to 5 minutes

Source: Adapted from instructional materials developed by Dr. Jerome Freiberg, Professor of Education, University of Houston. Used by permission.

CHAPTER 11

Reflective Teaching: Students as Shareholders

CHAPTER OUTCOMES

At the conclusion of this chapter you will be able to:

1. Develop a context for teaching and learning that supports learners as active participants in their own education.
2. Provide experiences that promote the learner's ability to take responsibility for learning, think inductively and critically, and solve problems.
3. Use the reflective teaching strategies of inquiry and guided discovery.

KEY TERMS AND CONCEPTS

Reflective Teaching Strategies
Climate of Trust
Constructivism
Shareholders
Active Participation
Brainstorming
Cone of Learning Experiences
Mapping
Deductive
Inductive
Critical Thinking
Problem Solving

INTRODUCTION

Have you ever patted yourself on the back thinking, "I did it," after assembling a new appliance that arrived without a set of directions? Have you ever smiled to yourself knowing, "I could explain that," as you listened to another person struggle to answer a question? Have you ever relaxed your face and neck muscles feeling, "Now I understand," while observing a situation similar to something previously studied? Have you ever resisted taking lessons being certain that, "I can learn it better on my own," because you've done it before and feel more comfortable with your own pace?

Reflective teaching strategies are approaches that support the kind of learning you have experienced if you answered "yes" to any of the above.

Definition

We are combining the characteristics of several descriptions (see Dunkin & Biddle, 1974) to create our definition of *reflective teaching strategies*: teaching strategies that stimulate students to use experiences to discover learning for themselves. Their discoveries may lead to knowledge, understandings, skills, and attitudes. They may discover how to solve problems, answer questions, draw conclusions, and take responsibility for their own learning. These strategies reflect a philosophy of education that views the learner as a source of knowledge rather than a blank slate upon which the teacher inscribes information. Because the learner determines the content of learning, it is relevant and important to him or her. These strategies lead learners beyond basic skills to higher levels of thinking and complex reasoning.

Rationale

In the progressive education envisioned by John Dewey in the 1930s and 1940s, the problems to be studied in schools were created from the everyday needs, interests, and, most importantly, experiences of the students (Dewey, 1938). That kind of curriculum development process can lead to the relevance that students have always demanded and needed. More recently, Harste, Short, and Burke (1988) urged us to make students "curricular informants," that is, the source of ideas, information, and problems to be explored. The reflective teaching strategies of this chapter support the learner role Harste and colleagues describe and the process Dewey envisioned.

In order to promote self-learning, your classroom context must be characterized by a climate of trust and the dimensions of constructivism. Learners will need to adjust to the role of shareholder in learning with expanded experiences and participation. The content of self-learning through reflective teaching strategies is not limited to any curricular area, but must include the processes of critical and inductive thinking as well as problem solving. Attention to the context, learner, and content will be important as you use the strategies of inquiry and guided discovery.

CONTEXT

Climate of Trust

For students to be able to take the risks required of them to be sources of learning, they need classrooms that feel safe. Let's return to the ideas we suggested in Chapters 5 and 6 for communicating protection and respect for your students' ideas: active listening, class meetings, and encouragement to name a few. When Mrs. Hathaway's students held a class meeting about playground problems, Omar was not afraid to suggest a "playground patrol" as a solution. She knew that everyone's ideas would be accepted as possibilities. When Ms. Conley-Trombley's students heard, "You paid attention to detail in your sketch," they felt respected.

In Chapter 10, we described the group norms that support a safe context—those of cooperation and respect. We suggested that your role is to promote and maintain the norms by prohibiting put-downs and discrimination, and by encouraging diverse opinions and ideas. Later, in Chapter 12, we will describe additional strategies for building a climate in which students can participate in roleplaying, simulations, and drama activities with comfort and trust.

We will now turn to some dimensions of constructivism—those that provide additional ways for you to support students as they develop ideas and solve problems.

Constructivism in Classrooms

Constructivism emerged from the observations of children at an early age as they construct knowledge from their world through various forms of interaction (touching, tasting, seeing, smelling, and hearing) (DeVries & Kohlberg, 1990). From the constructivist's standpoint, knowledge is built by the child through active participation in real-life situations and interactions with the environments of home, school, community, and the world.

Constructivism in the classroom incorporates three important dimensions: (1) valuing the student's point of view, (2) using higher-level questions to elicit student thoughts (see Chapter 8), and (3) valuing the process of student thinking rather than student answer or product.

Valuing the Students' Point of View

Students learn at an early age what adults expect to hear when they ask a question. Our favorite story is about a pastor giving a sermon to a group of children. She asked them to think about "something five or six inches high, sometimes brown and sometimes gray, with a big bushy tail, that scampers across the ground, climbs trees, and gathers nuts for the winter." Then she asked the children what it was. There was quiet. Finally, a child raised his hand and tentatively replied, "Well, ordinarily I'd think it was a squirrel, but I suppose you want me to say it was God" (Harste, Woodward, & Burke, 1984, p. xv).

You will need to encourage students to trust their own ideas in order to change established patterns like the one in our story. Your responses to their point of view can quickly communicate approval or disapproval. Listen to the following responses and decide which students feel valued for their thinking:

- "Giaccomo, it sounds like you support the tax increase because it's a fair approach to cut the deficit."
- "Andrea, are you sure you want to approach the recycling problem with a voluntary system? Have you looked at all the options?"
- "Matt, you sound sure of your interpretation of this formula. Have you thought about your ideas carefully?"
- "Class, we heard Carol's three reasons for why we should move the gerbil cage to the other self. She has been thinking about this problem all week."

Other examples of valuing responses to students are provided in Chapter 8.

Valuing the Process of Student Thinking

Initially your students may feel uncomfortable about responding, or unsure of how to provide reasons for their answers. Your patience and support will help them get started, and, in time, they will enjoy the opportunity to share their thinking processes. You will also benefit because teachers who practice this valuing process describe amazing student perspectives. Listen to Julie's ideas when asked about her thinking process:

> **TEACHER:** What are the Nacirema people like?
> **JULIE:** They are poor and not much like us.
> **TEACHER:** What in the story caused you to think they were poor?
> **JULIE:** They seemed to have many superstitions and usually poor people have more superstitions and they were afraid to throw away the charms. They do things differently than I do.
> **TEACHER:** You drew some conclusions I had not thought about. We are going to look at the Nacirema people more closely and think about their superstitions. We will also look for signs of poverty.

You will read a story about the people of Nacirema later in the chapter. When you do, you will see that Julie made a leap from the story to her own information. Without asking her, "What caused you to think they were poor?" you would think that she misread the story. Notice that her teacher's response to her thinking acknowledged and valued the process.

Student explanations offer important information about students. They provide you with the opportunity to see some of their inner-most thoughts. Getting close to their perspectives will help you support their role as "shareholder," while at the same time, expand their experiences and their participation in the learning process.

LEARNER

Teacher-directed strategies such as lecture or recitation require little of your learners. Although Denise may be thinking about the proper nouns you are defining during your lecture, Timothy may be thinking about his baseball game from the previous night. Reflective teaching strategies promote active participation of students. They require students to attend more, to recall previously learned ideas, to draw on existing information, to analyze, to synthesize, to draw conclusions, and to find solutions. In sum, "complex learning requires activity on the part of the learner" (Corno & Snow, 1986, p. 620). In order to achieve the kind of participation we have described, we suggest the role of *shareholder* for students.

Learners as Shareholders

To promote a shareholder role (that is, one in which students share in the planning and decision making), you will need to seek student input at different levels of your teaching. We describe three levels of input for you.

Learner Input in Planning

When you plan instruction, student ideas provide valuable information about previous learning, curiosities, and confusions. Listen to teachers seek student input.

TEACHER TALK

Class, we are going to develop a list of questions that you would like answered when we study about the planets next month. Move into your planning groups and come up with a list.

4th-Grade Teacher

This is an outline of the study of nutrition for six weeks. What are some learning activities you would like to have to help you learn and understand more about nutrition?

Middle-School Health Teacher

Learner Input during Instruction

When you are conducting a lesson, it is essential to seek student input to make those in-flight decisions we described in Chapter 2. Learners can inform you about the pace, the difficulty, the interest, and the need for clarification. Listen as teachers check with the shareholders.

TEACHER TALK

Class, we are going to spend about five more minutes practicing this computation. Is that enough time?

We have been working through this process for two days. How does it feel?

Rate this activity with your group members. Record each person's feelings about difficulty, interest, and involvement.

Before we go on, give a thumbs up if you understand the assignment, and a thumbs down if you would like more explanation.

It looks like many of you are confused. Yes, Roseanne? Roseanne says, "I figured it out. Would you like me to explain how I reached a solution?"

Secondary Math Teacher and Student

In classrooms where students begin to take ownership for learning, students like Roseanne are not self-conscious about helping find solutions to problems and sharing her thought process with others.

Learner Input in Assessment

When you are assessing what has been taught and learned, it is important to seek input from the learner. If you really want students to feel like shareholders in teaching and learning, it is important for them to have a voice in the entire process: in

planning, during instruction, and in assessment. You, of course, will benefit with insights for future planning and instruction. And students may develop different attitudes about the assessment process if they feel like shareholders.

To seek learner input in assessment, you may ask them to develop some questions for a test and give their answers. The process of test construction brings students to higher levels of thinking. Teachers from second grade through college who have tried this approach report positive results. You may also interview them for their ideas about the topic studied, and request their critique of the assessment measure (test, project, or paper). Essay-type questions that ask students to "describe three new ideas you learned about nutrition" or "write about how you will use your new computation skills outside of school" provide opportunity for student input.

Seeking their ideas for planning, instructing, and assessing promotes the shareholder role for learners, and begins the process of expanding experiences and participation.

Expanding Experiences and Participation

Reflective teaching strategies require students to recognize what they know and think about, and to process new information and ideas independently. It will be important to assure that your learners have experiences from which they can process information and ideas. And it will be important to provide some practice in the participation required for their role.

The vignette that follows describes a strategy called *active participation*, which can be used in any subject or grade level. It works toward increased participation from the entire class of students. From there, two more elaborate activities for expanding experiences and participation are *brainstorming* and *mapping*. These two activities have produced the independent thinking and the kind of reflection for which the shareholder role is designed. They are reasonably easy to implement in the classroom and are appropriate for learners from kindergarten to university classrooms.

Active Participation

This strategy is used to promote overt (easily seen) participation by students. It involves behavior such as writing, identifying, and responding with gestures. For example, when teaching a lesson about parts of speech, you may ask students to turn to a partner and give an example of a noun. When teaching a lesson in geology, you may ask students to write a term for a description you provide. When teaching a math computation process, you may ask students to hold up the number of fingers that corresponds to their answer.

Brainstorming

This activity needs a few ground rules if it is to promote participation and experience for all students. First, all ideas must be accepted. Second, the activity must be fast paced, like a "storm of the brain." Third, the ideas need to be recorded,

---

Elementary Research Vignette

INTRODUCTION

In 1986, Pratton and Hales designed a study to determine if active participation enhanced student learning. Observations had shown that the strategy promoted on-task behavior and focused student attention during a lesson.

STUDY DESIGN

Five teachers were selected and trained in the strategy of active participation. They were then scheduled to teach a 30-minute lesson to all fifth-grade classes (20 classes, 500 students) in a suburban school district. The lesson was developed on the subject of simple probability—a topic not ordinarily included in the fifth-grade math curriculum. Each of the five teachers taught four classes, two using active participation and two not using active participation.

To illustrate the difference in their teaching, one problem from the lesson plan was, "There are 5 checkers in a bag, 3 red and 2 black; what are my chances of getting a red." The nonactive participation teacher worked this example on the board, talking through the process. The active participation teacher told the students to solve the problem and indicate their answers by holding up the number of fingers corresponding to their choice. The teacher then visually checked for cor-

rect responses (Pratton & Hales, 1986, p. 212).

After the lesson, students took a multiple-choice test that was designed to include the six objectives of the lesson. Before data analysis, the lessons, which had been videotaped, were checked for consistency.

RESULTS

The class means on the test for the active participation group ranged from 78.4 to 87.2 percent. The class means on the test for the nonactive participation group ranged from 71.3 to 77.0 percent. In all cases, the class means were higher for the active participation group.

CONCLUSIONS AND IMPLICATIONS FOR PRACTICE

This study confirmed that active participation does make a difference in student learning, as measured by an immediate posttest. The researchers also noted that active participation was an efficient strategy, that it allowed teachers to monitor student understanding, and that it promoted student thinking and responding in overt ways.

This study provides a basic strategy for increasing student participation so that learners become comfortable with responding frequently.

---

and fourth, some of the ideas must be used. The following Snapshot provides a look at brainstorming used after an incident in which two students were nearly hit by a car. Notice the ground rules being established and followed.

SNAPSHOT: Elementary Classroom

The third-grade students in Mr. Gindele's class are talking among themselves about the near accident with excitement and anxiety in their voices. "Class, let's talk together about what happened to our friends yesterday. We know that the intersection of Vista and Sherwood is a very busy place, and the only help we have for crossing is a stop sign. Since so many of you use that route to go home, I would like us to work on the problem. We will begin by brainstorming suggestions for making the situation more safe. Remember to let yourself think of everything possible. We want to hear everyone's ideas. Rick, will you record ideas from this side of the room? Mei Ling, will you record ideas from this side of the room? Now spend a quiet minute getting suggestions ready." (pause) "OK, begin."

Every student's idea was recorded, and the process continued until the hum of brainstorming became still. Within three minutes, the lists were full. Some of the suggestions were:

Have students wear a red patch on their jackets so cars can see them.
Hire a crossing guard at the intersection.
Ask students to change their route home.
Ask older students to join a safety patrol for the intersection.
Ask a police officer to present a lesson on traffic safety.
Send a letter to the city council, asking them to add a stop light to the intersection.
Ask students' parents to drive them to and from school.
Have students take the bus.

Many other possibilities were listed. From there, Mr. Gindele asked one group to categorize the suggestions into long term and short term, one group to categorize the suggestions into practical and impractical, and one group to identify the five ideas that sounded safest. Following the group work, decisions were made about the "best" way to begin, and students volunteered spontaneously to carry out various responsibilities.

For some additional ideas on brainstorming, review the strategies suggested in Chapter 8. Those ideas will also be helpful for the next activity—mapping.

Mapping

This activity provides a visual image for learners as they think about and build relationships between ideas. In Figure 11.1, a student visualized the term *feudalism* as having three categories—guilds, kings, and church. From those "big ideas" about feudalism, he worked through "small ideas," such as fairs, monks, and manors. Another way of describing the picture in Figure 11.1 is a progression from main headings to subheadings, or from general to specific.

To use mapping with your students, start with simple examples. Have your students suggest words or terms related to feudalism, then write their suggestions in a format of relationships. In the example, crafts are related to guilds, and apprentice and journeyman are related to crafts.

Another example will help you see how relationships can be illustrated with mapping. In the map shown in Figure 11.2, a first-grade teacher began with the word *Spring* in preparation for a creative writing project. As you can see, young children come up with relationships quite different than those that you and I might build.

Mapping is an interesting way for students to process a story, a historical event, or a math problem. In the Samples and Examples section at the end of this chapter,

FIGURE 11.1 *Mapping Example 1*

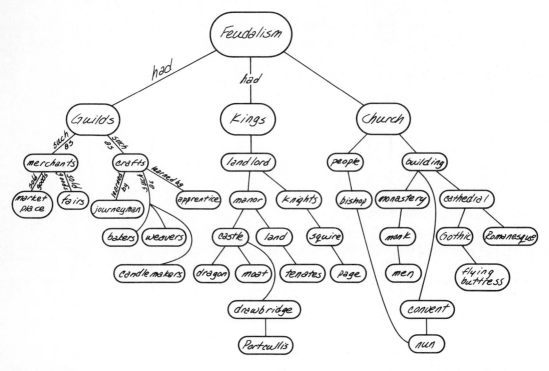

Source: Novak, J., & Gowan, D. (1984). *Learning how to learn*. London: Cambridge University Press. Used with permission.

we provide a format for mapping that is appropriate for secondary students, used for mapping information about a story or book character.

When McTighe and Lyman (1988) reviewed the research on mapping, they found it successful in improving learner retention of information. Their findings also yielded guidelines for your use of the process:

1. *Aid memory by giving tangible cues*, allowing students to focus more quickly on a topic or problem, and providing a visual representation of concepts.
2. *Provide a common frame of reference* by offering common terminology (heading, subheading) and specific cues for action (individual, small, or large group).
3. *Provide an incentive to act* by having students write out their thoughts, allowing teachers to see the results of the thought processes.
4. *Create permanence by imprinting in the mind* a variety of mapping options for transfer to other situations.

When Stahl and Vancil (1986/1987) studied student use of mapping, they con-

FIGURE 11.2 *Mapping Example 2*

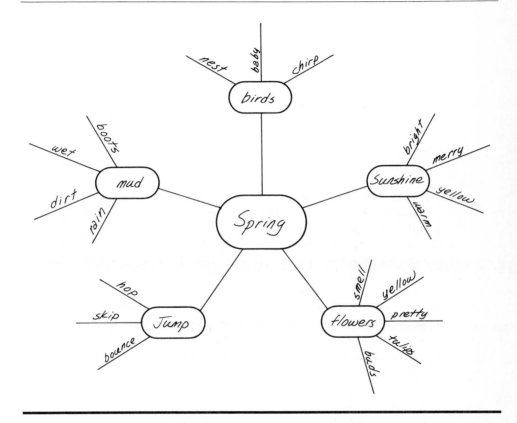

cluded that it was important for teachers to discuss the relationship between the words during the mapping process. So, a fifth guideline is:

5. *Promote relationships between ideas and information by questioning and discussion during mapping.*

As learners gain experience and expand their participation through brainstorming and mapping, they take on an authentic shareholder role in teaching and learning. They contribute to their own success in achieving understanding and skill. As we proceed to the content of reflective teaching strategies, you will see how important that success is for learners in today's world.

CONTENT

Whether you are teaching a senior high school economics course or a second-grade math lesson, the content of reflective teaching strategies is universal across the curriculum. Students will be developing inductive and critical thinking as well as problem-solving abilities.

Inductive Thinking

One approach to learning is through the deductive thinking of the teacher—that is, telling students facts, rules, principles, or generalizations, and then providing practice. Teaching the process of inductive thinking, however, requires you to provide students with a series of related examples or experiences, and supporting them emotionally and intellectually to discover the rules, principles, or generalizations. In this way, your students can create new knowledge from existing ideas and information.

Providing Experiences for Inductive Thinking

The type of experiences you create depends on the development of your learners; you will need to provide a range of experiences from which they produce ideas. The Cone of Learning Experiences in Figure 11.3 from Dale's (1954) model provides a representation of experiences that move from concrete to abstract, thus encouraging inductive thinking.

Young students need direct contact and experiences (e.g., a visit to the farm) and visual representations (e.g., photos of people from another culture). Older students gain experience from written symbols (e.g., a novel about Asian culture) and verbal symbols (e.g., a lecture on fusion), while continuing to need the more concrete experiences at the base of the cone.

Drawing Inferences from Experiences

A lesson on gravity in an inductive classroom would have students testing the law of physics related to objects of different weights falling at the same speed. They may decide to drop a 5-pound rock and a tennis ball from the top of a building at the same time, then develop their own inferences about the nature of gravity and the influence of shape on the rate of acceleration of an object.

Less exciting but appropriate for younger students is an experience with oranges, apples, pears, and grapes. After tasting and examining the seeds, five-year-olds begin to define fruit as "something sweet, with seeds in the middle, and a skin on the outside." Later, their definition is expanded with categories of fruit as they taste and examine bananas, kiwi, and pineapple.

Critical Thinking

This process begins with questioning by you and by your students. Together, you engage in analysis, synthesis, and evaluation of events, information, and ideas. The kind of thinking you do before making a major purchase is critical, because you look at options, weigh the advantages and disadvantages, determine the value of your choice, and reach a conclusion.

Critical thinking is a process for determining the value of an idea, a concept, a

FIGURE 11.3   *Pyramid of Learning Experiences*

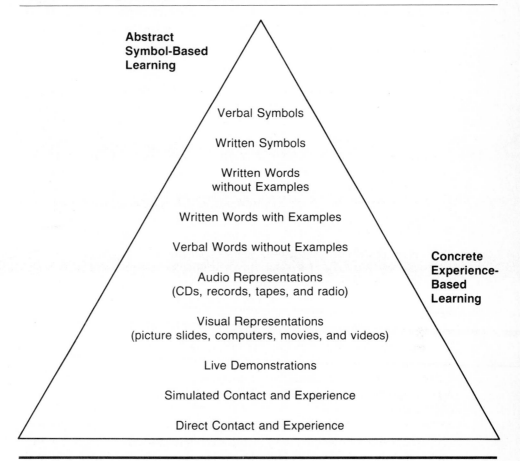

Abstract Symbol-Based Learning

Verbal Symbols

Written Symbols

Written Words without Examples

Written Words with Examples

Verbal Words without Examples

Audio Representations (CDs, records, tapes, and radio)

Concrete Experience-Based Learning

Visual Representations (picture slides, computers, movies, and videos)

Live Demonstrations

Simulated Contact and Experience

Direct Contact and Experience

Source: Adapted from Dale, E. (1954). *Audio-visual methods in teaching* (rev. ed.) (p. 43). New York: Dryden.

solution, or information. Beyer (1988) provided a list of eight actions you and your students could use to determine the worth of a statement or idea:

1. *Distinguishing between verifiable facts and value claims.*
2. *Distinguishing relevant from irrelevant information, claims, or reasons.*
3. *Determining the factual accuracy of a statement.*
4. *Determining the credibility of a source.*
5. *Identifying ambiguous claims or arguments.*
6. *Identifying unstated assumptions.*
7. *Detecting bias.*
8. *Determining the strength of an argument or a claim (p. 27).*

The list of actions for critical thinking are especially relevant to the needs of students faced with today's advertising. Consumer curriculum activities provide even very young children opportunities to detect bias and determine the factual accuracy of a statement. Look at the advertising claims for bottled water and purifying systems and use your critical thinking to:

1. *Distinguish between verifiable facts and value claims.*
   "This water purifier is designed to remove impurities from drinking water."
   "This water purifier will prevent cancer for those who drink from this product daily."
2. *Distinguish relevant from irrelevant information, claims, or reasons.*
   "Our water purifier system is in the homes of people just like you throughout the United States."
   "The water purifier uses charcoal, which is an effective source of removing common impurities."
3. *Determine the credibility of a source.*
   "In interviews with many of our customers, they state the health benefits derived from drinking our spring water."
   "A report from nonprofit and advertising-free magazines for consumers raises concerns that many water-purifying systems attached to the sink concentrate bacteria, which can be unhealthy."

In a review of the research on critical thinking, Norris (1985) concluded that "to think critically, one must have knowledge." So, your first responsibility to students' critical thinking is development of a knowledge base. Norris also concludes that "having a critical spirit is as important as thinking critically." A critical spirit, or the disposition (tendency) to think critically, is relevant for all aspects of life. It may require more sophistication to promote spirit than to provide a knowledge base, especially when students begin examining and questioning your ideas. As you promote this content of your reflective teaching, check your own awareness and ability to be open to critical thinking from your learners. The same sensitivity to thinking different from your own will be important as you teach the content of problem solving.

Problem Solving

Problem solving is one application or product of critical thinking. Once you make a conclusion about the value of information or ideas, you can use the information or ideas to solve a problem. The following list represents the most common steps used in problem solving:

1. Identify and describe the problem.
2. Gather information and/or possible responses.
3. Design a plan or solution.
4. Try out a plan or solution.

5. Check the results of the plan or solution.
6. Determine the effectiveness and select alternative plans if needed.

When students have not had experience with problem solving, you may have to develop the skills step by step. The "Finding an Apartment" exercise in the Samples and Examples section at the end of this chapter provides practice in steps 2 and 3. In the Snapshot presented earlier in this chapter, Mr. Gindele could have asked, "What is the problem?" before beginning the brainstorm. His students may struggle with, "Our friends nearly got hurt," and "Drivers aren't careful," and "I can't always see the cars coming," before arriving at, "The intersection of Vista and Sherwood is not safe" as the problem. The simplest strategy for achieving step 1 with students is to *ask* rather than tell whenever a problem situation arrives.

Once students have some beginning experiences, they can practice with classroom problems or community situations independently or as a group. Some examples of real-life problems that make sense to students include:

Needing money to finance a class trip
Vandalism on the school playground
Unattractive school hallways
Inefficient school lunch lines
Crowded conditions at the classroom resource shelves
Stray pets near the school grounds
Not enough puzzles for everyone

In Chapter 6, you watched a parent/teacher conference in which problem solving occurred. You also observed the class meeting about playground problems in Ms. Hathaway's room. Review the two illustrations to better understand how to use problem solving. Once you have learned the process, it can be modified by you and your students. Again, your acceptance and valuing of student ideas and the suggestions for promoting learners as shareholders will work toward competence in problem solving.

Notice that all of the content of reflective teaching strategies has relevance for learners and depends on their input. Notice that your teaching focuses on questioning and discussion techniques. You will continue to use those strategies as you teach with the reflective teaching strategies of inquiry and guided discovery.

REFLECTIVE TEACHING STRATEGIES

The two strategies discussed in this section, inquiry and guided discovery, are separated for in-depth description because they require a more subtle role for teachers. Their use requires indirect interaction with students but extensive preparation for the interaction. You are a kind of undercover agent with these strategies; that is, your work is not immediately recognized or easily noticed. Be ready to devote time to these strategies. They continue your support of the shareholder role for students, and promote inductive and critical thinking and problem solving.

Inquiry Approaches

Children are natural inquirers. They find something puzzling and they explore it for information. Teachers of young children need only to support the natural curiosity of students. However, as students get older, you may have to create conditions that stimulate an inquirying nature.

Steps of the Scientific Method of Inquiry

The following are six steps of the process that your students may follow when you teach with inquiry:

1. Forming and refining a question they wish to answer
2. Collecting instances and observing facts likely to be related to a possible answer
3. Putting facts or instances into a class or classes, and making generalizations about them
4. Making intelligent guesses (hypotheses) based on the facts to suggest possible explanations
5. Testing to see which hypothesis, if any, is the correct one
6. Using the new information as a basis for further reasoning

The following example from a 1917 textbook on science teaching (LaRue, pp. 16–18) serves as an excellent illustration of the process we are describing. The question to be answered is: What is the cause of dew? Before answering the question, we must know precisely what we mean by *dew*. Is it the moisture found sometimes on the outside of a pitcher, or on windows, or on water pipes? We end up with the definition of "the moisture that gathers on any substance exposed in the open air, when there is no rain or other apparent source for the dampness."

Our second step is to *get all possible facts with observations and experiments*. We notice that dew gathers on substances that are dry inside, substances that are damp, and objects that are under cover; it gathers on upper surfaces; and there is no dew on very cloudy nights.

Next, we *generalize* (that is, gather up our facts from all our observations) and notice that dew forms most freely on clear nights. Now, we make guesses, *hypotheses*, as to the probable cause of dew. With each hypothesis, we test it with what we know from our observations. Some examples are:

1. Dew may fall from the sky, as rain does. (No, this can't be because clear nights brought more dew than cloudy nights, and dew formed on our water pitcher, under cover, where anything like rain was out of the question.)
2. Dew may be forced out of the object on which it forms. (No, dew formed on objects that were dry through and through.)
3. Dew may come from the air and settle on objects. (But why does it not form on all objects all the time? We recall the coldness of dewed objects as compared with the temperature of the surrounding air. We know that cold contracts most things. Maybe it contracts the air and squeezes out the moisture, which then settles on whatever is near.)

We now have a hypothesis that the cooling of moist air by a comparatively cold object squeezes out particles of moisture and the particles unite to form drops on the object. We don't expect to find dew on objects that are warmer than the air, nor on any object surrounded by perfectly dry air. We experiment further and find that this third hypothesis holds under every test we can devise. We may use this "new truth" to answer further questions like, "Is there dew on the moon?" or "Could there be dew if there were no air?"

Teaching the Steps of Inquiry

As we suggested with mapping and problem solving, you may need to begin simply or with the individual steps of inquiry. The experience described in this Teacher Talk illustrates the work of a class on steps 1 and 2 (forming and refining questions to answer) and collecting instances and observing facts related to possible answers.

TEACHER TALK

It was December and we were studying the history of religions in our middle-school social studies class. I asked students what holidays were approaching. Many said, "Christmas." I asked if there were others. One student said, "Chanukah" (mispronouncing the word). I restated the word, using the correct pronounciation, and asked if they could tell me something about the holiday. It was quiet. The bell was about to ring. I suggested that they find out about Chanukah for our next class.

The next day, as class began, the students seemed anxious. Before I could ask, several students volunteered that they found out about Chanukah (pronouncing it correctly). They talked about the "holiday of lights," the story of the oil lasting eight days, the fight for freedom that the holiday represented, and the gift-giving customs. Some students had talked with their parents, two had called the local synagogue and asked for information, and others went to the library and looked up the holiday. There was a sense of pride as they described their searches for information.

Their experience with this "new knowledge" was a perfect start for their next assignment. They had two weeks to explore questions about religion, getting ready for a scheduled panel of experts. I had arranged for a Baptist minister, a Catholic priest, and a Jewish rabbi to come to class to discuss and respond to questions.

After much research in the library and discussions among individual students, the students were prepared for dialogue with the panel. The scheduled 45 minutes went on (with principal approval and extension) to an hour and a half. The three clergy indicated that they were totally impressed at the level of student questions. I was thrilled with the pride in students' eyes and the high level of thinking I observed that afternoon and for weeks after.

6th-Grade Teacher

The Teachers' Role in Inquiry

In inquiry, your role is quite different from the one you take when lecturing or conducting a demonstration. This role is like an iceberg. Only a small part of the effort is evident above the surface if viewed by the casual observer. Much work has been completed by the teacher before entering the classroom, and more work accompanies the student activity. The efforts are focused on creating the conditions necessary for a successful experience. The sixth-grade teacher in the preceding Teacher Talk guided students as they researched their questions, met with the principal to check policies related to the nature of the discussion and the panel members, scheduled the visits of the clergy, and briefed them on their roles.

Remember the climate of trust and respect we described early in this chapter? The climate in the sixth-grade classroom was one in which the students felt comfortable seeking answers and raising questions without worry of being considered silly or stupid. Groundwork for the dialogue with the panel members had focused on students' listening to each other, pride in the class group, and respect for diversity of opinion.

Did you notice that several weeks went into preparation for the panel? Probably for weeks afterwards, the processing of ideas and information continued. The climate and skills necessary for inquiry require time for development. The same conditions apply when you use guided discovery.

Guided Discovery

This strategy requires that you "examine the cognitive structure of the concepts to be taught and create a series of experiences for students to explore and discover the concepts for themselves" (Simon, 1986, p. 41). For example, when preparing to teach the concept and skill of estimation, you think about the definition of *estimation*, purposes of estimation, a variety of ways of estimating, situations in which estimation is appropriate and inappropriate, and some real-life examples of estimation.

The first experience you might provide would involve the placement of a large jar of jelly beans on display with a sign urging students to estimate how many. From there, a sequence of experiences would gradually guide students to discover that estimation is appropriate for some uses, that estimation is a calculated guess, that there are a number of ways to estimate, and so on.

Steps in Guided Discovery

This strategy draws on prior learning of students and requires active student participation toward a solution or an understanding. The following steps provide a framework for conducting guided discovery:

1. *Present a problem, question, or situation that is interesting or exciting, and will provoke student questions.*
2. *Ask students to define or explain terms, working toward a precise definition of the problem, question, or situation to be studied.*
3. *Aid students in the formulation of specific questions to focus the inquiry and facilitate the collection of data.*
4. *Guide students toward a variety of sources, including yourself and your students, to provide necessary data.*
5. *Assist students in checking the data by clarifying statements or judgments about the problem or situation.*
6. *Support the development of a number of solutions, from which choices can be made.*
7. *Provide opportunity for feedback and revision. Assist in testing the effectiveness of solutions.*
8. *Support the development of a plan of action (Freiberg, 1973).*

The context for these steps must be one of openness, and one in which students have consistent opportunities and encouragement to think and develop alternatives. The story of the People of Nacirema (Miner, 1956) provides an ideal step 1 as you see students listen to the story and show interest in the people. Read the story (in Figure 11.4) and then watch the fifth-grade students in the next Snapshot as they follow the steps of guided discovery.

FIGURE 11.4   *The People of Nacirema*

Anthropologists are so familiar with the many ways in which different groups of people behave, even the most exotic customs don't surprise them. Let's look at the Nacireman people, a group whose beliefs and practices show just how far human behavior can go.

The Nacireman culture has a highly developed economy. Although many people spend most of their time carrying on the business which makes up the economy, a large part of each day is spent in ritual activities. Their many rituals have to do with the human body. The people are very much concerned about their health and appearance. They believe that the body is ugly and is likely to become weak and diseased. This belief, itself, is not

continued

FIGURE 11.4   *(Continued)*

strange. However, the customs that surround this belief are what make it so unusual.

The Naciremans believe that because man is imprisoned in such a weak sickly body, man's only hope of life is through the powerful influences of his rituals and ceremonies. Every household has one or more shrines for this purpose. The more powerful people may have several shrines. In fact, many people feel the more shrines a family has, the richer it is.

The main item in the shrine is a box or chest that is built into the wall. In these chests are magical potions. No Nacireman believes he could live without these charms and potions. These things are gathered from many special people. The most powerful of these people are the medicine men. Help from a medicine man must be repaid with expensive gifts. The medicine men do not actually give the potions to their clients. What they do is decide what the client needs, and then write that down in a secret language. This writing is only understood by the medicine men and the herbalists, who for another gift will give the client the charm he needs.

The charm is not thrown away after its use. Instead it is placed in the charm box in the household shrine. Because there are different charms for different problems the charm box is usually full to overflowing. There are often so many charms in the charm box, that the Naciremans are afraid to use them again, but we get the idea they believe that just keeping the charm in the house will protect the worshipers.

Beneath the charm box is a small font, each day, one-at-a-time, each member of the family enters the shrine room, bows his head before the charm box, mixes holy water in the font, and does a short rite for cleansing. The holy water comes from the water temple of the community, where priests conduct ceremonies to make the water pure.

Just below the medicine men in importance are specialists known as the "holy mouth men." The Naciremans are almost mad when it comes to the mouth. They believe that the condition of the mouth has a supernatural effect on their relationships with people.

If it weren't for the holy mouth rituals, They believe that their teeth would fall out, their gums would bleed, their friends would desert them. In order to prevent all this from happening, they have one rite that is quite unusual. Each day they put what looks like a small bundle of hog hairs in their mouths along with some magic powder and move this all around. Doing this, they believe, is what saves them.

Besides that mouth rite they see a holy mouth man at least twice a year. These men have a frightening set of tools. These tools are used in an unbelievable ritual that at times is very painful. The holy mouth man uses these tools on decayed teeth. He makes holes in the teeth a little larger and puts in a magic substance. If there are no holes, the holy mouth man makes one. The Naciremans believe that this will help them win friends. In spite of how painful this rite is, it is so important that the Naciremans return to the holy mouth man year-after-year.

There is another ritual which is performed only by men. In this one, the men scrape and cut their faces each day. A rite by women includes having them bake their heads in a small oven for about an hour.

The Naciremans actually seem to enjoy pain. Looking at them from the safety of our civilization, we feel sorry for them, but we must understand that before we could be who we are today we were much like the Naciremans.

Source: Reproduced by permission of the American Anthropological Association from Horace Miner, "Body Ritual Among the Nacirema," *American Anthropologist*, 58(3), June 1956. Not for further reproduction.

SNAPSHOT: *Elementary Classroom*

After reading the story together, Ms. Stanich worked with students to under-line words that needed explanation. Students were then asked to write two questions they had about the people of Nacirema. The students had a library period during which they could search for information and definitions. A collection of resources on other cultures was set up in the classroom.

The next day, students worked in pairs, reading the story again and then drawing what they thought the Naciremans would look like. The students pre-sented their drawings to the class, and the class could ask questions. After much discussion of the "weird ways" of the Naciremans and some laughter, Ms. Stanich suggests that students take the word *Nacirema* and rearrange the letters backwards, which then spelled *American*. Once the students see the con-nection, the sounds of discovery ripple through the classroom. This is followed by a discussion about their perceptions of other cultures and the biases that accompany experiences with different ways.

Later, the students brainstormed ways to find better information about different cultures and to avoid stereotypes. They decided that they needed to share their discovery with other classes in the school, so they developed a slide tape about respecting other cultures and understanding your own biases.

Advantages of Guided Discovery

Notice again the time-consuming quality of the guided discovery strategy and the need to simultaneously use a number of strategies. On the surface, this kind of teach-ing looks easy, but, as in inquiry, you are a skillful "undercover agent," making sure that students are guided to their discoveries. With those challenges in mind, we point out the advantages of guided discovery:

1. Most students become more motivated due to greater participation in the learning process.
2. Students have the opportunity to think at more complex levels.
3. Students learn how to seek out information from a variety of sources to solve problems or develop ideas.
4. Students learn to be proactive learners producing new ideas and knowledge.

Your Role in Guided Discovery

You may have realized by now that the iceberg analogy is appropriate again. The role looks simple and easy, but below the surface, you have planned experiences, provided materials, and maintained a clear picture of the sequence and direction for which you have prepared (Houston, Clift, Freiberg, & Warner, 1988). When students discover irrelevant information, you may allow them to go off in an unin-tended direction, and later support their own redirection. You patiently allow the process of discovery to occur, maintaining the indirect role of guide.

SUMMARY

Reflective teaching strategies can elevate the level of intellectual processing and interaction in your classroom, and make learning more relevant to your students' lives. To achieve these goals, we remind you of the following:

1. Develop a *context* for teaching and learning that supports learners as active participants in their own education. The development must attend to a *climate of trust* and the dimensions of *constructivism*.
2. Provide experiences that promote the *learner's* ability to take responsibility for learning. Support them in a *shareholder* role by providing opportunities for input in planning, during instruction, and in assessment. *Expand their experiences and participation* through the strategies of active participation, brainstorming, and mapping.
3. Provide experiences that teach the *content* of inductive and critical thinking, and problem solving.
4. Use the reflective teaching strategies of *inquiry* and *guided discovery*.

We remind you that the activities and strategies of this chapter will take more preparation and time than other more direct teaching. You may feel insecure in your role in these strategies, because you must let go of your control of the teaching. Often, it will not feel comfortable to step back as learners direct their own learning, produce their own knowledge, and develop a high level of competence. Have courage and take risks—because you may get to experience the kind of teaching and learning that drew you to the profession. You heard a sixth-grade teacher in this chapter describe a "thrill" when observing student pride and their high level of thinking. Our hope is for you to feel that same excitement as you use the reflective teaching strategies.

REFERENCES

Beyer, B. (1988). Developing a scope and sequence for thinking skills instruction. *Educational Leadership, 45*(7), 27.

Corno, L., & Snow, R. E. (1986). Adapting teaching to individual differences in learners. In M. Wittrock (Ed.), *Handbook for research on teaching* (3rd ed.). New York: Macmillan.

Dale, E. (1954). *Audio-visual methods in teaching* (rev. ed.). New York: Collier.

DeVries, R., & Kohlberg, L. (1990). *Constructivist early education: Overview and comparison with other programs*. Washington, DC: National Association for the Education of Young Children.

Dewey, J. (1938). *Experience and education*. New York: Collier.

Dunkin, M. J., & Biddle, B. J. (1974). *The study of teaching*. New York: Holt, Rinehart & Winston.

Freiberg, H. J. (1973). Inquiry approach. In W. R. Houston & S. C. White (Eds.), *Professional development modules*. Houston: Professional Development Center, College of Education, University of Houston.

Freiberg, H. J. (1973). Recipe of classroom ideas. In W. R. Houston & S. C. White (Eds.), *Professional development modules*. Houston: Professional Development Center, College of Education, University of Houston.

Freiberg, H. J. (1988). *Generic teaching strategies.* Unpublished curriculum materials. Houston: University of Houston.

Freiberg, H. J. (1991). Consistency management: What to do the first days and weeks of school. *Consistency Management Training Booklet.* Houston: Consistency Management Associates.

Gowen, D. B., & Novak, J. D. (1984). *Learning to learn.* New York: Cambridge University Press.

Harste, J. C., Short, K. G., & Burke, C. (1988). *Creating classrooms for authors.* Portsmouth, NH: Heinemann.

Harste, J., Woodward, V. A., & Burke, C. (1984). *Language, stories and literacy lessons.* Portsmouth, NJ: Heinmann.

Houston, W. R., Clift, R. T., Freiberg, H. J., & Warner, A. R. (1988). *Touch the future—Teach!* St. Paul: West Publishing.

LaRue, D. W. (1917). *The science and art of teaching.* New York: American Book Company.

McTighe, J., & Lyman, F. T. (1988). Cueing thinking in the classroom: The promise of theory embedded tools. *Educational Leadership, 45*(7), 18–24.

Miner, H. (1956). Body ritual among the nacirema. *American Anthropologist, 58,* 503–507.

Norris, S. P. (1985). Synthesis of research on critical thinking. *Educational Leadership,* 40–45.

Novak, J., & Gowan, D. (1984). *Learning how to learn.* London: Cambridge University Press.

Pratton, J., & Hales, L. W. (1986). The effects of active participation on student learning. *Journal of Educational Research, 79*(4), 210–215.

Simon, H. (1986). The teacher's role in increasing student understanding of mathematics. *Educational Leadership, 43,* 40–43.

Stahl, S. A., & Vancil, S. J. (1986/1987). Discussion of what makes semantic maps work in vocabulary instruction. *The Reading Teacher, 40,* 62–67.

SAMPLES AND EXAMPLES

There are three Samples and Examples in this section.

- Finding an Apartment is provided as an example of how several different subject areas could be integrated into one activity.
- The Ready Reading Reference Bookmark is designed to be a reminder for students during reading activities.
- The Flowchart is an activity where students could map out the traits of a character related to the events in the story.

FINDING AN APARTMENT

Please review the apartment ads and, using the questions as a guide, select the best answer(s).

1. You have $200 a month to rent an apartment. Which of the nine apartments listed could you afford? Write in the space provided the location or two-word descriptor of the apartments (e.g., Montrose and Central/Air Heat) here. _____
   Yellowstone/Highway 288, Heights, and Galleria-Richmond first apartment.

2. How much more would you need to rent the Condo at 2121 Hepburn Street #308 near the medical center? _____ *$350.00*

3. Which apartments have two bedrooms? *Medical Center, Galleria-Richmond both apartments*
   and the Condo at Near Medical Center.

4. Which apartment is close to your school? *Yellowstone/Hwy 288*

5. Which apartment gives you the most information about the place and why? _____
   St. Thomas/Rice area. The owners need to fill the apartment which may be the reason for the
   free rent and all the information.

Source: Freiberg, H. J. (1988). *Generic Teaching Strategies.* Unpublished Curriculum Materials University of Houston.

NEAR MEDICAL CENTER. 2-2 condo, 2121 Hepburn #308. $550/month, $550 deposit. 2nd floor flat, stove, refrigerator, washer/dryer, fireplace, 24 hour guard. 528-5311. CLARK MCDOWELL.

YELOWSTONE/HWY 288: 1 bedroom, $150 monthly or $40 weekly. Individual. 748-8296.

HEIGHTS: NICE one bedroom apartment. Trees, yard, quiet. See what $160/month will rent in the Heights. 869-4516.

MONTROSE GARAGE APARTMENT. Large, clean, a/c. Near River Oaks Center. On bus line. $250 month. 665-3114.

MONTROSE/RICHMOND area. 417 W. Main. Ceiling fans, covered parking. 1 bedroom apartment. $225. Clean, hardwood floors, quiet complex, pets ok. 523-3121. MANAGER.

MEDICAL CENTER: 3607 Murworth. 2 bedroom, new carpet, mini-blinds, carport, downstairs. $300 a month. 984-9769.

CENTRAL AIR/HEAT. One bedroom in clean, quiet complex. Covered parking, laundry. New grey carpet, mini's. $250. 522-1565.

GALLERIA-RICHMOND two bedroom, $200. Covered parking. Two bedroom, $275. On-site manager at 4822 Merwin. Manager speaks Spanish. 439-1784. HYLTON MANAGEMENT.

ST. THOMAS/Rice area. Newly renovated 1 bedroom. All adult living, electronic gates, covered parking, mature landscaping, 24 hour emergency maintenance, mini-blinds, carpet, large walk-in closet, ceiling fan. Quiet neighborhood. Close to universities and downtown. $250. One month free! 528-5151. SOHO.

THE READY READING REFERENCE BOOKMARK

While you read—
Tell
yourself what the
author says.
Ask
yourself if what you are
reading makes sense.
Picture
what the author
describes.
Identify
the main ideas.
Predict
what will come next.

If you don't understand—
Identify
the problem.
Remind
yourself of what you want
to find out.
Look Back.
Look Ahead.
Slow Down.
Ask
for help.

After you read—
Retell
what you read in your own
words.
Summarize
the most important ideas.
Ask
yourself questions and
answer them.
Picture
in your mind what the
author described.
Decide
what was especially
interesting or enjoyable.

Source: Maryland State Department of Education. Reprinted by permission.

FLOWCHART

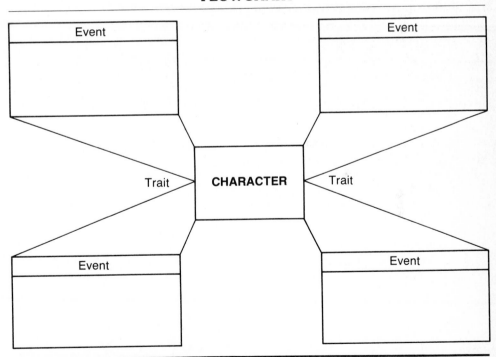

Source: J. McTighe & F. T. Lyman (1988). Cueing thinking in the classroom: The promise of theory embedded tools. *Educational Leadership 45*(7), 21–24. Reprinted with permission of the Association for Supervision and Curriculum Development. Copyright © 1985 by ASCD. All rights reserved.

CHAPTER 12

Roleplay, Simulation, and Drama: Making Learning Real

CHAPTER OUTCOMES

At the conclusion of this chapter you will be able to:

1. Consider the context, content, and learner in planning for roleplay, simulation, and drama.
2. Plan for and use roleplay, simulation, and drama with appropriate prerequisites, management, and other teaching strategies.

KEY TERMS AND CONCEPTS

Improvisation
Role Play
Simulation
Drama
Dramatic Play
Theater Games
Realia
Problem Solving
Decision Making
Facilitator
Coaching
Refereeing

INTRODUCTION

We offer three Snapshots as an introduction to the family of strategies in this chapter. In the first, a high-school class participates in a roleplay activity. In the second, a kindergarten snapshot, you will see a simulation strategy. A middle-school teacher uses the third strategy, drama.

SNAPSHOT: Middle School Classroom (Roleplay)

Eric Adams's environmental science class is studying ways to dispose of refuse. To develop understanding of the issues regarding use of landfills, he assigns roles to students and schedules a community forum. One group of students becomes property owners who live in the neighborhood of the proposed landfill site. A second group of students becomes the planning commission proposing the site. A third group is a hearing committee that will review the proposal and take testimony at the forum to make a decision. The last group of students are "interested observers": news reporters, chamber of commerce representatives, and business people.

During three days of research and preparation for the forum, Eric meets with each group to discuss what information they need, what sentiments are felt, and issues that have come up. At the Friday forum, each group speaks on the issues, raises questions, and pleads a case. Some roles are played with intensity for and against the landfill.

After the forum, the class meets for discussion. They respond to such questions as: What would you say to a community group that approached you for advice on this situation? Students write about what learning occurred during the roleplay, and how they learned.

SNAPSHOT: Elementary Classroom (Simulation)

As the kindergarten students arrive one morning, they are greeted by Mrs. Dunham, who points out the lines and arrows on the floor of their classroom. She instructs children to walk around the room only in the direction of the arrows.

When everyone has arrived, Mrs. Dunham reviews the walking instructions during "circle time," a time when students sit on the floor in a circle to talk. She refers to the walking arrangements as a new rule for the classroom. Within the first 10 minutes of activity time, students find the walking arrangements inconvenient and hard to follow. Mrs. Dunham waits another 10 minutes. She calls the class together for another "circle time" to discuss the new rule. She begins by saying that rules are made to help us work and play together well. She asks, "Is the new rule helping?" Most children say, "No," and she responds, "Rules can be changed."

When Mrs. Dunham asks for ideas for changing the rule, many students suggest turning the arrows the opposite way. She agrees, and students return to their activities.

Within a shorter time, students complain, and their teacher calls another discussion. Again she asks, "Is the new rule helping us work and play together?

The kindergarten class continues to negotiate and try out new walking rules. By the end of the morning, the students are talking about rules with a beginning understanding of the concept and the rule-making process.

SNAPSHOT: *Secondary Classroom (Drama)*

Sophomore students are studying the topic of drugs and the pressures for drug use. After filmstrips, readings, a speaker, and instruction, they form groups to develop play scripts about the pressures.

Groups may select a scenario for a play or create one of their own. For example, group 1 writes a script for a situation in which a popular older student approaches a younger student and offers drugs. After two days of script development, they rehearse for a day and then present to the other classes.

After the plays, the students discuss what they learned about drugs in their lives. Importantly, they talk about what it felt like to be offered drugs, to refuse drugs, the pressures to try drugs, and how different individuals influenced the feelings.

In this chapter you will learn how to use the three strategies observed in the snapshots in different contexts, with different content, and by different learners.

Definition of Terms

We combined roleplay, simulation, and drama in this chapter because of their similarities, but we needed a term to express all three. We came upon a teaching and learning strategy called *improvisation*, modeled in the British Infant Schools, and it described the strategies of this chapter. When we refer to them collectively, we will use improvisation. The strategies have in common the opportunity for students to:

1. Learn by doing, thinking, feeling, or responding.
2. Have a vicarious experience that takes the place of a firsthand experience.
3. Be involved in the development of content, understanding, skills, and attitudes.

As we define the individual strategies, you will see the individual uniqueness.

Roleplay

This is a strategy that enables participants to think, feel, and act as other persons. It is an enactment or rehearsal of behavior with some reality and with a safe environment for trying out new ideas and making mistakes. Eric Adams's students prepared for their roles to give them some reality, but at the same time, were able to play their roles spontaneously.

Simulation

This is a strategy that enables students to experience the consequence of their own and other's behaviors. Simulations are meant to represent reality as closely as possible. An important quality of simulations is the self-feedback provided by the person experiencing the behaviors or consequences. Mrs. Dunham's students gave their own feedback about the rules, and kept making changes based on the feedback.

Drama

A common definition of this strategy is a composition intended to portray life or a character or to tell a story, often with conflict, emotions, and action and dialogue. The story is intended for performance. The middle-school students composed their own stories to portray real-life pressures associated with drugs.

One form of drama, *dramatic play*, is an unrehearsed activity with props and accessories in which students play in real or unreal situations of their choice. A common example is found in early childhood settings, with children enacting roles of adults with props of a home.

Another form of drama is *theater games*. These are exercises or games that train participants in communication and theater techniques and skills. They are designed to stimulate action, spontaneity, and creativity. As games, they have a set of rules that keep the playing active.

Advantages of Improvisation

If you consider using improvisation in your classroom, and ask a colleague for an opinion, you may encounter the kind of comments that you hear in this Teacher Talk.

TEACHER TALK

I don't have enough time to do those activities.

Elementary Teacher

I'm uncomfortable, or my students are uncomfortable, with roleplaying.

Middle-School Teacher

I just don't get around to planning for drama. You know, having props ready, thinking through the routines, . . . there's so many other things to do.

Secondary Teacher

We think that there are lots of advantages for improvisation, and they are connected to the issues of the Teacher Talk: the time issue and the discomfort issue.

The Time Issue

Improvisational strategies do require more time than some other instructional strategies. The actual forum for roleplaying the landfill issues was scheduled for 55 minutes, and preparation took three days of class periods. The discussion that followed lasted another 55 minutes. So, the time issue is real.

A way to look at the time issue is to look at the additional learning benefits. During the 55-minute forum, students practiced public speaking, questioning, and use of data. They conducted research, used group processes, and planning.

A response to the time consumed as middle-school students wrote scripts, rehearsed, and presented their plays is that the time spent instructing on drug pressures could be lost if students do not get experience or practice responding to the pressures.

The Discomfort Issue

We advocate sensitivity to this issue. There are individuals who flourish when participating in improvisational strategies. There are also those who are shy and uncomfortable. We will describe how to provide different levels of participation in improvisation in our section called Learner.

The improvisation strategies offer roles, feelings, and situations not ordinarily available in classrooms. We think that you will find more advantages as we look at the context, content, and learner to make decisions about using these strategies for teaching and learning.

CONTEXT

Your community context provides planning information and resources, and your classroom context provides physical arrangements, an emotional climate, and a schedule to be considered. Begin by reviewing your advancework information about the community and your classroom.

Community Context

Community awareness is important when you use improvisation. You don't teach in isolation, so the "hows and whats" of your instruction must be sensitive to the attitudes and values of the community. You also need community resources for improvisation.

Community Attitudes and Values

The teaching strategies of this chapter have unpredictable outcomes. If students roleplay presidential candidates and reporters in a press conference, who knows what issues may be raised? If students participate in a simulation of world trade, moral and ethical decisions may arise. When young children engage in dramatic play of "mother and father," anything is possible.

Our advice is to anticipate some possible directions to which your activities may take students. What could happen? What might be said? What conclusions are possible? If you anticipate topics, feelings, or opinions that may offend students, parents, or community, you can decide whether the outcomes are worth the risk. If they do come up, you can be ready to talk about them with students. Discuss why they happened and how they conflict with community values or attitudes. Use caution not to sanction or judge them.

Our message in this section is not to stay on "safe ground," avoiding all controversial topics, but to be thoughtful and sensitive as you approach such topics. Being aware of community attitudes and values is your first step.

Community Resources

Go back to the Community Context Checklist in Chapter 5 and look for themes, props, and support persons for improvisation. Themes for your use of improvisation come from community issues, events, problems, and other situations. The landfill scenario came from a real-life situation occurring in Eric Adams's students' community.

Your community is a source of props: libraries, historical societies, chamber of commerce offices, hospitals, universities, realtors, restaurants, grocery stores, newspaper companies, and museums. Your school district may have a resource center. It is a matter of becoming familiar with what is available and being organized enough to schedule use of what you find.

One kind of prop for improvisation is *realia*, objects used to relate classroom teaching to the real life of people or situations studied. Some common examples of realia are costumes, tools, journals, maps, and household furnishings. The advantage of collecting and using realia is that items such as toys from colonial days can motivate authentic drama or roleplay. Students visualize life of the colonists when interacting with toy props.

Once you develop a list of needed items (props and realia), ask for help from parents and neighbors. Our experience has been that this is an easy kind of support for people to give. There is a request letter in the Samples and Examples section at the end of Chapter 10. If you have time, garage sales are goldmines for props.

The community also is a source of individuals or groups who can support your improvisational strategies. Consider using them for information, guidance, or as substitutes. The historical society guide can provide information with which to begin a roleplay of early settlers in your state. A construction company manager can provide real-life examples for your math simulations. The local drama group may have an individual who would enjoy coming to your class and conducting a drama activity.

For those of you who feel that discomfort we described earlier, many of these support persons can substitute for you while you gain experience and confidence. Chapter 13 offers you additional examples and sources for community resources.

Classroom Context

Room arrangements, emotional climate, and the schedule of your classroom context influence the effectiveness of your improvisational strategies. Each will be a consideration in your planning for teaching with improvisation.

Room Arrangement

Depending on the number of students in your class, the strategies of this chapter may require some extra classroom space. Students need to be seated or standing close to other students who are participating in the improvisation. If the entire class is not participating, the room may be arranged for separation of activities. Some improvisation requires additional space for physical movement.

Probably our best advice for your room arrangement is to have flexibility. Have an area or corner of the room that can be quickly cleared or set up for improvisation activities. Ideally, a student committee for "set-ups" can be organized in anticipating of the need for space. Decisions about location and student assistance can be made with students in a class discussion.

In addition to using actual classroom space, you will find alternative spaces outside the classroom. Your advancework will pay off as you locate hallways, play yards, and storage areas for rehearsal, planning discussions, and actual improvisation. Sometimes, the alternative spaces provide more supportive contexts than the classroom. When Mr. Hardt looked for a space similar to the living space on the *Mayflower*, he found an outdoor covered pavilion with a mast or support pole.

Emotional Climate

In all of the advice on using improvisation, there is a consistent theme of the importance of trust. If you are going to teach with improvisation, you must believe that individuals can and will succeed. You must also be clear that the enacted behavior is neither good nor bad. Along with your beliefs, you must provide the following in your classroom emotional climate:

1. Safety for exploration of feelings and behaviors
2. Permission to express all feelings
3. Respect for ideas and feelings of all

Shaftel and Shaftel (1982) recommend some procedures to help you provide such an environment. We describe them with some classroom examples:

1. *Demonstrate your acceptance of feelings or experiences.* Ms. Janes demonstrates to her third-grade class when she says, "Sometimes we feel afraid when we don't know anyone or enter a strange place. When I moved to Seattle two years ago, I was afraid. I didn't know anyone. I didn't know where the grocery store was located. I didn't even have the name of a doctor."
2. *Read and discuss stories of emotions, human traumas, relationships, and conflicts.* After sixth-grade students read a story of a moral dilemma, their discussion

comments could safely reflect the dilemma of the story's characters. It is secure to talk about, "Justin felt tempted to take the 50 dollars because he could be sure that no one would ever look for the money."

3. *Use active listening.* This kind of listening is described in the Teacher Effectiveness Training model in Chapter 5. As students begin to express feelings, ideas, or actions, you reflect back those same feelings, ideas, or actions, without any judgment. Mr. Rodriguez observed his first-graders roleplaying a library scene and reflected, "You feel angry when books aren't in the right place on the shelf."

4. *Provide guidance and be willing to explore topics in any direction.* When students in Ms. Schumanoff's history class became interested in societal attitudes about working women before and after World War II, she encouraged their research and drama for the rest of the class.

Classroom Schedules

Some suggestions to ease the time pressures of using improvisation include integration of curriculum and teaching strategies, and delegation of responsibilities to students. To be more efficient, you can design and use improvisation to teach more than one subject at once in elementary classrooms. A simulation about conservation of water can result in a discussion about water uses, effects of water shortages, charting of quantity of water use and frequency of use, and designing posters about water conservation (social studies, art, science, and math). In secondary classrooms, integrating curriculum is more difficult, but integrating teaching strategies is quite effective. When students participated in the forum on location of a landfill site and drama about pressures associated with drugs, their teachers conducted assessment, used peer teaching, and reviewed content.

For further efficiency, students can assume some of the responsibilities associated with use of improvisation: finding and organizing props, organizing each other into roles and responsibilities, and active listening. One of our most memorable teaching experiences was the Greek games staged by fourth-grade students who organized, prepared, and rehearsed independent of any assistance from us.

In sum, you and your students interact with the community's attitudes and values in improvisation, so awareness is important. Your classroom can support the strategy with its room arrangement, emotional climate, and use of time, but, again, you begin with awareness. That same awareness is important as you review your content to plan improvisation.

CONTENT

Some educators confine the use of roleplay, simulation, and drama to the social sciences—history, citizenship, economics, and so on. A creative teacher will find no curricular limits to use of improvisation. Some of our most memorable observations of teaching include:

- The preschool teacher whose four-year-old students roleplayed the artist Jackson Pollack and created "works of art."
- The first-grade teacher whose students simulated pairs for adding by twos.
- The sixth-grade class in which students dressed in costume and addressed the class in the role of the main character of their book reports.
- The chemistry teacher who had students wear nametags of various elements, and simulate compounds and equations.
- The education professor who had students roleplay parents and teachers meeting in conference about student problems or progress.
- The engineer trainer who simulated a steam pipe with body movement and sounds and brought both delight and understanding to his peers with his teaching.

So you see, art, math, science, language arts, education, and engineering can be taught with these strategies. We see no curricular or content limits. In addition, improvisation responds to a concern for significant curriculum that is "relevant and real life" content (Schaftel & Schaftel, 1982).

Roleplay, simulation, and drama are all process oriented. Processing is necessary for learning two real-life goals: problem solving and decision making. These two goals fit well in our content predictions for tomorrow.

Learning Problem Solving

Using improvisation to teach problem solving allows students to study serious problems, explore solutions, and make mistakes in the security of the classroom. They can learn from mistakes through followup discussions, feedback, and self-reflection. Your role is to prompt their learning with, "After looking at the economic situation, you decided that your solution wouldn't work. Why?"

Students can be guided through a sequence of problems over a period of months. They will need increasingly more difficult or complex problems for improvisation. Students gain insights when they try out previously successful solutions or responses on a new problem and are forced to rethink and create different ideas. Some examples of real-life situations for problem solving through improvisation are:

Being lost in the woods or in the city
Litter on the playground
No funds for school activities
Bully in the neighborhood
Stealing in the classroom
Competing with a best friend for a job

In the following vignette, we see how effectively roleplay activities assist in teaching problem solving and specific ways to use roleplay.

Secondary Research Vignette

INTRODUCTION

Researchers Glenn, Gregg, and Tipple (1982) studied the use of a roleplay activity to teach students to use a problem-solving strategy, specifically concerned with the efffects of variations of roleplay.

STUDY DESIGN

The researchers studied 18 classrooms of 307 senior high-school students, with teachers of comparable educational and experiential background, who trained in a roleplay workshop.

The classes were divided into three groups to test the use of specific strategies with the roleplay activities. An additional fourth group served as a comparison group, with no roleplay activity. The treatment groups were:

Group 1: Students received specific instruction about the steps of the problem-solving model on the day prior to the beginning of the roleplay activity. The instruction included a practice of the model with feedback. During the roleplay, students received specific feedback about the various steps in the model and how well they were following the model. During the debriefing session, students discussed the model and asked questions.

Group 2: Students received similar instructions with practice and feedback on the day prior to the beginning of the roleplay activity. The students did not receive any feedback during the actual roleplay activity. Debriefing included the same discussion and questions.

Group 3: Students did not receive any prior instruction about the model before the roleplay

activity. No feedback was given, and the debriefing was the same as the other groups.

Students in all four groups were pretested and posttested, using a Decision-Making Strategy Test, and scored on a scale indicating whether they followed the problem-solving strategy that was taught.

STUDY RESULTS

The first finding was expected; that is, the treatment groups followed the problem-solving model more closely than did the comparison group. A total of 29 percent of the students in the treatment groups followed the model exactly, whereas only 9 percent of the comparison group students did. In the pretest, there were no significant differences between the two groups.

In the comparison between the three treatment groups, there was a significant difference between group 1 and the other two groups. Students in group 1 scored significantly higher on the posttest. Some 57 percent of group 1 students followed the exact problem-solving model, 9 percent of group 2 students, and 10 percent of group 3 students, with no significant differences between the latter two groups.

When the pretest and posttest scores were compared, significant change was noted only for group 1, with a change from 6 percent to 57 percent of students following the model.

CONCLUSIONS AND IMPLICATIONS FOR PRACTICE

The researchers learned that roleplay activities can be effective for teaching students to follow a model. Roleplay activities combined with instruction, practice, and feedback are more effective.

As you plan to use roleplay, use the findings of this study to make improvisation more effective. Preview and clearly identify your content, provide practice opportunities, and give feedback on student performance.

Learning Decision Making

The younger the student, the fewer the opportunities to make decisions in real life, so the safety of the classroom offers the opportunity for repeated practices and mistakes. Mistakes in improvisation are not accompanied by failures, judgment, or rejection, as in the real world.

What is important in the decision making that occurs in improvisation is student awareness of process. As students talk about decisions with the reasons behind them, they develop awareness. Your input assists the awareness with, "When you were deciding to run for mayor, you paid attention to all the problems of holding office," or "Review the steps you took when you decided to talk with your parents."

Some classroom examples of opportunities to make decisions in improvisation are:

> Planning and building a city
> Selecting and buyiing a pet
> Having a child
> Choosing a career

In addition to these examples, there are plenty of real problems to solve and decisions to make in your students' lives. They can be used for practice in your classroom. Pulling the real-life dilemmas into the security of the classroom will allow students to put energy and emotion into the process without the worry of failure.

The content of improvisation is unlimited, and many real-life goals can be effectively met through roleplay, simulation, and drama. Content becomes relevant and memorable for the learner.

LEARNER

The strategies of improvisation require your sensitivity as you work with individual learners. You can adjust or vary the strategies for individual personalities and experiences.

Learner Personalities

With improvisation, there is often concern for the student who controls or dominates the drama, or for the student who is uncomfortable in the spotlight. We suggest that you accommodate individual personalities with improvisation by assigning roles some of the time, by having students select roles some of the time, and by rotating or reversing the roles some of the time.

TEACHER TALK

If I let them, two of my students would just take over the class. They are bright, clever, and well liked. I must admit, they get me laughing right along with the students. Whenever we have any kind of drama, it's just assumed that they will star. The other students seem to like it that way, but I sometimes wonder if there are others who would like to be in the center.

Middle-School Homeroom Teacher

Assigning Roles

At times, you may want to assign roles and confine the kind of students described in Teacher Talk to a specific role to limit involvement and provide other students opportunity to be in the spotlight. What is important is knowing your individual students. When you do, you can assign appropriate roles. You might also occasionally want the shy student to try out the extrovert role, and the outgoing student to roleplay the shy role. A friend, who teaches high school, encourages his students to try out roles in school that are quite different from their usual roles.

Student Selection of Roles

When you have a simulation developed about a neighborhood group working on a problem, you may say to students, "There is a variety of individuals in the group. Read the description of each and pick a role that sounds comfortable to you." Or you may say, "Pick a role that sounds comfortable to you, or very different from yourself." You and your students will gain understandings that go beyond the simulation— understandings of the students themselves.

There are always observer and reporter roles to be played. Some students may prefer to begin involvement with these roles. There can also be varied involvement in the processing that follows. Discussion of what happened in the neighborhood group problem solving can take place verbally in groups or in written form by individuals.

Rotation or Reversal of Roles

Another way to accommodate individuals is to begin the improvisation with only a few roles and many observers, then rotate learners into roles or add new roles as improvisation is repeated.

Role reversal will develop sensitivity and awareness in you and your students. Young students who play both the playground bully and later the child being bullied have described some profound understandings of the dynamics of that situation. Adolescents who play both the popular athlete and her best friend experience alternative explanations and understandings of behavior.

Learner Experiences

One of the best things about using improvisation is that your students bring such a range of different experiences. You will have students lacking in experience related to the theme of your improvisation, and students with vivid memories related to the theme. Observe some or all of the following approaches as you accommodate learner experiences.

Assess Student Experience

An efficient and organized way to find out the variety of experiences that students bring to your class is to survey such information at the beginning of the year. Your information gathering may be repeated throughout the year because student experiences change. Consider using:

Student interviews
Student life time lines
Student collages of life
Student bulletin boards of life stories
Student photo albums or scrapbooks

In Chapter 7, there was a Learner Profile that you can use to assess learner experiences, and in the Samples and Examples section of this chapter, there is a Student Survey and a Parent Survey to help you determine learner experience. When you read Chapters 14 and 15, you will find information about interviews, surveys, and questionnaires, all of which can be used to assess experiences for planning improvisation.

Notice Lack of Experience

Improvision actually helps you spot lack of experience. You will be able to hear and see misconceptions, confusion, and lack of insights as students participate.

When young children have never been on a farm, their dramatic play about farms is quite telling, and their lack of knowledge of farm life is evident. When older students have not experienced relationships with people of another culture, we are sometimes shocked by their misunderstandings and lack of sensitivity. What is important during these times is that you notice and use the information for your planning.

Use Student Experience

Students who have had experiences can be a resource to you and other students. For example, the student who has lived on a farm can describe the life there and roleplay with authenticity. The student who has lived in a culturally mixed neighborhood can dramatize the relationships and help other students gain experience.

The advice we shared from Shaftel and Shaftel (1982) for using literature and discussions is important for building student experience. In Chapter 13, we describe field trips, guest speakers and audiovisual experiences that can also supplement students' real-life experiences.

We have provided considerations for your planning and sensitivities for your use of roleplay, simulation, and drama. Now we will describe some models for teaching with improvisation.

TEACHING WITH IMPROVISATION

For the strategies of roleplay and simulation, there are models with specific phases and activities for teaching. We will describe those models and show you their use in classrooms. Drama does not have a specific model, but we will provide a set of recommendations. We conclude this section with descriptions of teaching roles to support improvisation activities: facilitator, supporter, and manager.

The Roleplay Model

For roleplay to be effective, two criteria must be met. First, students must act out the roles of the story or situation with believability. As we stated earlier, not all students have a dramatic flair or are comfortable with dramatic roles. However, the roles must be portrayed with quality in the enactment. Students themselves and their peers must be able to believe the role being played. Otherwise, little discussion of the role, feelings, and effects can take place. The second criteria is similar; that is, the role or situation must have a real-life quality. A connection to real life promotes interest and involvement of students. With the two criteria in mind, we turn to the model.

Joyce and Weil (1986, p. 245) describe nine phases for conducting a roleplay activity. Each of the phases is an important lead-in to the next phase, ultimately ensuring that discussions, evaluations, and generalizations are productive. We would like to take you through the phases of their roleplay model with a middle-school teacher. Her class has been studying the legal system in social studies/government and the use of alcohol in health, so she has integrated these curriculum topics into the roleplay.

Phase One: Warm Up

To warm up the group, Mrs. Fong describes a town in the northwest that prides itself on being beautiful and free from crime. The townspeople are involved in civic projects, sponsor many cultural events, and participate in educational activities. Mrs. Fong asks students to talk about what it would be like to live in such a place. Then she describes the mayor of the town, the first woman mayor, elected for the second time. The mayor has intense community support and an exemplary record of successes in her office.

"One evening the mayor is returning from a social event to honor an artist and is stopped by the police for reckless driving and possibly for being intoxicated. She describes a very exhausting work day, followed by an event that required her attendance. She did not have time for lunch or supper, but did have several drinks at the social.

"The police officer feels confused about what to do. The mayor asks him to forget the incident and she will take a cab home. She assures him that it won't happen again. He reluctantly agrees. The police officer discusses the incident with his superior officer. The mayor is troubled and discusses it with her major advisor."

Mrs. Fong stops her description and asks, "What are the issues in the situation?" She has students retell the story.

Phase Two: Participant Selection

Students then list the major players in the story and review what they know about each. Together with Mrs. Fong, they decide which students will play each role.

Phase Three: Set the Stage

Mrs. Fong states, "In order to roleplay this situation, what different settings will we need?" Students plan three settings in three corners of their classroom. Chairs are arranged to resemble a car, and a student's bike is brought in for the police officer. In another corner, a chair is pulled next to Mrs. Fong's desk for a setting with the police officer and a superior. In another corner, a conversational arrangement for the mayor and her advisor is set up.

Phase Four: Prepare the Observers

Those students who are not playing other roles are assigned observer roles. Three observers are to describe the feelings of the players, three are to define the goals of each player, and a pair is to critique the enactment for nonverbal expression. Other observers are to describe an alternative to the action when the roleplay is over. Others are charged, "Do you think that this could really happen?"

Phase Five: Enact the Story, Roles, and Situation

The students enact their roles as mayor, police officer, advisor, and superior officer through the plot described by Mrs. Fong. Others listen, observe, and take notes.

Phase Six: Discuss and Evaluate

At first, students talk excitedly about their reactions, some disagreeing with the actions and some commenting on how well the roles were played. Mrs. Fong allows the excitement to ease, then poses questions to help students think about the roles, the feelings and goals, and the interpretations of the behaviors. She asks, "What do you think the mayor intended with her plan?" As discussion slows, she asks, "What other options did these people have?" The class begins planning another enactment of the scenario with alternative actions.

Phase Seven: Enact Again

The situation can be reenacted any number of times, as long as new interpretations of the roles emerge or alternative actions are proposed. Because of time constraints, Mrs. Fong's class enacts the situation three times in small groups: once with the police officer releasing the story to the press, again with the police officer taking a "hard line" and ticketing the mayor for driving while possibly intoxicated, and again with the mayor taking action and meeting with the police to plan action.

Phase Eight: Discuss and Evaluate

Students responded intensely to each enactment, some with agreement and righteous defense of the police officer and some with disagreement and empathy for the mayor. They discussed the effects of alcohol, legal issues of driving under the influence of alcohol, and held some heated debates about implications for the mayor.

Phase Nine: Describe Experiences and Generalize

Mrs. Fong asked, "What advice would you give to public officials after your roleplay experiences?" Students offered advice and then were given the assignment, "I want you to think of a situation here at school that would be similar to our roleplay, and think of some individuals here who would experience the same kind of decisions."

The nine-phase model of roleplay from Joyce and Weil (1986, p. 245) gives you a sequence of specific activities. It will help you to have a model to follow when you first use roleplay. With experience, you may vary the model.

The Simulation Model

This model is simpler and has just four phases. To teach with simulation, select the activity and carefully direct students through the activities that you see in Mr. Cooley's classroom.

Phase One: Orientation

Mr. Cooley reviews the principles of effective management with students before describing the simulation. Then he proposes, "You are going to face a significant decision as members of the board of trustees of a major international corporation. The most important aspect of your task is to match the qualifications of the candidates with the projections for the corporation."

Mr. Cooley reviews the process of simulation and reminds students of a trade simulation experienced the month before. He then turns on an overhead of the organizational chart of the corporation. "The current president has resigned," he says as he points to the role on the chart. "These administrators are also on the board of trustees. These are not. Many have influential relationships with trustees. There are three candidates being considered, and you will have a resume for each."

Phase Two: Participant Training

Mr. Cooley informs the class that they will be moving to the board room down the hall to engage in the simulation. He encourages them to read the resumes quietly in their classroom and then join him in the board room. He proceeds to the board room and distributes copies of financial statements of the company and name cards at each place around the table. He places a second copy of the flowchart on an overhead projector at the back of the room.

Once students arrive and are ready for more direction, Mr. Cooley sets the schedule for the simulation. "We will be working on this decision for the remainder of the week. On Friday, we will vote for our choice. There will be some time that day for presenting a case for a candidate." Students are grouped into three different boards of trustees, and urged to meet and discuss the candidates. Each board receives a set of role cards with descriptions of board members.

Before dismissing the class, Mr. Cooley reviews the task, the roles, and the schedule for the simulation.

Phase Three: Simulation Operations

On Wednesday and Thursday, students meet in small groups, pairs, and with the candidates to discuss information and views. At the end of each class, Mr. Cooley spends 10 minutes checking on progress, needs, and directions. He asks, "What issue was important for your group today?" or "What success did your group have today?"

On Friday, the class meets with three boards, and votes are cast. Each board announces its decision and reason for candidate selection.

Phase Four: Participant Debriefing

After the decisions are announced, the groups compare their processes. Students are led through a discussion of the difficulties, insights, unexpected ideas, and a comparison of the simulation with real-world happenings. Mr. Cooley asks, "What information from this course helped your work in the simulation?" After a set of questions, students are assigned to write a critique of the simulation, assessing its effectiveness and making recommendations for revision.

In contrast to Mr. Cooley's work with secondary students, we see simulation used effectively to teach five-year-olds in the next vignette. As you read the vignette, you will get ideas for adding variation to the simulation model.

Drama

Drama provides the opportunity for your students to explore the concepts of fantasy and reality, cause and effect, and sequence. They can develop understanding and appreciation of literature by dramatizing a story or creating one of their own to perform. Concepts from most content areas can be explored in the form of drama, as you saw in the beginning Snapshot.

Guidelines for Using Drama

Before these experiences can occur, some prerequisites are necessary in your classroom. Practice opportunities in observation, creative movement, concentration, pantomine, and visualization will support success in drama. We remind you that a climate of trust is essential in your classroom if you want students to participate in drama.

In addition to the prerequisites, there are some simple guidelines to follow as you plan for drama:

1. Use as few props as possible to promote creativity, and be sure that players are familiar with the props.
2. Characters in a drama should be convincing and easy for students to identify with.
3. The story should be suitable in theme, length, and language for the age of students.
4. To rehearse students in parts, create emotional involvement with characters by discussing characters' goals and feelings.

It is recommended that students up to the age of 11 or 12 years participate in informal drama exclusively, that is, drama with minimal planning and spon-

Elementary Research Vignette

INTRODUCTION
A significant number of traffic-related injuries among young pedestrians prompted researchers Renaud and Stolovitch (1988) to evaluate the use of simulation on the attitudes and behaviors of five-year-olds with respect to traffic safety.

STUDY DESIGN
The sample was 136 five-year-olds from eight classes in four schools in Montreal. Students were randomly assigned to one of four groups. One group served as a control, and the other three were treatment groups with variations of simulation use. The procedures in the three treatment groups were as follows:

Group 1: The simulation game of traffic situations was played with roleplay and group dynamics in a group of six children. As children roleplayed "walking home from school," other children evaluated their safety behaviors and awarded them with "happy face" or "sad face" cards.

Group 2: One child plays the traffic simulation game with an adult. First, the adult explains traffic rules and shows the child what to do. The child then roleplays a pedestrian. In this simulation, there is behavior modeling, rehearsal, and feedback.

Group 3: This group combined the elements of the simulation use in the two previous groups. That is, six children played the game with one

adult. The adult explained the rules, demonstrated how to play, and modeled the behaviors. Children take turns roleplaying traffic behaviors, and receive evaluations with the face cards. Instruments were created for this study to measure attitudes by using photos to identify risks, to measure behaviors using questions about road pictures, and to measure transfer of learning using another simulation with life-size traffic models.

STUDY RESULTS
In the first analysis, the three treatment groups performed significantly better on all three tests than the control group. When the treatment groups were compared, group 1, the group that used simulation with roleplay and feedback, performed best on the behavior test. Group 2, the group that used behavior modeling and training, performed best on the transfer of learning test. There were no differences on the attitude test for the three treatment groups.

CONCLUSIONS AND IMPLICATIONS FOR PRACTICE
The study demonstrated the effectiveness of simulation for teaching young children a set of behaviors and promoting attitudes. Simulation also worked toward a transfer of learning. The researchers concluded that even if only some of the teaching strategies (roleplay, modeling, group dynamics, feedback) are combined with simulation, positive results can occur.

---

taneous action and dialogue. Older students can participate in rehearsed drama because they have the ability to think through dialogue and action and to perform with a greater degree of naturalness.

Sources for Drama
You have a wealth of literature to draw upon for drama: poetry, films, songs, legends, myths, short stories, novels, history, biographies, and current events. For original drama, you have students and content as sources. We urge you to consider beforehand what effect a story or drama may have on your class group as a whole and on individual students. Young students, especially, may be frightened or worried by

some literature. Remember to check your community context for other sensitivities in selecting a source for drama.

As you follow the models for roleplay and simulation, and the guidelines for drama, you will notice that you need to facilitate and support the learning as well as manage the activities. In the next section, we will describe how to be a facilitator, a support, and a manager with improvisation.

TEACHING ROLES FOR IMPROVISATION

The Facilitator Role

A *facilitator* is one who supports or makes something easier. When you facilitate improvisation, you make it easier for students to understand, to be involved, and to learn from the strategies. To do so, you guide students into the activity, through the activity, and in analysis of the activity. In addition, you will be explaining and rehearsing.

Guiding
To guide students through improvisation, you need the skills of a tightrope artist. You must be directing students and be nondirective at the same time. To begin this balancing act, start with your purpose. What do you intend for students to experience, feel, think?

If your goal is problem solving or the development of skills, you will provide direction with questions, focusing, and encouragement. If your goal is awareness or exploration of curriculum, you will limit your questions and focusing, and encourage students to determine focus and direction.

Your guidance will also take the form of listening—to the words and to the feelings. You will need active listening, which includes reflecting back to students their words and feelings. This requires time and concentration, free from interruptions, other tasks, and student distractions.

Explaining

In order for students to experience learning in improvisation, you must be clear in your explanations. The strategies of this chapter require some rules, procedures, mechanics, and roles, all of which will need explaining. When students do not understand what to do or how to do it, they will not gain much understanding or insight. Their concentration will be focused on their uncertainties.

Consider a rehearsal of your explanation to achieve clarity, and consider having students assist with some of the explaining. They are a good source of feedback on how understandable your explanations are. Listen as a fifth-grade teacher checks his explanations. "Tomas, explain what your group will be doing during the roleplay."

Rehearsing

This is another guidance behavior that contributes to student security and confidence. It can take the form of a routine that gets repeated or content that gets repeated. When routines are repeated, they are comfortable for students and students become proficient. For example, when you repeat the sequence of the roleplay model, students soon know what to expect. They gradually need fewer directions and can take over the leadership of the activity. It becomes a routine.

The other possibility for rehearsal is repetition of content. We saw this kind of rehearsal in the middle-school Snapshot. As students developed their skits, they rehearsed them. The dialogue became comfortable and their roles became believable. For rehearsal to occur, you must provide time, space, and some freedom to students.

Notice as you provide guidance, explanations, and rehearsals, students become more involved in the learning strategies. In time, they facilitate their own learning.

The Support Role

This role is essential to the success of improvisation because there are risks and fears associated with playing roles. To support students, use coaching and reacting.

Coaching

Think about a time when you observed a coach coaxing, advising, and encouraging his or her team. You may coax a student, "Use an angry voice to present your argument." You may advise students, "Stop and think about all the options before you as you decide." You may also encourage students with, "You played that role as if you were feeling the old man's pain."

The key in coaching students is that your advice, coaxing, and encouragement is offered, not required or demanded. Students make the decision to follow the advice, respond to the coaxing, or receive the encouragement.

Reacting

This behavior refers to the quality of the response that you give to students as they participate in roleplays, simulations, and drama. The appropriate reactions are nonevaluative or judgmental. Instead, communicate acceptance of and support for student efforts.

As students play a role or work toward a decision, your reactions will influence continued participation, risk taking, and whether students make their own judgments. If your reactions evaluate students and their learning processes, then they don't have to. A final reason for maintaining a nonevaluative reaction to students during improvisation is to keep the content free of teacher bias. If you want the content of a roleplay to emerge from students, you will "accept student responses in a nonevaluative manner" (Joyce & Weil, 1986). Additionally, you want to communicate to students with your reactions that there are many ways to play a role, different ways to solve a problem, and more ideas and perceptions to be explored.

In sum, your support for students in improvisation must be characterized by sensitivity and nurturance. To support them, coach their participation and learning, and react with acceptance.

The Manager Role

Did you notice the many details that were managed in Mr. Cooley's simulation activity? The board room was scheduled, transparencies were ready, and cards with descriptions of roles were prepared. Mr. Cooley was an effective manager and his simulation proceeded smoothly. As you manage improvisation, organize schedules, materials, and logistics, and be ready to referee when situations warrant.

Organizing

The time demands of improvisation require careful scheduling. These are not strategies that can be hurried, fit in, left unfinished, distracted, or interrupted. Some scheduling suggestions include:

- Schedule these activities for "quiet" times of day and in "quiet" places.
- Inform others of your need for undisturbed time.
- Schedule visually with a sign on your classroom door.
- Schedule time with students for a discussion of the importance of undisturbed time within the classroom.

A "quiet" time in elementary schools would be about an hour after everyone has arrived, or shortly after lunch. A "quiet" time in secondary schools would be shortly after classes have begun and well before class dismissal.

In addition to scheduling, think about space, materials, or props. Ask yourself: Where will this take place? Where will observers be? Would music add feeling to the drama? Involve students in the planning and organizing of materials and logistics, with room arrangement, gathering props, or listing necessary procedures.

Finally, you will need to be sure that your information is organized. Ask yourself: Do students know enough about slavery to enact this scene? or What data do students need to make this decision? or Will students be able to portray an architect with what they know about the profession? Once you organize what students already know and what they need to know, you can decide to review or teach additional content. When we described review in Chapter 9, we suggested application as part of the learning. Improvisation and review are an effective teaching and learning combination.

Refereeing

Because the strategies of improvisation call for freedom of movement, expression, and interaction, there is a need for refereeing behaviors. A *referee* is one who assures that rules are followed, keeps a game going, and keeps game behavior within limits. As students participate in improvisation, your refereeing will assure that the activities stay focused and keep going, that rules are followed, and that the enactments do not go beyond appropriate behavior.

Refereeing also protects students as they take risks. They need to hear you say, "Wait, that's not appropriate. You can respond only to the decision, not the individual." Physical safety needs attention during improvisation, especially when creative movement is involved. Students feel secure when they hear, "Let's move the chairs back a few feet so that if the molecules bounce off each other, there will be plenty of room."

Your refereeing will further ensure that students have equal opportunity to play and discuss the improvisation. As we suggested earlier, you may have to control the aggressive "stars" so that other students have a chance to play roles of choice. A combination of student selection, teacher selection, and random selection of roles and experiences is ideal.

In sum, your manager role calls for you to organize time and resources, and to referee student behavior for physical and emotional safety.

SUMMARY

The strategies of this chapter have the potential for powerful and dynamic teaching and learning. They also have the potential for risk taking and for unforeseen experiences and feelings. The flexibility and accommodation required by varied contexts, content, and learners give you good reason to use the strategies of this chapter. Those same foundations require your awareness and sensitivity.

Notice context for:

1. Community values and attitudes
2. Community resources
3. Classroom space and emotional climate
4. Classroom scheduling

Notice content for:

1. A full range of curriculum use
2. Making learning real
3. Opportunities for learning problem solving
4. Opportunities for learning decision making

Notice learners for:

1. Differences in personalities and experiences
2. Opportunities to develop group membership

With your awareness of context, content, and learner, you can proceed to the models for roleplay and simulation, and the guidelines for drama. You will expand your instructional role with the roles of facilitator, supporter, and manager.

The complexity of your instructional role in improvisation may be just what you need to be excited and challenged as a teacher. The unknown qualities of improvisation may intrigue you and your students. You may develop a closeness as you take risks together. Develop competence with roleplay, simulation, and drama by reading, observing other teachers, and participating in workshops. Practice with your students. Begin with a spirit of adventure, and make learning real.

REFERENCES

Glenn, A., Gregg, D., & Tipple, B. (1982). Using role play activities to teach problem solving. *Simulation & Games, 13*(2), 199–209.

Joyce, B., & Weil, M. (1986). *Models of teaching.* Englewood Cliffs, NJ: Prentice-Hall.

Lippit, R., Fox, R., & Schaible, L. (1969). *Social science laboratory units.* Chicago: Science Research Associates.

Renaud, L., & Stolovitch, H. (1988). Simulation gaming: An effective strategy for creating appropriate traffic safety behaviors in five year old children. *Simulation & Games, 19*(3), 328–345.

Schug, M., & Beery, R. (1987). *Teaching social studies in the elementary school: Issues and practices.* Glenview, IL: Scott, Foresman.

Shaftel, F. R., & Shaftel, G. (1982). *Role playing in the curriculum.* Englewood Cliffs, NJ: Prentice Hall.

_____*SAMPLES AND EXAMPLES*_____

The following are resources for you to draw from in developing your own improvisational strategies.

- The Selected List of Musical Recordings is a listing of mostly classical songs that stimulate the imagination of children.
- The Selected List of Stories, Anthologies, and Inspirations is a list of classic stories for elementary-grade students.
- The Parent and Student Surveys are inventories used to develop a curriculum with examples that could draw from positive student and parent experiences.

SELECTED LIST OF MUSICAL RECORDINGS

Excerpts from the recordings listed here have stimulated the imagination of children in the process of plot construction.

To use music for this purpose a teacher needs to listen to several recordings to find an excerpt that is appropriate both for a particular group of children and for plot construction. From the latter point of view, music needs to invite imaginative participation. It needs to be clearly structured to evoke "dramatic action" with beginning, middle, and ending action that occurs within a one- or two-minute period of time. Employing rhythm, mood, and melody, the music should begin at a comparatively high level of tension and rise in intensity as it moves toward a climax and resolution.

Adventures in Music (A New Record Library for Elementary Schools), produced by Peter Dellheim, National Symphony Orchestra, Howard Mitchell, Conductor; *Teacher's Guide* prepared by Gladys Tipton and Eleanor Tipton, RCA Corp, 1961.

Dukas, *Sorcerer's Apprentice.*

Grieg, *Peer Gynt Suite*, No. 1, "In the Hall of the Mountain King," "Morning."

Grofé, *Grand Canyon Suite*, "Cloudburst," "Sunrise."

Herbert, *Natoma*, "Dagger Dance."

Kabalevsky, *The Comedians*, "March and Comedians' Gallop," "Pantomime."

Kodaly, *Hary Janos Suite*, "Viennese Musical Clock."

Listen, Move and Dance, vol. 1, arranged and directed by Vera Gray, Electronic Sound Pictures, "A Wish and A Magic Journey," "Witches, Wizards, Alchemists, Sorcerers," "Journey Into Space," "Underwater Adventure," "Dreams."

Listen, Move and Dance, vol. 2, Electronic Sound Patterns.

Moussorgsky, *Night on Bald Mountain.*

Moussorgsky, *Pictures at an Exhibition*, "Ballet of the Unhatched Chicks," "Bydlo."

Popcorn, recorded by Hot Butter, "Popcorn" by Kingsley.

Saint-Saens, *Danse Macabre.*

Strauss, Richard, *Also Sprach Zarathustra*, opening theme.

Stravinsky, *The Firebird Suite*, "Infernal Dance of King Kastchei."

Vaughan Williams, *The Wasps*, "March Past of the Kitchen Utensils."

Wagner, *The Ring of the Nibelung*, "Magic Fire Music," "Ride of the Valkyries."

SELECTED LIST OF STORIES, ANTHOLOGIES, AND INSPIRATIONS

Arbuthnot, May Hill, ed., *The Arbuthnot Anthology of Children's Literature*, 4th ed., revised by Zena Sutherland, Chicago: Scott, Foresman, 1976.

Atwood, Ann, *My Own Rhythm: An Approach to Haiku*, New York: Scribner's, 1973.

Charlip, Remy, *Arm in Arm*, New York: Parent's Magazine Press, 1969.

Charlip, Remy, *Fortunately*, New York: Scholastic, 1966.

Charlip, Remy, Mary Beth, and George Ancona, *Handtalk: An ABC of Finger Spelling and Sign Language*, New York: Parent's Magazine Press, 1974.

Dunning, Stephen, Edward Lueders, and Hugh Smith, eds., *Reflections on a Gift of Watermelon Pickle*, New York: Lothrop, Lee and Shepard, 1966.

Dunning, Stephen, Edward Lueders, and Hugh Smith, eds., *Some Haystacks Don't Even Have Any Needle*, New York: Lothrop, Lee and Shepard, 1969.

Johnson, Edna, E. R. Sickels, and F. C. Sayers, eds., *Anthology of Children's Literature*, 4th rev. ed., Boston: Houghton Mifflin, 1970.

Saroyan, William, *Papa You're Crazy*, Boston: Little, Brown, 1956.

Schenck de Regniers, Beatrice, Eva Moore, and M. M. White, comp., *Poems Children Will Sit Still For: A Selection for the Primary Grades*, New York: Citation Press, 1969.

Sendak, Maurice, *Where the Wild Things Are*, New York: Harper & Row, 1963.

Dr. Seuss (Theodore Geisel), *The Foot Book* (A Bright and Early Book), New York: Random House, 1968.

Dr. Seuss (Theodore Geisel), *My Book About Me* (Beginner Books), New York: Random House, 1953.

Dr. Seuss (Theodore Geisel), *The Sneetches and Other Stories*, New York: Random House, 1953.

Siks, Geraldine B., *Children's Literature for Dramatization: An Anthology*, New York: Harper & Row, 1964.

Silverstein, Shel, *The Giving Tree*, New York: Harper & Row, 1964.

Steichen, Edward, created by, *The Family of Man*, New York: Maco Magazine Corp., 1955.

Ward, Winifred, ed., *Stories to Dramatize*, Anchorage, KY: Children's Theatre Press, 1952.

PARENT SURVEY

Name _____

Date _____

1. Describe some travel experiences of your family.

2. Describe some special family customs.

3. List some careers represented in your family (include aunts, uncles, etc.).

4. List some hobbies, crafts, or recreational interests of your family (include aunts, uncles, etc.).

5. What are some special events that your family has attended?

6. What are some common problems at your house? What are some common decisions?

STUDENT SURVEY

Name _____

Date _____

1. List some places to which you have traveled.

2. What are some special events you have attended?

3. Who are some famous people you have met, read about, heard about, or seen?

4. Have you had any dangerous experiences? Describe them.

5. Have you had any scary experiences? Describe them.

6. Have you had any sad experiences? Describe them.

7. Have you had any exceptionally happy experiences? Describe them.

8. Describe some big problems you have solved.

9. Describe some big decisions you have made.

10. What are some things you do well?

CHAPTER 13

Using Community Resources, Audiovisuals, and Computers: Varying the Stimuli

CHAPTER OUTCOMES
At the conclusion of this chapter you will be able to:

1. Describe purposes for using resources, audiovisuals, and computers for teaching and learning.
2. Consider the content, context, and learner when using resources, audiovisuals, and computers.
3. Describe how to use resources, audiovisuals, and computers effectively to vary the stimuli.

KEY TERMS AND CONCEPTS

Purpose of Stimuli
Selection of Stimuli
Content Match
Learner Match
Preview
Novelty
Variation
Interaction
Community Resources
Guest Speakers
Field Trips
Audiovisual Stimuli
Overhead Projector
Slide Projector
Television
Records and Audiotapes
Videotapes and Films
Bulletin Boards
Demonstrations
Computers

INTRODUCTION

Until now, we have shown you Snapshots of classrooms today, but for this chapter we are looking at a black and white photo in an old album. It captures an entire school. For those of you in our generation, the picture may bring nostalgia and chuckles. For those of who are too young (we envy you), the picture may bring disbelief.

SNAPSHOT: The Way We Were

It is a Friday afternoon in March at a small private elementary school in western New York. It has been snowing for weeks. At 2:00 PM, students from grades 1 through 8 file into the auditorium and seat themselves on metal folding chairs. The youngest take the seats in the front rows, and the oldest sit in the back rows.

When everyone is seated, the lights are turned off. There is an immediate ripple of talk and laughter, but some firm "Shs" bring quiet. On the large screen at the front, an image appears and "A Visit to the Andes" begins with music and titles. It is now 2:08 AM.

At 2:13, we see some of the first-grade students fidgeting and squirming in their chairs and some falling asleep. At 2:19, several third-grade students are scolded for talking. At the same time, we see two sixth-graders talking and pointing to the screen. They are heard discussing the condor, which they read about in their textbooks when they studied South America last fall.

At 2:26, there is a definite hum in the air—some muffled talk, shifting in chairs, and coughing. When the film ends at 2:34, there is quiet applause. The lights come on and the students leave, waving to friends and talking to each other. Back in the classroom, we observe quiet reading of library books, a health lesson, desk cleaning, and, in one classroom, a conversation about the Andes Mountains.

Lest you think that this is a unique Snapshot, let's go to another photo, another state, and look at a public school:

SNAPSHOT: The Way We Were

It is Friday afternoon again, and we're looking at a gymnasium in a rural elementary school in the midwest. The scenario is similar until the lights go off and the film begins. We see "Division of Fractions" and it lasts 18 minutes. This time, we see heads nodding and students shifting in chairs within the first three minutes of the film. The hum in the air is louder and lasts through most of the film.

What's wrong with this picture? It is an understatement to say that there has been no consideration of content, context, or learner in either Snapshot. You may also be wondering why the films were shown or maybe you know the reason. Let's look at the first Snapshot and analyze it together.

Content

Since we have no way of knowing the intent of the teachers for showing the film, or the curriculum being taught in the classrooms, we will look at the content of the film itself. "A Visit to the Andes" contained vocabulary such as *South America, Andeans, agriculture, subsistence farming, condor,* and *Aconcagua* (the highest peak in the mountains). The concept of weather, geography, culture, economics, and politics were described. Two maps of the mountains were shown. The narration drew several comparisons between life in the United States and life in the Andes Mountains. The content consisted of vocabulary, some concepts, facts, map skills, and comparisons.

If you were to ask some of the students, "What was the film about?", you would probably hear:

"The women carried baskets on their heads."
"The people were very poor."
"The weather in the Andes is hot and dry."
"They don't have cars or trucks."

You may hear a few facts, recognition of differences between life in the Andes and the students' life, and some misinterpretations. The content in this situation will vary from student to student, and from context to context.

Context

When we look at the immediate context, we see a large room with uncomfortable folding chairs and the lights out. It is Friday, after lunch, and students are sitting for 26 minutes. Put yourself in the context. How do you feel after lunch, in a darkened room? How are you on Friday afternoon?

Consider the community context: a small farming community of families who have lived there for generations and who have seen little outside of the community. This context influenced the film's effect, but even with this commonality of backgrounds, there are learner differences.

Learner

In the Snapshot you could see differences throughout the auditorium. The learners differed first in age and development, then in interest and understanding. If you could converse with the learners, you would find stark differences in their experience with and knowledge of South America, mountains, other cultures, and even with films.

As you watched the learners in the auditorium, you saw their differences exhibited in their responses to the film, a range from boredom and discomfort to interest and recognition. It would have been interesting to question them about why they were seeing the film, to explore the learner sense of purpose.

Purpose

Can you predict what teachers had in mind that Friday afternoon? We will venture a guess. With the time of year, with Friday afternoons, and with the effect of long-term winter weather, the film offered a break from routine. Beyond that purpose, it offered a look at another culture, a life that the students might never experience. It offered some entertainment, because students of all ages will be enthused about a movie, at least, for a while. There was probably an economic purpose for this small school with limited funding to show a film to all 130 students rather than a class of 25.

The film in the Snapshot is one kind of stimuli to use in your teaching. This chapter will describe a wide assortment of stimuli, including community resources, audiovisuals, and computers. In addition to the purposes suggested for "A Visit to the Andes," varying the stimuli can help you achieve these additional purposes:

1. *Developing concepts.* For a group of students studying Chile or Argentina, the film could help them understand concepts of poverty, subsistence farming, and survival, and the differences between urban and rural life in those countries. After the film, discussion and reading would further their understanding.
2. *Enriching experiences.* Enrichment is achieved through appeal to the senses. The film included animal and people sounds, and vivid pictures of mountains and people's faces.
3. *Extending experiences.* The film took students from a small farming community in New York to South America, and from a textbook to audiovisual representations.
4. *Stimulating interest.* The film offered variation from the usual classroom materials and teaching strategies, so there was initial curiosity, even for the youngest students.

Our old Snapshots demonstrated once again that planning to use stimuli begins with consideration of (1) *content*, in terms of vocabulary, concepts, maps or diagrams, skills, and information; (2) *context*, in terms of school, community, time needed for use, location of use, room arrangement, and climate inside and out; and (3) *learner*, in terms of development, interest, experiences, and previous knowledge and understanding.

We have a caution before we proceed with this chapter, and that is for you to plan to teach *with* stimuli. Stimuli will not teach for you. The idea of this chapter is to *vary the stimuli* for teaching and learning.

USING COMMUNITY RESOURCES, AUDIOVISUALS, AND COMPUTERS

To use stimuli effectively, there is some necessary preparation. We recommend a selection process and a preview process, so that your teaching will be varied with stimuli rather than distracted by stimuli.

TEACHER TALK

I heard that the videotape on space was great and that students really liked it. I ran out of time so I got the VCR and tape just before science. Well, I was having a bad day anyway, but when I turned on the television, the volume was all the way up. The class shrieked and laughed as I turned it on. There was a "soap" showing because I didn't have the right channel pressed. By the time I found the right one and the play button, I was frantic. We finally saw the tape and the class calmed down. I guess it was good, I don't really know. I couldn't concentrate after that.

8th-Grade Teacher

Selection of Stimuli

Both the videotape on space and the film on the Andes were selected with minimal criteria. We suggest that you match the stimuli with content and learner. To achieve a *content match*, the stimuli must:

1. Be directed to planned objectives or outcomes.
2. Fit the organization and sequence of your plans.
3. Be authentic and accurate.

Mr. Davenport looks for a content match in his choice of guest speakers. His students have been studying and practicing how to get a job, by responding to classified ads and applying to desired employers, as part of a study of "Finding a Job." Mr. Davenport has taught resumé development and interview skills, and now plans a simulation session in which all of the job-hunting efforts have been unsuccessful. His content now concerns using an employment agency, so he plans to bring in a guest speaker from an agency in the community.

Mr. Davenport checks with major employers in the area to assess agency reputations. He selects a recommended agency that is quite large and is located close to school. He sets up an appointment with the agency's representative and takes with him an outline of information. During the meeting with his intended speaker, he describes what students have been studying and what information they will be seeking.

Do you see the *content match* in this selection? The speaker will help Mr. Davenport's students meet objectives, so preparation matched stimuli with curriculum.

Next, work for a *learner match*. Begin by considering learner age, development, interest, experience, attention span, and needs:

Will this choice appeal to students of varied ability?

Will it bias student thinking?

Will it motivate learners to think, to want to learn more?

When Flora Weinland selected a visual for her seventh-grade biology class, she decided that her students needed to see pictures of the cell differentiation that they are studying. She finds slides, a filmstrip, and large photos in the media center. Which will be best for her class? Flora thinks of her students and says to herself: There's a lot of them—31 in the class. Management is always a challenge, but lately, I have been successful grouping them in learning teams to study.

She selects the large photographs, copies them to produce sets for each group, and prepares information cards for matching facts with photographs. She thinks to herself: These cards will give the students some control over the activity, and they can use them in different ways. Some students will focus on the information cards and some will focus on the pictures. She feels confident about the match of appropriateness for her learners.

As you watched Mr. Davenport and Ms. Weinland selecting stimuli by matching choices with content and learner, did you notice that they previewed their choices as they planned? *Preview* is the other step in preparation.

Preview of Stimuli

As presented in Teacher Talk, you can find yourself in embarrassing predicaments, losing students' attention and wasting frustrating amounts of time when you vary the stimuli. Previewing stimuli helps you avoid those situations. When you preview, check the content, quality, and potential for problems. For content, listen to the language, to the authenticity of information, to see if the information is up to date, and for evidence of bias. Will Mr. Davenport's speaker dress the part of an agency representative, speak in a pleasant voice, and present in a professional manner? When Flora copied her photographs, did the images remain clear and vivid?

In addition to checking content, quality, and potential for problems, we recommend a *rehearsal* or practice:

1. Check the seating arrangement of students in relation to the screen or board.
2. Locate the source of electricity.
3. Check the timing of the presentation.
4. Check the lighting.
5. Focus the projector.
6. Check the volume.

It can be exciting and satisfying when you use stimuli in your teaching if you have prepared. When you dramatically encourage your students to picture the enormity of Alaska, and smoothly pull down the U.S. map on which you have positioned a mileage indicator, it is effective. What is not effective is struggling to pull the map down or to find Alaska, or pulling down the wrong map. You will get student attention, but it will not be on the enormity of Alaska.

Even after selecting and previewing, varying the stimuli will require more decisions. We describe those decisions in the following sections.

Decisions for Varying the Stimuli

You make two important decisions when you plan to vary the stimuli: when to vary the stimuli and how to vary the stimuli. Additional decisions concern student involvement and evaluation for future planning.

Scheduling—When to Vary the Stimuli

Our worst fear is that you will slip into a routine for scheduling films or field trips, such as before a holiday, a Friday, or the first or last week of school. Instead, your decision should depend on your instructional intent. Look at what stimuli can do for your students:

1. *Stimuli can be used to introduce a topic.* At the beginning of a study of Monet, students view a display of the artist's work and a photo of Monet. Questions and discussions begin.
2. *Stimuli can be used to create interest in a topic.* Before beginning a study of Mexico, a display of photos and tapes of music are used to build enthusiasm in the coming unit.
3. *Stimuli can be used to restate or reinforce a process or skill.* During a lesson on using the encyclopedia, the librarian visits and demonstrates how to use it, followed by a filmstrip that restates the process.
4. *Stimuli can be used to summarize or review information or concepts.* After studying about the early pioneers, students use a computer program with a simulated pioneer journey to review.

You see that your scheduling decision depends on what you want the stimuli to do, so your teaching plan is a guide.

Deciding How to Use the Stimuli

Clark and Salomon (1986) concluded from their review of research on media use that stimuli "do not affect learning in and of themselves" (p. 474). So the decision of how to vary the stimuli is one of coordination with other teaching and learning strategies. Any of the other strategies in this book are appropriate to use with community resources, audiovisuals, and computers. Consider *novelty* and *interaction* as you combine stimuli with your teaching.

Novelty is the quality of variation or change; it is newness. Look at the following examples and determine which provide novelty and which do not.

EXAMPLE: In a high-school political science course, students watch a video-tape of a politician giving a speech immediately after a 20-minute teacher lecture. Is there variation?

EXAMPLE: In a high-school biology course, students watch a display of the heart with moving parts immediately after a 20-minute teacher lecture. Is there variation?

Interaction is mutual influencing or action. You will need a variety of other strategies to promote interaction between students and the stimuli. Listen as teachers encourage student interaction:

EXAMPLE: "As we study this unit on drugs and alcohol, one of our objectives is to identify appropriate community agencies and resources. We will visit a display to gather information about community agencies."

When students are aware of the purpose or objectives, they are more likely to interact.

EXAMPLE: "As you listen to the tape of ocean life, keep a list of the different sounds you encounter."

When students have an agenda or an advance organizer for the stimuli, they are more likely to interact.

EXAMPLE: "We are going to take a break halfway through our field trip to see if everyone understands how the production line works before continuing our tour. You will be able to ask questions and check on the terms used by our guide."

When students can check understanding or clarify information at intervals during stimuli use, they are more likely to interact.

Additional Decisions for Varying the Stimuli

As you continue planning for using stimuli in your teaching, you may question to what extent students can be involved. As far as students selecting stimuli, we know from research (Clark, 1982) that student criteria for making media choices are faulty and based on enjoyment alone. Our caution, then, is to involve students in selection only when they have criteria to follow. Begin by modeling your thinking and decision making for students: "I chose this film because it had such up-to-date photos of mass transportation, and because it organized information so clearly." Have class discussions about choosing a resource. Use a student feedback form, such as the one in Figure 13.1, to help students understand criteria for

FIGURE 13.1   *Student Feedback Form*

Date _____ Time _____ Subject _____

Describe the stimulus (title, type, length, subject).

_____

_____

What were the positive qualities of this stimulus?

_____

_____

What were the negative qualities of this stimulus?

_____

_____

What did you learn from this stimulus?

_____

_____

What questions do you have?

_____

_____

Rate your interest: 1   2   3   4   5
                       High   Low

Rate your learning: 1   2   3   4   5
                       High   Low

selection of stimuli. With your guidance, students can develop thinking appropriate for selection of stimuli.

For reasons that include efficiency, self-concept, and smoothness in management, it is to your advantage and to the advantage of your students to involve them in using stimuli. You will have assistance in your teaching and save time for other responsibilities. Even the youngest students (four-year-olds in our experience) are able to operate some audiovisual equipment and computers. Students need training in following directions, maintaining safety, and returning materials and equipment, but the learning will be used for a lifetime.

Once you have varied your teaching with stimuli, your last decision is an evaluative one. Ask yourself: Is the stimulus worth the time, expense, and effort?

Check your original criteria of content match and learner match. Set up a system for recording your critique of stimuli for future planning and use. (See the Samples and Examples section at the end of this chapter.)

Varying the stimuli will require complex decision making on your part: when, how, and why. In addition, you will be faced with stimulus alternatives from which to choose. Think of it as a shopping trip. Your shopping can even be done with a catalog, available at most district media centers, university and public libraries, and school supply facilities.

As you begin, consider the Pyramid of Learning Experiences that we described in Chapter 11. Use the pyramid to determine what kind of experience your choice will provide, to further assure your match with content and learner.

COMMUNITY RESOURCES

We begin with community resources—a broad category that could include objects, clothing, printed materials, models, displays, places, and people. We urge you to return to your Community Context Checklist (Chapter 5) to begin, and then move to the Yellow Pages of your telephone directory. Be certain of the learning outcomes you are seeking and have your instructional plan in mind. For this chapter, we will discuss the community resources of guest speakers and field trips.

Guest Speakers

Remember how Mr. Davenport checked with businesses to find out which employment agencies had good reputations? He also went to visit the person who would be meeting with his class. We suggest that you check on your potential speaker to be certain the person can present well, is personable, and is reputable.

Preparing the Guest Speaker

It is important to prepare your guest in order to achieve your teaching purposes. When you meet with your guest, provide some of the following information:

1. The objectives and expectations of his or her visit
2. Information that the students already know and that they are curious about
3. Classroom management routines (e.g., students will or will not raise hands to ask questions)
4. Plans for related teaching and learning experiences

Think about how comfortable your guest will be with this information, and how much better he or she will be able to relate information to the other experiences you have planned.

Preparing Students for the Guest Speaker

Preparing students for the guest can begin with the same information found in items 1, 2, and 3 above. Encourage them to develop questions beforehand, to discuss expectations, and to connect the speaker's visit with other learning experiences. With most students, you can share the responsibility of greeting the guest, introducing the guest, and expressing appreciation to the guest (verbally or in written form). Be sure to take care of school and district communications regarding your guest (e.g., forms and policies).

After a visit, guide students in processing the information. A discussion time or a writing experience will provide an opportunity for you and your students to hear each other's perceptions and information. You may structure it with directions such as, "List three things you learned from our guest, and three questions that weren't answered." You may simply ask students to write their thoughts about the presentation. Even the task of writing thank you letters will be a processing experience, especially if you ask students to describe specifics of the visit in their letters.

One of the benefits of using a speaker is the connection you make between your curriculum and the community. Field trips accomplish the same link.

Field Trips

A *field trip* is "a visit to a place outside the regular classroom designed to achieve certain objectives that cannot be achieved as well using other means" (Mason, 1977). Although this definition has been with us for some time, its specification, "that cannot be achieved as well using other means" is especially timely with today's limited budgets.

Selecting a Field Trip

School districts have limited resources for field trips, so make careful decisions about using trips to vary the stimuli. They have the potential for novelty and for unique firsthand experiences. You probably remember some from your own school memories.

In the case of field trips, our guidelines come from research. We have learned some lessons about the qualities of effective field trips from studying them. The vignettes suggest preparation and instructional planning.

When selecting a field trip, stop and consider whether the field trip will distract, disturb, or bore students. When you identify a trip that will stimulate, focus, and involve your students, then continue your preparation.

Preparing for a Field Trip

To prepare for a field trip, we suggest the following steps:

1. Schedule the location with your school or district, students, and parents.
2. Visit the location to preview what students will see, hear, and learn, to identify potential problems or dangers, and to assess for instructional planning.
3. Arrange for permission forms, transportation, and chaperones or assistance.

In addition to the basic steps, experienced teachers use creative preparations to make field trips even more successful.

Elementary Research Vignette

INTRODUCTION

Falk and Balling (1982) were interested in the effects of different kinds of field trips on student attitudes, behavior, and learning.

STUDY PROCEDURES

The researchers studied two kinds of field trip situations and their effects on third- and fifth-grade students. In their study, half of the 196 students went to a nature center and half went to a wooded area near the school. The two groups had equal representation of third- and fifth-graders. Observers watched students at both sites and recorded behaviors. Students were later asked questions about the trips, and tested on memory and recognition items on the day after the trip and one month later.

STUDY RESULTS

Third-grade students behaved, responded, and learned differently than the fifth-grade students. First, third-grade students "seemed overwhelmed by the field trip to the nature center," had more off-task behaviors at the nature center than at the wooded area near school, and learned more from the science activity conducted in the wooded area. In contrast, fifth-graders were "stimulated by the trip" and "bored by the activity" conducted in the wooded area. Their off-task behaviors were higher in the wooded area, and learning was higher for the nature center trip.

CONCLUSIONS AND IMPLICATIONS FOR PRACTICE

Younger students may be appropriately stimulated by less novelty in a field trip situation, whereas older students may need more novelty for stimulation. The learner should be a major consideration in selection of field trips. What is novel and stimulating for one learner can be distracting and uncomfortable for another. Although novelty is the quality for variation in your teaching, it is one of those qualities in which "more is not better."

TEACHER TALK

During my preparation visit to our field trip site, I took slides of the exhibits and the facilities that we would be seeing. I showed the slides to my class prior to the trip. Then, when we arrived at the site, there was a real excitement over finding the items we saw and talked about in class.

2nd-Grade Teacher

When we plan a field trip, I try to assign some of the preparation tasks to the students. One group writes a letter to be sent home that explains the trip. Another group works on logistics—schedule, maps, fees, parent assistance, and so on. Another group works on recording procedures for the trip, and I always have a group write the thank you letters.

Middle-School Civics Teacher

In addition to these logistical steps, we want to turn to some additional advice from research. Fortunately, the research on field trips has suggestions for some instructional preparations. Look at the next vignette to find out how to make a field trip as effective as possible.

Junior High School Research Vignette

INTRODUCTION
The study was conducted by E. E. Gennaro (1981) to assess the effect of other instructional materials on student learning from a field trip.

STUDY PROCEDURES
The researcher studied 10 eighth-grade earth science classes to determine the effect of using previsit instructional materials on student learning for a field trip experience. All of the students took a pretest to determine prior knowledge and to assure that the classes were similar in knowledge before the study began.

Five of the classes were then assigned to experimental instruction before the field trip. Their teachers used materials, study sheets, hands-on experiences, and demonstrations developed for the trip. They provided an overview of the trip and some "advance organizers" to get students ready for what they would see and learn at the museum. The five other classes were assigned to control groups; that is, their teachers maintained normal teaching and curriculum, and took their classes on the same field trip.

STUDY RESULTS
The experimental group scored significantly higher on a test administered after the trip.

CONCLUSIONS AND IMPLICATIONS FOR PRACTICE
The significant difference in test scores between a group of students who studied about the field trip, previewed it, and were "ready" for the experience when they went, and a group of students who went on the same field trip lead to the conclusion that field trip preparation must include instructional preparation.

Gennaro's results are not surprising. They remind us to make the most of our field trips by previewing with students, coordinating other learning activities, and even assessing the effects of a trip. With the cost and effort that go into a field trip, you want to be assured of maximum learning outcomes.

With all the caution we have expressed in this section, you may be thinking, "I'll just skip field trips—too much work, too risky." We want to share an excerpt from a student journal to offset those sentiments in your thinking. Journals were kept by fourth- and fifth-grade students during a visit to a Shakespearean festival in a college town. Before the trip, they studied the playwright, the plays to be seen, theater etiquette, and history and geography of the area where the festival was located. The students also raised money for the trip, developed budgets, and participated in making arrangements. Their journals contained a map of their travels, a three-day itinerary, some song sheets, and a packet of ticket stubs, brochures, and receipts.

STUDENT TALK

We are at the college, and it is nothing like I expected it to be. The rooms are very small, and there are two desks, two beds, and two closets. The rooms are kind of yucky. We have meal tickets, and whenever we eat, we take our meal tickets and show them to the people in the cafeteria. We can pick out anything we want, and they even have a salad bar.

Last night we saw *Pericles*, and it was really good. My favorite part was when the knights danced. There were palm trees and knights dressed up in

colorful clothes. They did a kind of modern-day dancing. I want to know—
how do they memorize those parts? Who makes all the props? Where do they
get the clothes?

4th-Grade Student (Jennifer, 1989)

The student journal provided a way of processing the trip's outcomes. We
recommend the same attention to processing of field trips that we described for
guest speakers—discussions, critiques, and writings. We have also seen students
take photographs, make tape recordings, and draw impressions of a field trip during
and after the experience.

These two community resources, guest speakers and field trips, provide exciting ways to vary the stimuli in your teaching. Our next type of variation, audiovisual
stimuli, requires the same careful preparation and processing.

AUDIOVISUAL STIMULI

Audiovisuals offer you both sound and pictures. We will look at your options, provide brief descriptions and guidelines for use, and suggest some unusual ways to
vary your teaching.

Overhead Projector

Notice that on the Pyramid of Learning Experiences (page 307) this stimulus generally provides high levels of abstraction to your teaching, so use it thoughtfully with younger students. The overhead projector projects a written or graphic image on a screen or wall. You can use it to display a study outline for your class or to list student ideas. Its uses are not limited to any curricular area, and it is easily transportable.

An overhead projector uses a sheet or a roll of transparent film, clear acetate. You can prepare a sheet ahead of time by using copy or thermal copy machines or writing with a transparency pen, or use commercially prepared materials. You may also write on the transparency while teaching, but it takes time and skill. An advantage of using the overhead projector is that it allows you to face students; however, if you write on it much during your teaching, you lose the advantage of seeing faces, questions, and behavior.

Using the Overhead Projector Effectively
Some guidelines for using an overhead projector are:

1. Keep your image simple and readable (too much information is distracting).
2. Turn the projector off when not in use (the noise and light are distracting).
3. Use a good quality pen for making sheets (black for most writing; color for interest only).
4. Check the seating of students for clear vision of the image (sit in a few desks to test out the image).
5. Use a piece of white cardboard to cover all the points or items except the one you are discussing.

Unusual Uses for the Overhead Projector
We have seen teachers use this stimulus for numerous activities:

1. *Play a recess game on rainy days.* Children take turns making shadow figures on the screen and the rest of the class guess the figure.
2. *Create suspense or a surprise.* To begin a unit on profit in an economics class, a large $ is drawn to fill the transparency and flashed on the screen.
3. *Provide memory practice.* A list of words is projected for a short time, and then students write all the words they can remember.
4. *Share a small number of materials or materials too small to be seen by many students.* With only one set of counting bears, a first-grade teacher places different quantities of them on the overhead for students to count, add, or subtract.

The overhead projector with transparencies offers stimuli to use with lecturing, discussion, questioning, and with other stimuli, useful for previewing, recording, posing questions, demonstrating, and organizing.

Slide Projector

This machine projects pictures with intense images and you can keep the room lights on. An additional advantage comes with your use of pictures of real people, places, and happenings. Slides can be taken by you, your students, parents, or purchased from commercial producers.

Using the Slide Projector Effectively

When you show slides, remember to:

1. Check the placement ahead of time (images are more effective when they are right side up).
2. Accompany the images with description and questions.
3. Check the vision of students seated in different locations around the classroom.

Slide projectors are lightweight, accessible, and fairly simple to use. You can have students handle the projection task and free yourself to lead a discussion to accompany the visual.

Using the Slide Projector in Unusual Ways

We have seen teachers use this stimulus for various activities:

1. *Develop sequence skills.* Show a small number of slides (3 to 6) in order and out of order.
2. *Develop student ability to predict.* Show a slide and ask, "What is happening here?" or "What may happen next?"
3. *Prompt creative writing.* Show a beautiful or provocative or inspiring picture as a stimulus for writing or drawing.
4. *Review a class project or trip.* Show slides of students to review information and perceptions.

Another advantage of using this stimulus comes with taking the slides. You and your students will gain insights and appreciations while you photograph your subjects.

Television

When you look at the number of hours our students already spend watching television outside of school, you probably question adding more viewing hours in school. We have two compelling reasons for urging your consideration of this stimulus. The first is that television is available in most classrooms, and with a wide selection of quality educational programming. The second is that your classroom use of television can model some good viewing habits for students.

Using Television Effectively
Those good viewing habits we mentioned are incorporated in the guidelines we suggest for use of television:

1. Discuss with students before and after viewing a television program (information, impressions, bias, hidden messages, and so on).
2. Check volume and image for students in different locations.
3. Eliminate distractions.
4. Watch the program with students (rather than work at your desk on some task).
5. Coordinate other learning activities with the program.

Using television to vary your instruction requires that you have a schedule and become familiar with various networks. Many programs are simply more lecture, so look for a demonstration or a drama.

Using Television in Unusual Ways
We have seen teachers use this stimulus for many activities:

1. Use regular network ads to teach advertising, listening, decision making, and so on.
2. Use only parts of a program (the beginning or ending of a story) and have students write or develop the missing section.
3. Have students plan and produce their own television program.
4. Assign a television program as homework (with parents' approval) and include processing tasks such as questions to raise or answer, or note taking.

It looks like television is here to stay, and we can best use our energy to make it work for our teaching.

Records and Audiotapes

Many of us limit our thinking for these stimuli to music, but there are excellent tapes and records for every curriculum area. Both record players and tape recorders are inexpensive and simple to operate.

Using Records and Audiotapes Effectively
With the addition of headphones, tapes and records can be used by one student or a group of students. Because of the simplicity of operation, there are few guidelines:

1. Check volume for different locations of the room.
2. Keep electrical cords flush with floor or wall so that you and your students don't trip.

3. Have the intended starting point positioned on the tape or record ahead of time.

Using Records and Audiotapes in Unusual Ways

To expand your thinking on potential uses, we urge you to consider different ways to vary these stimuli:

1. Coordinate musical or sound backgrounds with book reports, historical narratives, plays, or science demonstrations.
2. Provide background music for a particular learning center.
3. Have students record their own tapes as journals, correspondence with you or other students, self-evaluation, or progress reports.
4. Have student groups record problem-solving or decision-making sessions, and play back for analysis.

One of our favorite teachers writes the name of a musical composition on the chalkboard each morning and plays it as his students arrive. We have also heard teachers using recordings for management routines, clean-up, or transition.

Films and Videotapes

Both of these have appeal for students and can support learner motivation. Technology has simplified the use of equipment and has advanced the quality of programs.

Using Films and Videotapes Effectively

The same guidelines regarding vision and volume for students apply here. In addition, we want to focus on one major guideline for using films and videotapes, and that is to use them interactively. Remember that *interactive* means that your students must do more than listen and watch. They must respond to the tape or film, and you can make that happen with questions, advance organizers, and discussions.

Using Films and Videotapes in Unusual Ways

The following are some unusual ways to use movies and videotapes and make them interactive:

1. Use the film or tape without sound and ask students to supply the dialogue, predict what is happening, or act as an observer on the scene.
2. Stop the film or tape midway and have students dramatize or roleplay the ending, then compare it with the film or tape ending.
3. Have students watch different tapes or films on the same topic and compare information.
4. Have students make films or tapes to teach other students, present research, describe a group project, record class history, or advertise a class program.

Notice that with these unusual uses, you cannot sit at your desk and catch up on your work. Your involvement with questions and suggestions will be needed.

Chalkboards

Chalkboards are everywhere and they come in all sizes, shapes, and several colors. They do not need a bulb or an electrical outlet, and they say what *you* want them to say. You can prepare them ahead of time, or use them as you teach.

Using Chalkboards Effectively

Chalkboards get daily use in every classroom, but they also get misuse. Look at the guidelines for effectiveness:

1. Keep your words large enough, dark or white enough, and clear enough to be seen in locations around the classroom.
2. Avoid filling the board with so much writing that students get confused.
3. Protect the writing surface with proper cleaning and the appropriate writing materials (do your school advancework with the custodian).

Chalkboards offer generous amounts of space on which to write, and are often located in several sides of the classroom. You can move around as you teach, as we suggested in Chapter 6.

Using Chalkboards in Unusual Ways

You can also use the chalkboard creatively:

1. Use colored chalk occasionally to highlight or underline main ideas, or to border information.

FIGURE 13.2 *Sample of Unusual Chalkboard Message*

2. With tape or other devices, attach pictures and diagrams to the chalkboard with written descriptions, labels, or questions.
3. Reserve space for student messages.
4. On an infrequent basis, write your messages backwards, in a circle, or vertically. (See Figure 13.2.)

We have also seen teachers use a block of chalkboard space for a Thought for the Day, a riddle, a coded message, or a new vocabulary word. A daily or class schedule on the chalkboard is useful to you and your students. Reminders, directions, assignments and due dates, and announcements are all appropriate for chalkboard display. When you combine chalkboards with the other stimuli of this chapter, your teaching will be varied and will capture student attention.

Bulletin Boards

Bulletin boards come in different sizes and shapes. You hear teachers complain if they don't have one, and you hear teachers complain if they do. Like chalkboards, bulletin boards offer ease of use and accessibility.

Using Bulletin Boards Effectively

We have three simple guidelines for the use of bulletin boards:

1. Concern yourself with what your bulletin board says and does, rather than just how it looks.
2. Keep the display up to date, that is, connected to the theme of study, time of year, and so on.
3. Involve students in planning and producing displays.

We want to emphasize the first guideline with a reminder that we are talking about varying the stimuli in teaching. We have seen aesthetically arranged displays that are just part of the wall, never referred to in teaching, never discussed by students, and not connected to curriculum. The intent of these stimuli is to contribute to teaching.

The second guideline won't be a worry if your bulletin board is connected to your curriculum, and following the third guideline will help you keep your bulletin boards up to date.

Using Bulletin Boards in Unusual Ways

As we look at unusual ways to use bulletin boards, you will see the third guideline, students' involvement:

1. Students construct a bulletin board display of what they learned from a unit or course.
2. Each student is assigned a portion of a bulletin board to display what is happening in his or her life.

3. You construct a bulletin board related to future curriculum of unknown objects, places, and people for student guesses or predictions.
4. You and your students construct a bulletin board to communicate appreciation or honor to a student, parent, teacher, volunteer, or administrator.

In Chapter 14, you will see a bulletin board being used as part of assessment. With student involvement, bulletin boards can change from being a responsibility for you to an exciting way to vary the stimuli.

Demonstration

The word *demonstration* means to point out or show by display, so a demonstration helps you vary the stimuli by showing instead of telling. Demonstrations make information more concrete and are often interesting to students.

Using Demonstration Effectively

Figure 13.3 is an example of a rating form to use to evaluate a demonstration, specifically for science instruction (Gillen, Brown, & Williams, 1989).

The categories to be rated are our guidelines for using demonstrations effectively with any kind of curriculum:

1. Gain student attention immediately with an interesting title, some humor, an unexpected event, and your own interest and enthusiasm.
2. Check visibility so that all students can clearly see what is being shown.
3. Get students involved (interaction again!) by having them take notes, assist, predict, or ask questions.
4. Check that students understand what you demonstrated by asking questions, reviewing, or repeating parts of the demonstration.
5. Before you begin, familiarize students with the materials and equipment so that they can focus on the process or concept, follow safety procedures, and participate with competence.

When you teach with a demonstration, you can use the evaluation scheme as a checklist to get ready.

Using Demonstration in Unusual Ways

Take a look at how to demonstrate in unusual ways:

1. Demonstrate a cooking procedure or science process the first time with no explanations, in a pantomime, then repeat it with directions either from you or your students.
2. Demonstrate a familiar process or concept with some noticeable error, urging students to make corrections when needed.
3. Present a demonstration in a make-believe screen of a television, on a theater stage, or in costume.

FIGURE 13.3 *Rating Form for Evaluation of a Science Demonstration*

	Excellent 5	4	3	2	1	Poor 0
I. Captures Student Attention	___	___	___	___	___	___
II. Emphasizes Visibility	___	___	___	___	___	___
III. Obtains Student Participation	___	___	___	___	___	___
IV. Checks Concept Understanding	___	___	___	___	___	___

I. Captures Student Attention
1. The demonstration "hooks" student attention with a discrepant event, bright color or catchy title.
2. The volume of the teacher's voice is projected throughout the room.
3. The teacher is enthusiastic.
4. The teacher speaks with confidence.

Communication and audibility: total points earned ___

II. Emphasizes Visibility
1. The apparatus and materials being used are of adequate size for class size.
2. The room/demonstration is adequately lighted.
3. The demonstration can be easily seen throughout the room.
4. Materials are supported at an appropriate height from all areas of the room.
5. The teacher does not obstruct students' view.

Visibllity: total points earn ___

III. Obtains Student Participation
1. The teacher solicits student participation during the manipulations.
2. The teacher gets students to write their ideas down on paper.
3. Students respond to teacher questions and discuss concepts illustrated.
4. The teacher asks questions of both volunteers and nonvolunteers.
5. The teacher questions students throughout the room.
6. The teacher allows time for students to answer.

Student participation: total points earned ___

IV. Checks Concept Understanding
1. Asks questions at the appropriate cognitive levels to develop ideas, concepts and principles.

FIGURE 13.3 *(Continued)*

	Excellent					Poor
	5	4	3	2	1	0

2. Questions are probing in nature and stimulate students to think.
3. Questions direct students through a logical thought pattern.
4. Questions permit students to draw their own conclusions.
5. Questions stimulate students to initiate further investigations.

   Checks concept understanding: total points earned _____

V. Establishes Familiarity with Materials
   1. The teacher checks students for familiarity with materials and apparatus.
   2. Students show proficiency in being familiar with apparatus used through oral or written means.
   3. All materials and apparatus are readily available.
   4. Proper safety precautions have been followed.

   Preparation: total points earned _____

Total points earned _____
(Total points possible: 25)

Source: Gillen, A. L., Brown, W. E., & Williams, R. P. (1989). How-do-do-it: Developing dynamic demonstration. *American Biology Teacher, 51*(5), 306–311. Used by permission of National Association of Biology Teachers.

If there is a bit of "ham" in you, you will enjoy using demonstrations with your teaching. They are also an effective way to involve those community resources like postal service employees, cashiers, news forecasters, all of whom can demonstrate for students and enhance learning.

COMPUTERS

Writing a section, not a chapter or a book, about computers seems like an impossible task. We will limit our descriptions to what you can expect from computers, and some guidelines for their use. We will skim through an album of classroom snapshots for you to see a variety of ways in which teachers vary the stimuli with computers.

Expectations from Computers as Stimuli

In a list of "pervasive educational problems that school computers can help teachers address," Collis (1988) identified poor written communication skills, limited problem-solving skills, lack of organizational skills, and weak skills for finding and using information. Concern for student attitudes toward important curricular areas was also expressed as a potential target for computer assistance. As you use computers to vary the stimuli, we agree that their use can address those problems. As stimuli, you can expect computers to provide:

1. Opportunity for practice (students can use games or programs for recitation, review, and seatwork; review Chapter 9)
2. Opportunity for collaboration on problems, practice, and challenges
3. Simulated experiences for application of knowledge and skill
4. Individual assessment of student knowledge, skill, or attitude
5. Record keeping of student work, assessments, and progress

You will see examples of how you can use computers to meet these expectations as we describe the guidelines for use and as you scan the coming Snapshots.

Guidelines for Using Computers as Stimuli

Most of us began using computers with little direction or training. Some of the first classroom uses included extra practice for students having difficulty, remediation programs, and games for those students who finished their regular work quickly. These practices limited the effect of computers as stimuli, and few students were influenced. As we describe guidelines for using computers, our goal is variation for all students. We encourage you to:

1. Assure each student equitable acccess to equipment.
2. Plan for social interaction in computer use with pair assignments and tutor teams.
3. Connect computer use to whole class or small group instruction.
4. Preview and critique software yourself, and encourage student evaluation.

Following the four guidelines will take planning and management because schedules affect computer use. Many classrooms have only one or two computers, so following the first three guidelines may sound impossible. How do you find time for each student or a pair of students to use the computer even for a short period of time (maybe, 10 minutes) in conjunction with a one-hour lesson? It is not easy, but we will try to help you with some examples.

One example is to have five practice alternatives following your math demonstration: practice with manipulatives, practice with pencil and paper tasks, practice with games and card sets, practice with calculators, and practice with computers. The demonstration and practice can be repeated for three days to allow students to practice with each alternative.

Another way to follow the guidelines is to give ongoing assignments such as a research report for history or geography, a writing assignment, or data collection for science, to individual students, pairs of students, or small groups. Over the week of work on the assignment, each student or group has a time slot and is expected to complete part of the assignment on the computer.

Another way to meet the guidelines is to conduct several software evaluation sessions with students after they have all used some common programs. Or schedule preview times for small groups to critique and make recommendations about some new software.

As you look at the classroom Snapshots, you will get more ideas about how to follow the guidelines for using computers as stimuli.

Using Computers with Variation

We provide elementary, middle-school, and secondary classroom Snapshots to help you use computers with as much variation as possible.

SNAPSHOT: Secondary Classroom

In a geometry class, small groups of students are asked to create a family album for a specific geometric shape such as a polygon or quadrilateral. First, they use a computer to generate random samples of their group's shape and to obtain measures of specific attributes for each figure. Then they use a ruler and a protractor to reproduce the examples for their albums. Finally, they develop a list of properties for the shape they are investigating. As students construct their own descriptions for a particular geometric shape, there's enthusiasm and creative work. They are engaged in the "doing of mathematics" (Jensen, 1988).

This classroom computer use follows several guidelines with its collaborative use and connection with whole class instruction. It meets the expectations of computers to provide practice and application.

SNAPSHOT: Elementary Classroom

In a first grade, children participate in a class discussion about information such as names, birthdays, pets, favorite games, and holidays. After the discussion, each child completes an Information about Me worksheet. A template that duplicates the worksheet is created for the data base program. During the day, pairs of students come up to the computer and have their information typed in or type it in themselves.

When all the data are entered, children gather around the computer in small groups. They watch as each child's information is found. Children can compare their own information sheet with the information on the monitor. They also quickly learn how to find their own information. Later, questions such as, How many of our classmates have birthdays in March? can be posed and a computer list may be generated for monthly birthdays (Collis, 1988).

This classroom use is definitely a social activity, as well as an opportunity for practice, review, and individual assessment. Notice how classroom volunteers could be used effectively to assist the activity and how a variety of groups are possible for the viewing of data. Review those grouping possibilities in Chapter 10.

SNAPSHOT: *Middle-School Classroom*

In this English class, the teacher has prepared a format of a book summary using a data base program. Each time a student reads a book, he or she enters information about it in the data base. As the book report data base gets larger, students begin to access it for ideas of books to read. The teacher also uses it to get summaries of the types of books most popular with students to use in planning. Periodically the teacher searches the entries of each student and conferences with those who are not well represented in the data. Those students sometimes need suggestions for reading material.

FIGURE 13.4 *Book Summary Form for Computer Data Base*

1. Name of your book: _____

2. First author's last name: _____

3. First author's other names: _____

4. Are there other authors? (Y = yes, N = no) _____

5. If there are other authors, give their names here, last name(s) first:

   _____

6. Type of book? (N = novel, B = biography, I = information, S = short story,

   P = poems, O = other) _____

7. Your recommendation? (VG = very good, G = good, O = OK, N = not

   very good) _____

8. Would you like to read another book like this one? (Y = yes, N = no) _____

9. Complete this sentence (use at least ten words):

   This book is about _____

   _____

10. What is your last name? _____

11. What is your first name? _____

12. What is today's date? Month: _____ Day: _____ Year: _____

Figure 13.4 is a sample of a book summary. It could easily be adapted for students to use for reporting science experiments, software review, or other assignments. Notice how the data base provides you with assessment information.

Your options with computers are many. The bonus you will receive as you use them is that you will probably learn right along with your students, as you use computers to vary the stimuli.

SUMMARY

Did you feel a bit smug when you looked at the old school Snapshots? We have come a long way in our use of stimuli, but return in time with us once more. This time, we are skimming through an old teaching methods handbook. We find a page and a half under a heading, Handling Materials:

> *The problem of management in connection with the physical materials of instruction is growing more pressing, because the materials are growing more numerous. In the classroom today, to the regular texts have been added many supplementary texts; plasticine and clay and sand have their recognized place; paper and cardboard of various sizes and colors for cutting, folding, pasting, and drawing have come to stay. Photographs, stereoscopes, maps, charts, minerals and other specimens for geography and nature study are all making new demands on skills of the teacher. (Breed, 1922, p. 7).*

The picture sounded overwhelming and exciting in 1922 just as it does today. Substitute videotapes, computers, overhead projectors, and audiotapes and the rest of the narrative fits. There is a need for skills in using resources, audiovisuals, and computers to vary the stimuli.

We remind you to begin with your consideration of the *content, context,* and *learner* when you use stimuli. Your purpose(s) may be *to develop concepts, to enrich experiences, to extend experiences, to stimulate interest, to provide meaningful information,* or *to provide opportunities for practice.* Your selection of effective stimuli is based on *a match with content and learner.*

Once your selection is made, remember the importance of *preparation.* Include previewing a resource or audiovisual, arranging your classroom for its use, and practice using equipment. Your preparation continues with *scheduling decisions, decisions of how to use, decisions about involving students,* and decisions about future use.

From there, you have guidelines for the range of choices available to you. Whether you are using a field trip or a computer software program, the first guideline is that the stimuli are only part of your teaching. You will need to use other teaching strategies and to connect the stimuli to other learning experiences. A processing step for reviewing impressions, perceptions, understandings, and information is important after any stimuli use.

With most audiovisual materials and equipment, *visibility and clarity, volume, and student interaction* are essential. We have urged you to be creative and to discover unusual ways to vary the stimuli for your teaching. Resources, audiovisuals, and computers are constantly being developed and improved. With their use is support for learning and creative potential for your teaching. *Vary the stimuli!*

REFERENCES

Breed, F. S. (1922). *Public school methods.* Chicago: School Methods Publishing.

Clark, R. E. (1982). Antagonism between achievement and enjoyment in ATI studies. *Educational Psychologists, 17*(2), 92–101.

Clark, R. E., & Salomon, G. (1986). Media in teaching. In M. E. Wittrock (Ed.), *Handbook of research on teaching* (3rd ed.). New York: Macmillan.

Collis, B. (1988). *Computers, curriculum, and whole-class instruction.* Belmont, CA: Wadsworth.

Dale, E. (1969). *Audiovisual methods in teaching.* New York: Holt, Rinehart and Winston.

Falk, J. H., & Balling, J. D. (1982). The field trip milieu: Learning and behavior as a function of contextual events. *Journal of Research in Science Teaching, 76*(1), 22–28.

Gennaro, E. D. (1981). The effectiveness of using previsit instructional materials on learning for a museum field trip experience. *Journal of Research in Science Teaching, 18*(3), 275–279.

Gillen, A. L., Brown, W. E., & Williams, R. P. (1989). How-to-do-it: Developing dynamic demonstration. *The American Biology Teacher, 51*(5), 306–311.

Jensen, R. J. (1988). Teaching mathematics with technology. *Arithmetic Teacher, 35*(6), 4–46.

Mason, J. L. (1977). *Professional teacher education module series: Directing field trips.* Columbus, OH: National Center for Research in Vocational Education. (Eric Document Reproduction Service No. ED 149 065).

SAMPLES AND EXAMPLES

The following audio and visual Samples and Examples are included in this section:

- Penny Arcade is a writing activity for viewing films that involves the students.
- Historical Time Line of Political and Social Trends is a historical record in the form of songs that have played on the radio. They form the basis of a time line that traces historical events in our country. You may want to add other songs to the list like "Abraham, Martin, and John," which depicts the assassinations of Abraham Lincoln, Martin Luther King, and John F. Kennedy.
- The Audiovisual Assessment Form is a quick five-item assessment form to judge how effective a piece of audiovisual (e.g., film, videotape, etc.) material is.

PENNY ARCADE

Objective:
After viewing a portion of a film at the center, the student will write a conclusion to the film in a two-page paper, using dialogue and narration with descriptive words and variety in sentence structure.

Directions:
1. Turn on the projector and view the film for 10 minutes.
2. Stop the projector and rewind the film.
3. Now, write an ending to the film you have just seen by taking on the role of one of the characters. Your conclusion should be at least two pages in length. Be sure to use descriptive words and variety in sentence structure.
4. Place your paper in the box when you have completed the center.

Materials Teacher Provides:
The teacher should provide a story film and a projector for the student to view. The story should be at least 20 minutes long, so that after viewing the film for 10 minutes the student will be able to write an original ending to the film.

Source: From Don M. Beach, *Reaching Teenagers: Learning Centers for Secondary Classrooms* (Santa Monica, CA: Goodyear Publishing Co., 1977) pp. 48–49. Reprinted by permission.

A HISTORICAL TIME LINE OF POLITICAL AND SOCIAL TRENDS ILLUSTRATED BY SELECTED AMERICAN RECORDINGS, 1955–1987

Year	Political Events and Social Trends	Personalities Related to Events	Song Titles (Record Number)	Performing Artists (Year of Release)
1955	Walt Disney's television production of "Davy Crockett" sparked a national craze for coonskin caps and patriotic feelings about Texas and the Battle of the Alamo.	Fess Parker	"Ballad of Davy Crockett" (Columbia 40449) "The Ballad of Davy Crockett" (Cadence 1256) "The Yellow Rose of Texas" (Columbia 40540)	Fess Parker (1955) Bill Hayes (1955) Mitch Miller (1955)
1955	Rock 'n' roll music emerged as a teenage fad with performing idol Elvis Presley, the motion picture *Blackboard Jungle*, and a small group of raving disc jockeys gaining national attention.	Chuck Berry Elvis Presley Alan Freed	"Rock around the Clock" (Decca 29124) "Maybellene" (Chess 1604) "Heartbreak Hotel" (RCA 47-6420)	Bill Haley and His Comets (1955) Chuck Berry (1955) Elvis Presley (1956)
1956	The traditional pop music establishment, represented by major recording companies and their white singers, failed to halt the integration of black performers into the "Top 100" record charts.	Pat Boone Crew Cuts Diamonds Fontane Sisters Georgia Gibbs Gale Storm	"Tutti Frutti" (Specialty 561) "Tutti Frutti" (Dot 15443) "Why Do Fools Fall in Love?" (Gee 1002) "Why Do Fools Fall in Love?" (Mercury 70790)	Little Richard (1956) Pat Boone (1956) Frankie Lymon and the Teenagers (1956) The Diamonds (1956)
1957	The New York Yankees, following Don Larsen's perfect game victory in the 1956 World Series, continue to be baseball's most dominant team.	Mickey Mantle Whitey Ford Yogi Berra Casey Stengel	"Whatever Lola Wants" (Mercury 70595) "I Love Mickey" (Coral 61700)	Sarah Vaughan (1955) Teresa Brewer (1957)
1958	Rock 'n' roll idol Elvis Presley is	Elvis Presley	"The All-American Boy" (Fraternity 835)	Bill Parsons (1958)

Year	Political Events and Social Trends	Personalities Related to Events	Song Titles (Record Number)	Performing Artists (Year of Release)
	drafted into the U.S. Army and is stationed in West Germany.			
1958	The Hula-Hoop craze is at its peak, becoming one of the most prominent fads of the 1950s.	Millions of Americans swiveling hollow plastic rings around their waists	"Hoopa Hoola" (Atlanta 2002) "The Hula Hoop Song" (Roulette 4106) "The Hula Hoop Song" (Coral 62033)	Betty Johnson (1958) Georgia Gibbs (1958) Teresa Brewer (1958)
1959	Three young singers—Buddy Holly, Ritchie Valens, and the Big Bopper—are killed in a plane crash near Mason City, Iowa, on February 3, 1959.	Buddy Holly Ritchie Valens J. P. Richardson	"Three Stars" (Crest 1057) "American Pie" (Parts I & II) (United Artists 50856)	Tommy Dee (1959) Don McLean (1971)
1960	Congressional investigations into bribes and illegal payments made to station managers and disc jockeys to secure radio air-time for specific records.	Alan Freed Dick Clark	"The Old Payola Roll Blues" (Capitol 4329)	Stan Freberg (1960)
1973	The Watergate conspiracy, stemming from the unsuccessful attempt by members of the Nixon administration to cover up a 1972 break-in at Democratic National Headquarters in Washington, D.C., leads to the 1974 resignation of President Richard M. Nixon.	Richard Nixon John Dean Sam Ervin H. R. Haldeman John Ehrlichman Archibald Cox John Mitchell	"Elected" (Warner Brothers 7631) "Watergate" (Rainy Wednesday 202) "Sweet Home Alabama" (MCA 40258) "You Haven't Done Nothin'" (Tamla 54252)	Alice Cooper (1972) Dickie Goodman (1973) Lynyrd Skynyrd (1974) Stevie Wonder (1974)

continued

Year	Political Events and Social Trends	Personalities Related to Events	Song Titles (Record Number)	Performing Artists (Year of Release)
1974	The nadir of public confidence in the political honesty of American governmental leaders and anger over major economic difficulties caused by continuing oil shortages.	Richard Nixon Gerald Ford	"Masterpiece" (Gordy 7126) "The Americans (A Canadian's Opinion)" Energy Crisis '74" (Rainy Wednesday 206)	The Temptations (1973) Gordon Sinclair (1974) Dickie Goodman (1974)
1975	The Great Lakes ore vessel *Edmund Fitzgerald* sinks during a fierce storm on Lake Superior on November 11, 1975.	The crew of the *Edmund Fitzgerald* and their bereaved relatives	"The Wreck of the *Edmund Fitzgerald*" (Reprise 1369)	Gordon Lightfoot (1976)
1975	After generating a decade of public controversy, the man who is Cassius Clay, the "Louisville Lip," and Muhammad Ali wins the most dramatic prize fight of his brilliant boxing career in Manila against Joe Frazier.	Muhammad Ali Joe Frazier Howard Cosell	"Black Superman— 'Muhammad Ali' " (Pye 71012)	Johnny Wakelin and the Kinshasa Band (1975)
1976	The use of citizen band (C.B.) radio frequencies expands dramatically from truck drivers to the general automobile public.	C. W. McCall Dave Dudley	"Convoy" (MGM 14839) "C. B. Savage" (Plantation 144) "Teddy Bear" (Starday 142)	C. W. McCall (1976) Rod Hart (1976) Red Sovine (1976)
1977	The drug-related death of rock 'n' roll idol Elvis Presley at his mansion in	Elvis Presley Tom Parker	"The King Is Gone" (Scorpion 135) "From Graceland to the Promised Land" (MCA 40804)	Ronnie McDowell (1977) Merle Haggard (1977)

Year	Political Events and Social Trends	Personalities Related to Events	Song Titles (Record Number)	Performing Artists (Year of Release)
	Memphis, Tennessee, on August 16, 1977, shocks his fans.		"Are You Lonesome Tonight?" (RCA 47-7810)	Elvis Presley (1960)
			"My Way" (RCA PB-11165)	Elvis Presley (1977)
			"The Elvis Medley" (RCA PB-13351)	Elvis Presley (1982)
1978	The height of the disco craze which swept urban dance centers, the popular music industry, and motion picture screens as well.	John Travolta Barry Gibb Robin Gibb Maurice Gibb Donna Summer	"You Should Be Dancing" (RSO 853)	The Bee Gees (1976)
			"Stayin' Alive" (RSO 885)	The Bee Gees (1977)
			"Disco Inferno" (Atlantic 3389)	The Tramps (1977)
			"Last Dance" (Casablanca 926)	Donna Summer (1978)
1979	After the nuclear plant accident at Three Mile Island (T.M.I.) in Pennsylvania, the Musicians United for Safe Energy (M.U.S.E.) present a concert at Madison Square Garden to challenge the continued use of atomic energy even for peaceful means.	Jackson Browne Graham Nash John Hall	"Plutonium Is Forever" (M.U.S.E. Album)	John Hall (1979)
			"Power" (M.U.S.E. Album)	The Doobie Brothers with John Hall and James Taylor (1979)
			"We Almost Lost Detroit" (M.U.S.E. Album)	Gill Scott-Heron (1979)

See the original article for timeline to 1987.

Source: Cooper, B. L. (1989, January). *Social Education*, *53*(1): 34–40. Used by permission of National Council for the Social Studies.

AUDIOVISUAL ASSESSMENT FORM

Type	Title	Source	Quality	Student Response
Film	Your Health	Library	poor	bored, laughter
Photoset	Geometry	AV Center	Excellent	Entertained – interactive
Filmstrip	Dairy Farms	AVC	Very Good	Best used in small groups – with discussion
Large posters	Environment	Lib.	Very Good	Activity ideas on back – successful; high involvement

CHAPTER 14

Assessment of Learning: Let Me Count the Ways

CHAPTER OUTCOMES

At the conclusion of this chapter you will be able to:

1. Use and understand the language of assessment.
2. Describe and use assessment for multiple purposes.
3. Develop and use different assessment strategies.
4. Consider the content, context, and learner in assessment decisions.

KEY TERMS AND CONCEPTS

Evaluation
Assessment
Diagnostic Assessment
Formative Assessment
Summative Assessment
Informal Assessment
Formal Assessment
Criterion-Referenced Tests
Standardized Tests
Norm-Referenced Tests
Inquiry
Reliability/Validity
Teacher-Made Tests
Anecdotal Records
Checklists
Rating Scales
Fill in the Blank or Short Answer
True-False Tests
Multiple-Choice Tests
Matching Tests
Essay Tests
Questionnaire
Interview
Portfolio
Test Anxiety

INTRODUCTION

We begin this chapter with a Snapshot that shows you the dilemmas many teachers face when they assess student learning.

SNAPSHOT: *Elementary Classroom*

For the past week, Pam Rossio's students have been curious and responsive to a partial bulletin board labeled "Our Environment." On Monday she urged them to take time during the week to write questions related to the photographs and newspaper clippings, to add items of their own to the board, and to think and talk about the display. During the week she began planning a three-week unit on ecology. For the content of the unit, she emphasized conservation measures and the immediate environment of her students. She developed objectives, organized activities, and gathered resources from her files and the media center.

Today is Friday and Pam is putting the finishing touches on her plan. She reads the students' questions and thinks to herself: There's some curiosity about forestry and mining—I expected that. Some of these are very simple ideas, but a few questions get into complex ideas. Pam makes a note to check the content of her unit to see if the information will match the range of student understanding.

She thinks about a conversation she heard between Mona and Ardyth. Mona described a TV program about ecology and expressed a mature sensitivity and understanding. Pam noted the conversation because she was stunned by Mona's interest and knowledge, even some unusual vocabulary. Now she worries to herself: How can I provide Mona with a way to express this competence? She usually does so poorly on our written tests.

Pam schedules activities and content, then begins to work on the assessment part of her unit. She found three tests in the textbook that her students use. They are criterion referenced, and she plans to use one for each week of the unit. She has also sketched out a checklist for students to use in recording their own progress. She wonders how to assess the problem-solving skills will be assessed in the standardized tests used by her district and wants to be sure that her students master them.

A major goal of Pam's unit is to develop and improve attitudes toward ecology, and she has an intense commitment to this intent. She struggles with how to measure those attitudes and wonders if there is a formal evaluation tool available. She feels uncertain about how to find one. She thinks about doing a student interview. She thinks to herself: I don't know how I will find time, maybe I can use a questionnaire. It will be faster.

Language of Assessment

While you were reading the Snapshot, did you feel familiar with the terminology? Did you encounter labels that need definition? Not surprising! Assessment seems to have the most extensive set of language of any teaching and learning strategy.

It is going to be important to be able to talk about assessment using terms correctly and knowledgeably with other teachers, administrators, and parents. Therefore, we begin this chapter with assessment language. From there, we will work on the other assessment concerns and needs that you and Pam Rossio have.

Assessment terms are interrelated. Rather than give you a list of definitions, we will define the terms in a framework with examples. As you can see in Table 14.1, the starting point is *evaluation*; that is, the process of making a decision about student learning. Evaluation requires us to make a judgment about student knowledge, student behavior or performance, or student attitude. *Assessment* is a strategy for measuring that knowledge, behavior or performance, or attitude. It is a data-gathering strategy. The measurement or data you gain from assessment helps you make the decision of evaluation.

As you can see in the framework, teachers use three major kinds of assessment: *diagnostic, formative,* and *summative.* A simple way of thinking about and remembering these is that you must make decisions *before, during,* and *after* your instruction. Keep the framework in front of you as we describe each of the three kinds of assessment.

Diagnostic Assessment

Pam Rossio used her bulletin board for diagnostic assessment. She found out what students already knew and what they were curious about. She also listened to student conversations to find out who had some knowledge about ecology. When diagnostic assessment is used prior to teaching as in Pam's classroom, it provides planning information. Pam's strategies for diagnostic assessment were *informal*, that is, unstructured. Her alternative would have been a *formal* diagnostic assessment, that is, a scheduled and structured assessment. A commonly used formal diagnostic assessment is a *pretest*, which is a measure of student knowledge about information that is going to be taught before it is taught.

Using both formal and informal diagnostic assessments in your planning

TABLE 14.1 *Framework of Evaluation*

Diagnostic		Formative		Summative	
Formal	*Informal*	*Formal*	*Informal*	*Formal*	*Informal*
Standardized tests	Observations	Checklists	Journals	Inquiry	Discussion
Pretests	Discussions	Quizzes	Observations	Work projects	Observations
Placement tests		Ques. – answers	Ques. – answer	Standardized tests	Work Projects
Inquiry		Assignments	Student comments	Classroom tests	Student feedback
Questionnaires		Standardized tests	Assignments		
		Classroom tests			

process will give you a complete picture of student readiness and interest for your teaching. Diagnosis doesn't have to stop once plans are complete. Effective teachers continue to diagnose student understanding and interest throughout each lesson or unit of teaching. We call this ongoing assessment during teaching *formative assessment*.

Formative Assessment

Formative assessment is conducted during instruction, again either formally or informally. Both teachers and students receive information from this kind of assessment: information about problems, errors, misunderstandings, understandings, and progress. The textbook tests that Pam plans to use and the checklist she developed for student use will formally assess progress. Informally, Pam will listen to student comments and conversations during the activities for formative assessment.

The information you gather with formative assessment will help you revise your teaching plans to better match the learner, and will tell you whether your teaching has been effective. One possible outcome of Pam Rossio's use of textbook tests is that she will have to reteach a concept. One possible outcome of her use of student checklists is that she may have to change the pace of her unit. If students indicate problems or confusion, she may need to slow the pace; if students indicate boredom, she may have to speed it up. One possible outcome of listening to and observing students is that she may have to change or clarify content. You can see that it is important for Pam to use both formal and informal strategies because the data from her observations will support and explain the data from her tests and checklist, and vice versa.

Summative Assessment

Summative assessment is conducted at the end of a lesson, a unit, or a course. It is a final measure of what was learned. Most of us have taken numerous summative assessments in the form of final exams. As learners, they offer us the opportunity to demonstrate what we have learned. For teachers, they are, as Berliner (1987) puts it, the "moment of truth." If your summative assessment is well developed, it will tell you about your teaching as well as about your students' learning.

For her summative assessment, Pam Rossio plans to use a *criterion-referenced test*, which is a test that measures student learning according to a predetermined standard of achievement. Her predetermined standards include "understanding 90 percent of the terms," "explaining at least five conservation measures," and "demonstrating relationships by responding to five situations."

One of Pam's dilemmas is knowing how to measure the problem-solving skills of her unit. She feels that the skills require an assessment that goes beyond a test on paper. Like most teachers, she has had little experience or preparation for this task (Stiggins, 1988), so this is a difficult task. Pam's district will be using standardized tests in which students' problem-solving skills will be assessed. *Standardized tests* are commercially designed and administered in the same way to each student or group of students. They are usually nationally norm referenced; that is, they have been administered and scored for groups of students who represent the general population of students. Pam's students will take a standardized test that has been norm referenced on fourth-grade students.

Pam is also concerned about measuring student attitudes and is interested in using an inquiry assessment. *Inquiry* is the process of specifically asking students how they feel, what they think, what their likes and dislikes are, and probing their understanding. One possible inquiry strategy is an *interview*, a face-to-face meeting in which one person obtains information from another. Pam thought about asking everyone to respond to an environmental situation or picture. Because of time constraints, she also thought about using a *questionnaire*, which is another inquiry assessment. The efficiency of a questionnaire comes from its written form so that all students answer the questions at the same time, or at least independent of their teacher.

Thus far, we have described only formal summative assessments—tests, interviews, and questionnaires. Another formal possibility is a final project or paper. Informally, you will be observing students, conducting discussions, and studying student assignments and projects for summative assessment information. Pam Rossio's students may add pictures and comments to her partial bulletin board as their unit progresses. Such an unplanned event can provide informal assessment.

By now, the language may be sounding more comfortable for you. As we describe the purposes and uses of assessment, you will have a chance to check your understanding of terms. Our goal is to have the vocabulary used with ease and accuracy.

PURPOSES OF ASSESSMENT

Most teachers consider assessment an important part of teaching. The ultimate purpose is to measure student learning. The additional purposes are improvement of teaching, curriculum, and conditions for student learning. In today's trends of accountability and competitive test scores, it is easy to lose sight of those purposes. Stiggins (1988) recommends that you need to "learn about and become sensitive to a wide variety of purposes for classroom assessment." We agree; in fact, this chapter's title, Let Me Count the Ways, refers to both multiforms of assessment and multipurposes of assessment. We encourage your use of assessment for purposes of planning, purposes of decision making, purposes of motivating, and purposes of communicating.

Using Assessment Data for Planning

Before you plan a lesson, there is a variety of information that you must know about your students. To plan objectives, you must assess current levels of knowledge and skill. To plan activities, you must assess work habits, independence, interest, previous experiences, social relationships, and learning styles. To plan materials and resources, you must assess previous experiences, competence with materials, comprehension level, and interests.

A scenario of a substitute teacher in a second-grade math lesson illustrates the importance of assessment for planning. When Mr. Callahan noted the lesson on subtraction in the plan book, he immediately pulled out the unifix cubes for a practicing activity. What he didn't know was that the children hadn't used those manipulatives all year (which is a sad case in itself). Because of the novelty of the materials, the lesson became unfocused and the subtraction process became lost in play with the cubes.

What happened to this substitute teacher can happen in your classroom when your planning is done without ongoing assessment of your students. Keep some questions in mind:

- Do they like films and tapes?
- Do they have any research skills? Research experience?
- Can they work cooperatively?
- Who are the leaders and followers?
- What did they learn about the subject last year?
- Can they follow directions?
- What successes have they had? Problems?

Some of the questions are appropriate for group discussion and some need to be written into an assessment such as a questionnaire. Now, observe a scenario in which assessment is used for planning purposes.

On the first day of school, Ms. Lewelyn asked her students to complete a questionnaire about their literature preferences and reading experiences. Her year-long planning then reflected students' tastes in reading, and she used their previous experiences as starting points or comparisons for new literature. Her students showed high levels of interest in the class and participated enthusiastically in activities.

This teacher used assessment data for planning, and the result was appropriate curriculum and activities.

Using Assessment Data for Decision Making

Assessment for this purpose calls for the kind of reflection and responsible behaviors we observed in Pam Rossio. Many of the decisions made with assessment data have serious consequences for the lives of students and their families. Look at some of the most commonly made decisions using assessment data:

- Grouping and placement decisions (assignment of students to ability groups or classes for instruction)
- Identification of need for special services (referral of students to remedial or special classes)
- Grades (assignment of letter or number quantification on records and report cards)

- Promotion or retention, graduation, certification
- Educational and vocational counseling (advising for future study and work)
- Curricular decisions (to continue or discontinue a program of studies)
- Personnel decisions (to maintain or dismiss a teacher or other professional)

All seven of these decisions are influenced by data from both standardized tests and those tests that you develop. Although you do not determine the content of standardized assessments, you can influence how they are used if you have basic knowledge about the instruments. The power you hear in the Teacher Talk comes from that knowledge.

TEACHER TALK

We're frustrated with the standardized tests our district selected for language arts. The tests have little to do with how or what our students are learning. They don't describe understanding, and they don't consider attitudes.

The new assessment mandated for our state in writing is ridiculous. They found less than 1 percent correlation between the test items and the curricular approach being used to teach. We're going to write a statewide position paper.

4th-Grade Teachers

Here are some basic characteristics of standardized tests that you will need to understand:

1. *Reliability* is the consistency with which a test or items measures whatever it measures.
2. *Validity* defines whether an item or a test measures what it is intended to measure.
3. *Practicality* shows considerations of time, cost, difficulty of administration, and scoring to determine usability.
4. *Norm sample* or *standardized population* is the group whose scores are used as a comparison.
5. *Bias* shows items of test content that could discriminate against specific groups of students in terms of language, experiences, and tests.

These characteristics give you basic criteria with which to examine and discuss standardized assessments. We encourage you to study and develop understanding for using the tests. In this chapter we are also working on competence in developing assessments. The vignette demonstrates how critical your responsibility is when assessment data is used for decision making.

Elementary Research Vignette

INTRODUCTION

A significant decision made with assessment data is the promotion or retention of a student. Many teachers express concern about the emotional effects of grade retention. Byrnes and Yamamoto (1985) reviewed the research on effects of grade retention and found no information from students themselves in the literature.

STUDY PROCEDURES

The researchers interviewed 71 retained elementary students about their views on grade retention. The children were retained in grades 1, 3, and 6. Their responses were gained through structured personal interviews.

STUDY RESULTS

All students were introduced to the topic of retention in the following way: "Some students who need more time to learn spend another year in the same grade. Have you or any of the students in your class ever had that happen?" Of the 71 children who were repeating a grade, 74 percent named themselves. Only 57 percent of the girls included themselves, but 81 percent of the boys named themselves. First-graders, especially female students, were most likely not to include themselves, even with repeated questioning and clarification.

When students were asked how they "felt" or "would feel" about being retained, 84 percent shared feelings centered around "sad," "bad," and "upset." Students were also asked how their parents felt, and 46 percent said, "Mad."

Of the 55 children who admitted being retained, 47 percent said that they were punished. Punishments included being sent to one's room, getting a spanking, having allowance withheld, losing privileges, and cancellation of a family vacation.

When students were asked why they thought that they had been retained, their responses were diverse: "Not getting good grades" was the most common response (25 percent) and behavior reasons were next (14 percent)—"I talked too much," "I get in fights," "I played too much," and "I was standing up all the time." Work habits (13 percent), missing school (11 percent), and "not knowing English" (9 percent) were next in common responses.

All students were asked what they felt was the worst thing about not passing. The most common response was "being laughed at and teased" (22 percent), followed by "not being with friends" (16 percent). When asked about something good about not being promoted, most children found it difficult to think of something, and a number seemed to think that it was incredulous that they were even being asked.

CONCLUSIONS AND IMPLICATIONS FOR PRACTICE

Byrnes and Yamamoto summarized their study with a view that retention causes anxiety for children and intense concern about their status with peers and families. Their data indicated that children internalize some unintended messages from the practice of retention, most of which are negative and confusing.

Our purpose here is not to dispute the practices of promotion and retention. Our concern is with the data you will use to make those decisions. Consider the long-term effects of your assessment processes as well as your immediate needs for information.

Using Assessment Data for Motivating

Assessment is used in classrooms for two kinds of motivation. The first occurs because the assessment strategy gets students thinking about a topic or reviewing previous knowledge. As we described in Chapter 3, using an assessment to prompt thinking or review is an effective beginning for a lesson. Look at this teacher who is using assessment that motivates: Mrs. Holgate conducts a lively brainstorming session with her middle-school students on the topic of the Civil War. She begins with, "Think of all the information you know about the war." The lists of information give her data about what her students know, don't know, and have confusions about. The process also gets her students excited as they learn about the Civil War.

Remember Pam Rossio's bulletin board? While she was gathering information about what her students knew about ecology, they were thinking about ecology, developing curiosities and interest in it.

The second way in which assessment is used to motivate students is through the feedback they receive. Some of that feedback is in the form of grades, stickers, or comments. Our own philosophy makes us caution you in your use of assessment for motivation. We are not comfortable with students working only for stars, or happy faces, or 100s. We have seen students working in fierce competition with each other for grades or points. That competition may be contrary to the classroom climate we described in Chapters 5 and 6.

Students do need the feedback that is possible from assessment—information about their learning, information about their understanding, and information about their accomplishments. That information is necessary for learning and serves to motivate. We describe how to provide the feedback as we suggest how to communicate assessment data.

Using Assessment Data for Communicating

There are four major audiences for our communication of assessment data: *students, parents, school personnel,* and the *public.* For each of these audiences, your assessment data must be clearly communicated.

Student Audience

We begin with students. They have a right and a need to learn about their progress and achievement. Both written and verbal communication can provide such information. Students of all ages desire descriptive information along with grades.

STUDENT TALK

I hate it when I get a paper back and all it has on it is the grade. Even if it's an A, it doesn't matter. I want some feedback, some response to all the work I have done. I sometimes wonder if the teacher really read it completely.

High-School Senior

High-school students are not unique in this desire—all students want such communication. Be sure, however, that your communication is informative, helpful, specific, and unique to the student's work. Look at the contrasting examples for effective communication and ineffective communication to students:

GOOD WORK—NEAT PAPER

All of your multiplication problems have been done accurately. Your computation is easy to follow because numbers are clearly written.

Interesting paper!

You did extensive background reading before doing this paper. The details you provide on this topic made it both informative and entertaining to read.

Figure 14.1 provides an example appropriate for young children who are nonreaders.

Parent Audience

Parents are your next audience and, as we described in Chapter 6, your relationship with parents influences the teaching and learning in your classroom. It does take time to communicate well, but the payoffs are there for you and your students.

Whether writing or speaking to parents, we encourage you to follow the same advice we gave for communicating to students. Be informative, helpful, and specific, especially when communicating assessment data.

TEACHER TALK

When it comes to explaining test scores to parents, try to put it into words. People are easily threatened by numbers. The more you explain in words, the better off you are.

Listen as well as talk. Listen to the parents and their questions. Ask them to say the information back to you if you think that they may not understand. Say, "I don't know if I explained it well. Could you tell me what I said?"

Elementary Administrator (Henry, 1988)

We also encourage you to follow some guidelines for your written communication, whether you are writing informal notes or elaborate reports.

FIGURE 14.1 *Contrasting Examples of Assessment Communication to Young Children*

1. Make your notes neat and legible (no cross-outs or misspellings).
2. Be clear and concise (avoid long complicated sentences and jargon).
3. Present facts not impressions (avoid words such as *seemed, felt, appeared*).

These are basic, common-sense suggestions, but parents have complained and critiqued teachers when such guidelines are not followed.

School Personnel Audience

When communicating with the third audience, school personnel, we suggest the same guidelines we just listed for parents. We want to emphasize clarity. There is a tendency to use jargon because we think that other professionals will understand. They may or they may not. We know that educational jargon changes rapidly, so a current phrase may mean something different or nothing at all in a few years or in another part of the country.

When you communicate with other school personnel, it is also important to provide complete descriptions and not leave the reader with questions. Be cautious about your use of abbreviations, again, for clarity.

Finally, remember to include multiforms of assessment. Your professional audience will benefit when your data come from varied sources. Another teacher or administrator will understand the student better if the standardized test scores are accompanied by some observational data, a classroom checklist of work habits, and work samples.

Public Audience

Teachers do not usually communicate assessment data to the general public, partly because school districts and state departments of education generally take this responsibility. Standardized test scores are a regular media item, especially if there are gains or national prominence. What does not appear in the media very often are descriptive data from individual teachers.

For most teachers, this sounds like an overwhelming task, but listen to this teacher's experience. She decided that students' work needs to be communicated to her community.

TEACHER TALK

It's difficult for me to show off and I hate to use the phone, but I felt that my students were doing something worth mention. I checked with my district and was encouraged so I contacted the *Chronicle*. I explained what my fifth-graders were doing and checked possible dates with the paper. They said that someone would be there at a certain time and thought it was great news. The reporter talked with the students and took pictures. I was amazed at how easy it was. I will probably do it again.

5th-Grade Teacher

This teacher's experience is not unique. Most teachers are pleasantly surprised at how easy it is to communicate student assessment data to the public.

In sum, using assessment for communication has multiple audiences and therefore a need for multiple forms of assessment. When you look at all the purposes of assessment, you see the reasoning behind our theme, "let me count the ways."

HOW TO ASSESS LEARNING—LET ME COUNT THE WAYS

There are two major processes that comprise the assessment of learning. Both involve decision making. The first requires that you consider the *content*, and choose an appropriate way to assess. The second requires you to choose between using a ready-made test or developing one of your own.

Consider the Content

When you consider all the kinds of objectives you have for your teaching, you quickly see that one kind of assessment will not work for all the learning you intend. Think about the learning domains we described in Chapter 3. Your first assessment decision is to select the appropriate domain. Next, determine the appropriate level of the domain so that you can match it with an appropriate way to assess. We will look at each domain briefly to assist you with the matching process.

Assessing the Cognitive Domain

The *cognitive domain* is most often assessed with tests, especially for measuring knowledge, comprehension, analysis, and evaluation. Tests are systematic forms of measurement, either oral or written. At some levels, such as synthesis and application, specific kinds of tests, such as essay tests, are appropriate. For application, it is also appropriate to listen to or to observe students actually using knowledge. Table 14.2 gives you a list of appropriate options for the cognitive domain.

Assessing the Affective Domain

The *affective domain* is more difficult to assess because of the personal and internal qualities of affect. Again, the domain has levels of difficulty so that you can match your assessment to the level of learning. The inquiry strategy is most commonly used for the affective domain in Table 14.3

Assessing the Psychomotor Domain

In the *psychomotor domain*, you also have a hierarchy of difficulty levels, ranging from reflex movements to skilled movements. The levels in this domain are generally assessed by observation of either a behavior or performance. Observational data can be recorded as an anecdotal record, or with checklists or rating scales. In the following Snapshot, you see Mr. Whitfield making decisions as he considers the content for assessment.

TABLE 14.2   *Assessment Options for the Cognitive Domain*

Domain	Assessment Options
Knowledge	Written tests (fill in the blanks, matching, simple multiple choice) Observation of student recitations
Comprehension	Written tests (true-false, multiple choice, short answer) Student assignments (summaries, explanations) Observations of student discussions
Application	Written or oral problem solving Multiple-choice tests (with answers based on solving problems) Observation of simulations, roleplay
Analysis	Essay tests Multiple-choice tests that require classifying, coding, inferring, or using criteria Student assignments (comparisons)
Synthesis	Essay tests Student projects with a plan, product Written or oral problem solving

TABLE 14.3   *Assessment Options for the Affective Domain*

Domain	Assessment Options
Receiving	Observations of student discussions Questionnaires
Responding	Observation of student participation Interviews
Valuing	Interviews Questionnaires Essay tests
Organization	Observation of student choices
Characterization	Student responsibilities Student projects (taking a position) Student debates

---

SNAPSHOT: Secondary Classroom

It's time for first quarter grades and Mr. Whitfield looks at his data in anticipation of the decisions he must make. Most of the quarter has been spent in review of ideas and skills from previous basic art courses, so students have submitted only two products. Last year he developed a rating scale for use with student work. Other art teachers have critiqued the scale and students have provided comments about its helpfulness, so he feels confident using it. (See his rating scale in the Samples and Examples section at the end of this chapter.)

"The ratings don't seem enough," he thinks. He decides to observe his students for at least half of their work period each day for the next week. "I'm usually so busy talking to them about their work that I don't think I have really watched them." He jots a reminder to himself in his lesson plans.

On Monday, students begin working independently after a demonstration of a shading technique. Mr. Whitfield moves around the room in his usual way, commenting to several students and answering questions for about 10 minutes. Then he picks up a class list and begins recording what he sees . . .

Advanced Art 3—Mon., Nov. 12
11:10 AM, Rm. 29, Vista H. S.
Subject: shading, still life

Nathan: Seems unaware of other students; that is, works on his drawing for 12 minutes without looking around at other students. Pauses to look at arrangement; has a serious expression on his face.

Rochelle: Looks at the arrangement for a minute and a half, then holds up her pencil at several angles, looks at the arrangement again, then makes reference points on her paper, looking at the arrangement frequently. Asks Donna, "Do these look right to you?"

Donna: Responds, "Think about your proportions. The bowl is fat, the bottle is skinny. . . ." Turns back to her own work, sighs, looks up at the arrangement for a few seconds, then back to her lines. She uses repetitious lines, 5 or 6, for each surface. She moves her entire arm when making the lines.

After several days of writing the anecdotal records, Mr. Whitfield spends time reading his notes. Feeling anxious about his time, he decides to develop a checklist from the behavior he has already observed. "Next week I will use a checklist and see if each student is using the basic techniques." (The checklist is in the Samples and Examples section at the end of this chapter.)

Back to the psychomotor domain levels: reflex movements, basic fundamental movement, perceptual abilities, physical abilities, skilled movements, and nondiscursive communication—all can be assessed with Mr. Whitfield's observation strategy. You may not have noticed, but he followed some important guidelines, which will be helpful for your own classroom observation:

1. Observe students in natural environments or conditions.
2. Observe students in an unobtrusive manner.

3. Record exactly what students do and say.
4. Avoid using terms of judgment, nonspecific descriptions.
5. Provide contextual data (i.e., time, location).

Notice that Mr. Whitfield began observing students after they had been working for 10 minutes. He also moved about the room as he usually did during the work time. Notice, too, that he described Nathan as "Works on his drawing for 12 minutes without looking around at other students," which is more objective than his first comment, "Seems unaware of other students." When he recorded Donna's techniques, he didn't use "Good," or "Well," or even "Smooth." Instead, he described her technique with, "She used repetitious lines, 5 or 6, for each surface."

We began this section with the importance of matching the content of assessment with the *how* of assessment. Mr. Whitfield would have difficulty giving an essay exam on most of the content he teaches. In contrast, another teacher might faithfully observe her students each day and not have enough data to determine if each of her students can spell a specific list of words. After teachers consider the content and determine what kind of assessment is appropriate, they have another decision to make: selecting an assessment, or constructing an assessment.

Selecting an Assessment

Your first step in selection is to find out what is available. Remember Pam Rossio's dilemma? She was uncertain about where to find a test on student attitudes.

Locating Assessments

We suggest to Pam and to you that you begin with immediate resources: district media center, school resource personnel, textbook series, and/or curriculum guides. Be ready to be resourceful, because when Stiggins (1988) reviewed what was available to most teachers, he found that "districts simply have no one on hand with expertise in classroom assessment" (p. 366) to provide teachers with training, technical assistance, or support. Rather than be discouraged, we suggest that you turn to the following library (university or district level) sources for informative descriptions of many forms of assessment:

1. *Buros' Mental Measurements Yearbooks*
2. *Tests in Print*
3. *Test Collection Bulletin* (published by Educational Testing Service, Princeton, New Jersey)
4. Educational and psychological abstract indexes

If you have never looked at any of these sources, do yourself a favor and browse through them. You will gain both knowledge and a bit of expertise from them, and you may locate assessment tools. Your next step will be to appraise what you find, to be sure that it is an appropriate instrument or strategy.

Appraising Assessments

Ebel (1965) provided teachers with 10 qualities of a good test. The qualities are universal enough to apply to most assessments. Use them to pose the kind of questions we suggest for appraising an assessment:

1. *Relevance*. Do the items of this test match the objectives and content information of my teaching? Does this test measure the learning that I intended for my students?
2. *Balance*. Does this test represent all of the important content that I taught? Is important information given importance in the test items? Is any information given too much representation in the test items?
3. *Efficiency*. How much time will this test take? Is that amount of time appropriate or in proportion to the amount of time I spent teaching the content?
4. *Objectivity*. When I look at answers to the test items, are they fair?
5. *Specificity*. Is there a match between the curriculum information and the test items? Could a student who missed class do well on this test?
6. *Difficulty*. Can at least half of my students do very well on this test? Could each item be answered correctly by at least half of my students?
7. *Discrimination*. Will my students who worked hard, studied well, and are knowledgeable answer most of these items correctly? Will my students who put little effort, did minimal studying, and aren't knowledgeable answer most of these items incorrectly?
8. *Reliability*. Would my students score similarly if they took this test two days in a row? Does it matter who gives this test?
9. *Fairness*. Will all students have an equal chance on this test? Does it favor a particular group?
10. *Speed*. Will my slow-working students be penalized on this test? Will there be any problem with some students finishing this test?

Some of this information will be provided for you in the sources that we suggested. Otherwise, you will need to examine the assessment instrument itself. With appraising, you may decide that none of the available instruments are right for your purposes. Your next option is to construct one of your own.

Constructing an Assessment (Teacher-Made Tests)

As a starting point, think about your students and your intent for their learning. Consider the content with knowledge, skills, and attitudes. See if you can describe what you would like your assessment to measure. This is a good place to remind you to consider the content. Now you are ready to develop your instrument, probably in rough form. Review it, revise it, and use the 10 qualities we just discussed. Nitko (1983) suggests that you pilot the instrument with a group of students, and probably revise it again.

The process we just described is in contrast to a "throw it together the night before" test. We know that you are thinking about how long it will take to develop each assessment you may need. We offer some helpful advice: Give short tests and give them frequently. Be sure to review the time-saving ideas in Chapter 4.

You will also need some suggestions for the various specific kinds of assessments. We begin with the most commonly used paper-and-pencil tests and suggest some cautions:

1. Check your language, grammar, punctuation, and spelling. Avoid obscure or ambiguous vocabulary that could cause confusion.
2. Avoid "irrelevant cues" (Remmers, Gage, & Rummel, 1965) that trigger the correct response without any knowledge or skill on the part of the student.
3. Avoid interrelated items, that is, when the answer to one question furnishes the answer to another item.

As you read the three cautions, can you remember taking tests with such problems? Be sure that you don't repeat them with your own students. Now, we move to strategies for constructing specific paper-and-pencil tests.

Fill in the Blank or Short Answer

Provide enough information in a simple direct question or in a stem (part of a statement), as you see in the samples:

- Tests that _____ student scores are called *norm-referenced tests*.
- How do norm-referenced tests use student scores?

The first example has more than one possible answer (*compare* or *rank*). Be sure that if more than one answer is possible, you will accept more than one answer.

If you want a definition from students, ask for it directly. The item "Define *evaluation*" is better than "The process of making a decision about student learning is called _____." For this reason, a question form is preferable for this kind of test.

True-False Tests

This kind of test is efficient to score, but remember to avoid irrelevant cues. Look at the following samples;

- A pretest is always given before teaching occurs.
- A pretest can be given before teaching occurs.

Words like *always, none, all, never, might,* or *generally* give cues, or imply answers. Also, be sure that your "true" statements are absolutely true, and that your "false" statements are absolutely false. When they are not, they cause confusion and errors. Finally, we suggest that you work for a fairly equal number of true and false items. Due to the high levels of guessing, true-false tests should be used sparingly.

Multiple-Choice Tests

These tests ask students to select the answer from a set of alternatives. You provide a stem in the form of an incomplete statement or question. Your stem should be clear, direct, and singular in focus. A direct question is best. Consider our example:

- What is the most appropriate use for criterion-referenced tests?
  a. for a diagnosis of student interest in a topic.
  b. for a pass-fail assessment of student learning.
  c. for student information about progress.
  d. for planning information for teachers.

Notice that all of the alternatives are similar and parallel. Again, avoid irrelevant cues and use correct alternatives that are absolutely correct. Contrary to common use, the choice "none of the above" as an alternative answer is not useful. It does not provide enough information about student learning.

Matching Tests

Once again, have clarity in your criteria for matching and avoid irrelevant cues and absolute matches. This kind of test should not be too long (5 to 6 items for elementary students, 10 to 12 items for secondary students). It should be placed on a single page.

The left side of your matching items contains the *stimuli*, the information items that should prompt thinking and response. The right side lists *possible responses*. In order to assess learning accurately, more responses than stimuli should be provided. Haven't you been in the situation of matching 8 items, knowing 6 of the items and guessing correctly the last 2? If there were more than 8 responses provided, guessing would not be so effective.

Unlike most of the paper-and-pencil assessments, matching tests can be used with young students and nonreaders. The stimuli and responses can be provided with pictures and symbols instead of words.

Essay Tests

We repeat once more: Clear statements of the response expected and a singular focus are essential. Next, remember what is appropriate content for assessing with essay tests—problem solving, synthesis, commitment, and analysis. Be sure that your item asks students to use those criteria. Some other guidelines for writing essay tests include:

1. Provide several short essay items rather than a few long essay items (this will assess more learning).
2. Give students an indication of amount of time to spend or the value of an item (percentages or points).
3. Require all students to respond to the same question so that you have consistent information for all.
4. Decide beforehand what information and ideas you want to see in students' answers, and rate the worth of each in points or percentages.

Evaluation requires multiforms of assessment. Matching, essay, or fill-in-the-blank tests may not be appropriate for what you want to assess. You may need to construct checklists, rating scales, or questionnaires.

Checklists

Remember the checklist Mr. Whitfield used while observing students in his art class? Checklists are generally used during or after observation. To develop a checklist, begin by breaking down the skill or behavior that you intend to assess. The skill may have steps or it may have components. Ask yourself: When I watch a student performing this skill, what are all the behaviors I should see? If we were to observe you using the skills of this chapter, here is the beginning of a checklist we would use:

Name _____

Construction of Assessment

	Observed	Not Observed	Date
1. Reviews student characteristics	_____	_____	____
2. Considers curriculum	_____	_____	____
3. Describes purpose	_____	_____	____

To complete the checklist, we would continue listing the steps suggested for constructing an assessment. Remember: The purpose of a checklist is to indicate the presence or absence of a behavior or skill. You have choices in how you indicate—dating the observation of a skill, or checking that it was observed, or not checking when it was not observed.

Rating Scales

These are useful for assessing skills, student products, and behaviors. Again, you must break down the skill or behavior into steps, subskills, or components. From there, use either a qualitative scale or a frequency scale for each step or subskill. A *qualitative scale* uses terms such as "excellent to poor," a frequency scale uses terms such as "always to never." You can also develop specific descriptions for a scale that is tailored to the particular skill you are assessing. We demonstrate your three options in the samples that follow:

Rating Scale—Writing Fill-in-the-Blank Items

Name _____ Date _____

1. Writes definite and clear stems.

1	2	3	4	5	
Excellent				Poor	(Qualitative)

2. Uses questions instead of incomplete sentences.

1   2   3   4   5

Always   Never   (Frequency)

3. Gives credit to alternative answers.

_____ only when absolutely correct
_____ only when student demonstrates serious thinking
_____ only when many students give alternative answers
_____ only when it is acknowledged before the test is given
(Specific to the subskill)

Qualitative and frequency ratings work well for most of your student needs. When you use rating scales for your student products, you often use a "poor to excellent" rating scale or, as Mr. Whitfield did, a scale that reflects the criteria of assigned work.

Questionnaires

When you want to assess attitudes, opinions, and feelings, questionaires are more efficient than interviews and observational recordings. To design a questionnaire, first decide what kind of information you want. Then develop statements or questions to elicit the information.

In developing questionnaires, you have options for formatting questions and responses. Your choice will be related to the kind of information you are seeking. You may use a *simple checklist* or *open-ended questions*.

For the first option, begin constructing a checklist for your questionnaire by writing a stem and providing choices to complete the stem into a sentence, much like a multiple-choice item. This time, there is no right or wrong answer. Instead, you are looking for a preference, a feeling, or an opinion. Look at the sample:

• This chapter on assessment has made me feel:
_____ anxious
_____ confident
_____ committed
_____ ready
_____ bored

Your second option is a sentence completion format, or an open-ended form. You provide students with partial sentences and ask them to complete the sentences with words that best express their feelings, opinions, or thoughts. Look at the last sample:

• After reading this chapter on assessment, I feel _____
_____.

This concludes our suggestions for commonly used kinds of assessment. We want to describe two additional kinds, partly because of our commitment to multi-forms and partly because teachers are searching beyond the common forms. The first, an interview strategy, was mentioned previously, as Pam Rossio looked for a way to assess student attitudes. The second, a portfolio strategy, is currently being used for students of all ages for particular curricular areas.

Interviews

This strategy involves students in conversations to explore their thinking. Rather than seek right or wrong answers, interviews probe for understandings, feelings, opinions, and perceptions. You will generally begin with a developed question or set of questions, and proceed to spontaneously invented questions based on student response.

Interviewing requires sensitivity and will take practice before you are able to probe and develop spontaneous questions. As you begin, review your advancework information and establish rapport with your student. Prepare the student for the interview process by describing your procedures and introducing any materials being used, including recording equipment. Listen as the teacher in Teacher Talk begins an interview with a second-grader.

TEACHER TALK

I'm interested in talking to you to find out how you think about numbers. I've been talking to all the children and do you know what I've been finding out? Everybody doesn't think about numbers in the same way, so every boy and girl that talks to me teaches me something new. The things we'll be talking about may be things you have studied in school and others will be things you haven't studied. I'm not really interested in whether you know the right answer. I'm more interested in how you figure out your answer.

2nd-Grade Teacher (Labinowicz, 1985, p. 28)

It is essential that you provide an appropriate amount of time for students to think, so your "wait time" will affect the responses you hear. It is also recommended that you pause after a student's response to encourage more response or elaboration (Labinowicz, 1985). An additional consideration is your response to student answers. You will want to be aware of your body language, facial expressions, and verbal responses. It is recommended that you use a neutral acknowledgment, such as a repetition of the student's answer or a nod of the head. Finally, you will need to decide how to record student answers; you have several options: written notes, audiotapes, and videotapes.

Interviews have numerous benefits in addition to the opportunity to explore student thinking. They include relationships with students, one-to-one interactions with individuals, a chance to check misunderstandings, and an alternative form of assessment that meets learner differences.

"Well, it finally happened. Our evaluations show that 100% of the students interviewed couldn't care less about our new curriculum."

Portfolios

This strategy for gathering data on student performance is currently being used in the curriculum areas of reading and writing. Many teachers consider portfolios a way of "sampling student performance that is more closely linked to instruction" (Jongsma, 1989). They are a collection of work samples. For example, in language arts, portfolios contain samples of reading and writing.

Portfolios are usually developed by students. Guidelines are established at the beginning of the year for (1) content (criteria for including in portfolio) and (2) participation (teacher, student, parents).

If you decide to use portfolios, it will be important to schedule regular conferences with your students. These discussions can be both evaluative and instructional. They provide opportunity for students to self-evaluate, assess their own progress, plan for their own learning, and express ideas and opinions not usually gained in most assessment.

Portfolios offer a unique way to gather evaluation information, and are appropriate for many content areas.

FINAL CONSIDERATIONS FOR ASSESSMENT

We have already described how the content of your teaching influences your decisions about assessment. Now, as we have recommended with all of the instructional strategies, we will describe some sensitivities regarding the context and the learner.

Consider the Context

Does the following Student Talk sound familiar?

STUDENT TALK _____

I don't feel great about the test Monday afternoon. Being in that room with its closed windows and door makes me physically ill and I get headaches. I had a difficult time concentrating because of the heat.

High-School Junior

You may have the tendency to shrug off this student's sentiments as an excuse. However, if you have shared this experience, you know how real the effects of heat can be.

Environmental Factors

Environmental factors that require sensitivity include noise, interruptions, crowded conditions, temperature, and lighting. Even the time of day or day of the week can have an impact.

These factors affect students' physical state. Fatigue, hunger, and visual strain influence thinking processes. It is difficult to solve problems or analyze information when you are drowsy. There is also the effect of distraction. A new environment or constant interruptions cause students to slow down or lose ideas.

Preparing the Environment

Some strategies for avoiding the negative effects of contextual factors are:

1. Post a "Testing: Do Not Disturb" sign on your classroom door.
2. Clear a time frame for assessment with office and administration personnel to free your classroom from interruptions.
3. Avoid assessments at holiday times and just before or after recess, lunch, or dismissal.
4. Arrange classroom seating to give students space.
5. Have custodians check lighting and temperature if conditions warrant.

Conduct some classroom advancework before assessing learning and survey the environment for some of the factors we suggested. Consider discussing the factors with students: "Is there anything about our classroom that disturbs or distracts you when you are taking a test?" You may gain some helpful information, and, in the process, you will communicate concern to students. Your concern will work to dispel the often held belief of students that teachers are out to get them with tests. Let's continue with that same concern for the learner.

Consider the Learner

Our approach to assessment with "let me count the ways" is primarily due to concern for the many learners who will be affected. There are multiple ways to assess learning.

Accommodating Differences

In a class of 28 students, we know that there will be 14 who will easily demonstrate their learning on paper-and-pencil tests, 6 who will do so while being observed, 4 who can verbally do so in an interview, and so on. There must be other ways to assess. Just as we know that students learn differently, we know that they demonstrate learning differently. If you rely on a single form of assessment, you miss information about many of your students.

Test Anxiety

Another consideration for the learner is a sensitivity to test anxiety. We know that test anxiety can influence student performance on assessment measures. Guida, Ludlow, and Wilson (1985) found that "high anxiety" seventh-grade students spent much of their work time in self-preoccupied behaviors and worry. Other research studies have shown that anxiety interferes with retention and focusing. Some anxiety comes from repeated failures on tests, and some comes from the embarrassment and punishment that follows. A competitive climate can create pressure that results in test anxiety. When it comes to test anxiety, you can make a difference for your students. Figure 14.2 provides guidelines for your classroom, your teaching, and your assessment procedures.

We remind you to teach students how to review and study for tests and to encourage health habits (sleeping, eating) that could influence assessments. Discuss test-taking difficulties with students. Ask them what they have learned about being successful in assessment situations. Students usually say that it helps them to talk about anxiety and to hear other's feelings. Be sure that you communicate to them that there is a connection between assessment and learning. The discussion strategy is an important way to consider the learner as you conduct assessment.

SUMMARY

We began by looking into Pam Rossio's classroom and observing her need for "ways" of assessment and the importance of resources. As you read her story, you encountered the language of assessment, an extensive set of terminology. You learned about three major kinds of assessment: diagnostic, formative, and summative, and saw that you could choose formal or informal strategies for each.

From there, we urged you to "learn about and become sensitive to the wide variety of purposes of classroom assessment" (Stiggins, 1988). You saw that assessment data is used for planning, for decision making, for motivating, and for communicating.

FIGURE 14.2   *Guidelines Dealing with Anxiety*

Use competition carefully.
   Examples
   1. Monitor activities to make sure no students are being put under undue pressure.
   2. During competitive games, make sure all students involved have a reasonable chance of succeeding.

Avoid situations in which highly anxious students will have to perform in front of large groups.
   Examples
   1. Ask anxious students questions that can be answered with a simple yes or no, or some other brief reply.
   2. Give anxious students practice in speaking before smaller groups.

Make sure all instructions are clear.
   Examples
   1. Write test instructions on the board or on the test itself instead of giving them orally.
   2. Check with students to make sure they understand. Ask several students how they would do the first question of an exercise or the sample question on a test. Correct any misconceptions.
   3. If you are using a new format or starting a new type of task, give students examples or models to show how it is done.

Avoid unnecessary time pressures. ·
   Examples
   1. Give occasional take-home tests.
   2. Make sure all students can complete classroom tests within the period given.

Remove some of the pressures from major tests and exams.
   Examples
   1. Teach test-taking skills; give practice tests; provide study guides.
   2. Avoid basing most of a report-card grade on one test.
   3. Make extra-credit work available to add points to course grades.
   4. Use a variety of different types of items in testing, since some students have difficulty with certain types.

Source: Woolfolk, Anita E. *Educational psychology*, 4th ed. © 1990, p. 312. Reprinted by permission of Prentice Hall, Inc., Englewood Cliffs, New Jersey.

With the purposes of assessment in mind, you began making the decision of selecting your assessment strategy. The process calls for you to consider the content, starting with the learning domains in Chapter 3 for matching with appropriate assessment. You now have some resources for locating assessments and for appraising assessments (Ebel's 10 qualities). If you determine that none of the available assessments are right for your purposes, your next step is to construct one of your own.

Regardless of what type of assessment you plan to construct, we urge you to follow a construction sequence that begins with thinking about your students and your content. Be sure to question, edit, and revise the drafts of your assessment, and pilot it with students. For all types of assessment, check language, clarity, and irrelevant cues, and avoid ambiguity.

As you select or construct assessment, remember to "count the ways": paper-and-pencil tests, checklists and rating scales for observation, questionnaires and interviews for inquiry, and portfolios. Then, consider the context for conditions that will affect how students are able to think and perform the assessment tasks. Consider the learner and the need for assessment to meet individual needs and learning styles. Be sensitive to and discuss the anxiety that may accompany assessment for some learners.

You have plenty of ideas for your assessment work, but there will continue to be questions and concerns. When they appear, find an assessment expert in your school or among your colleagues and enlist their help and support. Continue reading about the topic, and keep some of our guidelines and recommendations nearby as you work.

REFERENCES

Berliner, D. C. (1987). But do they understand? In V. Koehler (Ed.), *Educator's handbook*. New York: Longman.

Byrnes, D. A., & Yamamoto, K. (1985). Academic retention of elementary pupils: An inside look. *Education, 106*(2), 208–214.

Ebel, R. L. (1965). *Measuring educational achievement*. Englewood Cliffs, NJ: Prentice-Hall.

Guida, F. V., Ludlow, L., & Wilson, M. (1985). The mediating effect of time-on-task on the academic anxiety/achievement interaction: A structural model. *Journal of Research and Development in Education, 19*(1), 21–26.

Henry, S. (1988). *Making the grade*. Charlotte, NC: Charlotte-Mecklenburg School.

Jongsma, K. (1989). Portfolio assessment. *The Reading Teacher, 43*(3), 264–265.

Labinowicz, E. (1985). *Learning from children: New beginnings for teaching numerical thinking*. New York: Addison-Wesley.

Nitko, A. (1983). *Educational tests and measurement*. Orlando, FL: Harcourt Brace Jovanovich.

Remmers, H. H., Gage, N. L., & Rummel, J. F. (1965). *A practical introduction to measurement and evaluation*. New York: Harper & Row.

Stiggins, R. J. (1988). Revitalizing classroom assessment: The highest instructional priority. *Kappan, 69*(5), 363–368.

Wolf, D. P. (1988). Opening up assessment. *Educational Leadership, 45*(4), 24–29.

Woolfolk, A. E. (1987). *Educational psychology*. Englewood Cliffs, NJ: Prentice-Hall.

SAMPLES AND EXAMPLES

The following examples and samples provide models of less common assessment and communication of assessment information:

- The Assessments for Drawings contains a scale and checklist for giving feedback for artwork.
- The Kindergarten Teacher Student Observation Scale is a 20-item scale that provides a limited profile for determining the level of functioning for kindergarten students.
- A syllabus is provided for Biology I, which provides assessment information to students and parents about teacher expectations for the course.

ASSESSMENTS FOR DRAWINGS

Rating Scale

Whitman—Advanced Art 3

Proportion	Appropriate				Inappropriate
	1	2	3	4	5
	Consistent				Inconsistent
	1	2	3	4	5
Composition	Symmetrical				Asymmetrical
	1	2	3	4	5
Chiaroscuro*	Accurate				Inaccurate
	1	2	3	4	5

Style

_____

_____

_____

*Chiaroscuro is the treatment of the light and shade on an object.

Checklist for Observation of Drawing Techniques

Technique	Observation Date	Description
Looks at subject matter regularly	_____	
Uses pencil to mesure proportions	_____	
Maps out proportions with reference points	_____	
Uses hard lines	_____	
Uses soft lines	_____	
Uses repeated lines	_____	

Source: Driscoll, K. (1990). Used by permission.

KINDERGARTEN TEACHER STUDENT OBSERVATION SCALE

Child's Name _____ Date Scale Completed _____

Teacher Completing Scale _____ Building _____

Directions: Put an X where applicable:

1. Attempts to follow directions   _____ _____ _____
2. Appears to think before acting   _____ _____ _____
3. Copes with something new without getting   _____ _____ _____
   nervous or upset
4. Is able to sit quietly   _____ _____ _____
5. Is willing to try on his own   _____ _____ _____
6. Seeks help when he cannot manage a task   _____ _____ _____
7. Shows by answers that he is giving attention   _____ _____ _____
8. Moves on easily from one task to another   _____ _____ _____
9. Stays with a task to completion   _____ _____ _____
10. Is able to wait his turn   _____ _____ _____
11. Attempts to contribute in group   _____ _____ _____
12. Can screen out distractions from surroundings   _____ _____ _____
13. Respects the rights and feelings of others in an   _____ _____ _____
    appropriate manner
14. Uses classroom materials appropriately   _____ _____ _____
15. Demonstrates a positive attitude toward school   _____ _____ _____
16. Accepts limits from adults   _____ _____ _____
17. Enjoys interacting with other children   _____ _____ _____
18. Separates easily from parents   _____ _____ _____
19. Appears rested   _____ _____ _____
20. Appears physically well   _____ _____ _____

Source: Dean, S. (1990). Evergreen School District, Evergreen, WA. Used by permission.

BIOLOGY I SYLLABUS

Course Outline:

Introduction to Biology
(Scientific Method, Lab Safety, Microscope Usage, Nature of Life)
Continuity of Life
(Cell growth and Reproduction, Heredity, Variation, and Diversity)
Microorganisms
(Viruses, Bacteria, Fungi, Protistans, Algae)
Animals
(Invertebrates and Vertebrates)
Multicellular Plants
(Mosses, Ferns, Seed Plants, Plant Growth and Responses, and Reproduction)
Ecological Relationships
(Biomes, Ecosystems, Populations, Environmental Concerns)

Grading Policy and System:

Students are responsible for keeping their own assignment sheets in their notebook at all times.
Overall grades are determined by points and percentage at the end of each quarter.
A list of Extra Credit Options is available for each semester.
Final grades are assigned using the following percents:

90—100% = A
80— 89% = B
70— 79% = C
60— 69% = D

Approximately 55% of a grade is determined by tests and quizzes.
Approximately 45% of a grade is determined by classroom work and homework.
Late work, not due to excused absences, will receive partial credit.
Make-up time for assignments missed because of excused absences will be equal to the amount of class time missed.
Students may be required to hand in their organized science notebook at the end of each nine weeks.

How Can a Parent Help?

Have a realistic grade expectation for your student.
Make it easy for your child to get help after school.
Offer a quiet place to study at home.
Contact me before a problem becomes a crisis.
Talk to and encourage your student. Be interested.
Help your student to be in class by discouraging trips and appointments during the school day.
Encourage your student to limit out of school obligations, such as jobs, on school nights.
Help your student with vocabulary practice, proofreading papers, checking worksheets, asking questions.
Encourage your child to ask for clarification regularly.

We have something very special in common—your child. I am excited about this school year, and I am looking forward to meeting many parents personally. Please feel free to call me about any school matter. I can be reached from 8 AM to 9 AM and after school until 4 PM on most days.

Source: Carol Tannenbaum, Staff Development Specialist, Mountain View School, Beaverton School District. Used with permission.

CHAPTER 15

Self-Improvement through Self-Assessment

CHAPTER OUTCOMES

At the conclusion of this chapter you will be able to:

1. Identify several sources of data to improve your teaching.
2. Use the Low Inference Self-Assessment Measure to analyze your teaching.
3. Use student feedback as a data source for your teaching.
4. Use peer observations with a student off-task seating chart to improve instruction.
5. Use the chapter checklists and self-assessment measures to reinforce the use of the teaching strategies presented in the text.

KEY TERMS AND CONCEPTS

Multiple Sources of Data
Creating Change from Within
Low Inference Self Assessment
   Measure (LISAM)
Audiotape Analysis
Guidelines for Effective Praise
Student Feedback
Student Messages
Our Class and Its Work (OCIW)
Teaching Effectiveness Questionnaire
   (TEQ)
Teacher-Developed Feedback
   Questionnaire
Off-Task Seating Chart
Consistency Checklist

> *A teacher affects eternity; you can never tell where*
> *your influence stops.*
> —Henry Adams

INTRODUCTION

Knowledge Is Power

We began *Universal Teaching Strategies* with a conviction that the teaching profession is facing its greatest challenge in modern history. The economic, social, and political fate of our country rests with the ability of our teachers, administrators, and other educators to enable all students to learn. The statement that "knowledge is power" is a truism that could be applied to both teachers and students.

The changing demographics of students in our classrooms requires both a broader range of teaching strategies and teachers who maintain their viability through the constant seeking of new knowledge. Although *knowledge is power*, knowledge about yourself is perhaps the greatest power. The power of discovering what you are doing and how you can change gives you control of your teaching life. In this concluding chapter of the text, we will provide instruments and measures designed to give you tools to assess your own teaching independent of others' evaluation. You will have the opportunity to reflect on information about your teaching that will ultimately improve your instruction.

How Am I Doing?

Teaching is at once a highly public profession, and a uniquely isolated profession, speaking everyday before 25 to 150 students, rarely meeting peers or other adults during the work day. From the student teacher to the 40-year veteran, the most common questions are: *How am I doing?* and *Where do I need improvement?* These important questions are only rarely answered to the satisfaction of most teachers. Accurate feedback is at the heart of change in teaching, but the process is always dependent on others.

The usual model of observation and feedback for secondary teachers consists of an administrator (principal, assistant principal, or department head) who visits one of six classroom periods from one to four times a year. Elementary teachers receive a similar visiting pattern, except the observations usually occur during reading or mathematics instruction. The administrator may use a checksheet, take notes, or simply observe what is occurring and share those perceptions with the teacher at a later date (Freiberg, 1987).

Providing information about teaching effectiveness may be called *supervision, feedback, assessment,* or *evaluation*. The end goal, however, should be to provide you with usable information about your teaching.

You need accurate information about what is going on in the classroom before you can begin to identify strengths and weaknesses and formulate a plan to institute change. It may not be an understatement to say that the entire school reform movement hinges on the ability of the profession to provide you meaningful data about what is occurring in the classroom and to create opportunities for all teachers to reflect on their teaching.

Sources of Data

There are several sources of information available to you about your teaching, including the following:

- Student gains on teacher-made tests
- Student gains on standardized tests
- Student feedback (verbal, nonverbal, and written)
- Systematic observation by supervisors or principals
- Administrative feedback
- Peer observation
- Self-assessment

In this chapter, self-assessment, using audiotape analysis, student feedback from written questionnaires, and classroom observation using an off-task seating chart will be presented as three viable ways of answering: How am I doing? and Where do I need improvement? Self-assessment, student feedback, and systematic observations represent three sources of data that are not used frequently in combination with each other but reflect an emerging trend toward teacher self-assessment (Freiberg & Waxman, 1988).

The seven potential sources of data are rarely collectively provided by schools. Generally, observations by an administrator are the most common source of data and feedback for teachers. Both administrators and teachers have questioned how accurately these brief observations represent the total teaching picture. The number of teachers in a school places limits on the quantity as well as the quality of feedback the principal can provide any one teacher. The average school year requires 1,080 hours of instruction (180 days × 6 hours a day). Most teachers are observed three times a year for 45 minutes each visit, totaling 2¼ hours a year, which represents a 0.2 percent sampling of instruction. Beyond the question of time, judging what is going on in the classroom is a difficult task. Simple checklists rarely provide an accurate picture of the fast-paced interaction of the classroom, and even the most detailed observation systems have their limitations (Stallings, 1986).

SELF-ASSESSMENT: CREATING CHANGE FROM WITHIN

Imagine an instructional conference between you and your principal. You confidently explain the areas of strength and weakness of a particular lesson, and focus on the types and quality of questions during instruction: "I used 30 percent higher order questions in my fifth-period tenth-grade literature class. This is a major improvement over the previous lesson whenI only used 7 percent higher-level questions. My motivating set was effective in gaining their attention but my closure was nonexistent—the bell rang before we had the chance to summarize the lesson. I need to pay more attention to my use of time."

The meeting continues for another 20 minutes as you and the principal review information of an audiotape analysis of a lesson you compiled and analyzed. The process described in this scenario is called *self-assessment*. In this example, the teacher met with the principal to discuss his or her analysis of a lesson, but this type of dialogue has also occurred between teachers meeting in small groups of 8 to 10 teachers as part of professional development activities (Freiberg, Orth, Stallings & Waxman, 1989).

Accuracy of Self-Assessment

Self-assessment without an objective data source is usually inaccurate. Being in the middle of a swirl of classroom interactions (up to 1,000 per hour) makes it difficult to reflect back and determine, for example, the level of questions being asked or the degree of teacher or student talk in the classroom. After a six-hour day of teaching, trying to make any accurate assessment of what happened in the morning during a reading activity or in a first-period mathematics is rather futile. The research is consistent about our inability, as teachers, to assess accurately teaching effectiveness through self-perceptive data when compared to direct observations of the same lesson (Hook & Rosenshine, 1979).

Audiotape versus Videotape

During the past two decades, teachers across the United States have had the opportunity to analyze their teaching by tape recording or videotaping their classes and coding the frequency of different teaching actions (e.g., number of times teacher praises a student) onto a data sheet. The information collected on a data sheet can then be analyzed by the teacher, and areas of strength and weakness may be identified with the intent of enhancing areas of strength and improving areas of weakness.

The question of whether to use audiotape or videotape to collect the data may be determined by the classroom context. The comparisons made between video and audiotaping in Figure 15.1 reflect the advantages and disadvantages of both systems. Review the advantages and limitations for your own setting and decide which technology would be mose effective. Our experience has been that audiotaping a lesson seems to be less obtrusive and more convenient than videotaping. But each classroom setting is unique. If your goal is to focus on verbal classroom interaction then the audiotaping technology may provide greater flexibility in listening and analyzing a lesson. Videotaping will provide more visual and nonverbal clues about your teaching and classroom interaction.

LISAM

Audiotaping allows for greater flexibility in listening and analyzing a lesson. The Low Inference Self-Assessment Measure, or LISAM (Freiberg, 1987; Freiberg, Wax-

FIGURE 15.1   *Scoring Strengths and Weaknesses of the Videotape and Audiotape Recorder in Teacher Self-Assessment*

Directions: Place a plus (+) for a strength oror a minus (−) for a limitation in each area associated with the type of media: audiotape or videotape recorder.

Videotape Recorder	*Audiotape Recorder*
_____ 1. Audio and video qualities	_____ 1. Audio qualities
_____ 2. Large	_____ 2. Small
_____ 3. Setup time: approximately 10–15 minutes	_____ 3. Setup time: less than 5 minutes
_____ 4. High visibility to students	_____ 4. Low visibility to students
_____ 5. Permanent record	_____ 5. Permanent record
_____ 6. Moderately portable	_____ 6. Highly portable
_____ 7. Moderately expensive	_____ 7. Relatively inexpensive
_____ 8. Mechanical operation, fairly complex	_____ 8. Mechanical operation, fairly simple
_____ 9. Accessibility	_____ 9. Accessibility
_____ TOTAL SCORE	_____ TOTAL SCORE

Source: Gerald D. Bailey (1981). Teacher Self-Assessment: A Means for Improving Classroom Instruction. © 1981, National Educational Association. Reprinted by permission.

man, & Houston, 1987), focuses on verbal interaction in the classroom. You tape-record your class and then listen for and code specific categories of teaching. Studies on changes in teaching behaviors (Freiberg, Waxman, & Houston, 1987) and teacher feedback support using the LISAM (pronounced *leesam*) as a highly effective and efficient self-assessment tool for analyzing teacher-student verbal interaction in the classroom. This section, which describes the use of the LISAM instrument, is adopted from an article that appeared in a journal for the National Association of Secondary School Principals entitled, "Teacher Self-Evaluation and Principal Supervision" (Freiberg, 1987).

Common Agreement

The "Low Inference" title of the instrument is derived from the fact that two people listening to the same tape could reach common agreement on what was occurring in the classroom. The LISAM has been used with student teachers, veteran teachers, and beginning teachers at the elementary, middle, or high-school levels.

From Questioning to Use of Student Ideas

The six items on the LISAM instrument (see Figure 15.2) were selected to provide a clear indication of teaching behaviors in key instructional areas. The LISAM instrument focuses on instructional areas that have been highlighted throughout the text (e.g., wait time, questioning, set induction, closure and praise). The instrument builds on the early work of Flanders' (1965) 10-item observation instrument.

LISAM is not the whole picture, but rather a slice of classroom interaction. By listening to the tape and then transferring the spoken words into frequency counts

(which are recorded on the LISAM coding instrument), a dimension of objective self-assessment that is missing from other feedback procedures is added.

The audiotaping provides you with an opportunity for reflective inquiry into the teaching process based on specific data. Listening to yourself also adds a perspective that goes beyond the six items on the instrument. Teachers commented about their tone of voice or the dominance of some students in the classroom during questioning and discussion.

The following describes how to use the six elements: (1) questioning skills (recall to opinion), (2) teacher and student talk, (3) set induction and closure, (4) wait time, (5) praise, and (6) use of student ideas of the LISAM coding instrument presented in Figure 15.2.

1. *Questioning skills.* Chapter 8 supports both the advantages and limitations of questioning. Being able to determine the level and tone of your questions will provide an important insight into this dominate instructional strategy.

A balance of 60–40 percent, or 50–50 percent between factual questions (e.g., yes-no and short answer) and higher cognitive questions (e.g., comparison and opinion) may be appropriate for many discussion and question-and-answer lessons. Although LISAM uses only four levels of questions, other levels of questions may be substituted by using, for example, the five levels in Bloom's Taxonomy (see Chapter 3).

FIGURE 15.2 *Audiotape Analysis Coding Instrument*

1. *Questioning Skills*   TOTAL = _____ = _____ %
   Yes-No: (Recall/Informational)   TOTAL = _____ = _____ %
   Short Answer: TOTAL = _____ = _____ %
   Comparison: (Reflective/Thought Provoking)   TOTAL = _____ = _____ %
   Opinions:
2. *Teacher Talk/Student Talk*

Teacher:	Student:	Other
Total (T) = _____ %	Total (S) = _____ %	(e.g., Independent Activities with no Interaction):
Teacher = _____	Student = _____	Total _____ %

3. *Identification of Motivating Set and Closure*
   Describe each from the tape:
       Set-Induction (Focus):

       Closure (Ending):

4. *Wait-Time*
   Time between teacher question and next teacher statement:
                                 Average Time = _____ Seconds
   Place a (*) next to all higher-level questions (comparison and opinion).

5. *Identify Number of Positive Statements Made by Teacher*
   Praise or encouragement

   Class _____ Individual _____ Uses student name _____ Total = _____

   Identify the praise or encouragement statements directed both toward the entire class and individuals. Also tally the number of times students' names are used with praise statements.
6. *Identify the Number of Times the Teacher Uses Student Ideas*
   Including referring by name to other student's idea:
                                         Total = _____

Source: Adopted from H. J. Freiberg (1987). Teacher self-assessment and principal supervision. *NASSP Bulletin, 71*(498), 85–92. Reprinted by permission.

Many teachers, who before listening to themselves were sure they were asking higher-order questions, were truly shocked to find a void of those questions. Recall-type questions are on the lowest levels of Bloom's Taxonomy and require a recall response from the student. Some forms of questioning appear to be verbal forms of worksheets. There is only one answer the teacher is expecting or accepting. Comparison questions require students to sythesize information before a conclusion could be reached. Opinion questions ask students to express their views on a particular issue. Although student opinion should have some foundation or basis for its response, you should not have a predetermined correct answer in mind. Examples of the four types of questions are provided on the next page.

a. Yes-No   Was George Washington the first president of the United States?

b. Short Answer   Who was the first president of the United States?

c. Comparison   What were the similarities and differences between the inaugural addresses of George Washington's and John F. Kennedy's?

d. Opinion   Which president (from Washington to Bush) do you think provided the best leadership for the United States?

In the LISAM analysis Example I of Teacher A's seventh-grade social studies classroom (see Figure 15.3), the teacher uses 94.8 percent lower-level questions and only 5.2 percent higher-level questions. She commented in her self-assessment, "My overuse of lower-level questions was inappropriate, given the goal to stimulate thinking in my students." The need to provide a balance of questions becomes greater as you move from checking for recall of information to critical thinking.

The questioning levels are not absolute. Determining where a question should be placed is relative to the learner, context, and content of the class. A recall question for a fifth-grader may be a higher-level question for a second-grader. In deciding the best placement for the question on the LISAM, determine what information the question seeks to answer and the mental processes the student needs to achieve to answer the question.

> **PROCEDURE:** To complete the questioning section, place a mark (1) next to the appropriate question for each occurrence (see Figure 15.3). Percentages are calculated for each type of question asked, and a total is given for the actual number of questions.

2. *Teacher talk/student talk.* The teacher talk/student talk balance is an important element in understanding the level of classroom interaction. Teacher talk in secondary classrooms in 1965 was between 80 and 85 percent in math classes, and between 70 and 73 percent in social studies classrooms (Brophy & Good, 1986). Those same figures are consistent with Goodlad's (1983) findings in classrooms of the 80s. Depending on the learner, content, and context, the degree of teacher talk should vary from lesson to lesson.

An introductory lesson designed to give an overview of a unit may require more teacher talk than a lesson that seeks to stimulate student thinking and dialogue. Teacher dominance, which becomes evident in high levels of teacher talk (85 to 100 percent), could inhibit student participation and diminish opportunities for students to take greater responsibility for their learning.

Once the data have been coded onto the LISAM instrument, the analysis of the information is the next step. The low levels of questioning, combined with high degrees of teacher talk (87 percent), produced the following analysis from Teacher A, which is presented in the Snapshot.

FIGURE 15.3 *Audiotape Analysis, Teacher A, Example I, 45-Minute Seventh-Grade Social Studies Lesson*

1. *Questioning Skills*
   Yes-No: 1111 1111 1111 1111 1   TOTAL = 15 = 39.5%
   Short Answer: 1111 1111 1111   TOTAL = 21 = 55.3%
   Comprison: 11   TOTAL = 0 =   0%
   Opinions: 0   TOTAL = 2 = 5.2%

2. *Teacher Talk/Student Talk*

Teacher:	Student:		Other
Total (T) = 470	Total (S) = 70	(T) + (S) = 540	(e.g., Independent
Teacher = 87%	Student = 13%	393 58 = 14.7%	Activities with

   Other (e.g., Independent Activities with no Interaction):
   Total 0
        0%

3. *Identification of Motivating Set and Closure*
   Describe each from the tape:
      Set-Induction:
      I summarized for the students the issues related to the Lincoln-Douglas debates which had been discussed the previous day.

      Closure: The bell rang before I had time to bring closure to the lesson.

4. *Wait-Time*
   Time between teacher question and next teacher statement:

1	1	2	2	1	3	.5
.5	2	2	2	1	*2	
1	3	2	2	2	*1	

   Average Time = 1.63 Seconds

5. *Identify Number of Positive Statements Made by Teacher*   Total = 5
   Praise or encouragement
   2 to the class
   3 to individuals (using students' names twice)

6. *Identify the Number of Times the Teacher Uses Student Ideas*   Total = 5

SNAPSHOT

Teacher A, Seventh-Grade Social Studies (Figure 15.3)
My domination of the classroom discussion is evident from the high teacher talk. This class is the second lesson in a unit on the pre-Civil War period and was designed to give a sense of the issues in the presidential election prior to the Civil War. I need to consider other strategies in addition to lecture. For example, the students rather than I could have summarized the issues we discussed from the previous day. I realize using original documents that actually show the issues of the time from the Lincoln-Douglas debates would also be

more effective. The students could read the materials and first discuss the issues in groups of two, then have a total classroom discussion.

My lack of higher-level questions was surprising. It is easier to think you are asking higher-level questions than to implement them. There seems to be little time to think about questions during the lesson; it's simply a good habit I have not developed effectively. When I did ask higher-level questions, I rushed the students' answers with 1 or 2 seconds wait time. I always feel rushed to cover the content in class, but the audiotape analysis was an eye opener. I need to give more time to being sure my students have some involvement in the class.

I could also improve the quality and quantity of praise statements. I was tired of hearing myself say "good" all the time. I am pleased that of the few responses the students made that I was able to integrate their ideas into the class. Greater opportunities for use of ideas will come with more higher-level questions. I was never a high-praise person, but I feel comfortable with using the students' ideas.

The ability to be self-analytical is the first step on the road to being independent and creating change from within. Teacher A began to explore areas in which a supervisor would need to overcome potential resistence to create the same insight for Teacher A.

In another analysis, a high-school Spanish teacher who used the LISAM coding instrument found that he was talking 90 percent of the time. Given the instructional focus for student use of language in the classroom, he decided that the level of teacher talk was too high. He reduced it for many lessons to 70 percent teacher talk and a corresponding 30 percent student talk. This was accomplished by varying his instructional strategies. He reduced the amount of pure lecture and increased small group activities where the students could practice their Spanish in twos and fours.

PROCEDURE: Using a watch with a second hand or a digital watch, place a checkmark (✔) every five seconds either under the teacher or student column, depending on who is talking. If the students are working in groups, consider it student talk. If the students are doing seatwork and are not talking with each other or the teacher, enter a mark under the other column. You should have 12 marks for each minute if there is continuous interaction in the classroom, or approximately 600 marks for a 50-minute period.

3. *Identification of motivating set and closure.* A set induction, sponge, motivating set, or other focusing activity at the beginning of the lesson has been found by researchers (see Chapter 3) to be highly effective in creating student gains when compared to no formalized instructional beginning (Schuck, 1981). Teacher A (see Figure 15.3) used an uninspiring set for the students. Reading a brief section from the original Lincoln-Douglas debates or incorporating the Go-Around System into the start of the lesson (see Chapter 8) may have been a better strategy for gaining the students interest and attention.

Closure is any device used by the teacher to summarize, review, or bring some finality to the content or procedures being studied or presented. This process usually occurs at the end of a lesson but may take place at several points during the lesson or day. For secondary students, the main points of the lesson should be reviewed before the students move on to the next lesson or unit. Teacher A allowed the bell for change of classes to be the closure for the lesson. Asking a student to provide a nonverbal clue to alert the teacher five minutes before the end of class has been an effective strategy for many secondary teachers. A kitchen timer has been a useful strategy for many elementary teachers to indicate change in subject areas.

> **PROCEDURE:** Describe in writing your set induction and closure for the lesson.

4. *Wait time.* Research generally supports waiting three to five seconds for the student to respond after the teacher asks a question (see Chapter 8). This is of particular importance when the teacher is asking higher-order questions. Veteran teachers have reported counting silently for three or four seconds before making another statement or asking a question.

> **PROCEDURE:** Time the interval between your question and any teacher statement prior to the student's response. Identify the actual wait time provided for students to answer each higher-order question by using an (*) asterisk (See Figure 15.3).

5. *Identify number of positive statements made by teacher.* Flanders (1965) determined that only 1.28 percent of the classroom interaction he observed could be characterized as praising or encouraging. Goodlad's (1983) look at secondary schools in the 80s also concluded that little praise was being used by secondary teachers. Although elementary teachers use greater numbers of praise statements, there is a tendency to use the same phrases repeatedly.

Table 15.1 provides guidelines for the use of praise as determined by extensive research conducted by Jere Brophy (1981). Praise reinforces students' responses and, because of the public nature of the classroom, signals to other students the correctness of the response. The quality of praise is as important as the quantity. A series of "oks" or "goods" provides little to the students. The tone of voice and facial expression also communicate much to the student and the class about the value of students' statement. Students will determine a statement to be negative if either the tone or facial expression is negative regardless of the spoken words. A variety of praise statements (Freiberg, 1991) is provided in the Samples and Examples section of this chapter.

> **PROCEDURE:** Count the number of total praise or encouraging statements made during the lesson. Also calculate the number of statements directed to the entire class and individuals and the frequency that student names are incorporated into the positive statements.

TEACHER TALK

Praise is very hard for me to give. Although I increased the number of comments to 10, they were poor expressions that I used of the lowest caliber. I also realize that I tried to teach too much too quickly. If I were to reteach the lesson I would divide the content into two lessons.

High-School Math Teacher

My most glaring weakness, in my opinion, is my tendency to *tell* instead of *ask*, and I frequently restated or answered my own questions without having allowed sufficient time for student thought.

Middle-School English Teacher

6. *Identify the number of times the teacher uses student ideas.* The use of student ideas received some early support from a series of studies reviewed by Dunkin and Biddle (1974). Although the early studies were not always conclusive, the direction for use of student ideas was encouraging. Morine-Dershimer (1982) indicates in her research that students answers that are expanded or extended by the teacher may signal to students that the answer has greater importance.

More recently, Brophy and Good (1986) stated:

Teachers should answer relevant student questions or redirect them to the class, and incorporate relevent student comments into the lesson. Such use of student ideas appears to become more important with each succeeding grade level, as students become both more able to contribute useful ideas and more sensitive to whether teachers treat their ideas with interest and respect (p. 364).

> **PROCEDURE:** Calculate the total number of times student ideas were incorporated into the lesson. For example, a tenth-grade mathematics teacher said, "Sarah's idea of constructing a city of geometric shapes is an excellent way to show how geometry is part of our everyday lives." The teacher was able to make the connection between Sarah's comment and the content being discussed. It is important that the student's name (or the names of several students) be used to indicate where the idea originated.

LISAM Summary

Once the criteria for coding the frequencies of each of the six elements of the LISAM are understood, the following steps should be followed.

1. Determine which class will be taped.
2. Prepare a detailed lesson plan to be used for comparison or as a frame of reference while listening to the tape. (See Chapter 3 for possible lesson plan formats.)
3. Tape the class for the entire period or for a complete lesson of 30 to 50 minutes.
4. Using the LISAM sheet, listen for each item. (For example, listen to the types of questions asked and complete the frequencies for item 1, then return to the tape and listen for the frequency of teacher talk to student talk.)

TABLE 15.1 *Guidelines for Effective Praise*

Effective Praise	Ineffective Praise
1. Is delivered contingently.	1. Is delivered randomly or unsystematically.
2. Specifies the particulars of the accomplishment.	2. Is restricted to global positive reactions.
3. Shows spontaneity, variety, and other signs of credibility; suggests clear attention to the student's accomplishments.	3. Shows a bland uniformity that suggests a conditioned response made with minimal attention to the student's accomplishment.
4. Rewards attainment of specified performance criteria (which can include effort criteria, however).	4. Rewards mere participation, without consideration of performance processes or outcomes.
5. Provides information to students about their competence or the value of their accomplishments.	5. Provides no information at all or gives students information about their status.
6. Orients students toward better appreciation of their own task-related behavior and thinking about problem solving.	6. Orients students toward comparing themselves with others and thinking about competing.
7. Uses students' own prior accomplishments as the context for describing present accomplishments.	7. Uses the accomplishments of peers as the context for describing student's present accomplishments.
8. Is given in recognitionof noteworthy effort or success at difficult (for *this* student) tasks.	8. Is given without regard to the effort expended or the meaning of the accomplishment.
9. Attributes success to effort and ability, implying that similar successes can be expected in the future.	9. Attributes success to ability alone or to external factors such as luck or (easy) task difficulty.
10. Fosters endogenous attributions (students believe that they expend effort on the task because they enjoy the task and/or want to develop task-relevant skills).	10. Fosters exogenous attributions (students believe that they expend effort on the task they expend effort on the task for external reasons—to please the teacher, win a competition or reward, etc.).
11. Focuses students' attention on their own task-relevant behavior.	11. Focuses students' attention on the teacher as an external authority figure who is manipulating them.
12. Fosters appreciation of, and desirable attributions about, task-relevant behavior after the process is completed.	12. Intrudes into the ongoing process, distracting attention from task-relevant behavior.

Source: From J. Brophy, "Teacher Praise: A Functional Analysis," *Review of Educational Research, 51* (1981), pp. 5–32. Copyright 1981 by the American Educational Research Association. Reprinted by permission of the publisher.

5. Complete the frequency counts for items 1, 2, 4, 5, and 6. Describe the set induction and closure for number 3.
6. Complete all percentages, as described in Figure 15.3.
7. Analyze each of the six elements in the LISAM based on the frequencies collected from the audiotaping.
8. Provide a summary of strengths and weaknesses for the lesson.

9. Describe the changes you would make if you were to reteach the lesson.
10. Provide some conclusions (or lessons learned) about your teaching analysis.

Theory into Practice

You are encouraged to use the LISAM several times during the school year. The LISAM has been implemented in real as well as simulated teaching situations. It has been used in peer teaching situations where teachers in training teach a group of five or six other peers a 10- or 20-minute lesson. The "teacher" records the simulated teaching event and analyses the lesson. Peers may give feedback using the Peer Feedback Sheet provided in the Samples and Examples section of this chapter.

A second use of the LISAM is during student teaching. The LISAM has proven to be highly effective in enabling student teachers to reflect and change their instruction during student teaching (Freiberg, Waxman, & Houston, 1987). The student teacher tapes and then analyzes the lesson. The analysis could be shared with the cooperating teacher and/or supervisor. The *student teacher is not graded* on the effectiveness of the lesson but on the ability to analyze and reflect on their teaching. The emphasis is placed on learning how to be self-analytical rather than being judged on a single teaching episode.

The LISAM has been used extensively with experienced teachers in Texas, California, West Virginia, and Missouri with gratifying results. Veteran teachers who have used the LISAM described the experience as "enlightening," "challenging," "sobering," "exciting," "beneficial," and "encouraging." We have included two additional examples of self-assessments from a high-school geometry teacher and a fifth-grade teacher. The LISAM data sheets and their analyses of their teaching are included. Examine the data sheets (see Figures 15.4 and 15.5) and compare your analysis with that of the two teachers presented in the Teacher Talks that follow.

TWO TEACHERS ANALYZE THEIR CLASSROOMS

The LISAM analysis of an eleventh-grade geometry class and a fifth-grade class are presented to provide additional perspectives on the process of self-improvement through self-assessment for different grade levels.

Teacher B's Eleventh-Grade Class

Teacher B teaches geometry to eleventh-grade inner-city students. She has analyzed her geometry classroom twice using the LISAM audiotape analysis. Teacher B's second critique of her class is presented in the Teacher Talk* section after her LISAM audiotape analysis (see Figure 15.4).

*Kathleen Gandin-Russell. Used by permission.

FIGURE 15.4 *Audiotape Analysis, Teacher B, Example 2, Eleventh-Grade Geometry Lesson*

1. *Questioning Skills*
   Yes-No: TOTAL = 16 = 31%
   Short Answer: TOTAL = 20 = 38%
   Comparison: TOTAL = 16 = 31%
   Opinions: TOTAL = 0 = 0%
2. *Teacher Talk/Student Talk*

Teacher:	Student:	Other
Total (T) = 147	Total (S) = 42	(e.g., Independent
Teacher = 78%	Student = 22%	Activities with no
		Interaction):
		Total = 0
		0%

3. *Identification of Motivating Set and Closure*
   Describe each from the tape:
   > Set-Induction: As the students walked into the classroom they were each handed an orange card with a geometrical figure on each.

   > Closure: They raised their cards in order to identify polygons—convex or concave.

4. *Wait-Time*
   Time between teacher question and next teacher statement:
   Average Time = 1.69 seconds

5. *Identify Number of Positive Statements Made by Teacher*
   Praise, encouragement, suggestions, etc.
   Total = 38

6. *Identify the Number of Times the Teacher Uses Student Ideas*
   Including referring by name to other student's idea:
   Total = 1

Note: Teacher B completed an earlier LISAM version which did not include the identifying of higher level questions or whether the individual or group was receiving praise.

Source: Kathleen Gandin-Russell. Used by permission.

TEACHER TALK

Teacher B, Eleventh-Grade Geometry Lesson (Figure 15.4)
I asked a majority of lower-level questions; however, I did ask more higher-level questions than last time. I asked yes/no questions 31 percent of the time, and short-answer questions 38 percent of the time. In this lesson I asked 31 percent of comparison questions, which was better than last time's 3 percent. I still feel that I could have asked more had I consciously prepared the questions. Again, I asked no opinion questions. I now see the importance of preparing questions ahead of time at all levels. When you are actively teaching you do not always have time to ponder or remember to ask higher-order questions. I am sure, in retrospect, that I could have come up with at least one

opinion question; for example, "Why do you suppose it is important to classify polygons?"

My *teacher talk/student talk* ratio leaned a bit more to the student's side the second time around, but not much. This time I had 78 percent of teacher talk to 22 percent of student talk, as opposed to last time I had 80 percent teacher talk and 20 percent student talk. My students talked a whole 2 percent more than before. Even though the data do not support it, the students were more involved in this lesson. Many of my questions had silent responses and therefore the students were participating, even though they were not verbalizing it in order to verify it on tape. Many questions they answered by showing me cards that matched the descriptions I was looking for. So, even though student talk appears low on the data sheet, the students were actively involved.

Since the *set induction* that I had originally planned on was not very motivating, I changed it. Originally I was going to have the geometrical figures drawn on the chalkboard. Instead, I drew them on orange cards and handed each student one as they walked in the door. This little change in the set induction had a tremendous effect on the rest of the lesson. Active planning went into effect and the lesson took a 180 degree turn for the better.

Actually having the figures in their hands caused them to actively discuss their figures before class even started. Since they had the figures, when it was time to discuss the difference between a polygon or not a polygon I had them raise their cards to participate in the answers. Thus, the new *set induction* helped increase class participation. After we discussed the definition of a polygon, we talked about how to classify the polygon as convex or concave and by the number of its sides. Again, they raised their cards in response to the questions. Then an in-flight idea came to me—to group them to practice the new concepts. This worked very well.

The *closure* was also altered because of the set induction. Since they had the cards in their hands, they again raised them at the appropriate times to prove that they had or had not mastered the difference between a polygon and that they could classify the polygons as convex or concave and by the number of its sides. The evaluation was also different in that they classified figures in their textbook.

I am not sure how I feel about the *wait time* data. My wait time on questions went from 2.14 seconds to 1.69 seconds. I realize the ideal is 3.0 seconds and that I went further away from that, but they quickly answered many of the questions and more wait time was not always appropriate. Longer wait time is appropriate for higher-level questions. Fast-paced drill will give you shorter times. I felt that I waited sufficient time when necessary. However, I notice that now I am constantly aware of my wait time in class and frequently try to glance at my watch without the students knowing about it.

The number of *positive statements* that I made increased greatly from last time. I made 38 positive statements; last time I made 9. Unfortunately, I decreased in the number of times that I used student ideas. Only once did I refer to a *student's idea*, as compared to last time with 16. I feel that this new lesson did not lend itself well to my being able to use student ideas. However, if I had really put my mind to it, I'm sure that I could have done better.

If I were to reteach the lesson, I would make sure that I prepared higher-order questions ahead of time. I would use the same set induction (motivating), stimulus variation, and closure as before. But I would see to it that I improved on the items mentioned as my weaknesses.

I see how important it is to have a motivating set induction; it could be the difference between a good and bad lesson. I also see how important it is to be flexible. I feel that analyzing my teaching has helped me to improve greatly.

Kathleen Gandin-Russell

Small Changes

Small changes can produce great results. The movement of the geometric figures from the chalkboard to cards in the students' hands created greater stimulus variation (see Chapter 13) and higher levels of student involvement. The point of nonverbal student response is a limitation of the audiotape, but the teacher is aware of the discrepancy. It is evident from Teacher B's description of the lesson that student learning and involvement also produced high levels of involvement and satisfaction for the teacher. She also used a student feedback instrument at the conclusion of the lesson, which is included in this chapter (see Figure 15.8). The student assessment of the class was very positive and validates the data from the audiotape analysis.

Teacher C's Fifth-Grade Class

Teacher C, who is teaching a fifth-grade mathematics lesson on perimeters for advanced students, was less satisfied with his lesson. The audiotape analysis (see Figure 15.5) highlighted areas he wanted to change in future lessons.

TEACHER TALK

Teacher C, Fifth-Grade Math Lesson (Figure 15.5)
The objective for this lesson was to have the students calculate the perimeter of any rectangle or square. I decided to ask the students to build a fence around a small plot of land the class would buy. This plot of land would be used later to build a house and determine the land area needed for the house and other possible improvements.

- *Questioning skills.* I was pleased with the overall coverage of the four different types of questions but higher-level questions only accounted for 22 percent of the total.

- *Teacher/student talk*. My balance of teacher to student talk was much better than in previous lessons. However, in listening to the tape I felt the lack of patience on my part inhibited some student discussion.

- *Identification of motivating set and closure*. The set induction was mediocre at best. The idea was good, but the delivery was poor. After listening to the tape, I realized the set was rushed and poorly organized. I realize the importance of more planning time in developing a motivating or facilitating set. The closure was sidetracked. One of the students did not understand the entire lesson. I spent the time allocated for closure using the example of a football field to explain the idea of perimeter to David, who wants to be a football player. He finally understood the example, but we had to move on to PE (physical education).

- *Number of teacher positive statements*. I was surprised by the lack of positive statements (only 6). Also, listening to the tape, the statements I did use came across as very impersonal (e.g., yes, good, ok). I definitely need to take care to personally give more positive recognition to the students.

- *Teacher use of student ideas*. I need to be more responsive to students' ideas. I was set to plow through the lesson as I had imagined it should go and gave little thought to increasing student contributions to the lesson.

- *Student feedback on the TEQ*. I had the students complete the *Teaching Effectiveness Questionnaire* (see Figure 15.7). Of the 16 items, the students gave high marks on 13 items. The three lowest items, although above the mean, included "preparation," "attitude" and "what is expected of student." The fact some students saw me as somewhat biased was an eye-opener. I need to use a place on the board for assignments and help the students, perhaps through a syllabus or outline on the board, understand what is expected of them.

There are several changes I would make in a future lesson. First, I would give more thought and planning to the set induction. For example, after listening to the tape I realized that we could have used our classroom to measure the perimeter. I need to help the students learn how to learn and be successful in my classroom. When I was a student I disliked trying to guess what the teacher wanted, and here I am doing the same thing. I like the idea of using an outline on the board and providing opportunities for greater student involvement in the lessons.

Teacher C is perhaps harder on himself than necessary but self-assessment has the potential to create greater change because the change comes from within. When this realization that change is needed is combined with effective inservice programs or college classes, continued professional growth can be achieved.

Conditions for Success

There are several ways the LISAM can be used. You may use the LISAM as an ongoing professional development activity, where a group of teachers meet once a month

FIGURE 15.5 *Audiotape Analysis, Teacher C, Example 3, Fifth-Grade Mathematics Lesson*

1. *Questioning Skills*
   Yes-No: TOTAL =   7 = 12.1%
   Short Answer: TOTAL = 38 = 65.5%
   Comparison: TOTAL =   5 =   8.6%
   Opinions: TOTAL =   8 = 13.8%
2. *Teacher Talk/Student Talk*

Teacher:	Student:	Other
Total (T) = 83	Total (S) = 71	(e.g., Independent
Teacher = 53.9%	Student = 46.1%	Activities with no
		Interaction):
		Total = 0
		0%

3. *Identification of Motivating Set and Closure*
   Describe each from the tape:
      Set-Induction: The class purchased some land. Fences had to be built as well as other improvements.
      Closure: A short quiz spanning the material covered

4. *Wait-Time*
   Time between teacher question and next teacher statement:
                                    Average Time = 4 seconds

5. *Identify Number of Positive Statements Made by Teacher*
   Praise, encouragement, suggestions, etc.
                                    Total = 6

6. *Identify the Number of Times the Teacher Uses Student Ideas*
   Including referring by name to other student's idea:
                                    Total = 3

Note: Teacher B completed the original LISAM version which did not include the identifying of higher-level questions or whether the individual or group was receiving praise.

to share their audiotape analyses and propose solutions for each other. However, certain conditions are necessary if the use of LISAM is to be successful.

- A climate to learn and an opportunity to share both successes and failures should be supported by your principal, other teachers, and the district administration.
- You should be willing to make changes in your instructional approaches based on actual classroom data analyzed from the LISAM.
- Discussions between you and other teachers relating to the LISAM analysis should be held in confidence.
- Staff development activities should support teachers who use the self-assessment instrument.

Critical Insight

Self-assessment can be done independently or with the support of your principal or other teachers. The audiotape analysis enables you to examine one aspect of classroom life.

Self-assessment, using objective sources of information, empowers teachers to be more reflective and self-analytical. The comments in the Teacher Talks highlight this willingness to explore teaching from a more introspective and reflective basis. The insights and critical analysis provided by the teachers are far beyond what any administrator would give in the normal course of providing feedback.

STUDENT FEEDBACK

The greatest source for feedback on the effects of teaching sits directly in front of you each day—your students. However, they are rarely tapped as a data source. Within the classroom setting, you measure the reactions of the students to lessons, content, and strategies, and other elements of teaching on an instantaneous basis but little time is available for reflective and measured responses. Students are constantly giving nonverbal and, in some instances, verbal clues and messages about their level of comfort (or discomfort) to instructional activities in the classroom. Reading these messages can provide a valuable source of information to both neophyte and veteran teachers.

Student Messages

Once routines and teaching patterns are established during the first few weeks of school (see Chapters 5 and 6), changes in the content, context, or instructional strategies could result in mixed reactions by the students. "The stronger the student response, either positive or negative, the stronger the message to the teacher about his or her performance" (Smylie, 1985, p. 10). An example of this interaction between teacher and student is evident when teachers begin to move away from worksheets to more interactive, reflective instructional activities.

Teachers report students, and particularly lower-achieving students, as being resistant to changes that require more thinking and a greater risk of failure in the highly public classroom environment. Worksheets require less risk (students are rarely asked to read from the sheet) and minimize interactions with both peers and teachers (students work independently at their seats). The tradeoff of using worksheets for both teacher and students is a lack of opportunity to think and interact with others. Introducing activities that require greater "academic exposure" and new skills (e.g., working in groups, thinking aloud for answers, problem solving, and brainstorming) require the teacher to be a careful observer of student responses to change. The following list should be considered in identifying students' messages as you introduce instructional changes into the classroom.

Student Concern Messages

_____ Students are excessively fidgety prior to and during highly interactive activities, including grouping, discussion, and reports to the class.

_____ Students are very quiet when asked to think aloud or explain an answer to the class.

_____ Students are less willing to participate when called on or volunteer to answer.

_____ Students begin acting out, including calling out, tapping pencils, rocking chairs, tapping fingers.

_____ Students look down when class discussion is about to occur.

_____ Students stare blankly at objects around the room.

_____ Students allow themselves to be distracted more easily.

Student messages are signals that teachers may use to make in-flight corrections during instruction. However, some teachers are overwhelmed by students' responses or miss the meaning of some messages.

Student Change

There is an assumption that the young respond to change more readily and with greater comfort than adults. There is no evidence to support this assumption. Presenting an unknown situation for some students is seen as a challenge to be tackled, while others see potential failure. Link these negative experiences together and *some students will seek monotony over challenge and worksheets over dialogue.*

Student negative messages may indicate a degree of anxiety or discomfort with a new procedure or instructional strategy that is requiring rapid change and adjustments. Preparing students for changes will diminish or alleviate the sources of many messages on the list. For example, preparing students for working in groups (see Chapter 10) through practice, assigning specific roles, reporting and grading procedures, and gradually increasing the difficulty of the task to be solved will make the unknown known and lessen the impact of change on students. The transition is gradual and ordered, allowing students to progress at a reasonable rate.

Formal and Informal Messages

There is a need for some disequilibrium in which students' notions are challenged and ideas are tested, but there is no requirement that students become frustrated, inhibited, and alienated from learning. Being aware of student messages is an important source of information about your effectiveness and the comfort level of your students. Other forms of student feedback, including surveys and questionnaires, are also available to you. Although observing student messages are informal and ongoing, survey feedback is more formalized and would occur less frequently (a few times a year). The advantages of using student surveys of classroom environment or specific teaching areas is realized by the opportunity to reflect on the information and prepare some specific planned changes. If student messages influence in-flight corrections, then student surveys influence both post-(future) and preplanning. Three examples of student questionnaires are discussed in the chapter.

THREE STUDENT FEEDBACK INSTRUMENTS

Three student feedback instruments are presented here. The first is a questionnaire entitled *Our Class and Its Work* (OCIW). The OCIW (Eash & Waxman, 1983) is a 40-item questionnaire that has been used effectively in research and as a self-assessment instrument for teachers. The items build from the research on effective teaching. The second instrument, entitled *Teaching Effectiveness Questionnaire* (TEQ), (Freiberg, 1972) is a 16-item bipolar (e.g., from good to bad) adjective (e.g., preparation, organization, and subject matter knowledge) questionnaire. The TEQ has been used in research and practice with students in elementary, middle, and high-school classrooms. The third instrument is a 21-item teacher-developed questionnaire designed from the TEQ by the geometry teacher (B) highlighted in a Teacher Talk. She used the questionnaire with her eleventh-grade students. The OCIW questionnaire, developed by Eash and Waxman (1983), is valid and reliable for use with students in upper-elementary through high school. The OCIW (see Figure 15.6) measures teaching qualities that research on teaching supports as being effective in improving student achievement. The administrative suggestions, procedures, and scoring are provided in the Sample and Examples section at the end of this chapter.

FIGURE 15.6 *Our Class and Its Work*

Student Identification Number _____ Boy _____ Girl _____

Birth Date _____

Directions: This is not a test. The statements inside are to find out what your class is like. Please answer all the statements. If the statement describes your class well, circle SA, Strongly Agree. If the statement describes how your class is a lot of the time, circle A, Agree. If the statement does not describe how your class is a lot of the time, circle D, Disagree. If the statement does not describe your class at all, circle SD, Strongly Disagree.

Example

		Mark your answer			
1. Our classroom is noisy. If you think that your classroom is noisy almost all the time, circle SA like this:		(SA)	A	D	SD
1. Our classroom is noisy. If you think that your classroom is noisy but not all the time, circle A like this:		SA	(A)	D	SD

1. Our classroom is noisy. SA   A   Ⓓ   SD
   If you think that your classroom is not usually noisy, circle D like this:

1. Our classroom is noisy. SA   A   D   ⊚SD⊚
   If you think that your classroom is not noisy at any time, circle SD like this:

1. Our teacher brings new and different materials into the classroom. SA   A   D   SD

2. Our teacher spends too much time asking questions.

3. Our teacher carefully checks all our work. SA   A   D   SD

4. Some students bother the class when we're working.

5. Our teacher thinks it's more important to learn than to have fun at school. SA   A   D   SD

6. Before we start a lesson, our teacher tells us that we will enjoy it. SA   A   D   SD

7. We all understand what our teacher is talking about. SA   A   D   SD

8. Students usually get to work with other students. SA   A   D   SD

9. There are many interruptions in our classroom. SA   A   D   SD

10. Students should only do things according to the teacher's way. SA   A   D   SD

11. Our teacher gives us work that is too easy for us. SA   A   D   SD

12. Our teacher lets us know when we act well in class. SA   A   D   SD

13. Our teacher lets us do things on our own. SA   A   D   SD

14. Our teacher immediately tells students if their answers are right or wrong. SA   A   D   SD

15. Our teacher always rushes us to finish our work. SA   A   D   SD

16. Many students do not finish all their work. SA   A   D   SD

17. After we've read a lesson, our teacher asks us what we think. SA   A   D   SD

18. Our teacher lets us know what we'll do tomorrow. SA   A   D   SD

19. Our teacher spends too much time going over work. SA   A   D   SD

20. Students do get a chance to ask questions in our class. SA   A   D   SD

21. We always spend a lot of time doing our schoolwork. SA   A   D   SD

22. We waste a lot of time in school. SA   A   Ⓓ   SD

23. Our teacher never lets us know when we do good work. SA   A   D   SD

24. Our teacher assigns us a lot of work to do. SA   A   D   SD

25. Students are allowed to select activities on their own. SA   A   D   SD

26. Our teacher often reviews yesterday's work. SA   A   D   SD

27. Our teacher asks us questions which are too difficult to answer. SA   A   D   SD

28. We try new and different things in the classroom. SA   A   D   SD

continued

FIGURE 15.6 *(Continued)*

29. We always have an assignment to work on.	SA	A	D	SD
30. Our teacher lets us know if the questions we answer are right or wrong.	SA	A	D	SD
31. Our teacher gets excited about things that he or she teaches.	SA	A	D	SD
32. It's difficult for our class to get down to work.	SA	A	D	SD
33. We always have enough time to do our schoolwork.	SA	A	D	SD
34. Our class assignments are very interesting.	SA	A	D	SD
35. Our teacher lets us play a lot of games in school.	SA	A	D	SD
36. Our teacher always gives us homework.	SA	A	D	SD
37. Our teacher has us work too slowly in reading and math.	SA	A	D	SD
38. We always have to wait for the teacher to tell us what to do before we can get started on our work.	SA	A	D	SD
39. Our teacher usually teaches the whole class at once.	SA	A	D	SD
40. We are always working in our class.	SA	A	D	SD

Source: Eash, M. J., & Waxman, H. C. (1983). *Our class and its work (OCIW) user manual.* Chicago: University of Illinois at Chicago, Office of Evaluation and Research. Used by permission.

Background of the OCIW Instrument

No scientific work stands alone; it profits from and builds upon previous work in the field. This instrument is no exception. The first versions of OCIW were developed as an effort to measure the nine theoretical constructs on teacher behavior identified by Rosenshine and Furst (1973) as being related to student academic achievement. Building upon the research work of other investigators—Talmage, Walberg, Gage, McDonald, Medley, Good, Brophy, Steele, Berliner, Staybrook, Madaus and many others—items were revised, new scales and items were added. After successive revisions of the original instrument based on the results of field tests, the following series of scales emerged:

1. Didactic Instruction—implies that the teacher directs the instruction for all students in the class. Students are involved in whole class instruction.

2. Enthusiasm—considers the extent to which the student sees the teacher exhibit excitement and interest in teaching.

3. Feedback—describes the extent to which teachers respond to students' answers and provide students with feedback about their schoolwork.

4. Instructional Time—refers to the time students spend learning or being engaged in learning. It includes the notions of both engaged time (i.e., the time students are engaging or participating in their schoolwork) and allocated time (i.e., the amount of time the teacher allocates for student learning).

5. Opportunity to Learn—indicates how well the teacher provides opportunities for all students to learn or cover the criterion material. It deals with the extent to which teachers limit classroom misbehavior and make sure students cover the assigned content by finishing their work.

6. Pacing—deals with whether or not the classroom work is at the appropriate level of dif-

ficulty for students in the class. It is also concerned with how rapidly the teacher goes over and/or covers the material.

7. *Structuring Comments—refers to whether the teacher provides overviews at the beginning and ending of instructional sequences and whether or not students understand what the teacher is talking about.*

8. *Task Orientation—indicates the extent to which the classroom is "businesslike" and whether students have appropriate amount schoolwork assigned to them. (Eash & Waxman, 1983, pp. 1–2)*

Teaching Effectiveness Questionnaire

The *Teaching Effectiveness Questionnaire* (see Figure 15.7) is based on similar research findings as the OCIW. The TEQ uses a seven-point scale and is a shorter instrument than the OCIW, with 16 verses and 40 questions. It has been determined to be valid and reliable for use with students in grades 6 through 12 as a feedback measure of teaching effectiveness (Freiberg, 1972).

Scoring Procedures

The examples and samples section of this chapter has a template that can be used for scoring this instrument. To eliminate the possibility of a student checking down one side or the other, the poles (e.g., thorough-unprepared) have been reversed for items #2, 5, 7, 8, 10, 12, and 15. The template should be made into an overhead transparency and placed on top of each completed questionnaire. The scores for each line would be written on the right side. The highest score possible will be 112. A score above 80 should be considered good, although you may want to examine any trends for a particular item. You may also want to add one open-ended question (e.g., What do you like best or least about this class?) in the space provided at the bottom of the page. The students should not place their names on the questionnaires.

Modified TEQ

A third questionnaire was designed by Teacher B for her eleventh-grade geometry class (see Figure 15.8). She modified the TEQ to a five-point scale and added smiley faces to indicate the range of responses. It has "face validity" (no pun intended) for the teacher who designed it. The questions have meaning for the teacher and provide a measure of feedback to the quesiton: How am I doing? Teacher B received feedback from 25 eleventh-grade geometry students. One of the students wrote in the open comment section: "I wish she would teach me all the subjects. This is a great teacher. I really never liked math but the way she teaches it makes it interesting. I really enjoy coming to this class. I look forward to it throughout the whole day." It is clear from the student's comments that his or her teacher has made a difference in geometry. Teachers who seek to meet the needs of their students and are willing to learn from mistakes and capitalize on success can increase their effectiveness and improve their own satisfaction with teaching and student motivation for learning.

FIGURE 15.7 *Teaching Effectiveness Questionnaire*

Teacher: _____ Expected Final Grade _____ Grade Level _____

Instructions: The following lines represent traits commonly noted by students when describing their teachers. Please place a checkmark (✔) on that part of the line which would indicate how you would rate your teacher. Please read each question carefully as the words on each end of the line have been reversed for specific questions (e.g., thorough-unprepared). Each line should be checked.

| Poor | Organization | Good |

| Thorough | Preparation | Unprepared |

| Limited | Subject matter knowledge | Current |

| Dull | Presentation | Interesting |

| Open minded | Attitude | Biased |

| No | Sense of Humor | Yes |

| Interesting | Personality | Poor |

| Encourages | Discussion | Prohibits |

Boring	Speaker	Effective

Respects	Student	Belittles

Ignores	Student's needs	Recognizes

Clear	What is expected of student	Unclear

Unfair	Fairness	Fair

Not	Warmth	Very

Very	Flexible	Not

Not	Enthusiastic	Very

Comments:

What did you like most about this class?

Source: Freiberg, H. J. (1972). *An investigation of similar and different ability groups in secondary classrooms.* Amherst: University of Massachusetts. Used by permission.

FIGURE 15.8 *Teacher B Feedback Sheet*

Teacher Name: _____ Expected grade: _____ Grade level: _____

Instructions: Please place a checkmark (✓) on the face that best tells how you feel about each statement.

1. My teacher is well organized. ☺☺☺☹☹
2. My teacher is well prepared. ☺☺☺☹☹
3. My teacher is knowledgeable about the subject he or she is teaching. ☺☺☺☹☹
4. My teacher presented the lesson in an interesting way. ☺☺☺☹☹
5. My teacher has an open-minded attitude. ☺☺☺☹☹
6. My teacher has a sense of humor.
7. My teacher has an interesting personality. ☺☺☺☹☹
8. My teacher is happy when we ask questions. ☺☺☺☹☹
9. My teacher is an effective speaker. ☺☺☺☹☹
10. My teacher respects students. ☺☺☺☹☹
11. My teacher recognizes students' needs. ☺☺☺☹☹
12. My teacher is very clear about telling us exactly what he or she expects of us. ☺☺☺☹☹
13. My teacher is fair. ☺☺☺☹☹
14. My teacher is a warm individual. ☺☺☺☹☹
15. My teacher is flexible. ☺☺☺☹☹
16. My teacher is enthusiastic about teaching. ☺☺☺☹☹
17. I understand what my teacher just taught us. ☺☺☺☹☹
18. If I had to grade my teacher I would give him or her a(n) _____. ☺☺☺☹☹
19. I would like to take another class from this teacher. ☺☺☺☹☹
20. I enjoy coming to class. ☺☺☺☹☹
21. I have always liked math. ☺☺☺☹☹

Additional Comments:

Source: Kathleen Gandin-Russell. Used by permission.

Summary

Each of the instruments provides an element of feedback to judge the effectiveness of your teaching. You may wish to adapt an instrument for your particular class. Students are a valuable source for data about your teaching and their learning, and they should become part of your repertoire for teaching.

The LISAM and the student questionnaires are sources of data that you may implement without assistance from other teachers or administrators. You may wish to share this information with others in your school who also receive feedback from their students and talk about strategies for improving instruction. A third source of data about your teaching may be derived from an off-task seating chart, which requires the assistance of a colleague to collect the information. However, only you should analyze it and make any final assessments about your ability to focus student attention.

DATA FROM PEER OBSERVATIONS

Colleagues can provide an important source of data for you. School systems throughout the United States are moving to peer coaching and collegial teams (Joyce & Showers, 1988). However, many teachers feel uncomfortable giving feedback to a colleague or receiving it. The difficulty rests with the perception that feedback is an evaluation about one's teaching from one's peer. If, however, the colleague is a data gatherer, not an evaluator, then the peer can be an invaluable source of information in answering the questions: *How am I doing?* and *Where do I need improvement?* The off-task seating chart developed by Jane Stallings (1986) is effective in identifying off-task student behavior. The feedback and analysis of the seating chart has shown to be effective for increasing teaching academic time and reducing organizing time (Freiberg et al., 1989; Stallings, Goodman, & Johnson, 1986). (See the Research Vignette on page 445.)

Off-Task Seating Chart

The use of the off-task seating chart requires another person (teacher, administrator, parent, or high-school student) to code what the students are doing when the teacher is involved in various instructional activities. The teacher, for example, is instructing and 25 students are listening, but 2 students are chatting and 2 are uninvolved during the presentation.

Sweeps

The observer begins with a seating chart of the class and "sweeps" (or looks) from left to right in the classroom and notes what the teacher is doing (e.g., instruction [I]) and where the teacher is located on the seating chart (e.g., T1). There are 10 sweeps per observation. If the class is 50 minutes in length, each sweep is 5 minutes (50 minutes ÷ 10 sweeps = 5 minutes per sweep). If the class is 60 minutes or 55 minutes, then the sweeps would be 6 minutes and 5.5 minutes respectively. For an elementary-school lesson, the time period can be decided prior to the observation. The observer codes only those students on the seating chart who are off-task during instruction. In the case of the example (see Figure 15.9), Joshua, Matthew, and Ann during instruction (I) are uninvolved in sweep #1, the first five minutes of class. In the case of Joshua, a *1 U/I* is placed in his seating chart box. The number *1* indicates the first sweep, the *U* shows uninvolvement, and the *I* identifies the types of instructional activity, which in this case is *instruction*.

FIGURE 15.9 *Off-Task Seating Chart #1*

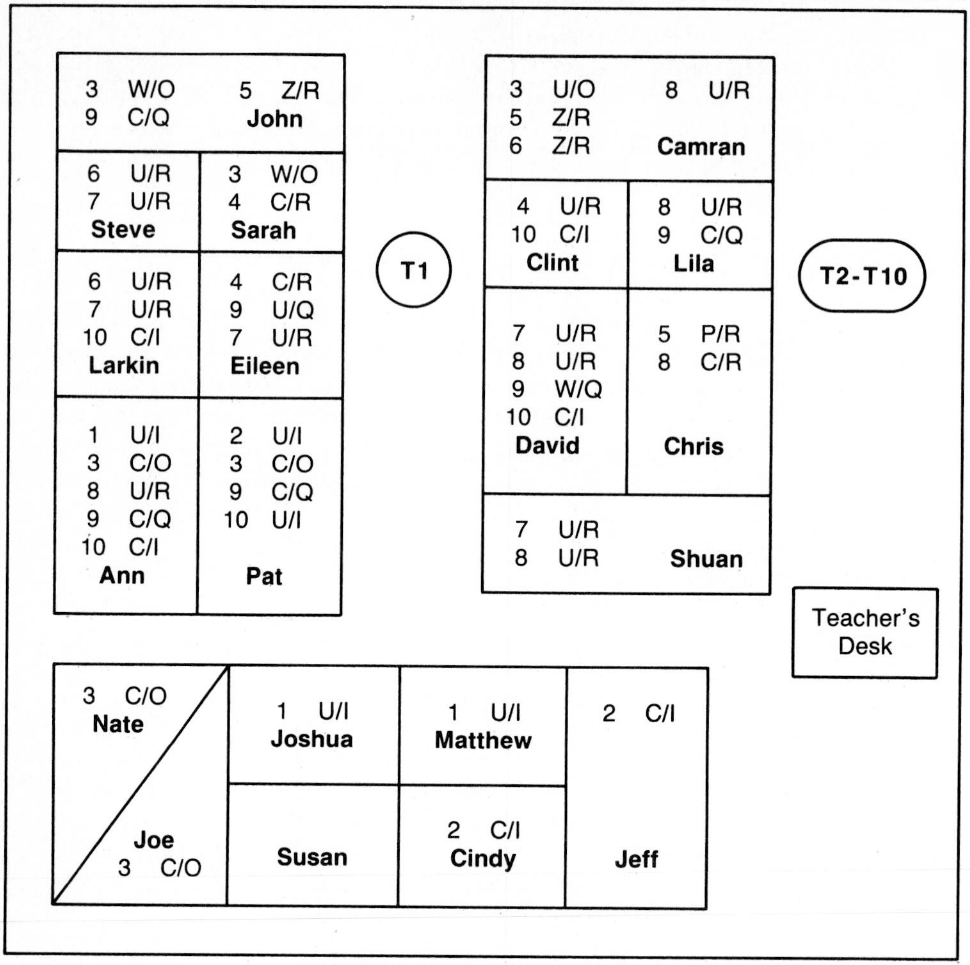

Teacher Activity During Sweep

Organizing = 3   Oral Reading = 4, 5, 6, 7, 8 Cooperative Groups
Instruction = 1, 2, 10 Seatwork
Question/Answer = 9   Games

Off Task: C = Chatting   U = Uninvolved
           D = Disruptive   W = Waiting
           P = Personal   Z = Sleeping
               Needs

Activity: S = Seatwork   R = Reading Aloud
           O = Organizing   Q = Question/Answer
           I = Instruction   G = Game
                                 C = Cooperative Group

Source: Jane Stallings. Used by permission.

Instructional Activity Codes

The instructional activity codes reflect seven common instructional practices:

C—Cooperative group   Q—Question/Answer
G—Games   R—Oral Reading
I—Instruction   S—Seatwork
O—Organizing

Each of the criteria for coding the activity codes follow.

The teacher may be *instructing (I)*, which includes lecture, explaining, or presenting; *organizing (O)*, including passing out papers, taking attendance, or grading papers in class; *question/answer (Q)*, including teacher's questions, fast-paced oral drill, and student responses; *oral reading (R)*, including reading aloud; *seatwork (S)*, including students working independently at their seats, reading or writing; *games (G)* for the entire class, including board games, teacher-made games, and computer games; and *cooperative group (C)*, including students working in groups of two, four, or six on academic tasks.

Off-Tasks Codes

There are six off-task codes:

C—Chatting   U—Uninvolved
D—Disruptive   W—Waiting
P—Personal needs   Z—Sleeping

Chatting (C) is any conversation between students during instructional time that is not sanctioned by the teacher and is unrelated to the task. *Disruptive (D)* behavior is coded when the teacher needs to stop instructional activities and respond to a student or when the disruptive student is drawing attention from other students in the classroom. *Personal needs (P)* represent students going to the bathroom, combing hair, applying make-up, or other grooming activities during instructional time. *Uninvolved (U)* students are identified by their lack of focus on the teacher or instructional activities. Students reading a book during a teacher's or other student's presentation, doing homework for another class, looking out the window, and involved in activities indicate they are not focusing on the lesson. A student who is looking down or glances off away from the teacher may be involved. Some judgment may be required. If the observer is unsure, then the student should not be coded as uninvolved. *Waiting (W)* cannotes the student waiting in line to see the teacher, raising a hand during seatwork until the teacher is able to respond, or other behaviors that indicate the student is waiting to proceed. *Sleeping (Z)*, which is maybe more common at the secondary level (student working the late shift), is a particularly troublesome off-task behavior and is provided a separate code.

Off-Task Behavior Summary

Figure 15.10 provides a summary of off-task behaviors. We can see from Figure 15.10 that there are 44 off-task behaviors in a 50-minute time period. The most common

FIGURE 15.10 *Seating Chart #1: Summary of Off-Task Behaviors*

Sweeps	1	2	3	4	5	6	7	8	9	10	
Observation #1	3	3	7	3	3	3	5	6	6	5	= 44

Behaviors	Chatting	Disruptive	Personal Needs	Uninvolved	Waiting	Sleeping	
Observation #1	17	0	1	20	3	3	= 44

Activities	Organizing	Instruction	Question/ Answer Discussion	Oral Reading	Seatwork	Games	Cooperative Groups	
Observation #1	7	11	6	20	0	0	0	= 44

GRADE 3 READING CLASS, Stallings Observation System

Source: Jane Stallings. Used by permission.

off-task behaviors are chatting (17) and uninvolved (20) in this classroom. Students were off-task most often during oral reading (20) and instruction (11), with teacher organizing attributing to some (7) students also being off task. Determining the percentage of time the students were off task requires inserting the numbers from the summary of off-task behavior into the formula below.

$$\frac{\text{number of off-task behaviors}}{\text{number of students} \times \text{number of sweeps}} = \% \text{ Off task}$$

Going back to Figure 15.10, we see the following:

$$\frac{\text{number of off-task behaviors (44)}}{\substack{\text{number of students} \times \text{number of sweeps} \\ (20) \times (10) = (200)}} = 22\% \text{ Off task}$$

Junior High School Research Vignette

INTRODUCTION

A study conducted by Georgia G. Mohlman (1982) and presented at the annual meeting of the American Educational Research Association examined which of the three different approaches increased teacher use of academic time with 20 junior high-school teachers of English and mathematics teachers of low-achieving students.

STUDY DESIGN

The 20 teachers were divided into three groups for a series of workshops entitled the Effective Use of Time (Stallings, Needles, & Stayrook, 1978). The 2½-hour workshops, conducted each week for four weeks, focused on student time on task. Each group received training using presentation strategies, demonstration practice, and feedback. Group 2 ($N = 7$) received *peer observations* using, for example, the off-task seating chart (see Figure 15.9). Group 3 ($N = 6$) received on two occasions *coaching* by the trainer in their classrooms. Group 1 ($N = 7$) only received the original four-week in-service workshops.

A control group of 17 teachers who did not attend the workshop and the treatment group of 20 teachers were observed before the workshops, using the Stallings Observation Instrument, which codes teacher/student interactions and how teachers use their time in the classroom. A second observation was conducted after the workshops in January and February, and a follow-up observation was conducted with two teachers from each group. Interviews were also conducted with each group of teachers.

RESULTS

The results show that Group 2 with *peer obser-*

vations using the student off-task seating chart and a second interactive seating chart created the most gain in the use of academic time in the classroom as measured by Stallings Observation System. The control group regressed from the beginning of the observation period to the second observation.

		Use of Academic Time
Control group gain	($N = 17$)	−11%
Group 1 gain	($N = 6$)	+ 9%
Group 2 gain	($N = 7$)	+16%
Group 3 gain	($N = 6$)	+ 7%

The third group with trainer coaching had the least gain of the three groups. Group 1, which only received four workshops without the off-task seating charts or peer coaching, gained slightly more use of their academic time than Group 3.

DISCUSSION AND IMPLICATIONS FOR PRACTICE

The research study by Georgia G. Mohlman (1982) has some limitations. The number of teachers in each group is small and the statistical procedures are descriptive. But the results lend some support for peer observation using instruments that are student focused. The information from the instruments were analyzed and critiqued by the teachers being observed. The peer was only collecting the data to be analyzed. Although better controlled studies needed to be conducted with different formats, the use of student focused observation systems as a source of data for teachers is helpful.

The off-task behavior for this third grade classroom was 22 percent, which is high. The goal for off-task behavior should be 3 percent or less (Stallings, 1986).

Possible Solutions

Off-task behavior is both a teacher and student concern. Mrs. Smith spent 25 minutes in oral reading (5 minutes × 5 sweeps). This may be too long for the 20 third-graders. The teacher could have shorter oral reading sessions or ask the students to read to each other in pairs for part of the oral reading time while the teacher works with small groups. The teacher used three instructional strategies: instructing, question and answer, and oral reading. A better balance of the two and the addition of other strategies like cooperative groups, discussion, and five minutes of guided or independent practice could add greatly to the interaction in the classroom.

Procedures for Observers

- Remind the observer of strict confidentiality prior to the seating chart activity. If students will be moving to a laboratory setting, learning centers, or cooperative groups, then name tags are placed on the back of the students with high-mobility activities.
- Provide a seating chart of the students in the classroom to your colleague.
- Remind the observer that he or she is only a collector of data and should not make value judgments about what is being observed.
- Analyze your own data and complete the formula to determine the percentage of off-task behavior.
- Share your chart and discuss possible solutions with another teacher who you are observing.

Our experiences with the seating charts and the teachers who have worked with them have proven to be very positive. As with the other feedback tools for answering the questions, "How am I doing? and How may I do better?, the off-task seating chart is but another sliver of life in the classroom.

SUMMARY

This chapter is designed to give you independent measures of your own effectiveness. You, your students, and your colleagues are valuable sources of data that may be tapped to gain an insight to your teaching. The instruments included in this chapter are selected to foster independence and reflection, and are based on a belief that learning to be an effective teacher is a lifelong pursuit, requiring a variety of sources of information.

The LISAM should give you a measure of how the students hear you and an indication of how you are doing in six areas of instruction. The Snapshot and Teacher Talks of the chapter were devoted to elementary, middle, and high-school teachers analyzing and critiquing their own instruction.

The student feedback instruments, OCIW, TEQ, and Teacher B's Questionnaire, are designed to provide different measures for both classroom instruction and climate.

The off-task seating chart (Stallings, 1986) is included to give you an opportunity to see your classroom from the eyes of an observer using a systematic observation instrument.

Key Points

The instruments individually and collectively will enable you to test the influence of using different strategies with your students. The following list of concepts and terms highlight the key points of the chapter.

- Knowledge is power, but knowledge about yourself is the greatest power of all.
- There are at least seven sources of data about your teaching.
- Self-assessment is not accurate without an objective source of data.
- Audiotaping and videotaping are effective tools for collecting information about your teaching. Generally, audiotaping is less obtrusive in the classroom.
- The LISAM focuses on six areas of instruction, including questioning, teacher/student talk, set and closure, wait time, praise and encouragement, and use of student ideas.
- The research supports 12 guidelines for effective praise.
- Student messages about your teaching are constantly being provided during instruction.
- Students need to be prepared for change in the classroom.
- Student feedback is an important but neglected source of information about your teaching.
- Formal student feedback can be acquired by presenting student questionnaires.
- Off-task seating charts will enable you to measure the amount of time and during what instructional activities students are most frequently engaged in learning.
- Learning to be an effective teacher is a lifelong pursuit and requires a variety of information sources.

Consistency Checklist

We conclude this chapter with a summary checklist for the text. The 30-item checklist (Figure 15.11) brings together activities that reinforce many of the management and organizational strategies from the text. The checklist is designed to provide another means for maintaining a high level of transfer from your reading of the *Universal Teaching Strategies* to your own instructional setting.

FIGURE 15.11   *Consistency Management Checklist*

Please check which of the following you have completed. If there are areas which remain unchecked, consider includiing these activities in future lessons.

_____ I have sent at least five positive postcards to the parents of my students.

_____ I have developed an absence packet for students who miss class.

_____ I ask questions using popsicle sticks or 3 × 5 index cards with the students' names on them to balance the questioning and responses in the classroom.

_____ I allow the students to pass on a question and raise their hands later to answer.

_____ I try to catch the students being good and use positive behavior as the model in the classroom.

_____ I spend more time rewarding the students than focusing on the consequences of inappropriate behavior.

_____ When I need to reprimand a student I emphasize the behavior that was inappro-priate rather than the student.

_____ I have something ready for the students when they walk in the door.

_____ I try to say something genuine and positive to each student every day.

_____ I review the instruction from the previous day before beginning the lesson for the day. This could be done by having the students telling me one thing they learned from yesterday.

_____ I have the students review at the end of a 50 minute instructional period.

_____ I have started peer tutoring activities where both students are the teacher at some point during the day.

_____ I have begun to include some cooperative grouping activities for simple tasks.

_____ I teach the students how to work cooperatively in groups through simple activities like drawing a picture together.

_____ I am beginning to ask a range of questions from yes-no to short answer to com-parison to opinion.

_____ I post the students' work in the room.

_____ I include at least five students each day in helping activities in the class (e.g., line leaders, room organizer, etc.).

_____ I review the classroom rules on Mondays or as needed.

_____ I recognize other students or classes when they are displaying appropriate behavior in the halls and other common areas.

_____ I send home a schedule of when homework and other assignments are given on a weekly or monthly calendar.

_____ I prepare the students for field trips by visiting the location in advance and taking slides and incorporating the slides into a lesson about the trip.

_____ I create a warm positive feeling in the classroom for learning.

_____ I spend more time in teaching and less time in organizing.

_____ The students spend little time waiting for me to begin a lesson.

_____ I try to guide the students when they have a difficult time in answering a question.

_____ If I am with one group of students, I will have a table or group leader for each of the other groups who are working independently at their seats. The group leader will answer the questions before a student will interrupt my teaching.

_____ The students work in pairs to do oral reading.

_____ I provide richness to my instruction by including examples which go beyond the textbook.

_____ I will think "success" when working with my students and work together with my colleagues to have a great year!!!

Source: Freiberg, H. J. (1987). *Consistency management checklist.* Consistency Management Associates, Houston, Texas. © Used by permission.

REFERENCES

Brophy, J. (1981). Teacher praise statements: A functional analysis. *Review of Educational Research, 51,* 5–32.

Brophy, J. E., & Good, T. L. (1986). Teacher behavior and student achievement. In M. C. Wittrock (Ed.), *Handbook on research and teaching.* New York: Macmillan.

Coker, H., & Coker, J. G. (1982). *Classroom observations keyed for effective research.* Atlanta, GA: Georgia State University.

Dunkin, M., & Biddle, B. (1974). *The study of teaching.* New York: Holt, Rinehart and Winston.

Eash, M. J., & Waxman, H. C. (1983). *Our class and its work (OCIW) user manual.* Chicago: University of Illinois at Chicago, Office of Evaluation Research.

Flanders, N. (1965). *Teacher influence, pupil attitudes and achievement.* Cooperative Research Monograph No. 12. Washington, DC: U. S. Office of Education.

Freiberg, H. J. (1972). *An investigation of similar and different ability groups in secondary classrooms.* Amherst: University of Massachusetts.

Freiberg, H. J. (1987). Teacher self-evaluation and priniciple supervision. *NASSP Bulletin, 71*(498), 85–92.

Freiberg, H. J. (1991). Consistency management: What to do the first days and weeks of school. *Consistency Management Training Booklet.* Houston: Consistency Management Associates.

Freiberg, H. J., Orth, L., Stallings, J., & Waxman, H. (1989, March). *Improving the effectiveness of veteran teachers.* Paper presented at the annual meeting of the American Educational Research Association, San Francisco, California.

Freiberg, H. J., & Waxman, H. C. (1988). Alternative feedback approaches for improving student teachers' classroom instruction. *Journal of Teacher Education, 39*(4), 8–14.

Freiberg, H. J., Waxman, H., & Houston, W. R. (1987). Enriching feedback to student teachers through small group discussion. *Teacher Education Quarterly, 14*(3), 71–81.

Goldhammer, R. (1969). *Clinical supervision.* New York: Holt, Rinehart and Winston.

Goodlad, J. (1983). *A place called school. Prospects for the future.* New York: McGraw-Hill.

Hook, C., & Rosenshine, B. (1979). Accuracy of teacher reports of their classroom behavior. *Review of Educational Research, 49,* 1–12.

Joyce, B., & Showers, B. (1988). *Student achievement through staff development.* White Plains, NY: Longman.

Mohlman, G. (1982, March). *Assessing the impact of three inservice teacher training models.* Paper presented at the annual meeting of the American Educational Research Association, New York.

Morine-Dirshimer, G. (1982). Pupil perceptions of teacher praise. *Elementary School Journal, 82,* 421–434.

Redfield, D., & Rousseau, E. (1981). A meta-analysis of experimental research on teacher questioning behavior. *Review of Educational Research, 51,* 273–245.

Rosenshine, B., & Furst, N. (1973). The use of direct observation to study teaching. In R. Travers (Ed.), *Second handbook for research on teaching.* Chicago: Rand McNally.

Shuck, R. (1981). The impact of set induction on student achievement and retention. *Journal of Educational Research, 74,* 227–232.

Smylie, M. (1985, April). *Improving the accuracy of teacher self-evaluation through staff development.* Paper presented at the annual meeting

of the American Educational Research Association, Chicago.

Stallings, J. (1985). *Effective use of time program: Notes for trainers.* Nashville: Peabody Center for Effective Teaching, Vanderbilt University.

Stallings, J. (1986). Using time effectively: A self-analytical approach. In K. Zumwalt (Ed.), *Improving teaching. ASCD yearbook.* Alexandria, VA: Association for Supervision and Curriculum Development.

Stallings, J., Goodman, J., & Johnson, R. (1986). Engaged rates: Does grade level make a difference? *Journal of Research in Childhood Education, 1*(1), 22–27.

Stallings, J., Needles, M., & Stayrook, N. (1978). *How to change the process of teaching basic reading skills in secondary schools.* Final Report to the National Institute of Education. Menlo Park, CA: SRI International.

SAMPLES AND EXAMPLES

There are three samples and examples in this section.

- Administration of Our Class and Its Work describes the OCIW.
- A template for scoring the Teaching Effectiveness Questionnaire (see Figure 15.7).
- 70 Ways to Vary Your Praise.
- Peer Feedback Sheet.

ADMINISTRATION OF OUR CLASS AND ITS WORK (OCIW)

OCIW Administration Suggestions. The OCIW can be used for several purposes. We would recommend its use where classroom teachers are involved in a cooperative effort to improve student achievement through more effective instructional behaviors by teachers. It may also figure in research and evaluation studies where a group measure of classroom performance is needed to accompany analysis of student achievement data and the supervision of instruction. Where its use involves instructional improvement the usual admonitions concerning sensitivity to faculty morale and using implementation strategies capitalizing on cooperative rather than adversarial approaches be heeded. Our experience has found that the instrument can be incorporated into an inservice program without threatening teachers. Moreover, when properly administered students find it an interesting and comfortable instrument to use. The instrument has been used from grades 3–12.

Preferably, the instrument should be administered by a staff member other than the regular classroom teacher (i.e., another teacher, counselor, adjustment teacher) to facilitate confidentiality of responses by students. If possible, the regular classroom teacher should be out of the room when the instrument is administered.

Procedure

1. Each student is given a copy of the instrument with his/her identification number on the top sheet. This identification number is the one given to the student during the first enrollment. The student's name is not to appear anywhere on the instrument.
2. Each student is to have a pencil with an eraser.
3. Review the sample on the top sheet with emphasis on the meanings of SA, A, D, SD. Allow students to express their own interpretations of the letters. Answers such as YES for AGREE and NO for DISAGREE are often mentioned. Also, discuss AGREE meaning: "That's the way it is even though we might want it another way." The same idea may be explained for DISAGREE. Remind students that this inventory requests their observations—not what should be.
4. Read aloud: "I shall read each statement twice, and you are to circle one of the answers for each statement—after I read the statement. Only one of the four answers is to be marked for each statement: SA for Strongly Agree, A for Agree, D for Disagree, SD for Strongly Disagree."
5. Remind students: "Remember this is not a test—only you know what is on your paper. Your teacher will not be shown your paper at any time."
6. Statements are to be read slowly and then repeated. After the repeated statement: "Mark your answer for number _____. Do you Strongly Agree, Agree, Disagree, or Strongly Disagree? Circle the one answer for number _____." This is to be done for each of the forty statements. Students should use a marker to follow each statement.
7. As students place answers on the sheets, the monitor should check for placement of only one answer next to each statement. No information is to be given to students about the instrument's contents and/or meanings of words.

Scoring. The OCIW is scored as follows:

Strongly Agree	4
Agree	3
Disagree	2
Strongly Disagree	1

The scores are then added cumulatively to produce a total score. If used over time with a number of cases, local norms are advised. In the absence of local norms, the following scale can be used for normative interpretation of a single score.

- Upper ranges of raw scores (120–160)—The teacher probably obtains increased achievement from most students.
- Middle ranges of raw scores (80–120)—The teacher is somewhat inconsistent in obtaining increased achievement from students.
- Lower ranges of raw scores (Below 80)—The teacher probably does *not* obtain increased achievement from most students.

In all cases attention should be given to the scores obtained on the separate scales and separate item responses as these give clues to teaching behaviors and how they are perceived and offer opportunity for specific changes. Thus a total score and individual scale scores should be computed as well as individual item scores reviewed.

Caution: In scoring the questionnaire the following items (2, 4, 8, 9, 11, 13, 15, 16, 19, 22, 23, 25, 27, 32, 35, 37, and 38) have been given negative polarities to prevent response sets and the scale should be given the exact reverse values, Strongly Disagree = 4; Disagree = 3; Agree = 2; and Strongly Agree = 1.

Source: Eash, M. J., & Waxman, H. C. (1983). *Our Class and its work (OCIW) user manual*. Chicago: University of Illinois at Chicago, Office of Evaluation Research.

SCORING TEMPLATE FOR FIGURE 15.7: TEACHING EFFECTIVENESS QUESTIONNAIRE

Teacher: _____ Expected Final Grade _____ Grade Level _____

Instructions: The following lines represent traits commonly noted by students when describing their teachers. Please place a checkmark (✔) on that part of the line which would indicate how you would rate your teacher. Each line should be checked.

1	2	3	4	5	6	7

Poor			Organization			Good
7	6	5	4	3	2	1

Thorough			Preparation			Unprepared
1	2	3	4	5	6	7

Limited		Subject matter knowledge				Current
1	2	3	4	5	6	7

Dull			Presentation			Interesting
7	6	5	4	3	2	1

Open minded			Attitude			Biased
1	2	3	4	5	6	7

No			Sense of Humor			Yes
7	6	5	4	3	2	1

Interesting			Personality			Poor
7	6	5	4	3	2	1

Encourages			Discussion			Prohibits
1	2	3	4	5	6	7

Boring			Speaker			Effective
7	6	5	4	3	2	1

Respects			Student			Belittles
1	2	3	4	5	6	7

Ignores			Student's needs			Recognizes
7	6	5	4	3	2	1

Clear			What is expected of student			Unclear
1	2	3	4	5	6	7

Unfair			Fairness			Fair
1	2	3	4	5	6	7

Not			Warmth			Very
7	6	5	4	3	2	1

Very			Flexible			Not
1	2	3	4	5	6	7

Not			Enthusiastic			Very

70 WAYS TO VARY YOUR PRAISE

Always use the student's name in providing praise. You may *acknowledge effort, praise a positive result,* or give a *brief acknowledgment.* The following are examples of each area.

Brief Acknowledgments

OK	Sensational	Correct	Outstanding
Fine	Superb	Accurate	Standout
Great	Astonishing	Perfect	Important
Super	Incredible	True	Noteworthy
Yes	Marvelous	Precisely	Remarkable
I see	Beautiful	Truly	Notable
Nice	Grand	Agreed	Key point
Wonderful	Impressive	All Right	Main point
Much better	Magnificent	Positively	Keep it up
Exactly	Splendid	Noted	Keep up the great work
Excellent	Dazzling	Splendid	Keep up the good work
Tremendous	Brilliant	Better	Your on target
Surely	Good	Much improved	Very nice
Right	Very Good	Superior	Congratulations

Acknowledge Specific Effort
- Bill, I like the way you are using your time to study.
- Jose, You have really focused on the lesson.
- Sarah, I see you have tried very hard to complete this English assignment.
- Don, the extra time you are spending on your homework will make a difference in your class work.
- Jasmine, I like seeing you come to class on time.
- Jamie, you almost have it completed.
- Manuel, you are this close (teacher gestures) to finishing your assignment.

Extended Praise
- Juan, excellent, this is the best paper you have written this year in my class.
- Bill, nice job of getting your assignments in on time and putting thought into your work.
- Rose, congratulations, you really discovered another answer to the problem.
- Sarah, great job of completing your Civil War assignment.
- Sam, you really mastered the beginning structure of a topic sentence for your news article.
- David, much better us of first person in your writing.
- Linda, exactly, your answers show you understand and can give examples which explain the concept of gravity.

Source: Freiberg, H. J. (1991). Consistency management: What to do the first days and weeks of school. *Training Booklet.* Copyright 1991 Consistency Management Associates Houston, Texas. Used with permission.

PEER FEEDBACK SHEET

After participating a simulated teaching situation, please provide the following information to the "teacher."

Identify up to three strategies used by the teacher in this simulated lesson.

(Please check)

_____ Lecture

_____ Questioning

_____ Discussion

_____ Drill/Recitation

_____ Cooperative Grouping

_____ Reflective Teaching (Discovery, Inquiry, and Problem Solving)

_____ Roleplay

_____ Simulation

_____ Drama

_____ Media

_____ Computers

_____ Assessment

Please be specific (e.g., using the diagram helped me visualize the concept) in giving feedback.

1. Describe the set induction (beginning) and the closure (ending) of the lesson.

2. Describe a strength of the lesson.

3. If the lesson was to be retaught, what changes would you recommend?

Use the other side for additional comments.

Author Index

Subject Index